Leading

with the Future in Mind

Knowledge and Emergent Leadership

by
Dr. Alex Bennet and Dr. David Bennet
with Dr. John Lewis

Mountain Quest Institute and CoHero Institute

MQIPress (2018)
Frost, West Virginia
ISBN 978-1-949829-27-3

The New Reality Series

We exist in a new reality, a global world where the individuated power of the mind/brain offers possibilities beyond our imagination. It is within this framework that thought leading emerges, and when married to a collaborative nature, makes the impossible an everyday occurrence. *Together we dream the future.*

MQIPress
Frost, West Virginia
303 Mountain Quest Lane, Marlinton, WV 24954
United States of America
Telephone: 304-799-7267

eMail: alex@mountainquestinstitute.com
www.mountainquestinstitute.com
www.mountainquestinn.com
www.MQIPress.com
www.Myst-Art.com

ISBN 978-1-949829-27-3

Graphics by Fleur Flohil

Table of Contents

Figures

Figure 1-1: The fields of collaborative competition and competitive collaboration.

Figure 2-1: Usage of terms in literature over the years.

Figure 2-2: Knowledge (Informing) and Knowledge (Proceeding)

Figure 3-1: The Learning-Knowledge Loop

Figure 3-2: Exploring the relationships among information, knowledge, creativity and innovation.

Figure 5-1: Value creation has moved from knowledge of how to hunt game to development of deep intellectual capital.

Figure 6-1: Knowledge and authority in literature over the years.

Figure 7-1: Classical management approaches will not work in a CUCA world.

Figure 7-2: The relationship among the eight emergent characteristics of the ICAS.

Figure 8-1: Six types of leadership that can contribute to collaborative leadership.

Figure 8-2: Six types of leadership and their aspects that contribute to collaborative leadership.

Figure 8-3: The mesh serves as a framework for the immediate gathering of collaborative leaders from different knowledge domains to handle an immediate challenge or opportunity.

Figure 9-1: Representative characteristics, activities, values and foundational concepts that characterize the lived experience of the collaborative leader.

Figure 10-1: A knowledge taxonomy for grouping types of knowledge from the viewpoint of what knowledge is needed to do a particular type of work or take a particular action (Bennet & Bennet, 2007; 2015a).

Tables

In Appreciation

There are so many that have contributed to the learning and stories in this book, many unnamed in their short interactions, yet creating a lasting impact with their ideas and responses. We are all indeed one, sharing ideas in groups and communities, face-to-face and virtual, appearing and connecting where they will, in our continuous expansion toward intelligent activity.

We would also like to give a very special thanks to our colleagues in Singapore who inspired us to bring all of this together for the 2015 Information & Knowledge Society Conference; a special thanks to Bob Turner, who again embraced the role of editor as he visited Mountain Quest; and a special thanks to our friend and graphic artist, Fleur Flohil, who designed the cover graphic many years ago for our Knowledge Mobilization book. That graphic found its leading place today in this book.

And we could not think the thoughts we think and act on them without the day-to-day support of Andrew Dean, the Bennet's son and the Manager of the Mountain Quest Inn and Retreat Center situated in the middle of the Allegheny Mountains of West Virginia.

A deep appreciation to those professionals, colleagues and knowledge thought leaders who have worked with Alex, David and John through the years in developing their understanding of thought leadership. Among others, including participants in the KMTL study, our deep thanks to Dorothy Agger-Gupta, Verna Allee, Debra Amidon, Gil Ariely, Joyce Avedisian, Ramon Barquin, Surinder Kumar Batra, David Bennet, Steven Bennet, Prem Bhatia, Juanita Brown, John Seely Brown, Barbara Bullard, Frada Burstein, Frank Calabrese, Francisco Javier Carrillo, Robert Cross, Cam Danielson, Raj Datta, Tom Davenport, Ross Dawson, Steve Denning, Charles Dhewa, Anthony DiBella, Nancy Dixon, Jo Dunning, Susan Dreiband, Leif Edvinsson, Kent Greenes, David Gurteen, Susan Hanley, Jack Hawxhurst, Esther Hicks, Jeanne Holme, Clyde Holsapple, Esko Kilpi, Lowell Lannert, WB Lee, Dorothy Leonard, Geoff Malafsky, Martha Manning, Tom McCabe, Robert Meagher, Doug Moran, Mother Theresa, Art Murray, Neo Kim Hai, Brian Newman, Carla O'Dell, Edna Pasher, Barnett Pearce, Dan Porter, Larry Prusak, Karuna Ramanathan, Virginia Ramos, Madanmohan Rao, Vincent Ribiere, Tomasz Rudolf, Melissie Rumizen, Hubert Saint-Onge, Judi Sandrock, John Schlichter, Charles Seashore, Peter Senge, Arthur Shelley, William Sioris, Dave Snowden, Milton Sousa, Michael Stankosky, Tom Stewart, Michael J.D. Sutton, Karl-Erik Sveiby, Eric Tsui, Jane Turner, Robert Turner, Steve Wallis, Doug Weidner, Steve Weineke, Etienne Wenger-Trayner, Richard Werling, Karl Wiig and Norman Wright.

Our appreciation for all those whose lives that have touched us, and from whom we have learned as we moved through our professional careers in the government and private sectors and continue our learning from students in university settings around the world.

With Love, Alex, David and John

Preface

Through the past 20 years we have engaged in extensive research—much of it experiential in nature—which has led us to break through life-long perceived limits and shift and expand our beliefs about Life and the world of which we are a part. In 2004 the Bennets published a new theory of the firm, *Organizational Survival in the New World: The Intelligent Complex Adaptive System*, followed in 2007 by *Knowledge Mobilization in the Social Sciences and Humanities: Moving from Research to Action*. John Lewis' book *The Explanation Age* became a reality in 2010 as a visualization of the new learning organization, with the third edition released in 2013.

The advent of self-publishing virtual books has opened the door to share a larger segment of this learning. In 2013 the Bennets published an extensive treatment on *Decision-Making in The New Reality: Complexity, Knowledge and Knowing*. In 2015 they published two large bodies of work that have been underway for a number of years: *The Course of Knowledge: A 21st Century Theory* and *Expanding the Self: The Intelligent Complex Adaptive Learning System*. It was then that the focus turned to the powerful relationship of knowledge and leadership and this book was born.

Leadership has always been a popular subject for debate and discussion and is probably the most widely studied aspect of organizations. Many thousands of books have been written on the subject over the past century, and undoubtedly many others before that. We sometimes give leaders great credit for success and intense ridicule for failure, believing that these outcomes are due to their leadership alone. This book explores the long-term relationship between knowledge and leadership, highlighting the force of knowledge in human development, the changing roles that knowledge has played throughout history, and the more recent focus on thought leadership.

To begin, we offer the following assumptions:

Assumption 1: Knowledge has a direct relationship to action. We consider knowledge as a human capacity, *the capacity (potential or actual) to take effective action in varied and uncertain situations* (Bennet and Bennet, 2004). Knowledge consists of understanding, insights, meaning, intuition, creativity, judgment, and the ability to anticipate the outcome of our actions. Characteristics of knowledge are described in Chapter 2. For an in-depth treatment see Bennet and Bennet (2015a).

Assumption 2: The human mind is an associative patterner that is continuously re-creating knowledge for the situation at hand. Knowledge exists in the human brain in the form of stored or expressed neural patterns that may be selected, activated, mixed and/or reflected upon through thought. Incoming information is associated with stored information. From this mixing process new patterns are created that may represent understanding, meaning and the capacity to anticipate (to various degrees) the results of potential actions. Thus, knowledge is context sensitive and situation dependent, with the mind continuously growing, restructuring and creating increased organization (information) and knowledge for the moment at hand. While an in-depth treatment of the workings of the mind/brain is not included in this book, the concept of associative patterning will be addressed where appropriate.

Assumption 3: We are social creatures who live in an entangled world; our brains are linked together. We are in continuous interaction with those around us, and the brain is continuously changing in response (Bennet & Bennet, 2015). Further, over the course of evolution, mechanisms have developed in our brains to enable us to learn through social interactions. This impacts significantly on leadership approaches. See Chapter 8 on Collaborative Leadership.

Assumption 4: Leadership is a quality of what it is to be human. Every individual has some potential for leadership in some area of knowledge. This point will be made in both Chapter 8 on Collaborative Leadership and in Chapter 15 on Thought Leadership.

Assumption 5: Knowledge and leadership have always been in relationship. However, the significant mental growth emerging throughout the 20th century—where individuals at all levels began to expand their individual capacity to learn—and the expansion of the capacity for social knowledge in the interconnected world of the 21st century have plummeted humanity into a new age where knowledge—and the responsibility for how that knowledge is used—sits squarely on the shoulders of leadership at all levels.

Assumption 6: Human beings and the organizations we create are complex adaptive systems. A complex adaptive system (CAS) contains many parts that interact with each other. Complex adaptive systems are partially ordered systems that unfold and evolve through time. They are mostly self-organizing, learning and adaptive—thus their name. To survive and thrive, they are always creating new ideas, scanning the environment, trying new approaches, observing the results, and changing the way they operate. To continuously adapt, they must operate in perpetual disequilibrium, which can result in unpredictable behavior. Having nonlinear relationships, the CAS creates global properties that are called emergent because they seem to emerge from the multitude of elements within the system and the relationships among these elements. Examples are life, ecosystems, economies, organizations and cultures. The intelligent complex adaptive system model for organizations is introduced in Chapter 7.

Assumption 7: The New Reality. The world we live in is ever changing, uncertain and increasing in complexity (see Chapter 12). In other words, things are just as they should be, offering our organizations and leaders the opportunity to co-evolve with our Earth as the Golden Age of Humanity unfolds.

Building on these assumptions, the focus of this book is knowledge and leadership.

Section I, *Creating a Foundation*, lays the groundwork for understanding the material in the following sections. We begin with an Introduction, identifying three underlying issues that provide the incentive for this work. In Chapter 2 we address the terms of reference, specifically, leadership, management, information, knowledge and learning. Chapter 3 considers the force of knowledge from five frames of reference: (1) knowledge as the offspring of learning in relationship to making decisions, taking actions and learning; (2) knowledge as an imperfect and/or incomplete resource; (3) knowledge as a bounded resource supporting our beliefs and values; (4) deep knowledge as a limiting frame; and (5) knowledge as the action lever for creativity.

Section II, *Moving from the Past*, first looks at the historical connections between knowledge and leadership, beginning with the early hunter gatherer, circa 35,000 B.C., quickly moving to China and the beginnings of bureaucracy, touching on knowledge and the papacy, then fast-forwarding to the industrial age and into the 20th century. We then look specifically at the movement from management to leadership, focusing on the role knowledge plays. Finally we address the long-standing relationship between knowledge and power.

Section III, *Today and Tomorrow*, briefly presents the ICAS organizational model. In this section we first present a short overview of the intelligent complex adaptive system (ICAS) model for organizations, a model that enables organizations to react more quickly and fluidly to today's fast-changing, dynamic business environment (Bennet & Bennet, 2004). With the stage set, we ask is there an historic leadership style or approach that would meet the needs of the ICAS? We focus on collaborative leaders, those individuals *throughout the organization* who have the initiative, competency, and connections to mold, support, and guide their part of the organization's structure, culture, and execution competency to achieve high performance, then share some foundational concepts before exploring the knowledges leaders need in terms of types and variety. Finally, we address the leader as learner.

Section IV, *Intelligent Activity*, begins with examples of sustainability competences that support flexibility, quick response, resilience, robustness and continuous learning. In Chapter 13 we explore knowledge capacities, sets of ideas and ways of acting that are more general in nature than competencies. In Chapter 14 we delve into the leadership phenomenon of complexity driven simplicity.

Section V, *Thought Leadership*, is built out of the rich findings of research involving 34 thought leaders from four continents. This is the first time much of this material has been made generally available. Chapter 15 first explores the concept of thought leader, taking a closer look at various characteristics before delving into the effects of being a thought leader. The Leader Within, the title of Chapter 16, refers to the belief and value set of thought leaders. Chapter 17 deals with ideas, the offspring of thought leaders, exploring the mind/brain as an associative patterner, then looking at where thought leaders get their inspiration and how they feel about their ideas once they are out there in the general public. In Chapter 18—and in Appendix E and Appendix F supporting it—we first explore the construct of passion, then specifically look at the passions driving thought leaders.

Yours in learning, Alex, David and John

The Drs. Bennet live at the Mountain Quest Institute, situated on a 450-acre farm in the Allegheny Mountains of West Virginia. See www.mountainquestinstitute.com They may be reached at alex@mountainquestinstitute.com Dr. Lewis lives in Richmond, Virginia, where he is co-founder at the CoHero Institute. See www.cohero-institute.com. John can be reached at john@cohero-institute.com.

ADDENDUM: In 2017 the Bennets were joined by Dr. Arthur Shelley, Dr. Theresa Bullard, Dr. John Lewis and Dr. Donna Panucci in developing and expanding what has become known as the Intelligent Social Change Journey. This word was first published in five parts as *The Profundity and Bifurcation of Change.* Part I is Laying the Groundwork; Part II focuses on Learning from the Past, assuming that for every effect there is an originating cause; Part III focuses on Learning in the Present, co-evolving with the environment; Part IV is about Co-Creating the Future, learning to fully embrace our role as co-creator; and Part V is Living the Future.

Twenty-two core concepts emerging from this work are the focus of the Conscious Look Books entitled *Possibilities that are YOU!* Each volume of this title presents seven ideas in a conversational format, with exercises, stories and examples. There is also a Conscious Look Book entitled *The Intelligent Social Change Journey*, which was published in 2019. We hope this body of work is of service to you.

Section I
Creating a Foundation

You bring amazing capabilities and capacities with you as you sit down at your reader or computer to scan this book. We're counting on it, because we're going to take a consilience approach to this material, integrating findings from business, psychology, education, philosophy, neuroscience and spirituality, to name a few fields. You're going to be bombarded with old stuff and new stuff banged together with a third kind of stuff—which doesn't even have a name yet—that's going to be emerging in YOUR head. And THAT's the stuff ideas are made of. Welcome to the world of thought leading!

As if that's not enough, we're going to ask you to share your ideas, and this book as you see fit, with others. Create the conversation, join the conversation, and enjoy the conversation!

In this section we lay the foundation for the book. We begin with an Introduction, exploring the emergence of collaboration as we moved into a global world. In Chapter 2 we slow down a bit to address the terms of reference, specifically, leadership, management, information, knowledge and learning. Revving back up, Chapter 3 considers the *force of knowledge* from five frames of reference: (1) knowledge as the offspring of learning in relationship to making decisions, taking actions and learning; (2) knowledge as an imperfect and/or incomplete resource; (3) knowledge as a bounded resource supporting our beliefs and values; (4) deep knowledge as a limiting frame; and (5) knowledge as the action lever for creativity.

Thank you all for joining us on this journey. As you can see, we're all about building the skills and knowledge that can change the world!

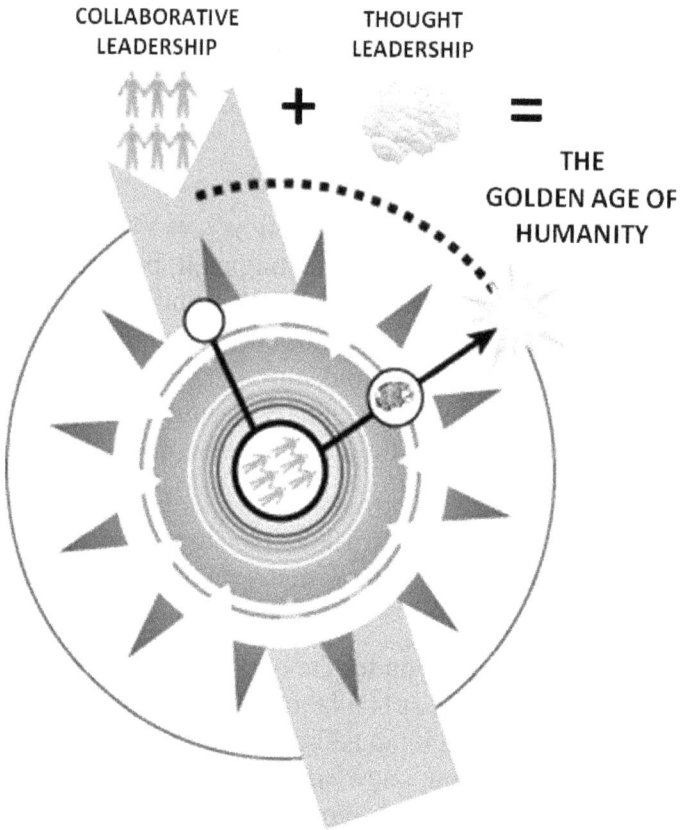

COLLABORATIVE
LEADERSHIP

THOUGHT
LEADERSHIP

THE
GOLDEN AGE OF
HUMANITY

Together we dream the future ...

Chapter 1
Introduction

The increase in world and local dynamics, uncertainty, and complexity is impacting citizens throughout the globe. Having moved from the information age to the knowledge age, everything moves faster, farther, and gets intertwined with other people, societies, and technology. Companies collaborate instantly around the world, people work from home, virtual connectivity gets heavier, money moves faster among nations, and organizations move from control oriented to empowered workforces. To operate successfully leaders at all levels must deal with the increasing speed, unpredictability, and complexity of their environment.

While some levels of complexity have existed throughout history, the explosion of information, communication speed, and networking is moving the world toward an increasingly complex state. The saying complexity begets complexity (Battram, 1996) has proven itself over the past few decades in such examples as the Internet, electric power grids, international finance and market flows (Friedman, 2005; Kurzweil, 2005). While complexity has historically built upon complexity because of the competitive nature of the world, this phenomenon also occurs through creativity and collaboration, creating a collaborative entanglement that erases cause and effect relationships. All of this is at play in the current environment. This global trend can be characterized as increasing **Change**, rising **Uncertainty**, growing **Complexity**, and ubiquitous **Anxiety**— or **CUCA** (Bennet & Bennet, 2004; 2007). This term is used throughout this book.

Never has there been a time when the call to leadership is more compelling, more needed, a leadership with knowledge generation at its very core. For the first time in history, the idea of global touches every country and every culture, offering the potential to reach every organization and every person. The principles of diversity, universal access, freedom of expression, and

> There has never been a time when the call to leadership is more compelling, more needed.

education for all ride upon a foundation of pluralism, inclusion, equity and openness, all forming the building blocks of knowledge creation, preservation, dissemination and utilization (UNESCO, 2005; Souter, 2010). Societal values, structural frameworks and individual capabilities and capacities are merging with knowledge processes and tangible and intangible assets to achieve societal economic, social and environmental goals (Hector, 2015).

And in the midst of this journey toward intelligent activity, ideas are sparked and knowledge emerges, and people come together to pursue the ever-larger dream. In the conversations the leaders emerge, in their communities, in their organizations, sharing their thoughts and passions, igniting the flame of collaboration.

From Competition to Collaboration

When Darwin first published his book in 1859, *On the Origin of Species,* he voiced conclusions regarding the superior strength of individuals. His conclusion was "survival of the fittest" became an accepted business mantra leading to and supporting hard competition. What is lesser known is that later in life in his book, *The Descent of Man*, Darwin had realized his mistake. As he summarized, "Those communities which included the greatest number of the most sympathetic members would flourish best and rear the greatest number of offspring." (Darwin, 1998, p. 110) It was too late. Darwin's early work had become a meme, taking on a life of its own and steering businesses away from cooperation and goodness.

In the early 20th century, Russian naturalist Peter Kropotkin had discovered from his own observations that "cooperation and unity, rather than survival of the fittest, are the keys to the success of a species." (Kropotkin, 1902) As John Swomley, a professor emeritus of Social Ethics at the St. Paul School of Theology, bluntly stated in direct contradiction to Darwin's earlier work that cooperation is the "key factor in evolution and survival." (Swomley, 2000, p. 20). But in the world of business, where hard competition was rearing its head and roaring its way to winning regardless of direct or collateral damage, power, control and the accumulation of wealth had gained a toehold for those who had the unique abilities and mindsets to plunge forward at all costs.

Recognition that competition was not the best answer to the American Dream was emerging long before we had the language of complexity to describe the shifting environment and develop a new business model for an information-rich global society. As early as 1912 the limitations of competition were publicly recognized. At a speech at the People's Forum in Troy, New York, on March 3, 1912, President Franklin Roosevelt stated, "Competition has been shown to be useful up to a certain point and no further, but cooperation, which is the thing we must strive for today, begins where competition leaves off." (Rosenberg, 2015) As early as 1912 it was already clear that competition would not take us the distance.

Competition has historically been viewed in terms of soft and hard. Soft competition is based primarily on reputation; in individuals (and sometimes organizations) this translates to ego-driving urges to be "better than", the "best". Hard competition has been a part of our dog-eat-dog world. This approach is based more on power, control, and "survival of the fittest" in what has been perceived as a bounded market and economy of limits.

Collaboration is the process where two or more people and/or organizations work together towards achieving mutually beneficial goals and objectives. This is the co-creation of value through open sharing, the leveraging of existing resources and creating new insights through the bisociation of ideas. During the course of interaction there emerges a *collaborative entanglement*, a dynamic process of mixing, analyzing, discussing, perceiving and interpreting knowledge from different perspectives with emergent patterns. *Collaborative advantage* can be described in terms of open communications, shared understanding, and decision-making that collectively and equitably moves collaborators in an agreed-upon direction.

And as we moved into Internet dominance, concepts and terms began to emerge that tempered the hard edge of competition with elements of cooperation and collaboration. An early concept was co-opetition. Applying game theory to business—with money representing points won or lost—co-opetition is described by Brandenburger and Nalebuff (1997) as part cooperation and part competition, creating a new dynamic to generate more profits and change the nature of the business environment. The underlying premise is that

> As we moved into Internet dominance, concepts and terms began to emerge that tempered the hard edge of competition with elements of cooperation and collaboration.

companies can achieve sustainable competitive advantage by changing the game to their own advantage, cooperating and/or competing where appropriate for maximum gains. Long-term gains come not only from competing successfully in the current environment, but from being an active participant in shaping the future environment and creating expanded opportunities.

Amazon is an excellent example of co-opetition. Amazon works closely with other companies while also competing with them. For example, the Amazon Marketplace enables competitors of any size to use Amazon's online platform and technological capabilities to present millions of new, used, and rare books and other products to millions of customers. Competitor's products are displayed right next to similar products sold by Amazon.

Enter the new century. Different combinations of competition and collaboration comprise the interim currency of today as we move toward ever-increasing connection and collaboration in our global world. Figure 1-1 looks at the characteristics of competition and collaboration in terms of inside or outside organizational boundaries. Dependent on the primary focus—competition or collaboration—we can describe combinations as collaborative competition or competitive collaboration, respectively. Note that while innovation can occur in all four sectors, we now recognize that innovation is a highly interactive, multidisciplinary process that increasingly involves cooperation and partnerships between a growing and diverse network of individuals and organizations (Kapeleris, 2012).

Collaborative competition is a developed skill set that supports relationship building and leverages collaboration strengths. This approach cultivates a strategic mindset and a personalized, healthy approach to competition (Mayer, 2009). It can inspire, spark creativity, and make work fun. For example, Dr. Kenneth Cohn (2008), a specialist in physician-administrator communication issues, shares two stories focused on enhanced healthcare collaboration. In the first story, a cardiologist kept track of starting times in the catheterization lab and used healthy competition to motivate other cardiologists to show up on time. He noted, "Cardiologists are a lot like alpha dogs who, when a bone is tossed their way, are eager to fetch." (Cohn, 2008)

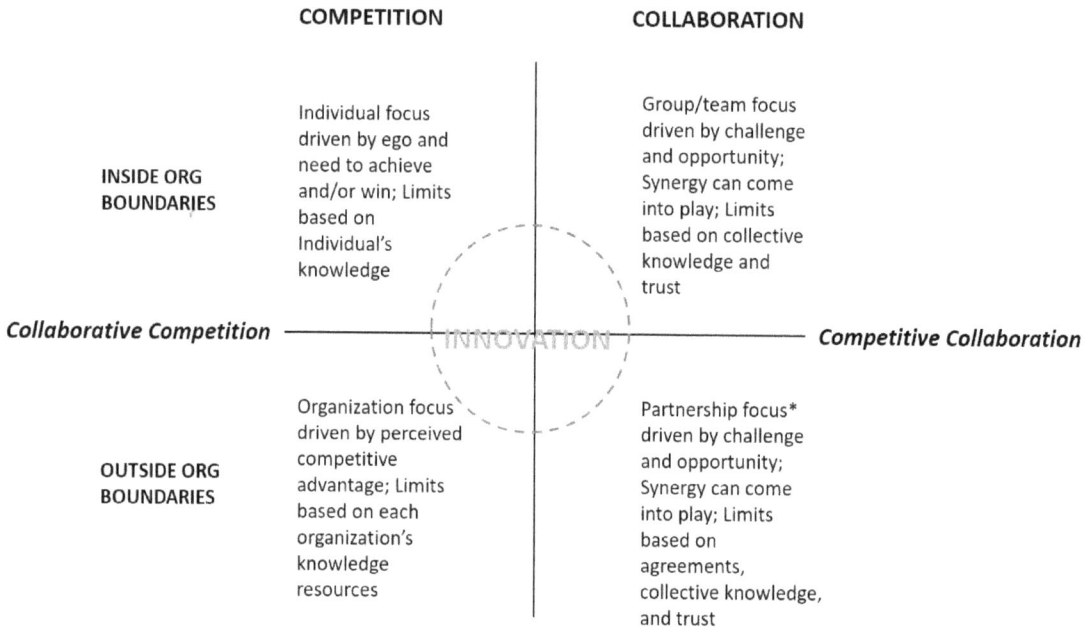

Figure 1-1. *The fields of collaborative competition and competitive collaboration.* *Note: Teaming, partnering, and alliances are terms given to more formal relationships between organizations. They imply the intent of one or more organizations to work together to improve the effectiveness and efficiency of a common goal, and to reduce the costs of disagreements.*

Another example of collaborative competition is the Northwrite 2013 exercise. Sponsored by the New Zealand Society of Authors, Northland Branch, the focus of this competition was on writers working with writers, with the choice of collaboration approaches left up to the participants. The judges were pleased with the variety.

> We discovered stories and poetry woven together; we witnessed cases of experimentation with language and form; we admired pieces that explored variety in voice and tone. From humor to suspense to the esoteric, these entries captivated and challenged us as readers, and as competition judges. (Northwrite, 2013)

Their bottom line is that the process of collaboration changes the outcome, takes the creative endeavor in new directions and creates something altogether original and surprising.

Competitive collaboration is when companies channel their competitive energy towards a common goal. It is a style of cooperation that demands real commitment and deep engagement from both parties.

Competition is a valuable human behavior. It is a great motivator ... Rather than ignore this dynamic and expect purely altruistic motives, organizations are wise to work with it. Channel the competitive energies toward collaborative behaviors that drive innovation. (Carpenter, 2014)

A key principle is to recognize and reward people for contributions that help advance ideas as much as the people who originate the ideas. Carpenter (2014) says there are three design principles required for the effective application of this approach: (1) Enable the provision and visibility of feedback; (2) recognize those who do it well; and (3) provide tangible incentives for collaborative behavior. For example, in the U.S. Department of Navy a community of practice provided awards to all participants who contributed to finding solutions to problems or issues addressed by the community (Porter, et al., 2002). Since the community interacted on a virtual platform, it was quite easy to observe member contributions. This could also be achieved through the process of peer ratings.

Singapore Airlines (SA) chose a competitive collaboration approach in the process of launching a full-service carrier in a 49:51 joint venture with Tata Group. Tata-SIA airline submitted its application for the grant of Air Operator's Permit in April 2015. Tata found an opportunity in new areas of business by collaborating with SIA. SIA recognized the synergy in this relationship. As Tan Pee Teck, SIA Senior VP for Product Services, says, "I think there is some compatibility obviously in the relationship ... There is competitive collaboration and adversarial competition." (Teck, 2015)

In the interconnected world of today this approach can never again gain a long-term foothold. As can be seen, the journey away from seeking competitive advantage to seeking collaborative advantage is well underway, a journey that produces win-wins instead of winners and losers, a journey where collaborative leadership at all levels of the organization, community, country and world emerges.

The Search for Transcendent Themes

As William Gibson puts it, "The future has already happened, it's just unequally distributed." (Hamel, 2000, p. 128) From our viewpoints down in the middle of the thicket, immersed in a world that we perceive as continuously changing, becoming more and more complex, and increasingly uncertain (Bennet & Bennet, 2004), it is difficult to integrate the patterns that are emerging in our own organizations, much less in leadership. Yet, here is one more requirement for leaders, the search for transcendent themes. As Hamel explains, "One of the reasons many people fail to fully appreciate what's changing is because they're down at ground level, lost in a thicket of confusing, conflicting data. You have to make time to step back and ask yourself, what's the big story that cuts across all these little facts?" (Hamel, 2000, p. 128) Since answers may close thinking while questions open possibilities we begin with Hamel's question: So, what's the big story that cuts across all these little facts?

Once upon a time there was a young leader who began to realize that she didn't know everything she needed to know. She began her leadership journey by making a conscious effort to fully understand her *self*, exploring her spirituality and her relationship to nature. Over time, she began to build relationships with others holding similar moral values who could contribute to her knowledge and knowing, and to whom she could contribute. As these relationships continued, this group moved from mutual respect to trust, and developed into a living network. Their curiosity and continuous sharing unleashed new ideas, spurring individual and collective learning. They began to recognize patterns and connections among things. They grew into a global community and, as they began to recognize knowledge as a limitless resource, they individually and collectively integrated their holistic self into the workings of their work, rotating leadership according to their knowledge, passions and the community needs. And through the multidimensionality of their transcendent feeling and thinking, they began to change the world.

This is what is happening in our organizations today. And while there is no one way to capture this, to describe this, to share this, we will make humble attempts to do so, focusing on the collaborative nature of leadership and the unbounded potential of the mind/brain.

Chapter 2
Terms of Reference

Since the terms leadership and knowledge are used repeatedly in describing the movement from *physical* demonstration of power to *knowledge* as power, some working definitions of these terms are provided. We also provide definitions for management, information and learning—terms closely aligned with leadership and knowledge. Throughout this book we continue to clarify these concepts, providing context to develop and expand the rich meaning of each.

Leadership

Leadership, as a quality of the organization, is an institutional capacity to organize, energize and synergize to take effective action. There are as many definitions of leadership as there are people who have attempted to define the concept. Stogdill's Handbook of Leadership explores "leadership" as: a focus of group processes, personality and its effects, the art of inducing compliance, the exercise of influence, an act or behavior, a form of

> As a quality of the organization, leadership is an institutional capacity to organize, energize and synergize to take effective action.

persuasion, a power relation, an instrument of goal achievement, an emerging effect of interaction, a differentiated role, and the initiation of structure (Bass, 1981). As a working definition, we consider leadership to be **the process of giving meaningful direction to collective effort and causing willing effort to be expended to achieve collective goals** (Jacobs & Jaques, 1991).

We contend that *effective* leadership in today's global world is, by necessity, *spiritual in nature*. Using Google's Ngram Viewer, we can see the rise and fall in the usage of terms within books over the years. As we consider the trends for the usage of the terms spiritual, leadership, and collaboration, we find that the terms collaboration and leadership were virtually not used in print media in 1880, while the term spiritual was used frequently. See Figure 2-1.

Now, in addition to the upward trend in the use of the term collaboration, we also see a recent crossover between spiritual and leadership. As we consider where we turn to for knowledge, guidance, and inspiration, it appears we have begun to turn away from the type of leadership, as a standalone term, that dominated since the 1960's, and are moving towards a spiritual and collaborative approach towards gaining knowledge, guidance, and inspiration.

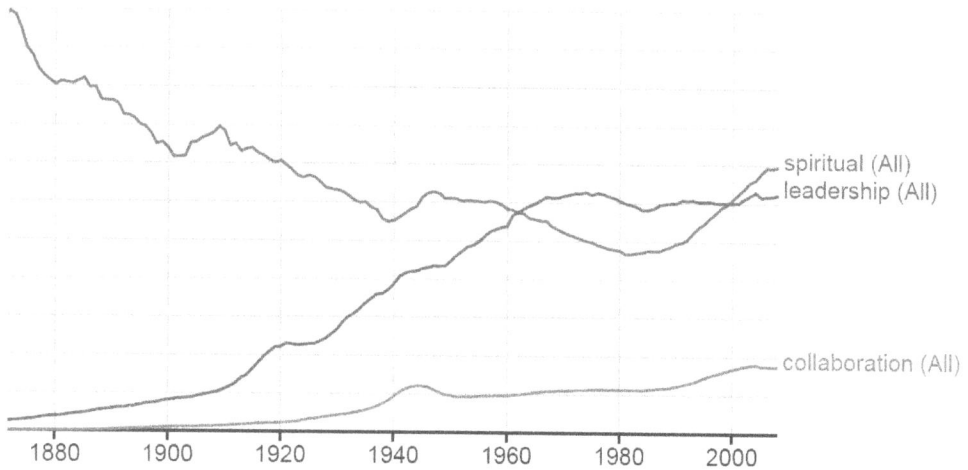

Figure 2-1. *Usage of terms in literature over the years*

The term spiritual is taken to mean pertaining to the soul, or "standing in relationship to another based on matters of the soul" (*Oxford*, 2002, p. 2963). Soul represents the animating principle of human life in terms of thought and action, specifically focused on **its moral aspects, the emotional part of human nature, and higher development of the mental faculties**. From the philosophical aspect, it is the vital, sensitive or rational principle in human beings (*Oxford*, 2002, p., 2928). Csikszentmihalyi says that "an enduring vision in both work and life derives its power from soul—the energy a person or organization devotes to purposes beyond itself." (Csikszentmihalyi, 2003, p. 19) An alternative definition of spiritual is **of or pertaining to the intellect** (intellectual, the capacity for knowledge and understanding, the ability to think abstractly or profoundly) (*American Heritage*, 2000, p. 910) **and of the mind** (in terms of highly refined, sensitive and not concerned with material things) (*Oxford*, 2002, p. 2963).

The importance of this concept is recognition of the interconnection of humanity in a global setting, and the responsibility to ensure the health of our world today and the sustainability of our world for future generations. When we refer to the greater good throughout this book, this is the essence of that state of being.

Some may wonder why the terms leadership and spiritual are so intertwined. The collaborative leadership model taught at the CoHero Institute operates with "workability beliefs" at the core. For any given topic or project, there will always be people that believe that it works and those that believe that it won't work. But the same is true for the workability belief that we rarely mention, where all projects and stories spend a significant amount of time: *could work*. It is within this workability belief that we spend most of our efforts working towards transformational change. And in here, to effectively lead, we have to reflectively state the ideas we are going to put our faith in. It is not a matter of having fact or having faith, which is a false dichotomy since we all put our faith in some idea when in the state of *could work*. When working through "could work," trying to reach "does work," we need to actively state that we are putting our faith in something or someone, which could be our own strategy, our weapons systems, our own strength, a new consultant, our leaders, our government, or a higher source. In the struggle to reach "does work," sometimes we find that we have to change what we put our faith in within "could work," and leadership provides guidance, to a new, changed, *does work*.

Management

Although the terms management and leadership are often intermixed—in today's world, and in this book—they can represent significant differences. Since World War II management has been closely tied to planning, organizing, staffing, directing and controlling, the classical POSDC found in many management textbooks of that era. Managers achieved goals by creating an organizational infrastructure and a set of specific jobs for accomplishing plan milestones, staffing the jobs with qualified people and developing systems to carefully monitor and measure progress. Leaders were expected to energize and align people by creating a vision that motivates and inspires. But these differences in terminology and focus are relatively recent. In Chapter 4 we provide a broad brush of the evolution of the relationship between management and leadership.

Information

Information and knowledge are concepts that have long histories and multiple interpretations, making it difficult to communicate their meaning within a given context. Theoretical biologist Tom Stonier (1997) defined information in the following way:

> Specifically, a system may be said to contain information if such a system exhibits organization. That is, just as mass is a reflection of a system containing matter, and heat is a reflection of a system containing energy, so is organization a reflection of a system containing information. (p. 14)

By organization, Stonier means the *existence of non-random patterns*. From Stonier's perspective, information is a fundamental property of the universe and takes equal status with energy and matter (Stonier, 1990; 1997). Embracing Stonier's work, *we take information to be a measure of the degree of organization expressed by any non-random pattern or set of patterns*. The order within a system is a reflection of the information content of the system. Data, a subset of information, is factual information organized for analyses. In computer science, it is used to describe numerical or other information represented in a form suitable for processing by computers. The term is also used to represent values derived from scientific experiments (*American Heritage*

Dictionary, 1992). While data and information are both patterns, they have no meaning until some organism recognizes and interprets the patterns (Stonier, 1997; Bennet & Bennet, 2008b). Thus, information exists in the human brain in the form of stored or expressed neuronal patterns that may be activated and reflected upon through conscious thought.

This interpretation of information offers three advantages. First, it recognizes the foundational nature of the concept and, as such, information becomes a part of all life and the physical world, as we understand it at this time. Second, information is precisely defined such that the definition circumvents the confusion of multiple interpretations. Third, this definition should be applicable to both the natural sciences and the humanities, at least to the extent that where interpretations contradict each other they can be recognized and acknowledged as personal opinion.

Knowledge

As we shall see in this book, knowledge has turned—and continues to turn—the role of leadership upside down. Knowledge has an interesting history beginning with Plato and Aristotle up to the present. The early definition authored by Plato, which is still used by many people today, is knowledge as justified true belief. In other words if someone believed A, and could justify their belief and demonstrate that A was true, then that person had knowledge of A. For example, if we said that Austin was the capital of Texas and showed it to you on a map to justify the statement, and you went to Austin, Texas, and validated that truly there was an Austin, Texas, then we would both agree we had knowledge of the existence of Austin, Texas. While we do not take issue with the justified true belief approach, and certainly it served humanity well in beginning the conversation around knowledge, we define knowledge in a different manner such that it represents a more relevant and significantly important concept for the modern age.

As a functional definition, *knowledge is considered the capacity (potential or actual) to take effective action in varied and uncertain situations* (Bennet & Bennet, 2004); a human capacity that may consist of understanding, insights, meaning, intuition, creativity, judgment, and the ability to anticipate the outcome of our actions.

> Knowledge is considered the capacity (potential or actual) to take effective action in varied and uncertain situations.

Understanding includes the description of the situation and its information content that provides the *who, what, where* and *when*. It involves the frame of reference of the observer, including assumptions and presuppositions. This can be referred to as surface knowledge (Moon, 2004; Bennet & Bennet, 2008b; 2015a). Meaning is the significance created in the mind/brain of the knower by relating the incoming information of a perceived situation to the current cognitive structures of the learner. Thus, meaning can be determined only by the learner and can result from the situation, its history, and/or the implications of the situation as affecting the future (Edelman & Tononi, 2000; Sousa, 2006; Stonier, 1997).

Insight is taken to mean, "The capacity to discern the true nature of a situation; penetration. The act or outcome of grasping the inward or hidden nature of things or of perceiving in an intuitive manner" (*American Heritage Dictionary*, 2006, p. 906). Intuition is the act or faculty of knowing or sensing without the use of rational processes; immediate cognition (*American Heritage Dictionary*, 2006, p. 919). From another perspective, insight is also the result of searching for new relationships between concepts in one domain with those in another domain (Crandall et al., 2006). It creates a recognition and understanding of a problem within the situation, including the how and why of the past and current behavior of the situation. It is often the result of intuition, competence, and the identification of patterns, themes and cue sets (Crandall et al., 2006). Insight may also provide patterns and relationships that will anticipate the future behavior of the situation. Creativity is the emergence of new or original patterns (ideas, concepts, or actions) that "typically have three components: originality, utility and some kind of product" (Andreasen, 2005, p. 17).

As used here, prediction is the anticipation or expectation of solutions to, and the results of, proposed actions on some situation. Prediction does not imply certainty but rather is the best estimate, expectation, or probability that an individual has for anticipating the outcome of his or her actions. For a complicated situation it may come from identifying and understanding the causal relationships within the situation and their influence in the future. For a complex system it may come from intuition, pattern recognition, creative exploration, and an awareness of approaches to influencing such systems. It could also include past experience with, and an understanding of, complex systems theory and practice (Bennet & Bennet, 2004; 2007; 2013). An advantage of these definitions of information and knowledge is that their meaning can be applied in terms of the mind/brain and in social communication.

Knowledge (Informing and Proceeding)

While knowledge has an information component called Knowledge (Informing), it also has a process component called Knowledge (Proceeding) that consists of the capacity to put information together in different ways by recalling, selecting, combining, and integrating internal and external information to create and implement effective actions (Bennet & Bennet, 2015a). This builds on the distinction made by Ryle (1949) between "knowing that" and "knowing how" (the potential and actual capacity to take effective action).

Knowledge (Informing) is the *information (or content)* part of knowledge. While this information part of knowledge is still generically information (organized patterns), it is special because of its structure and relationships with other information. Knowledge (Informing) consists of information that may represent understanding, meaning, insights, expectations, intuition, theories and principles that support or lead to effective action. When viewed separately this is information even though it *may* lead to effective action. It is considered knowledge when used as *part of the knowledge process*. In this context, the same thought may be information in one situation and knowledge in another situation.

Knowledge (Proceeding), represents the *process* and *action* part of knowledge. It is the process of selecting and associating or applying the relevant information, or Knowledge (Informing), from which specific actions can be identified and implemented, that is, actions that result in some level of anticipated outcome. There is considerable precedent for considering knowledge as a process versus an outcome of some action. For example, Kolb (1984) forwards in his theory of experiential learning that knowledge retrieval, creation and application requires engaging knowledge as a process, *not* a product. Bohm reminds us that "the actuality of knowledge is a living process that is taking place right now" and that we are taking part in this process (Bohm, 1980, p. 64). Note that the process our minds use to find, create and semantically mix the information needed to take effective action is often unconscious and difficult to communicate to someone else; therefore, by definition, tacit.

Figure 2-2 shows the relationships among Knowledge (Informing) and Knowledge (Proceeding). "Justified True Beliefs"—the definition of knowledge credited to Plato and his dialogues (Fine, 2003)—represents the theories, values and beliefs of an individual that are generally developed over time and often tacit, that is, difficult to express.

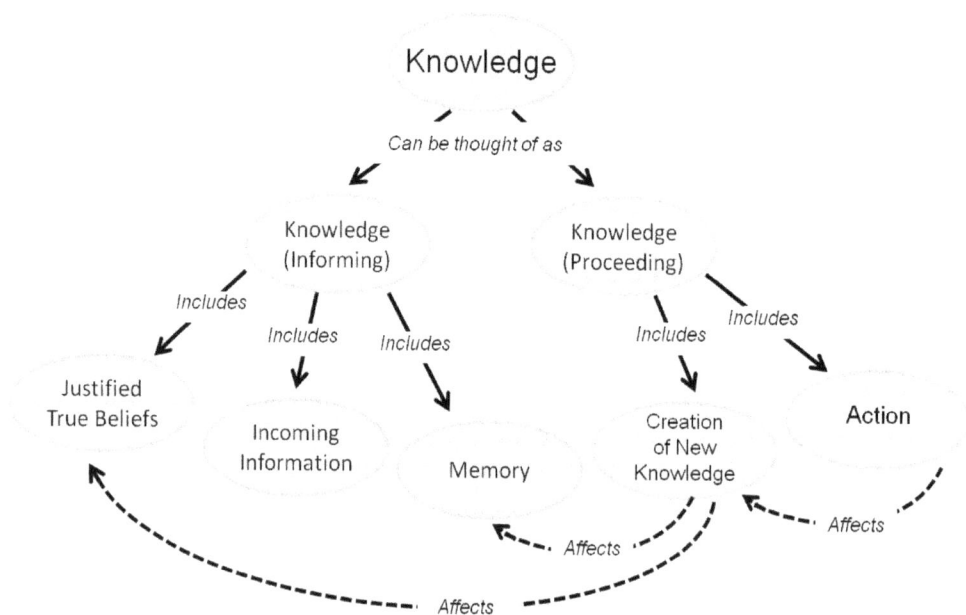

Figure 2-2. *Knowledge (Informing) and Knowledge (Proceeding)*

Note that justified true belief represents an *individual's* truth, that is, whether judging my

personal experience or judging the experience of others, the beliefs and values that make up our

personal theories, all developed and reinforced by personal life experiences, impact that

judgment. Therefore, it is acknowledged that an individual's justified true belief may be based on

a falsehood (Gettier, 1963). However, if it is used to take effective action in terms of the user's

expectations of outcomes, then *it is considered knowledge from that individual's viewpoint.*

Building on the definitions of Knowledge (Informing) and Knowledge (Proceeding) introduced above, it is also useful to think about knowledge in terms of three levels: surface, shallow and deep. Recognizing any model is an artificial construct, the focus on three levels (as a continuum) is consistent with a focus on simple, complicated and complex systems (Bennet & Bennet, 2013; 2008b) and appropriate in the context of its initial use with the U.S Department of the Navy (DON), the first government organization to be named as a Most Admired Knowledge Enterprise for their extensive work in Knowledge Management and organizational learning.

Levels of Knowledge

Surface knowledge is predominantly but not exclusively simple information (used to take effective action). Answering the question of what, when, where and who, it is primarily explicit, and represents visible choices that require minimum understanding. Surface knowledge in the form of information can be stored in books and computers. Because it has little meaning to improve recall, and few connections to other stored memories, surface knowledge is frequently difficult to remember and easy to forget (Sousa, 2006). **Shallow knowledge** includes information that has some depth of understanding, meaning and sense-making. To make meaning requires context, which the individual creates from mixing incoming information with their own internally-stored information, a process of creating Knowledge (Proceeding). Meaning can be created via logic, analysis, observation, reflection, and even—to some extent—prediction. Shallow knowledge is the realm of social knowledge, and as such this focus of KM overlaps with social learning theory (Bennet & Bennet, 2010; 2007a). For example, organizations that embrace the use of teams and communities facilitate the mobilization of surface and shallow knowledge (context rich) and the creation of new ideas as individuals interact, learn and create new ideas in these groups.

For **deep knowledge** the decision-maker has developed and integrated many if not all of the following seven components: understanding, meaning, intuition, insight, creativity, judgment, and the ability to anticipate the outcome of our actions. Deep knowledge within a knowledge domain represents the ability to shift our frame of reference as the context and situation shift. Since Knowledge (Proceeding) must be created in order to know when and how to take effective action, the unconscious plays a large role, with much of deep knowledge tacit. This is the realm of the expert who has learned to detect patterns and evaluate their importance in anticipating the behavior of situations that are too complex for the conscious mind to understand. During the lengthy period of practice (lived experience) needed to develop deep knowledge in the domain of focus, *experts have developed internal theories* that guide their Knowledge (Proceeding) (Bennet & Bennet, 2015a; 2008b).

Learning

Building on the definition of knowledge, *learning is considered an increase in the capacity (potential or actual) to take effective action, that is, knowledge*. From a neuroscience perspective, this means that learning is the identification, selection and mixing of the relevant neural patterns (information) within the learner's mind with the information from an external situation and its environment to create understanding, meaning and anticipation of the results of selected actions (Bennet & Bennet, 2008e). Each learning experience builds on its predecessor by broadening the sources of knowledge creation and the capacity to create knowledge in different ways. When an individual has deep knowledge, more and more of their learning will continuously build up in the unconscious. In other words, in the area of focus, knowledge begets knowledge.

In Chapter 3 we introduce the learning-knowledge loop to expand on the steps within the cycle where knowledge begets knowledge. The more that is understood, the more that can be created and understood, relegating more to the unconscious to free the conscious mind to address the instant at hand. The wider the scope of application and feedback, the greater the

> In the learning-knowledge loop, the more that is understood, the more that can be created and understood.

potential to identify second order patterns, which in the largest aggregate lead to the phenomena of Big Data (Mayer-Schönberger & Cukier, 2013). Figure 2-1 is an example of using *big data*, that is, a very large data set, to produce second order patterns. Lewis (2013) defines learning as "the gaining of knowing, satisfied with some degree of reason." As leadership and learning become more collaborative, the reasons that satisfy what we know will move beyond the authoritative "because the leader/teacher said so," and beyond the principles and probabilities, and finally towards the questions that we would dare ask. This book seeks to develop the knowledge, and the questions, that allow us to lead with the future in mind.

Final Thoughts

One final term for this chapter is *linguistic relativity*, which is the idea that the terms a person speaks with has an influence on this person's cognition. Words are not just outputs of thought; they are also input toward what a person can think. This is why an introduction to key terms is near the front of this book, not at the end, so that you have a strong foundation in the deep meanings of terms like leadership and knowledge, with the following chapters developing and expanding on the principle that knowledge begets knowledge.

Chapter 3
The Force of Knowledge

Knowledge has played and continues to play a large role in the human drama of growth and expansion. In this drama, knowledge itself is neither true nor false, and its value in terms of good or poor is difficult to measure other than by the outcomes of its actions. Knowledge includes a special form of information and all information is energy; how it is used determines its value. Hence, good knowledge would have a high probability of producing the desired and anticipated outcome, and poor knowledge would have a low probability of producing the expected result. Note that the concept of "good" or "bad" is not connected to morality but to anticipated outcome of the user. For complex situations, the quality of knowledge (from good to poor, relative to each specific situation) may be hard to estimate before the action is taken because of the situation's unpredictability. After the outcome has occurred, the quality of knowledge can be assessed by comparing the actual outcome to the anticipated outcome.

However, as knowledge is connected to other knowledge, shared and expanded, there is an emergent quality of "goodness" in terms of the greater good, which concept was described in Chapter 2. This is because the sharing of knowledge—that is, bringing knowledges together which are imperfect or incomplete—move the individuals, organizations or countries who are sharing toward intelligent activity, with the result of taking action that has a higher potential for effectiveness. In addition, the concept of "effectiveness" is now a shared intent, with the "goodness" of the result perceived by multiple individuals, organizations or countries. This is why *intelligent activity is described as a perfect state of interaction where intent, purpose, direction, values and expected outcomes are clearly understood and communicated among all parties, reflecting wisdom and achieving a higher truth.*

> As knowledge is connected to other knowledge, shared and expanded, there is an emergent quality of "goodness" in terms of the greater good.

To aid leaders at all levels in understanding and potentially harnessing knowledge, we shall explore the force of knowledge from five frames of reference: (1) knowledge as the offspring of learning in relationship to making decisions and taking actions; (2) knowledge as an imperfect and/or incomplete resource; (3) knowledge as a bounded resource supporting our beliefs and values; (4) deep knowledge as a limiting frame; and (5) knowledge as the action lever for creativity and innovation.

From Learning to Knowledge

Knowledge determines the quality of every single decision we make. We are continuously informed from without and within and by uniquely sifting through, focusing, and connecting the stream of information that informs our knowledge and drives our actions. Sometimes we recognize our choices, and sometimes they are beyond our conscious awareness, that is, buried in the unconscious. The knowledge we can create is both triggered by external events and very much determined by our past experiences and current state of learning, what is called the process of associative patterning.

While individual experience is the primary facet for human learning (Bennet & Bennet, 2015b), learning does not occur in isolation, that is, we are social creatures who live in an entangled world. Thus the model showing the learning-knowledge loop—focused on the learning environment—begins with experience directly impacting learning. Simultaneously, it acknowledges that social interaction (social engagement) and thinking (cognitive processes) also directly impact the learning experience, all combining to create knowledge, *the capacity to take effective action.* See Figure 3-1.

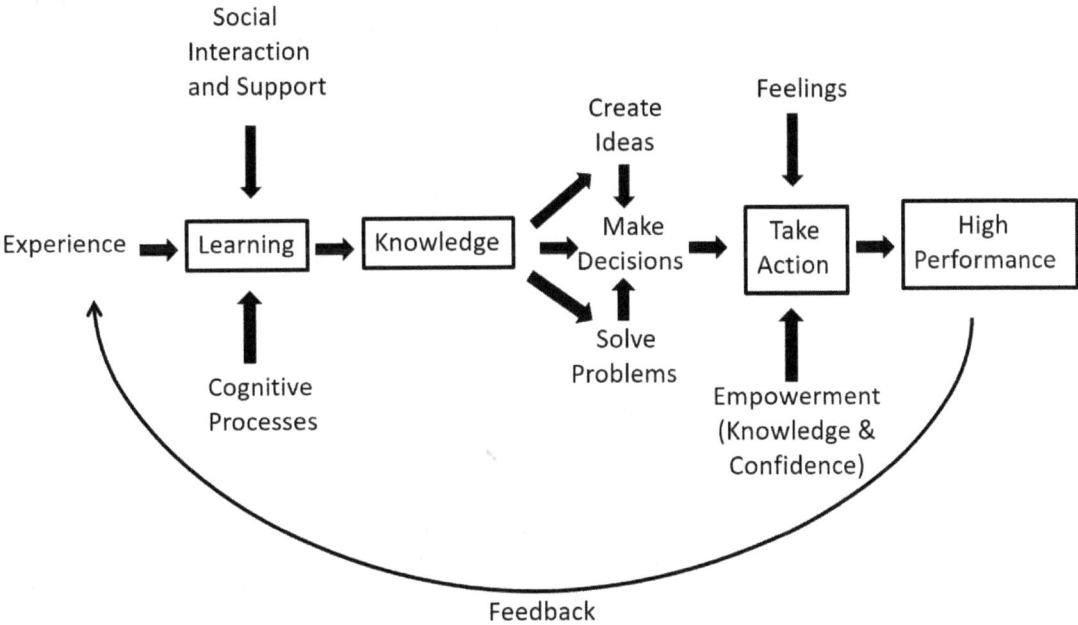

Figure 3-1. *The Learning-Knowledge Loop*

The Learning-Knowledge Loop can be viewed from the framework of the individual self or an organization. From the viewpoint of the organization, we start with the question: What completely determines the performance of an organization on any given day? We propose that the answer is: The actions taken by every employee on any given day determines the performance of the organization that day. We then ask: What determines the actions an employee takes? This is where thoughts and feelings come into play, both the thoughts and feelings emerging from within the individual (conscious and unconscious cognitive processes) and the thoughts and feelings triggered by the external environment (social interaction and social support) (Bennet & Bennet, 2015b). It is these thoughts and feelings, Knowledge (Informing), complexed with incoming information about the environment and situations, also Knowledge (Informing), that influence the perception and effectiveness of the actions that are taken, Knowledge (Proceeding).

Think about all of the relationships and activities that occur on a given day. While these activities often seem minimal in the course of life, over time they completely determine the performance, and success, of the organization. The same set of questions and comments can be applied to the individual. From this viewpoint we can see that daily actions taken become extremely important for achievement of long-term goals and sustainability. And all these actions are based on our knowledge, what we have learned from past experiences (including beliefs and values), what we know about the current situation, and the anticipated outcome of our actions. The force of our knowledge, then, is highly dependent on our capacity to learn.

> The force of our knowledge is highly dependent on our capacity to learn.

As we consider individuals and organizational cultures the "regulators" in this capacity to learn, there are two primary orientations to consider. One orientation is a "learner" who leans towards curiosity and moves with the flow of knowledge and feedback. Another orientation is a "knower" who leans towards conviction, learning something new only when forced just to return to their home base of knowing as quickly as possible. Compared to the "learner," a "knower" has more cognitive laziness and defensiveness due to confirmation seeking. This use of the label "knower" refers to subconscious knowing, that is, a limited knowing based on a set of bounded past experiences heavily tied to our personal comfort zone, which would include our beliefs and values and the limits they set. (See Chapter 114 for a discussion of knowing as a higher order energy flow emerging from the collaboration of the subconscious *and* the superconscious). Historically, the pace of change was slow enough to allow us to remain what we will call "subknowers" (a knowing supported in the subconscious) throughout our lives. We could learn a skill early in life, and then practice what we know for the duration of our career. But as we move into the age of knowledge, we as individuals, and especially as leaders, need to first be "learners" in that we are able to continually learn as our home base, and only stop periodically to "know" in the context of subknowing. This is primarily necessary, not due to our current truths proving false, but due to our current truths *finding a higher truth*. (See Chapter 16.)

Knowledge as an Imperfect or Incomplete Resource

All knowledge is imperfect and/or incomplete intelligence. Intelligent activity represents a perfect state of interaction where intent, purpose, direction, values and expected outcomes are clearly understood and communicated among all parties, reflecting wisdom and achieving a higher truth. Let's explore the characteristic of knowledge as imperfect and/or incomplete from several frames of reference.

First, we recognize that knowledge is context sensitive and situation dependent, that is, since each situation and its context are different, the knowledge needed to take effective action is different. The more complex the environment, the more difficult it is to take effective action. Complexity is considered as the condition of a system, situation, or organization that is integrated with some degree of order, but has too many elements and relationships to understand in simple analytic or logical ways (Bennet & Bennet, 2004). In such a situation there are few clear cause-and-effect relationships between actions and desired outcomes. Every decision has hidden within it a guess about the future. In anticipating the results of an action, we are in fact making a guess, howbeit educated or not, about what the consequences will be. This guess has many assumptions relative to the complex situation or its environment, and, as Axelrod and Cohen so succinctly summarize, "the hard reality is that the world in which we must act is beyond our understanding" (Axelrod & Cohen, 1999, p. xvii). In other words, we can never fully understand a complex situation and its context; therefore, our knowledge is imperfect and/or incomplete.

> Every decision has hidden within it a guess about the future.

Second, people are complex adaptive systems, each having both a personal model of how we view the world and a threshold for learning (a focus) as we interact with the world. At any given moment, each individual and each organization functions from a very definable band or region of thinking, talking and acting. Within this threshold knowledge and events make sense to us. If a proposed new idea or strategy or initiative is above our threshold, it is not comprehended and has no perceived value. If a proposed new idea or strategy or initiative is below our threshold, it is so well-understood that it may be dismissed as unimportant.

What we believe in and how we view the world is always reflected in what we think about, what we talk about, and what we do. We are expressing what we believe to be important based on our personal values and beliefs, which are knowledge (Bennet & Bennet, 2015a). Pushing the edges of this threshold produces discomfort, and we seek to bring our environment and our values and beliefs back into balance. As we are able to integrate new experiences and knowledge into our threshold, our understanding increases and, by definition, our threshold moves.

Considering the external shifting and changing and the consequent internal connecting and learning, knowledge is continuously being created within the individual. Thus, at any single instant, knowledge is imperfect or incomplete.

Recognizing that knowledge is situation dependent and context sensitive, and incomplete and/or imperfect, there is a *continuous incentive to learn* in order to make the best possible decision for the situation at hand and to take the best possible action to move toward the desired outcome. See Bennet and Bennet (2013), which details the process of complex decision-making in a complex, uncertain and changing environment.

Knowledge as a Bounded Resource Supporting Our Beliefs and Values

Each individual's (or organization's, or country's) threshold includes deep pockets of focus, that is, areas that are of particular interest (or passion) to the individual (or organization, or country). For example, a concert pianist may have a deep focus on a specific kind of music with a developed set of preferences and beliefs around the value of other music. A farm growing organic crops will have a bounded focus on the methodologies, with a strong prejudice against insecticides, etc. An IT organization may have deep knowledge that is bounded by a focus on non-Apple products (or vice versa), supporting their belief in the value of one over the other. A state or country with high elevation would have a focus on winter sports and would, most likely, value winter sports over other sports in terms of fitness, etc.; the focus and beliefs of those living on a Caribbean island would be quite different.

With beliefs and values come strong emotional "tags", that is, they carry with them a sense of conviction that drives decisions and actions. While these can be visible in the form of emotions, they can also take the form of affective tacit knowledge, feelings that are not expressed—perhaps not even recognized (Bennet & Bennet, 2015a). Let's briefly explore this concept.

Strong emotional tags come with beliefs and values.

Information that comes into the brain moves through the amygdala where an emotional tag is attached. If this information is perceived as life threatening, then the amygdala takes control, making a decision and acting on that decision before conscious awareness of a threat. Thus, the success of our ancestors in escaping from a hungry tiger!

Haberlandt (1998) goes so far as to say that there is no such thing as a behavior or thought not impacted by emotions in some way. Even simple responses to information signals can be linked to multiple emotional neurotransmitters. Thus, affective tacit knowledge is attached to other types or aspects of knowledge. As Mulvihill states,

Because the neurotransmitters which carry messages of emotion are integrally linked with the information during both the initial processing and the linking with information from the different senses, it becomes clear that there is no thought, memory, or knowledge which is 'objective,' or 'detached' from the personal experience of knowing. (Mulvihill, 2003, p. 322)

Beliefs and values are knowledge and, as such, are context sensitive and situation dependent (Avedisian & Bennet, 2010). They can be considered as a "preference, multiplied by its priority" (Henderson & Thompson, 2003, p. 15). Built up over time, beliefs and values provide guidelines around what is important and not important, and how to get things done to meet performance objectives and cope with the environment. See Bennet and Bennet (2015a) for an in-depth treatment of values as knowledge. The emotional tags related to beliefs and values are strengthened as those beliefs and values are used (as knowledge) to guide decisions and actions, and feedback reinforces their "rightness" and usefulness.

Now, juxtapose two different sets of people whose knowledge (including beliefs and values) is focused on specific cultural, religious and economic preferences that are quite different. Each set of people is "right" within the perspective of their threshold and areas of focus (bounded domains of knowledge), yet their desired outcomes may be diametrically opposed. Thus, knowledge is the force used by these sets of people (such as countries) to initiate conflict.

Deep Knowledge as a Limiting Frame

Even deep knowledge does not represent a perfect state of interaction, that is, intelligent activity, and deep knowledge potentially carries with it the perceptual burden of ownership. Since knowledge is a capacity, continuously emerging in individuals and social settings in response to a shifting, changing environment, no one can own or control knowledge in terms of singular ownership. Although, admittedly, the bureaucratic model attempted this approach, and some organizations of today still attempt to follow it (see Chapter 4).

Let's explore this concept a bit more deeply. In addition to potentially limiting our frame of reference (by choice and focus), an inherent difficulty with deep knowledge is communicating it and having others understand it. Because of this, a separation occurs, and there is the ever-present danger that the "expert" ceases to interact with others and the environment, bounding the domain and perceiving the self *as* the knowledge instead of the creator and user of knowledge. As this behavior is reinforced by others' reliance on the expert, *being* the knowledge can lead to pushing, directing or ordering—and perhaps even controlling—others' actions because of a perceived superiority. Further, when an expert is cut off from the environment there is a diminishment of situational and experiential learning related to that environment, which eventually leads to a lack of effectiveness in that environment, no matter how good the knowledge is perceived to be. Some of the ways to mitigate such situations are to remain a continuous learner, ensure social engagement in the environment in which you work, engaging in conversations with experts in similar and other domains, and fully participating in mentoring experiences, both as the expert and as the learner. This means staying open to new ways of seeing and thinking ... and remembering that we are not our knowledge; rather, knowledge is a capacity. **We are a verb, not a noun**, ever learning and expanding.

Knowledge as the Action Lever for Creativity

Creativity comes exclusively from people, a capacity to see new ideas from associating internal and external information. As defined by Andreason (2005), **creativity** is emerging new or original ideas or seeing new patterns in some domain of knowledge. In other words, creativity can be considered as the *ability to perceive new relationships and new possibilities*, see things from a different frame of reference, or realize new ways of understanding/having insight or portraying something.

Some experts believe that creativity should also have utility and lead to a new product or process, that is, innovation. Innovation means the creation of new ideas *and* the transformation of those ideas into useful applications; thus, the combination of creativity and contribution as operational values promote innovation. A creative environment is fueled by the values of integrity, empathy, transparency, collaboration, learning, and contribution that foster trust and a spirit of collaborative success (Avedisian & Bennet, 2010).

> The combination of creativity and contribution as operational values promote innovation.

All individuals are creative. For simplicity, we can consider two groups of creative people. Most people are considered to have ordinary creativity. Whenever one talks, drives home a different way, or solves a problem they are being creative—doing something that they may have never done before. A smaller group of people is considered to have extraordinary creativity. These are the few who are known as geniuses, who create brilliant new ideas and products. However, this can be very misleading, because we all have the capacity to be very creative in some way in some areas at some times, and these people are just the ones who have been recognized, or perceived, as the originators of some new idea. While there may well be many others who are doing the same thing in different parts of the world, it is the first person who is publicized that gets the glory!

In addition to the type of creativity associated with creating something new, leaders can exercise other types of creativity. From the leadership assessments administered by The CoHero Institute, every leadership profile has some specific creative aspect. Some are creative in seeing the opportunities over the problems, some are creative in how a solution is built and delivered, and some are creative in how they find added efficiency and effectiveness while just "running the engine."

Knowledge and creativity are both capacities which can be applied in the present or engaged in the future. Further, they both emerge from the associative patterning process of the brain, that is, the unique complexing of external and internal information (organized patterns). In Figure 3-2 we draw a dotted line between knowledge and creativity, which when combined lead to innovation. Note that innovation is not necessarily an immediate result. As Fritz Machlup said in the early 1960's as found in his seminal work on the knowledge economy, "We shall have to bring out clearly that this is not a simple unidirectional flow from one stage to the next, from inception to development, to eventual adoption, but there are usually cross-currents, eddies, and whirlpools." (Machlup, 1962, p. 179)

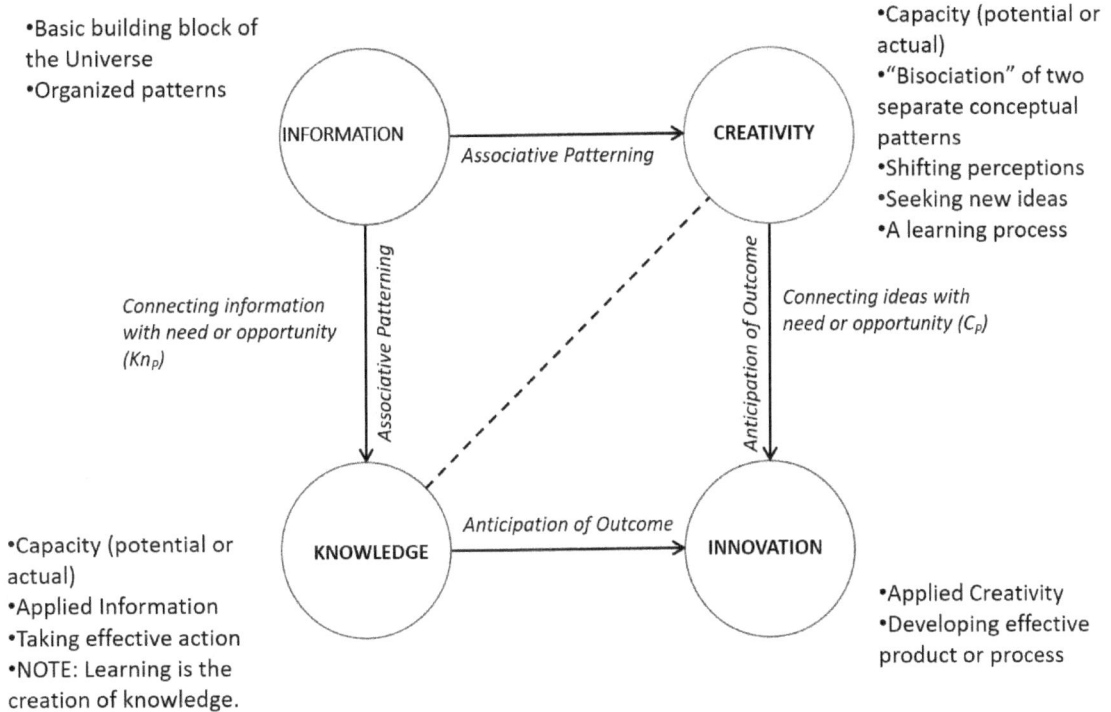

Figure 3-2. *Exploring the relationships among information, knowledge, creativity and innovation.*

Past experiences, feelings, knowledge, goals and the situation at hand all influence how creative an individual will or can be. It is the context of the activity or situation at hand (need, challenge, etc.) that triggers the putting things together in an unusual way to create (and recognize) something that may be new and potentially useful (innovation). Thus knowledge—context sensitive and situation dependent—is the action lever for creativity.

Extraordinary creativity can be developed. Since a basic operation of the brain is that of associating patterns within the mind to create new patterns thoughts, ideas, and concepts; this can be referred to as ordinary creativity. Andreasen (2005) believes that everyone possesses ordinary creativity: the creation of new ways of doing things in their daily lives through discussing new ideas and developing insights and deeper understanding. We agree. In this sense all learning is creating. *Extraordinary creativity* refers to highly creative people who often receive ideas through flashes of insights and moments of inspiration. Extraordinarily creative people "go into a state at the edge of chaos, where ideas float, soar, collide and collect" (Andreasen, 2005, p.159).

Final Thoughts

As can be seen, knowledge can serve as a powerful expander or limiter, highly dependent on the user's openness to learning. Further, the incompleteness of knowledge that is never perfect serves as an incentive for the continuous human journey of learning and the exploration of new ideas. It is important for leaders to understand these forces so that by choice they can be engaged, or not engaged, for the greater good. In the next section we take a closer look at historical connections and, through history, the expanding role of knowledge and power.

Section II
Moving from the Past

Are you still with us? We're about to take a little detour into the past, looking at the historical connections between knowledge and leadership. We're going to go WAY back, because knowledge and leadership have been around a long, long time! We begin with the early hunter gatherer, circa 35,000 B.C., quickly move to China and the beginnings of bureaucracy, touch on knowledge and the papacy along the way, then fast-forwarding to the industrial age and into the 20th century. So imagine yourself watching a PBS special or engrossed in one of those historical fiction kind of movies, or, even better, hack into the rolling pictures in your mind. Our mind talks in pictures and symbols, so dive into this material with your imagination on high. Can you see it? By the time you go to the next page, just maybe ...

As you will see in Chapter 4, historical examples and recent research indicate that the social surroundings, sources and nature of power, personality of the leader, and characteristics of followers all come into play. The role and influence of knowledge on leadership has significantly increased over the past century as the information age moved into the age of knowledge and complexity!

The idea of management pops its head into this material as well. Now, by management we don't mean control in the sense of strong authority and direction. This style of management fails with knowledge, because *no one can control another person's mind* where knowledge resides. While this has not always been the case historically, increasingly the intent is that managers strive to create and nurture a culture and an infrastructure that stimulates workers to create, use and share their knowledge! This kind of environment supports the freedom to self-organize and act effectively over a broad range of situations. We're going to take a close look at the movement from management to leadership, focusing on the role knowledge plays in this movement.

Finally, we address the long-standing relationship between knowledge and power. You'll notice we ended the first section with a chapter on knowledge and power, and we're ending this one with a chapter on the force of knowledge. Are you finding a commonality here? A core idea? If so, then you're right on track.

Now, run the movie in your head ...

Chapter 4
Historical Connections[1]

Since the early hunter gatherer, circa 35,000 B.C., the success of small bands of humans gathering berries, leaves and grubs and occasionally hunting larger animals is indicated from the world-wide distribution of archeological sites where human colonies lived. Environmental forces demanded specific actions for survival, leading to the development of culture via the need and propensity to cooperate, and propelled by Darwinian variation and selection of the fittest. The fittest of the fittest (the strongest and/or smartest) became the natural leaders of the group.

About 12,000 years ago, as the sea level rose due to the end of the ice age, Homo Sapiens Sapiens found a new way to get food (Roaf, 1999). By cultivating plants and domesticating animals humans could, and did for the most part, stop their continuous roaming, build houses, and, with the development of language, settle into longer-term social and cultural relationships. While work continued to be mostly dependent on physical strength, knowledge was clearly at the core of this activity (Corbin, 2000). With the definition of geographical boundaries came the building of more permanent relationships that opened the door to the creation of leaders and followers. This also spurred the need for learning, and the use of new materials and technologies such as pottery making, stone carving and metalworking.

Beginning in the fertile ground between the Euphrates and Tigris rivers in Mesopotamia, the spread of farming throughout the world was quickly followed by the first Neolithic villages and then (in 4,000-3,000 B.C.) by the urban explosion. This transformation involved the development of cities, with large numbers of people living in small areas, many of whom did not farm. Ties of kinship became important, class distinctions arose, and leaders achieved and kept power through religious, military and/or political means.

The expansion of knowledge beyond survival needs has continued throughout our history. In early Egypt, circa 1150 to 1069 B.C., knowledge became synonymous with leadership. For example, one man, the Overseer of All the King's Works, directed the massive labor force required to build a pyramid. "His position required him to be a man of science, an architect and a figure of commanding authority and outstanding leadership abilities." (Silverman, 1997, p. 174) The ruling official was a scribe. "[h]is palette and papyrus scroll were symbols of the authority of knowledge, and bureaucratic lists and registers were the tools of political and economic power." (Silverman, 1997, p. 90) Literature was prized because of its influence over others, and brought fame to the scribe. In short, knowledge, demonstrated by writing, was considered an authority, whether it took the form of literature, a medical recipe, or a list.

China: Knowledge and the Beginnings of Bureaucracy

Leapfrogging 3,000 years of history and landing in China, the beginnings of a bureaucracy became visible alongside the supposed feudal order. By the reign of Taizong (626-649 AD)—which is considered the golden age in Chinese imperial history—the central government was comprised of the secretariat (which drafted edicts), the chancellery (which reviewed them), and the department of state affairs (which put them into effect).

Taizong worked to firmly establish his Imperial family line as superior to that of other leading Chinese families. "His actions relating to education and scholarship suggest a motive." (Roberts, 1999, p. 54) Taizong instituted a system of state schools and colleges, one of which was reserved for children of the Imperial family and those of the highest Imperial officials. Following the advent of regular examinations, many of the highest positions in the government tended to go to those who passed these literary exams. Thus, the value of learning and knowledge was recognized and used to expand the Imperial family's influence throughout the bureaucracy and as a gateway for hopeful young leaders.

The success of this monarchical bureaucratic government was a direct result of Taizong's strong leadership and management approaches built on a solid cultural and military base, and his careful avoidance of alienation with the Buddhist Community until he was firmly ensconced as emperor. His thinking is captured in a text written by him in 648 AD, "Emperor Taizong on Effective Government." This text appears to represent what could be considered his guiding principles or, from a different perspective, the key success factors in his reign as emperor. Under the heading of esteem culture, Taizong says that nothing is better than literature to spread manners and guide customs; nothing is better than schooling to propagate regulations and educate people. The "Way" is spread through culture; fame is gained through learning. Without visiting a deep ravine, one cannot understand how deep the earth is; without learning the arts, one cannot realize the source of wisdom. Neither military nor culture can the country do without; which to emphasize depends on circumstances (Ebrey, 1993). This early reference appears to actually extol the virtue of *sharing knowledge and understanding* as an important element of effective leadership.

However, as his flexibility tightened, and the separation between his Imperial bloodline and other Chinese families increased, the effectiveness of Taizong's bureaucracy began to decline. By the time of his death in 649 AD, his foreign wars and extravagant building had drawn him into difficulties in court. At a memorial, his mentor, Wei Zheng, said of him: "In the early years of his reign the emperor had always made righteousness and virtue his central concern … [but now he] had become increasingly arrogant, wasteful and self-satisfied." (Roberts, 1999, p. 55) Apparently the keys to success were lost in the exuberance of authority and power. We've seen similar stories more recently in the *Wall Street Journal* and *Forbes*. We now step forward *in time* and move from China to Rome *in space*.

Knowledge and the Papacy

The Papacy is the central governing institution of the Roman Catholic Church under the leadership of the Pope. The origin of power of the Bishop of Rome comes from the teaching that Jesus Christ directly bestowed ruling and teaching authority (knowledge) on the apostle Peter. This supreme power was then passed on to his successors, the Bishops of Rome. Recognizing the importance of environmental forces, in 313 AD the church granted toleration of all religions and allowed Christians to worship freely. This early part of the Middle Ages underwent a backward shift from towns to rural villages, and hence became a more agrarian society, as violence and political turmoil increased with the influx of Germanic tribes.

The Papacy was as unable to lead the peasants as were the emperors. Both vied for authority with no clear winner. During the period from the 6th to the 15th Century, the papacy varied in their power from being subservient to the power of emperors to negotiating peace treaties and alliances with nations and kingdoms. The church reached its height of power circa 1200 AD during the Pontificate of Innocent III when the papacy experienced almost universal power and supervised the religious, social, and political life in the western world. The papacy governed through a centralized administration that ensured its power over the bishops by tapping the church's financial resources. Thus the key success factors were money and power, with direct knowledge of God's will and rituals serving as the framework and justification for authority. The role of knowledge had succumbed to the power of religions and dogma.

The Industrial Age

With the advent of the Industrial Age, implementation of the bureaucratic model reached its full height. The seeds were sown in the use of the scientific view over the religious, moving from the magical and mythical portrayal of knowledge to a growing rational pattern of thinking, still exclusive to leaders, but no longer bounded by lineage or physical strength. The bureaucratic framework cited by Max Weber (1864-1920) called for a hierarchical structure, clear division of labor, rule and process orientation, impersonal administration, rewards based on merit, decisions and rules in writing, and management separated from ownership (Cummings & Huse, 1989). Conflict is a theme throughout this model, postulating that forces exist in organizations that perpetuate conflict and class separation. Weber dealt primarily with the conflict of capitalist and worker, the owner of the means of production versus the producer of labor, differentiating these "classes." He also believed that the ever-increasing importance of expert and specialized knowledge created a conflict between the "specialist type of man" and the older type of "cultivated man" (management) (Gerth & Mills, 1946, p. 243).

Yet the bureaucratic model was built on management power over workers in what Weber called "imperative control," with legitimacy as the common ground for maintaining imperative control. "Although domination or authority may be based," Weber says, "on custom, interest, affectual or 'value-rational' motives, a secure order is usually characterized by a belief in its legitimacy." (Outhwaite & Bottomore, 1993, p. 38) Although Weber did not see knowledge as a form of legitimacy, he did *link knowledge with power*. He believed that, "Every bureaucracy seeks to increase the superiority of the professionally informed by keeping their knowledge and intentions secret." (Gerth & Mills, 1946, p. 233) This observation indicates clearly that knowledge was valued and used as power.

Into the 20th Century

While the word "leader" has been present in historical writings as early as the year 1300 (*Oxford English Dictionary*, 1933), it wasn't until the first half of the nineteenth century in writings about political influence and control of the British Parliament that the word "leadership" showed up (Bass, 1981). This "leadership" term appears to have emerged during the mechanical age when people began to recognize the need to acquire new skills and knowledge to increase their effectiveness and career prospects. While "knowledge of how to hunt for certain game or how to run machines was necessary for success down through the ages … not until about 100 years ago did work become highly intellectual." (Corbin, 2000 p. 168)

With the rise of large corporations in the early twentieth century came a strong interest in research in fields such as leadership, management, organizational theory, and capitalism. Frederick Taylor, Henri Fayol, Mary Parker Follet, Chester Bernard, Adam Smith, Herbert Simon, and Abraham Maslow, all contributed to the foundational research and set of organizational and leadership concepts of the early to mid 20th century. This era created the formal foundation of management. Although the origins lay in Weber's bureaucracy, church and state autocracy, and military leadership, these were all modified by the social, political and capitalistic drives in the free world after World War II. The new theories and concepts such as Theory X, Theory Y, Theory Z,

Charismatic and Transformational Leadership, General Systems Theory, and Organizational Linking Pins became popular and a noticeable shift began from the management control of bureaucracy toward a more benign and malleable management and leadership structure.

Tools such as Total Quality, Business Process Reengineering, Management by Exception, Span of Control, Kurt Lewin's Force Field Analysis, and Taichi Ohno's Toyota Production Line techniques helped both managers and workers implement change throughout their organizations. While some changes occurred, most organizations continued to be both hierarchical in form and bureaucratic in function and, as Whyte noted in his widely-read *Organization Man,* large organizations were still forcing people into molds and stereotypes (Whyte, 1956). As they still *represented power and authority*, knowledge and information were held close by supervisors and managers and protected. Economic progress was relatively steady and, until the 1970s, fairly predictable. During this post bureaucratic era the key factors were a combination of Taylor's time and motion studies and participative management, slowly bringing some of the workforce into the arena of worker responsibility and empowerment.

As the affluence, mobility and expectations of the workforce in developed countries continued to rise, coupled with the explosive growth of information and communication technologies and of the creation of knowledge, organizations found themselves in situations of restructure or collapse. The old mechanical metaphor could no longer function in the non-linear, dynamic, complex global web of the mid 1990s. Many organizations failed, many were acquired, and the best of them tried to achieve the popular vision of the "world-class" corporation. The stage was now set for the rise of the information and knowledge organizations. Information organizations took the lead via computers and communications technology in the early 1980s and 1990s, and the knowledge organization, currently in its early form, was focused on networking and knowledge creation, sharing and application (Bennet & Bennet, 2004). Simultaneously, the world was becoming more complex. With the rise of new ways of doing business came a new way of managing and leading, and new relationships between leaders and knowledge. The shrinking, flat world was beginning to show its new muscles.

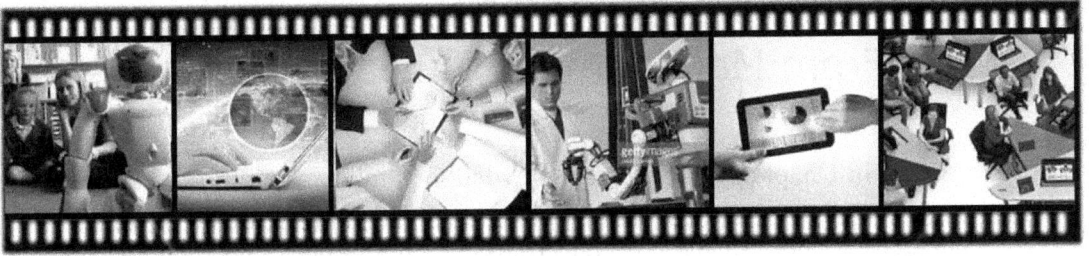

Chapter 5
From Management to Leadership

As can be seen in Chapter 4, the role of knowledge is interwoven throughout history with the concept of power, and historically connected with management and leadership. Management, historically the word used to frame many of those things now considered part of leadership, has always been in relationship with knowledge. "Managers have always been concerned with making sure that they have the necessary skills to do their jobs … In their attempts to mobilize action, managers rely upon their knowledge at every turn." (Eccles & Nohria, 1992, p. 174)

Management was once tangible or "so we were led to believe … and if it wasn't, managers tried their hardest to make it so. They produced reports, budgets, strategic plans, memos, directives, rules and minutes. It didn't work. The decisions are bigger, the information more complex and the time scales shorter." (White et al., 1996, p. 192)

The Management Shake-up

In 1998 a picture of management guru Peter Drucker was featured on the cover of *Forbes* magazine with the words in large print "Everything you learned is wrong." Inside the magazine, Drucker talks about the impact of the rise of knowledge workers, and how this will eliminate the concept of "subordinates." He explains that the increasing use of the word "associate" is not just polite, but a recognition of reality. Further, Drucker points out that "knowledge workers must know more about their job than their boss does—or what good are they?" (Drucker, 1998, pp. 152-176)

Belasco describes a reversal of roles occurring, that in this upside-down world leaders lead and employees manage. "[T]he employees who hold the intellectual capital do the managerial work of planning, organizing, commanding, coordinating, and controlling. Leaders perform the leadership tasks of changing your own leadership behavior first, making your customer the boss, thinking strategically, transferring ownership and learning continuously." (Belasco, 1997, p. 37-38)

> In this upside-down world leaders lead and employees manage.

Even as these roles were changing, Davenport insisted that management and managers will continue to exist, although not necessarily in recognizable form.

The old model of the manager who sits in an office staring down at toiling workers and occasionally makes a visit to the factory floor is now officially obsolete. The new managers look suspiciously like knowledge workers, but do more than day-to-day knowledge work … Rather than sitting at the top of the hierarchy, the new managers must subsume their own egos to those of the knowledge workers they manage. (Davenport, 2001, p. 58)

Bennis, Parikh and Lessem describe the new managerial role in terms of knowing enough about the organization, and the internal dynamics of the organization, to be able to create harmony between the two.

As such a new-paradigm manager, firstly you possess general insights into people, things, ideas, and events, as well as particular professional and managerial know-how. Secondly, you have greater insight into environmental forces and trends than is required for everyday business and management functions. Thirdly, you have in-depth insights into your own inner dynamics, covering the functioning of your body, mind, emotions, neurosensory system, and states of consciousness. (Bennis, 1995, p. 37-38)

Davenport proposed that managers in the future must adapt their activities to the new challenges they face. They must move:

from overseeing work *to* doing it

from organizing hierarchies *to* organizing communities

from imposing work designs and methods *to* understanding them

from hiring and firing workers *to* recruiting and retaining them

from building manual skills *to* building knowledge skills

from evaluating visible job performance *to* assessing invisible knowledge achievements

from ignoring culture *to* building a knowledge-friendly culture

from supporting the bureaucracy *to* fending it off

(Davenport, 2001, p. 47) [Emphasis added]

Knowledge Workers

From the above it can be seen that knowledge plays a primary role in new ways of thinking about management. The concepts of knowledge workers and the manager as a knowledge worker have been introduced and will be further explored below. But while the authors cited above have used the terms "manager" and "management," most of the current literature focuses on the terms "leader" and "leadership," with knowledge as a central theme.

By the turn of the century, many organizations recognized knowledge as the new bottom line. For example, Skandia Insurance in Stockholm created what it calls "future accounting," in which "knowledge is more valuable than physical objects, and intangible assets are the leading indicators of future success" (Rosen et al., 2000, p. 352). Dauphinais (2000, p. 322) believes that, ultimately, if the organization is to operate successfully in this new knowledge economy, "Its CEO and senior managers on down need to develop a culture that values knowledge and, most important, knowledge sharing."

What is it that has brought knowledge so strongly into this discussion of leadership? It is because ideas have replaced physical goods, becoming the most valued commodities in the global market place. See Figure 5-1. As Tichy et al. state, "Brains, energy and talent—human capital—have replaced plant and equipment—physical capital—as the primary source of value creation" (Tichy et al., 2002, p. 226). The role of leadership, then, has become that of *developing knowledge assets* integral to a company's success in the marketplace. "The business plan must clearly embody the expectation that knowledge will be stewarded and increased, in the same way that increased revenue is an explicit goal." (Dauphinais et al., 2000, p. 321)

When you actually think of the knowledge base in an organization, it's just impossible for the top twenty people to know what's down there. You've got to believe that unleashing knowledge at all levels is crucial for the success of the business. And you need leadership skills to make that happen. (Rosen, et al., 2000)

Corbin contends that the numbers of knowledge workers are growing exponentially. He defines knowledge workers as those "who earn their living by analyzing, managing, and making judgments based on knowledge extracted from information" and states that "these types of workers will be called on to exhibit leadership skills at one time or another" (Corbin, 2000, p. 5). He goes on to say that, "Thus, in increasing numbers of cases, leaders are also considered to be workers. The line between leaders and workers is blurring. The only difference may lie in the type of work or function that each category performs" (Corbin, 2000, p. 6). Davenport (2001) introduces the term *knowledge work manager* to identify the individual who does the following work or functions: builds knowledge work communities, redesigns and improves knowledge work, recruits and retains the best knowledge workers, builds and propagates knowledge skills, evaluates knowledge effectiveness, and creates a knowledge-friendly culture.

According to Corbin, great leaders are those who understand and provide five specific needs to knowledge workers: knowledge, vision, hope, harmony and a sense of control. As he asserts,

Knowledge workers are more productive when they set mutual goals with organizational leaders. The tougher the goal, the greater the challenge to knowledge workers. They enjoy solving challenging problems or stretching to reach their goals; the feeling of accomplishment is exhilarating. (Corbin, 2000, p. 136)

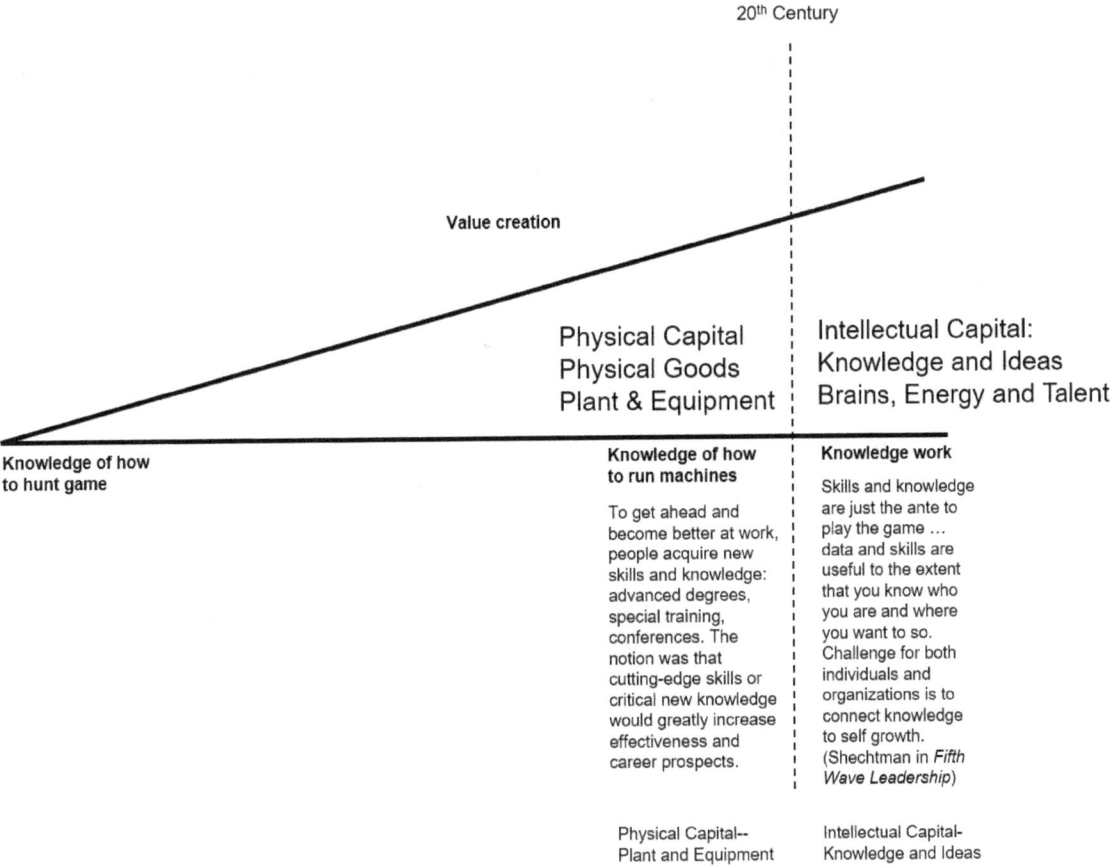

20th Century

Value creation

Physical Capital
Physical Goods
Plant & Equipment

Intellectual Capital:
Knowledge and Ideas
Brains, Energy and Talent

Knowledge of how
to hunt game

**Knowledge of how
to run machines**

To get ahead and
become better at work,
people acquire new
skills and knowledge:
advanced degrees,
special training,
conferences. The
notion was that
cutting-edge skills or
critical new knowledge
would greatly increase
effectiveness and
career prospects.

Knowledge work

Skills and knowledge
are just the ante to
play the game …
data and skills are
useful to the extent
that you know who
you are and where
you want to so.
Challenge for both
individuals and
organizations is to
connect knowledge
to self growth.
(Shechtman in *Fifth
Wave Leadership*)

Physical Capital--
Plant and Equipment

Intellectual Capital-
Knowledge and Ideas

Figure 5-1: *Value creation has moved from knowledge of how to hunt game to development of deep intellectual capital.*

Corbin (2000) cites 5 common themes that appeared in a study of three universities (Arizona State, University of Southern California and George Washington University) in how they led their knowledge workers. These were: (1) recognition for accomplishments in their areas of expertise; (2) freedom in selecting how they work and what they work on; (3) evaluation by peers and customers; (4) buy-in to the mission and the organization's strategic plan; and (5) a highly variable time factor (flexible hours).

With knowledge leaders and workers doing knowledge work, there is a growing emphasis on the role of teams. While a deep discussion of teams is not the focus of this book, teams (and communities and networks) are recognized as a significant contributor to the links between knowledge and leadership. Helgesen views teams as a shift in the distribution of power.

A team is not simply a task force, for task-force members are appointed by their superiors, who define their mission and set the criteria for judging its fulfillment. A true team, by contrast, both defines its objectives and finds ways to meet them, integrating the conception of tasks with their execution. Since teams in the knowledge organization set their own goals, they are also free to use any new information that comes their way to refine their methods and objectives as they do their work. Autonomous teams thus enable people at the grass roots to organize themselves in ways that permit real-time use of information technology. (Helgesen, 1999, p. 21)

Corbin points out that while project teams may be assembled by team leaders, just as often a knowledge worker is asked to build his or her own team, with mutually agreed upon checkpoints and availability of the team leader to correct direction when a team gets off track. "In empowered organizations, knowledge workers discover a problem, assemble an ad hoc team to fix it, and then report the results without the necessity of submitting to bureaucratic procedures." (Corbin, 2000, p. 136)

Following Peter Drucker's introduction of the knowledge worker more than a decade ago, Robert Kelley was perhaps the first author to recognize that these knowledge workers are a different breed, thus requiring a different type of leadership. Kelly called for organizations to adapt to special knowledge worker needs and demands, emphasizing that the new worker deals in knowledge, not just physical labor or goods and services (Kelley, 1985). He describes these new knowledge workers as,

> Knowledge workers are a different breed, thus requiring different leadership.

> ... imaginative and original ... They engage in complex problem solving, not bureaucratic drudgery or mechanical routine ... and have little tolerance for boredom. [They demand] interesting work and satisfying emotional relationship ... [and] psychic and social stimulation on the [job] ... Taking orders ... insults their intelligence and often results in a creative shutdown ... [They prefer to] manage themselves. (Dunlap, 1996, p. 127)

Knowledge Leaders

What leadership works best with these knowledge workers? Goldsmith and Walt believe that old models of leadership will not work, that a shared leadership is necessary. "In a world where leading across a fluid network may become more important than leading from the top of a fixed hierarchy, being able to effectively share leadership is a requirement, not an option" (Goldsmith & Walt, 1999, pp 164-5). They go on to point out that this approach requires new values of cooperation and rotational leadership, knowing when strengths and weaknesses need balancing, thinking globally and appreciating cultural diversity, building partnerships, and having the ability to fully utilize technology. These are "competencies that many leaders do not have or do not even realize are important. They are also skills that most future leaders will need and must recognize as essential to the success of development programs" (Goldsmith & Walt, 1999, p. 165).

Manz and Sims believe that the best approach to managing knowledge is the implementation of a system that not only values each knowledge worker, but aims at making each worker a knowledge leader.

> We believe first that the ultimate control comes from within—that the essence of leadership in today's information age is to develop the capacity of people to lead themselves. The real challenge is to maximize the potential of human capital by unleashing this inner self-leadership. (Manz & Sims, 2000, p. 13)

In addition to valuing all knowledge workers, establishing a nurturing environment for self-leaders, and setting up knowledge within an organization so that it can be efficiently accessed by all employees, the approach they suggest involves building natural rewards into tasks such that employees are motivated to share large amounts of knowledge with minimal guidance. An example would be the intrinsic rewards in knowing the value of your work (Manz & Sims, 2000).

There is clearly a strong correlation between high-performing leaders and their management of knowledge. Menkes goes so far as to say that for executives, questions of intelligence must focus on how well a manager uses or manipulates information and knowledge.

> Cognitive ability, or intelligence, has been proven to be one of the most powerful predictors of managerial success … The distinction between knowledge and intelligence is frequently blurred … [they are] interdependent … Knowledge provides essential clues to the best way to handle a particular situation, yet this information is useful only to the degree that it is skillfully applied. Intelligence is the information processor that determines how deftly one's knowledge will be used… Just as knowledge is not useful if it cannot be intelligently applied, intelligence is useless without sufficient knowledge to process. (Menkes, 2005, pp. 210-218)

Drath suggests that leadership definitions and styles have given way to knowledge principles, a set of ideas and rules about the nature of reality and life that are taken for granted to be true.

> Right away, the difference between a knowledge principle and a definition becomes apparent, because most definitions of something as complex as leadership are by their nature subject to debate, doubt, and challenge. Knowledge principles, on the other hand, comprise sets of taken-for-granted truths, truths that are obvious to those who hold them. (Drath, 2001, p. 7)

In our day-to-day life we use knowledge principles. For example, someone might say, "God is good" or "nature is beautiful" or "killing is evil." Drath (2001, p. 10) continues, "A leadership [knowledge] principle is what gives meaning to definitions and styles in the sense that a principle is required for people to recognize and understand that leadership is what is happening." An example of a knowledge leadership principle might refer to the power of networks or the importance of building trust to knowledge sharing.

To this point, we have been primarily concerned with the concepts of management and leadership (and their relationship to knowledge) in terms of organizations. But today, not only is the term leadership used in many different ways, but almost everyone acts as a leader in some context or situation. Leaders are literally emerging everywhere. For example, Cleveland sees the growth rate of leaders in the USA in the same light as the growth rate of knowledge:

> Almost everyone acts as a leader in some context or situation.

> I have tried several times to count the number of leaders in the USA. In the mid-1950s, because I was publisher of a magazine I wanted them to buy, I counted 555,000 "opinion leaders." A 1971 extrapolation of that figure came out at about a million. Seven out of ten of these were executive leaders of many kinds of organizations; this "aristocracy of achievement" was estimated in 1985 at one out of every two hundred Americans. After that I gave up: the knowledge revolution keeps multiplying the number of Americans who take the opportunity to lead, at one time or another, on one issue or another, in one community or another … The galloping rate of growth of complexity means that a growth curve of the requirement for leaders if anyone were clever enough to construct such an index would show a steeper climb than any other growth rate in our political economy. (Cleveland, 2002, p. 6)

The importance and value of knowledge becomes clear when we remind ourselves that knowledge is the capacity to take effective action. Action is the only way to make any change in our organizations. Knowledge leaders determine the actions taken by their organization, while the actions determine the success or failure of the organization.

Final Thoughts

With ideas and knowledge becoming the raw materials of work, and all workers more focused on knowledge and performing in more leadership roles, the terms knowledge and leadership cannot be addressed adequately as standalone terms. It is not enough to be a collaborative leader in a knowledge world, and it is not enough to be a thought leader without the ability to share these thoughts. We are, whether we intended to become or not, multidimensional in nature. What fun to bring this into our awareness, to be conscious of our multidimensionality!

Chapter 6
Knowledge and Power

Throughout the history of our business, social and governmental organizations there has been a continual growth of the individual leader's power. Simultaneously, "small amounts of knowledge were gradually diffusing outward and downward, primarily as the results of advances in communications, which provided access to greater and greater numbers of knowledge" (Hesselbein, et al., 2002, p. 192). But the technology explosion has changed this. Suddenly all have access to everything, allowing self-empowerment and the growth of all people who chose this path.

> The massive increase in individual empowerment made possible over the last decade ... has had a centrifugal, fragmenting influence ... Corporations and social institutions that do not respond to the new obligation to release power outward will find themselves rejected in the marketplace and the ballot box. As we move into the twenty-first century, and technology taps the awesome potential talent of the penumbra of nearly five billion previously disenfranchised intelligences on the planet, the Paleolithic concept of single-issue, top-down leadership needs to be redefined. The old reductionist division of labor, which solved problems one at a time, will not be able to keep pace with the demand for simultaneity and flexibility in the new dynamic business and political environment ... In this new world of personal empowerment, the all-seeing visionary leader, pointing the way to the future, is an obsolete anachronism to be replaced perhaps by facilitators, acting as mentors rather than commanders. Knowledge is power, and for the first time it is becoming freely available to the many rather than the few. (Hesselbein et al., 2002, pp. 192-193)

While this quote is rather long, it hit the mark, building to recognition that *knowledge is power and that it was now freely available to all*. This shift of power was echoed by nearly every leading author in the field as each struggled to define exactly what this shift entailed.

The Decline of Hierarchy

Rosabeth Kanter (1997, p. 141) stated, "As hierarchies are deemphasized, the formal authority derived from hierarchy is less important than professional expertise in gaining the respect required for influence and leadership." Formal power, then, becomes less important than expert power.

Komives sees the bases of social power as expert power, referent power, legitimate power, coercive power and reward power. Expert power, described as the power of information or knowledge, can come from formal education, professional development, possessing specific information, or extended experience. "We trust experts," Komives et al. (1998, p. 78) state, "and give them power over us, based on their assumed higher level of knowledge or experience." Supporting the need to trust external sources for their knowledge needs, Zand (1997, p. 158) says that it is becoming "increasingly common for leaders with formal power to have little expertise and for experts to have little formal power." He further states that knowledge acts as a source of power when a person knows so much about a specific problem or subject that people willingly accept his influence.

> Even if a person lacks formal authority, people will seek and defer to his knowledge in certain circumstances; people let physicians prescribe remedies for their ailments, lawyers write their contracts, and accountants prepare their tax returns. These are common examples of experts who have knowledge but not formal authority. People grant expert power to individuals who do not have legitimate position power because they believe that they will make a better decision with the expert's knowledge than without it. (Zand, 1997, p. 158)

As we consider the trends for the usage of the terms knowledge and authority within books over the years, we find that they were used almost equally in 1850. But over time, and especially in recent times, the term knowledge is used more than authority. See Figure 6-1.

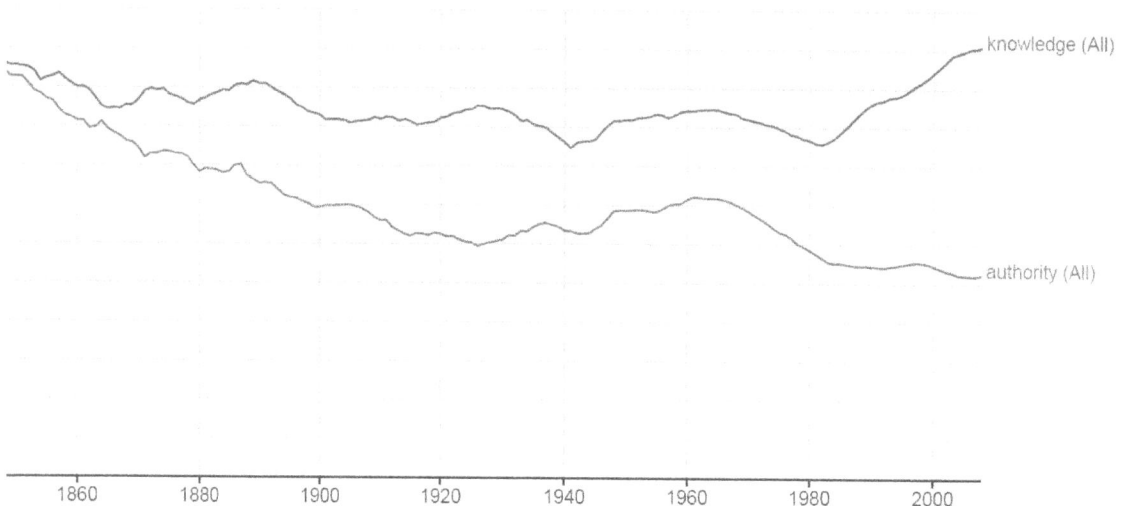

Figure 6-1. *Knowledge and authority in literature over the years.*

Cleveland states that as information and knowledge empowers the many, leaders are no longer seen as authoritative sources.

> [T]he spread of knowledge, the widening of educational opportunities, the proliferation of educated people around the world has made it harder and harder for power to be wielded by leaders on the grounds that they understand, let alone control, mysteries that are inaccessible to people in general. In the societies with the largest numbers of educated people, the spreading skepticism about authority figures—political leaders, corporate executives, media moguls, religious leaders, lawyers, physicians, scientists, and other experts—is overwhelmingly documented in survey research … The spread of education around the world eroded the pyramids of power and wealth and discrimination that looked like granite but turned out to be porous sandstone, crumbling under pressure. (Cleveland, 2002, pp. 40-41)

In an organizational setting, with knowledge (representing power) vested more widely throughout, this translates into less emphasis on positional power. Helgesen (1996, p. 54) notes that this reflects the "shift in the balance of power from organizations to individuals."

Traditional power-centered leadership will not work. Indeed, Zand contends that it often achieves the opposite of what is intended.

> Leaders who do not understand this new world try to remedy their declining effectiveness by using power to squash dissent and by imposing tighter controls. Caught in a vicious cycle of decreasing access to knowledge and increasing use of power, they are puzzled by the organization's unrelenting downward spiral in performance. (Zand, 1997, p. 23)

He explains further that leaders need to understand the new conditions of leadership, that knowledge drives competition [and collaboration] and that knowledge is in people's heads, therefore elusive, difficult to access and nonlinear. "Position power is in eclipse as leaders increasingly need to depend on others for the knowledge to make good decisions … Leadership in knowledge organizations is the ability to harness, and integrate three interdependent forces—knowledge, trust, and power." (Zand, 1997, p. 23)

In the earlier discussion of knowledge sharing we introduced the relationship of trust and knowledge. In terms of power, Zand emphasizes that trust and knowledge are critical to leadership power.

> Leaders may have formal power, but without knowledge and trust they become martinets, leading people on meaningless forays … Some leaders may have both formal power and knowledge, but if they are mistrusted, they too distort leadership, becoming cold, inaccessible taskmasters … Effective leadership in the new world depends as much on knowledge and trust as it does on formal power. A deficiency

in any of these dimensions distorts leadership and reduces the leader's effectiveness. (Zand, 1997, p. 22-23)

Building trust and *using power sensitively* are the other two dimensions (with knowledge, each interacting with the other) of Zand's leadership model. "When leaders have and use relevant knowledge, people trust them and grant them power because they have confidence that the leaders know what they are doing." (Zand, 1997, p. 22) When people trust their leaders, they are willing to disclose their knowledge. Thus knowledge, trust and power are not only tightly coupled, but mutually reinforce each other.

Similarly, Lee sees knowledge as one element of principle-centered power, what he calls a mark of quality, distinction, and excellence in all relationships.

It is based on honor, with the leader honoring the follower and the follower choosing to contribute because the leader is also honored ... specifically, acquiring accurate information and perspectives about followers ... while being worthy of respect for what they are now, regardless of what they own, control, or do, giving full consideration to their intentions, desires, values, and goals rather than focusing elusively on their behavior. (Lee, 1997, pp. 223-4)

In this book, knowledge and leadership have moved into closer and closer relationship, and the understanding of leadership in a knowledge era has substantially expanded to encompass nearly every human being in some situation or context. While the recognized power of knowledge has grown, knowledge as power has remained consistent, and—as it is shared, understood and used—*the whole concept of leadership is changing.*

Sharing Knowledge and Power

Historically, holding knowledge close, keeping things secret, was the key to the power and success of managers. What we have discovered along the way is that, "Knowledge is improved through the act of sharing ... It is through ... cooperation and sharing that knowledge as a resource grows more abundant for everyone." (Ury, 2003, p. 46) As Cleveland explains,

Information is shared (not "exchanged") ... information by its nature cannot give rise to exchange transactions, only to sharing transactions ... If I sell you an idea, we both have it. If I give you a fact or tell you a story, it's like a good kiss: sharing the thrill enhances it ... If it's a thing, it's exchanged; if it's information, it's shared. The difference is fundamental. It's what is inducing much rethinking of theory and practice, of law and custom, as well as the people of every state, every nation, every government, every company, every kind of organization come to terms—gradually, as in any major cultural transformation—with the fact that the worlds key resource is now a sharing resource. (Cleveland, 2002, p. 41)

A future world where knowledge shared becomes power clearly breaks away from the bureaucratic model described in the beginning of this chapter. In fact, it is in direct conflict with Weber's bureaucratic notion of the professionally informed keeping their knowledge and intentions secret. In this new world there is clearly a shift in authority from upper and middle management and leadership to the workforce, which essentially means that management and leadership give up some authority while maintaining responsibility—

> A future world where knowledge shared becomes power clearly breaks away from the Weber's bureaucratic model.

something historically very few people are willing to do. Yet, for leaders to successfully unleash the worker's knowledge and experience for organizational improvement, the context, direction and authority to make local decisions must be made available to all personnel. Ultimately, it's not a matter of how much power the leader has, rather it's a matter of how much power the organization has. This is the grist of the recent movement toward what is called collaborative leadership (Bennet & Bennet, 2004). In 2004 the Bennets designed a new theory of the firm based on the intelligent complex adaptive system (ICAS) model that embraces collaborative leadership. In the ICAS environment, which will be detailed in Chapter 7, leaders emerge at all levels.

As we saw graphically at the beginning of Chapter 2, in the 1960s the term "leadership" became a dominant way to convey where we turned to for knowledge, guidance, and inspiration. Not surprisingly, the 1960's also saw the rise of the phrase "Question Authority!" Whether the influence of power was *derived* from hierarchy or expertise, the *delivery* was the same, which was authoritative rather than collaborative. So, there are two sides to this equation, and they are therefore related. Understanding how the power is derived is just as important as how it is applied. As Lewis (2013) states, we should say "Question Authorization!" An authorization process is how one is placed in a position of power. The initiative to overthrow monarchies was through this lens, since "birthright" became a questionable authorization process. If the authorization process for establishing leaders required not just expert knowledge, but also expertise in the *process* of gaining and sharing knowledge, then we could expect to see more collaborative leadership.

Gaining Knowledge

A recent study published in *Fortune* (Colvin, 2015, p. 108) asked employers which skills they need the most over the next 10 years. Interestingly, the answers did not focus on "left-brain thinking skills that computers handle well." Instead, the focus is on "relationship building, teaming, co-creativity, brainstorming, cultural sensitivity, and the ability to manage diverse employees—right brain skills of social interaction."

Gaining the needed knowledge and skills is now easier than ever. Rather than travelling to a brick and mortar school, we can connect with classes online. And rather than paying hefty school fees, some classes are now free. We are now in the latest stage of open educational resources, with the advent of the MOOC, a Massive Open Online Course. The goal is unlimited participation, giving free access to top university courses to anyone with an Internet connection. After all, technology and access are the only things holding most people back from gaining knowledge. At least, that was the thinking. But so far, that is not how it has turned out. As reported in *Nature* (Ezekiel, 2013, p. 342), "A survey of active MOOC users in more than 200 countries and territories has revealed that most students on these courses are already well educated — and that they are predominantly young males seeking to advance their careers." Rather than the MOOC reaching the disadvantaged, they are widening the gap between the uneducated and the highly educated. There is still a leadership role to be played, which provides curiosity, hope, and encouragement—even with the access to technology!

Putting Knowledge in its Place

One compelling question a leader can ask within any organization is "where is the knowledge and where should it be?" Maybe the organization has the knowledge, but the reason it does not have the power is because of where the knowledge resides. It resides in people, and it could reside within the minds of a few workers who are about to retire. If it is surface knowledge, it could be documented yet reside deep inside a document management system, such that the author is still the only one who really has access to it. Or it could reside within the training materials of one department, when it should be shared online with everyone, or even codified within the business rules of a production system. For codified knowledge, the issue is one of locating it and accessing it. But there are larger issues.

Over the past ten years—built on an increasing understanding of the deep knowledge developed by leaders over the course of their careers—there has been a lot of focus on succession management and knowledge retention. These are systems issues. Recall in Chapter 2 the discussion of Knowledge (Informing) and Knowledge (Proceeding). Knowledge (Proceeding) is the way Knowledge (Informing) is put together or complexed in order to take action, and this is unique to each decision-maker! Certainly, explicit actions in terms of process can be codified, but the deeper knowledge that understands the patterns of the situation at hand cannot be easily captured or shared. However, it often can be developed over time through mentoring, shadowing and, generally, experiencing. There are several very large questions that have to be addressed. First, with the discoveries and technological advances happening every day, what is the shelf life of this knowledge I am trying to capture. Second, am I really able to codify the deep knowledge reflected in this leader's decision-making? These are critical questions to explore. The answer is not always to capture knowledge, but perhaps in expanding the boundaries of the organization. In the military they use an interesting model. Retirement is not retirement, just a shift in focus. If a "retired" decision-maker is needed, they will be called back into service for the time of that requirement.

How might we learn from that model? One option is waved retirement, positionally releasing the leader while retaining him/her for a period of months as an internal consultant, with a slow "phase out" over a period of months. Another option is a one-year external consulting agreement with a minimum/maximum to working hours. A third option is having the retired leader continue as a virtual member of a community of practice designed around his domain of expertise. And there are many more creative ways to ensure the expertise of a leader is available on demand as needed for a period of time equivalent to the shelf life of his/her expertise.

> In the military model, retirement is not retirement, just a shift in focus.

Clever consulting firms have developed a myriad of approaches to this very real issue. For example, recognizing that capturing knowledge is not the key to success, Shelley (2016) has developed an approach called KNOWledge SUCCESSion that facilitates releasing knowledge internally so it can be reapplied, reworked, adapted for new contexts and sometime even decommissioned because newer and better knowledge has been created and can be leveraged across people as they transition through roles. Focusing on simplifying behavioral interactions and making it easier for people to see the impacts of behavior, Shelley uses the metaphor of the organizational zoo, engaging people to represent each behavior as an animal character and to explore the impacts each has on the other animals in the zoo (Shelley, 2007). As an aside, when participating with a group using the organizational zoo cards that are part of this learning experience, it was noted that most senior leaders identified with the eagle, which is described as an inspirational leader, knowing what they want and soaring well above the rest. This is a power animal who is visionary, strong, focused, inspiring and confident.

What is important about this example is that it is very much based on building relationships and the sharing of knowledge in a climate of trust. Thus, the power of knowledge is *not* in the capture of it, but in the ability to share it across the organization, to collaborate.

Final Thoughts

How do we contemplate power? Knowledge is power, but is it controlling power or collective power? Knowledge can create win-lose situations or win-win situations. As has been demonstrated in the way bureaucracies were managed during the past century, when there is an attempt to control knowledge there is a separation that occurs. When people *become* their knowledge, making decisions for others based on their belief that they know better what is the right thing, they cease to learn. But we have choice.

We can show up for work, from a primary underlying question of "What's in it for me (WIIFM)?" or one that asks "What's in it for us (WIIFU)?" Lewis (2013, p. 112) observes that "in building highly productive teams, this approach [WIIFM] can be counterproductive because people recognize they are in a competitive rather than collaborative environment and make decisions that help themselves over the team's goals." Too many people know better for us to turn back the clock. Too many people are learning and expanding and adding their amazingly diverse ways of thinking and knowing to the larger global picture. How do we collectively tap into that expanding knowledge? It is with that thought in mind that we briefly introduce the intelligent complex adaptive system, a knowledge-based organization that can co-evolve with its environment.

Section III
Today and Tomorrow

The development of true understanding, meaning and vision **requires a human mind**, one that has the confidence, competence, freedom and support to venture into the unknown and comprehend ambiguity, uncertainty and complexity. A mind just like yours! But to activate this mind requires a supportive environment, structure, culture and leadership style that is not static. As hard as it is to imagine, all of these are living things, as is the organization or community that they support! Why? Because they all involve people.

As the markets and customers in the environment change, so must the organization adapt and change. Every living system must be flexible and adapt to its environment if it is to succeed and survive. This holds true for a human cell, a fish, an individual, an organization, a society or a nation. In a stable world adaptation may be small, perhaps unnoticeable. But in a dynamic world, only the adaptive will survive and be around for the future.

So we begin with a short overview that describes an organization that can co-evolve with its environment, the intelligent complex adaptive system (ICAS) model for organizations. This model enables organizations to react more quickly and fluidly to today's fast-changing, dynamic business environment. With the stage set, we now ask: Is there an historic leadership style or approach that would meet the needs of the ICAS?

During the past several decades *knowledge leadership* has begun to emerge, and along with it new relationships among leaders, followers, and knowledge. Today, leadership is no longer out in front of the crowd; leadership is in the middle of the crowd in the setting of collaboration.

We focus on collaborative leaders, those individuals *throughout the organization* who have the insights, initiative, competency, and connections to mold, support, and guide their own part of the organization's structure, culture, and execution competency to achieve high performance. They work collaboratively toward achieving intelligent activity.

After exploring some concepts foundational to collaborative leadership, and recognizing that all models are artificial constructs, we address the issue of multiple categories of knowledge and their effect on leadership. We explore the *knowledges* leaders need in terms of types and variety, and then specifically focus on concepts important to leaders as learners: experiential learning, continuous learning, spiritual learning, leaders as teachers, social learning, the Net and Millennial generations and the search for transcendent themes.

Chapter 7
The ICAS Organization[1]

Over the last half of the 20th Century, the industrial age has gradually morphed into the information age, resulting in a plethora of information that become so intense and ubiquitous that it often overwhelmed decision-makers. Information feeds on information, ergo its exponential rise. However, information also feeds complexity as systems compete and knowledge advances through the learning stimulated by the availability of information and competition. A corollary phenomenon of these processes is the increasing need and value of knowledge. Examples are smart cars, market versus book value of corporations such as Microsoft, and the Internet explosion with its new ways of doing business.

As we continue to create multi-networked, flexible, national and global organizations it is becoming clear that information alone cannot provide the understanding and meaning needed to solve problems, make decisions, and take effective actions. Such a milieu requires a different organizational paradigm and with it, a new perspective on leaders and leadership. The paradigm selected for this paper is The Intelligent Complex Adaptive System, (ICAS), a nominal organization designed within a framework and set of concepts that combine to create and maintain sustainable high performance in a rapidly **C**hanging, **U**ncertain, **C**omplex and **A**nxiety prone environment, what we call CUCA.[2]

For decades, senior managers have felt compelled to develop detailed plans and strategies to define a vision, objectives, and a pathway to achieve those objectives for their organizations to guide them into the future. The standard procedure is to study the environment, find the major trends, and develop a vision of what the organization should be to achieve a competitive advantage. Then these same senior managers analyze the current status of the organization, lay out the difference between what currently is and the vision (identifying the gap as it is commonly called), and prepare

> It was assumed that the future would be quite like the present, or at least that the future was predictable.

the strategy, tactics, and operational actions to close the gap. The often-unstated assumption is that the future will be quite like the present, or at least that the future is predictable and they have a good idea of what it will be. After decades of thinking efficiency, stability, quality, and optimization, and trying every new idea in management, senior managers look for another new idea, work harder, and continue to do what they have always done: identify the gap, write the strategy, and implement according to plan. This approach worked well when the environment was stable and the assumptions were right.

Classical management approaches will not work in a CUCA world. In a CUCA environment it is impossible to forecast the future. The questions faced by leading edge corporations operating in a complex environment are not so much what products to make or what processes are the most efficient, although both of these are important. The critical questions become considerations such as how to capitalize on relationships, how to build and keep trust, how to determine future wants and needs, how to predict the consequences of our actions, how to develop our people with a high turnover rate, where to find managers smart enough to run their departments when things are happening so fast that no one can know enough to make effective decisions, and so forth.

Historically, during times of intense competition and rapid change the corporate response has been to increase control so that the organization reacts faster, but this only works where those in control know what the right decisions are. In a fast-paced, confusing and unpredictable marketplace, how do we know what are the right decisions and actions? What level of decisions is appropriate for senior managers to make?

There is another way to approach the problem. If we cannot know what the future will bring, then what strategy, if any, will best prepare an organization for surviving and maintaining competitive advantage? Or, are our assumptions wrong? With this question the focus now shifts away from how can we do better what we have been doing in the past to how can we *create an organization that does not need to be able to second guess the future*?

REFLECT:

How has this environment impacted me?

Am I ready to do things differently?

As we entered the 21st century, we spent a great deal of time exploring the shifting environment of business and life, and exploring the emergent properties within organizations that would serve them to sustain and grow in that shifting environment. The resulting organization was what we term an Intelligent Complex Adaptive System with the properties of organizational intelligence, unity and shared purpose, optimum complexity, selectivity, knowledge centricity, flow, permeable boundaries and multidimensionality (Bennet & Bennet, 2004). An organization capable of surviving in a CUCA environment (increasing Change, Uncertainty, Complexity and the resulting human Anxiety) was described as one moving from competitive advantage to collaborative advantage. See Figure 7-1.

Note that while accountability, responsibility and authority (ARA) carry across these models, there are definite shifts away from the "Planning, Managing, Staffing,

Directing and Controlling" model of business management skills in a bureaucracy, to collaborative leadership and empowered team-based decision networks. There is also recognition that the Plan of Action and Milestones is part of a larger direction cone. As an organization learns and adapts to the challenges and opportunities, decisions and actions also shift and change as part of a larger decision journey. In the U.S. Department of the Navy we described this as a *connectedness of choices*, noting that while our decisions and actions may differ at different parts of the organization, they are heading us in the desired direction (Porter, et al., 2002). Excitingly, with increasing awareness of the importance of information and knowledge this includes a shift from repetitive work patterns to the emergence of ever-changing challenges and opportunities.

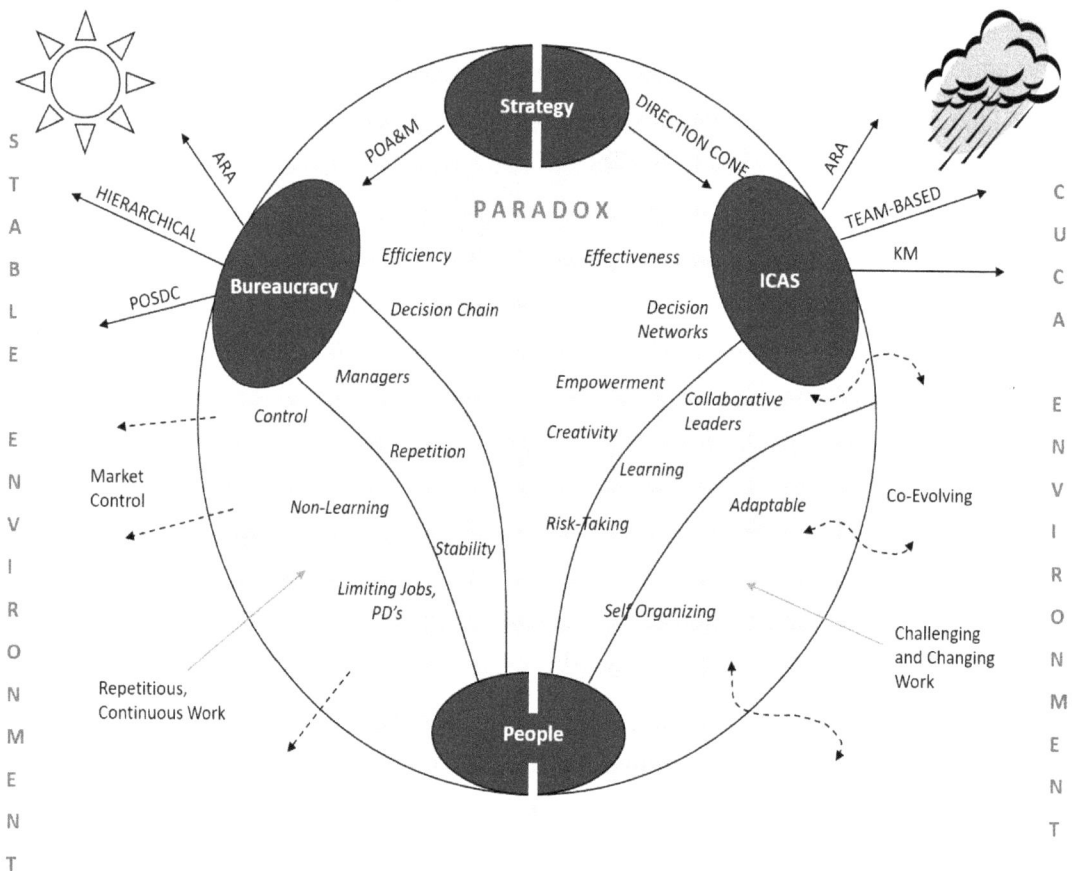

Figure 7-1. *Classical management approaches will not work in a CUCA world.*

Introducing ICAS

The Intelligent Complex Adaptive System is an organization designed to behave similar to an autopoietic system, meaning the structure of ICAS may change but its identity remains. Von Krogh and Roos describe this well when they say that, "...autopoietic systems are systems of a certain organization, independent of its components but dependent on their interrelations. Thus, over time an autopoietic system changes its components but maintains its organization." They also note, "The theory of autopoiesis refers not only to self-production as such, but also to the characteristic of living systems continuously renewing themselves in a way that allows them to maintain the integrity of their structure...then the system must allow for the interrelations between that define it as a unity." (von Krogh & Roos, 1995, p. 36)

In the ICAS organization, the most significant relationships are those between, and among knowledge workers. With the increase in global complexity, competitiveness and information, human capital is becoming *the source of choice* for creating value. As Lawler suggests, "The era of human capital has finally arrived." (Lawler, 2001) As we will discuss below, collaborative leaders play a big role in creating value from human capital. ICAS was created on the presumption that an organization can best survive by possessing a number of specific capabilities and competencies not usually found in industrial or bureaucratic enterprises. The

> Collaborative leaders play a big role in creating value from human capital.

organization, with its identity, competencies, and internal relationships, is the primary source of long-term performance and survival—its products, services and markets will almost surely change. Even if its structure, culture and processes change over time the unity, identity, or alignment of the institution should remain the same. This is so because it is the unity of ICAS that represents the nature and character of the organization such that it has the characteristics necessary for survival in an unpredictable world, see below. The ICAS is an organization that co-evolves with its environment through autopoietic structural adaptation (Maturana & Varela, 1987); and continuously learns, creates, manages and applies knowledge that can deal with change, complexity, and uncertainty. In this organization,

STATEMENT 1: The sum of the daily actions of employees determines the ICAS performance, thus people with their knowledge, competency, and relationships are its most important asset.

STATEMENT 2: The major functions of *senior leadership* are to set the direction, vision, and purpose of the organization and to direct and allocate resources at the highest level.

STATEMENT 3: The major function of *collaborative leaders* is to support, energize, and empower the workforce (primarily knowledge workers) so they can respond quickly and effectively to environmental opportunities and threats.

STATEMENT 4: The major function of *collaborative leadership* (the emergent collective effect of collaborative leaders) is to ensure organizational alignment while modulating the structure, culture, and local directions to achieve sustainable high performance.

REFLECT:

Am I carrying any old ways of thinking into the future?

How adaptable am I in the workplace?

Dynamic Balancing

In an organization, "everything is exactly as it should be." The interpretation here implies that the organization is the result of a balance of forces among many different interacting individuals and artifacts. When things are moving and changing within the organization, there is an unbalance of forces creating this movement. In order to be successful in the turbulent world, the ICAS must be a robust organization capable of changing within itself and being able to respond to many different and surprising events in the environment. At the same time, when things are relatively stable, the organization must be capable of maximizing its output performance and maintaining a steady state or system that is pretty much in balance.

To be able to handle both of these conditions—relative stability and expected agility, and flexibility and adaptiveness—requires *dynamic balancing*. The concept of dynamic balancing means that leaders and workers, throughout the organization, will continuously balance a number of opposing forces or demands such as control versus freedom, short-term versus long-term, information versus knowledge, stakeholder needs, corporate alignment versus local responsiveness, and generic versus individualized learning. Thee balances will rarely remain constant for very long, hence leaders will continuously monitor and change the balance of forces in their areas of responsibility to maintain local effectiveness.

The Eight Emergent Characteristics of the ICAS

The foundation of the ICAS organization is built upon eight characteristics. As introduced above, these emergent characteristics are *permeable boundaries, selectivity, flow, optimum complexity, knowledge centricity, multidimensionality, shared purpose*, and *organizational intelligence.* (Bennet & Bennet, 2004) Each characteristic contributes to the capacity of the organization to survive and adapt in a highly uncertain environment. For example, *permeable boundaries* address the mechanisms of exerting influences across boundaries and ensuring that the organization remains open to changes in its environment while continuously interacting with, and responding to external forces, customers and markets. (Gold & Douvan, 1997) *Selectivity* denotes the capacity to scan and select only those environmental events and trends that are of interest to the organization—thereby filtering and simplifying external complexity, minimizing cost and focusing effort. This also serves as a basis for forecasting future trends and creating possible scenarios and strategies. (Makridakis, 1990) To do these well requires continuous learning through effortful, reflective experience and a well-developed, context oriented intuition and judgment.

Flow as used here is an expansion of Csikszentmihali's concept of optimal (autotelic) experience to encompass the continuing movement of people, ideas, and resources to provide the local capacity to handle opportunities and threats. (Csikszentmihali, 1990) *Optimum complexity* is a concept that helps organizations deal with complexity and is based on Ross Ashby's law of requisite variety. (Ashby, 1964) It gives visibility to, and addresses the management of, different levels of internal complexity to help deal with external complexity. For example, there are many actions that a facilitator or a team can take to vary the diversity and number of ideas, solutions or actions to consider when solving a complex problem or making a decision within a complex situation. Nonaka says,

> The more variety the market generates, the more information and decision burdens increase; the more variety each firm faces, the more variety of information it needs to record, monitor, and interpret for decision-making…A way to cope with this variety is to respond in kind by creating variety in one's own organization structure. This is a fundamental principle called the law of requisite variety, first proposed by Ashby. (Nonaka & Scharmer, 1996 p. 2)

Knowledge centricity puts knowledge in the middle of the organization and promotes its capacity to create, manage, leverage and apply knowledge. *Multidimensionality* (also called integrative competencies) addresses the need for knowledge workers to expand their competency beyond their own discipline so they develop a broader perspective and understand the impact of their actions on other parts of the organization. It includes competencies such as system and complexity thinking, relationship network management, the risk of poor leadership and information literacy. *Shared purpose* represents the grounding for ICAS existence and is a resource for aligning and energizing the workforce and their daily actions. *Organizational intelligence* represents the ability of ICAS to plan, set and achieve goals and objectives. The underlying theme of these eight characteristics is to use learning, knowledge, collaboration, empowerment and a systems perspective to support and unleash the energy and potential of knowledge workers. The objective is to take effective local actions that are in concert with the organization's direction, values and purpose, while being able to respond quickly to surprising local threats and opportunities.

Figure 7-2 shows the major characteristics in the ICAS model and the top-level conceptual relationships among them. The box to the side identifies the four major processes and their broad relationships to each other. It also shows that organizational intelligence has a major role in the quality of those processes. The middle rectangle identifies the eight emergent characteristics of the ICAS organization, together with their major relationships. The bottom two rectangles represent the major characteristics in the external environment.

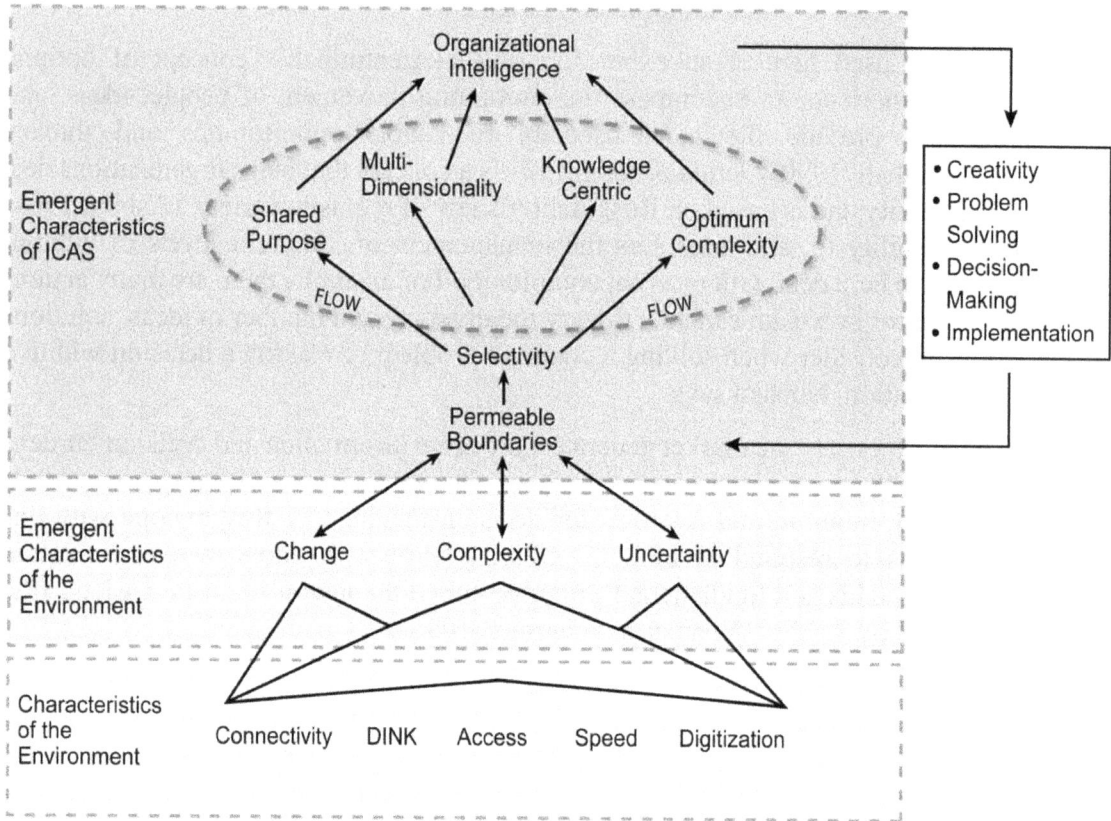

Figure 7-2. *The relationship among the eight emergent characteristics of the ICAS.*

Organizations take inputs from their environment, transform those inputs into higher-value outputs and provide these to the environment. They do this by using internal and external resources in efficient and effective ways that create added value above and beyond the value of the incoming resources. While this sequence is easy to describe, it becomes very complex and challenging in the real world, particularly when things are moving quickly, the problem is not well understood, there are many opinions, and a successful outcome is dependent on external events such as the relationship among the eight emergent characteristics of the ICAS.

These eight characteristics cannot be decreed by management, but rather will emerge in the organization as a result of the day-to-day leadership, management and working environment. These characteristics, taken together, are mutually supportive in creating and maintaining the ICAS organization as a complex adaptive system. To facilitate the emergence of these characteristics requires a new way of thinking about structure, culture, major processes and leadership.

Structure and Culture

Neither the classic bureaucratic nor the flat organization could provide both the unity and selectivity necessary for the ICAS. A different structure is needed to create an organizational system that can enter into a symbiotic relationship with its cooperative enterprise, virtual alliances, and external environment while simultaneously retaining unity of purpose and selectivity of incoming threats and opportunities. This organization is a living system composed of other living systems—teams within teams, interacting communities, self-organization within organization—that combine and interact to provide the capabilities of an advanced, intelligent techno-sociological adaptive enterprise.

The objective of structure is to provide a framework and foundation for the workforce to meet its mission/vision and business goals. The structure must align with the vision and strategy over the long term while at the same time supporting the immediate needs of all people in the organization and in the stakeholder community. In a turbulent world, strategy is more a direction than an end goal and vision is a characterization of the future firm rather than a detailed description.

The *learning structure* is designed to ensure continuous learning and rapid response to external events. The basic structure consists of the use of teams within teams and communities to facilitate collaboration and leverage knowledge. The existence of an Operations Center—together with a Knowledge Center, Learning Center and Career Management Center—helps ensure unity of the ICAS actions, effective use of knowledge and continuous learning. Action teams, communities, and networks are embedded throughout the structure to provide rapid and diverse response. The levels and balance of authority, responsibility and accountability given to leaders, managers, and workers is designed to provide the right balance between the occasional need for hierarchical decision-making and the continuous need for collaboration and local empowerment and decision-making.

> The learning structure uses teams within teams and communities to facilitate collaboration and leverage knowledge.

The *action culture* is the invisible medium through which the ICAS knowledge worker seeks, interprets, and analyzes information, creates and shares knowledge, makes decisions, and takes action on issues and market opportunities. This culture plays a significant role in energizing and helping each worker make the right decisions and take the best actions. The action culture has the characteristics of widespread trust, continuous learning, high integrity, and fair treatment of all people. In addition, it encourages creativity, allows a high degree of self-determination, and supports knowledge sharing and collaboration, all within an equalitarian base. The culture is action-oriented, flexible, and cannot be predetermined; the action is nurtured guided and supported in a manner that will push it in the right direction.

Basic assumptions for the ICAS culture include: The future is unknowable, individual action makes the difference, all individuals are creative and can learn and develop knowledge, no one individual possesses the information or knowledge to completely understand complex situations, knowledge can be leveraged through strategy, structure and collaboration; trust, mutual respect, fairness and collaboration are critical for leveraging knowledge; and strong control is a myth, influence is possible, and dialogue is essential. As can be seen, the ICAS sets the stage for the emergence of collaborative leadership. See Bennet and Bennet (2004) for a more in-depth treatment.

The four major organizational processes—creativity, problem solving, decision-making, and implementation—are embedded within the ICAS culture and become a natural part of how the work gets done. By formalizing and inculcating these processes throughout the ICAS, knowledge workers and teams are able to leverage knowledge quickly and efficiently and greatly improve their adaptivity and response.

> The four major organizational processes are embedded within the ICAS culture and become a natural part of how the work gets done.

To ensure that the ICAS workforce possesses the knowledge, experience, freedom and self-confidence to identify problems and take effective action in their area of responsibility, leadership must take on a significantly different role than that presented in classical organizational theory. Two major differences are: (1) leadership cannot be controlling, but rather must be nurturing, supportive, and collaborative, and (2) leadership must be implemented at all levels throughout the organization. This collaborative leadership, while maintaining accountability and responsibility, shares authority with knowledge workers and, through fostering a collaborative workplace, ensures the ability to make decisions and quickly respond at the point of action.

The Correlation of Forces

An important aspect of strategy in the ICAS organization is the correlation of forces. A good strategy identifies the major strengths, or forces within the organization, and those that meet day-to-day changing external threats and opportunities. Senior management should recognize and monitor the fundamental forces within the organization to ensure that these forces are aligned to maximize their effectiveness in creating sustainable competitive advantage. This alignment means that the forces are moving the organization in the same direction and that they are coordinated so that together they reinforce each other.

In a complex organization there are many forces at work. By harnessing, directing, and/or nurturing the major forces, the organization can correlate its major resources to achieve maximum effectiveness. The correlated organization may perform at a point on the operational spectrum that utilizes less of one resource and more of another, achieving a higher gain than if these resources were added separately. This is what could be called organizational synergy through the correlation of resources. This correlation is not static, but may be responsive to external pressures.

The forces the ICAS needs to correlate are considered in light of the following: (1) The short-term effectiveness of an organization depends on the actions of all of its employees; and (2) the long-term health (sustainability) of an organization is determined by the same set of actions of all employees seen from their consequences and implications for the future.

Being able to take effective actions every day is a function of the knowledge and intent of knowledge workers. The environment and the organization's knowledge would be correlated when that knowledge as applied by the workforce is directly related to those areas in the environment consistent with the organization's direction, that is, knowledge created and used by knowledge workers is within the knowledge space of the organization.

> Being able to take effective actions every day is a function of the knowledge and intent of knowledge workers.

The strength of the ICAS organization is a combination of four forces that directly influence the organization's success. These four forces are the *Force of Direction*, the *Force of Intent*, the *Force of Knowledge*, and the *Force of Knowing*.

The fundamental force of the organization is the **Force of Knowledge**. This consists of the creation, sharing, dissemination, leveraging, and application of knowledge. The strength of the Force of Knowledge is measured by capacity, capability, connectivity, and flow. What is the knowledge capacity of the organization? What abilities does the organization have to create, leverage, and apply knowledge? How do technology, structure, culture, and leadership support this force? How does the organization ensure connectivity of its knowledge workers with each other and with the external environment? How does the organizational structure and culture facilitate flow in terms of data, information, and knowledge; in terms of people; and in terms of autotelic work? How does the organization engage social networking? Does the hiring, movement, and learning of workers support the long-term needs of the ICAS? Is knowledge recognized for its strong role in the organization's success? The weaving of knowledge and leadership is a core theme throughout this book. For an in-depth treatment of knowledge see Bennet and Bennet (2015a).

The second force is the **Force of Intent**. Intention is the source with which we are doing something, the act or instance of mentally and emotionally setting a specific course of action or result, a determination to act in some specific way. It includes the purpose and attitude toward the *effect* of one's action, the outcome, with purpose implying having a goal or the determination to achieve something and attitude encompassing loyalty and dedication. Intent focuses energy and knowledge; knowledge is the "know how" and intent is the power to focus the knowledge and maintain direction toward a vision of the future. It can take the form of a declaration (often in the form of action), a directive, an assertion, a prayer, a cry for help, a wish, a visualization, a thought or an affirmation.

From the mind/brain frame of reference, intention is a determinate of success. Back in the 1940's, Henry Ford is credited with saying *If you think you can or you think you can't, you're right.* Whether he actually said this or not, by the late 1990's neuroscience findings proved this statement right. *What we believe leads to what we think leads to our knowledge base which leads to our actions, which determines success* (Bennet & Bennet, 2015b; Begley, 2007; Lipton, 2005; Rose, 2005; Bownds, 1999). In terms of self, just understanding, believing and acting upon this one finding can change the course of our learning journey.

In focusing the energy and knowledge of the organization, intent is the power and consistency that gains the admiration of the marketplace. The strength of the Force of Intent is measured by the desire, willingness, and energy of every member of the organization. How does the work get done? Where do people focus their attention? Are knowledge workers excited about their work? Is there strong competition among team leaders that weakens intent and drains energy? Does senior leadership act consistently with the stated direction and value set of the organization?

REFLECT:

Do I understand that I am the captain of my ship?

How can I best use my intent to achieve my dreams?

The third force is the ***Force of Direction***. Direction serves as the compass for the organization as it moves into an uncharted and uncharitable future. It both limits ICAS activities within some action space surrounding the chosen direction and conserves energy by defining what areas the ICAS is not interested in. With any direction comes a purpose and a vision of what is required to make the journey. In that regard direction acts on organizational reason for being and provides spirit and purpose to all employees. It also is used to explain why the ICAS must be as it is—providing sound reasons for collaboration, empowerment, etc.

The strength of the Force of Direction is measured by organizational cohesion, the line of sight, and the connectedness of choices. The level of communication, the alignment of work activities, and the effectiveness of the Operations Center all impact the Force of Direction. Are the organization's resource allocations consistent with the mission? Do knowledge workers have access and two-way communication with leaders? Are decisions at every level geared toward achieving a common direction, a connectedness of choices? Why are *we* going in this direction? Why do we think this is the best direction? What happens to us if the environment drastically changes? Does our direction include my own pet idea? Is everyone expected to go in that direction? What about new ideas and opportunities? What do we need to learn to contribute to the direction? What could happen that will make us change directions?

The fourth force is the ***Force of Knowing***. Knowing is a blending of the cognitive capabilities of observing and perceiving a situation, the cognitive processing that must occur to understand the external world and make maximum use of our intuition and experiences, and the faculty for creating deep knowledge and acting on that knowledge. See Bennet and Bennet (2013; 2015a) for an in-depth treatment of knowing.

Knowing can be elevated to the organizational level by using and combining the insights and experiences of individuals through dialogue and collaboration within teams, groups, and communities. Such efforts significantly improve the quality of understanding and responsiveness of actions of the organization. It also greatly expands the scope of complex situations that can be handled through knowing because of the great resources brought to bear. Knowing is the tip of the ICAS spear, penetrating the haze of complexity by allowing workers to think beyond normal perception and dig into the meaning and hidden patterns in a complex world. Knowing represents the fog lights into the future. The strength of the Force of Knowing is measured by the organization's ability to perceive, interpret, and make sense of the environment and take the most effective actions. How is the organization supporting learning? Are teams and communities supported and rewarded? Are knowledge workers achieving integrative competencies? Do knowledge workers trust their intuition and act accordingly? Are decision feedback loops in place?

In a turbulent environment there are holes that offer opportunities, what we call the environmental opportunity space, a window of opportunity in terms of space and time. A correlated organization has a consistent direction and a comprehension from what knowing has provided about the environment. While the company may not be able to define this space, nor can it go there before it exists, the organization's direction is such that it can take advantage of the environmental opportunity space as it emerges, and does so. Intuition, judgment, and insight do not just happen in particular minds. They can be studied, developed, and practiced over time and within domains of interest.

Here is where the organizational forces come into play. Most opportunities and threats in the environment are "sensed" (through the sense of knowing) prior to actuality. Defining and understanding the environmental landscape is necessary before the organization can set its direction to move in. Success is then dependent on employees having the intention to take advantage of that window, and creating, leveraging, and applying the right knowledge to do so. Knowledge enables workers to continuously make sense of and track the window. Learning (open system) and knowledge provide the flexibility to keep up with (or ahead of) changes inside the window. Knowing creates the opportunity to see beyond the window. These forces are the tools of leadership that support the emergence of the eight characteristics of the ICAS organization.

Final Thoughts

Consider the four Forces: Direction, Intent, Knowledge, and Knowing. *Direction* sets the compass, gives meaning to the trip and offers a vision of what to strive for. *Intent* provides the energy and consistency of movement. *Knowledge* provides the competency to take the right actions. *Knowing* provides a deeper understanding of the environment and how to deal with it. These forces are aligned when: Direction is set and understood; Intent moves the organization in the desired direction; Knowledge ensures actions follow intent and direction; and Knowing improves knowledge, bolsters intent, and signals the ICAS whether the actions and directions are on track.

When you close your eyes and picture your organization, what do you see? A building? A logo? An organization chart? If these are your references, then the activities you encounter daily are through the lens of these limiting perspectives. Image your perspective now aligning with what is actually taking place—operating inside an Intelligent Complex Adaptive System. The entire experience changes from a feeling of "box-checking" to "sense-making." Instead of seeing the information and digging for the explanations, the user interface becomes the explanations—beyond just more information. Could we call it *The Explanation Age*? (Lewis, 2013)

We've only tasted the possibilities in this chapter, although it is clear that the themes of collaboration and learning and knowledge thread throughout the ICAS organization, and pointing that out was the intent of this chapter.

Chapter 8
Collaborative Leadership

Given the functional requirements needed for survival and the changing knowledge worker values and attitudes, is there an historic leadership style or approach that would meet the needs of the ICAS? The classical autocratic leader would not be successful, because no individual knows enough to second-guess the environment, whether it is global or local. The charismatic leader is unlikely to be effective because knowledge workers, while inspired by passion, also demand respect and freedom of choice. They want to participate, not just follow. It is also becoming clear to many workers that while energy is needed, it is not sufficient for effective actions—working smarter is clearly better that working harder. Since they lead by personality and image, strong, individualistic leaders want and expect control and visibility.

The nature of ICAS is best fulfilled by leadership distributed throughout its structure to aid in cohesion, alignment, rapid responsiveness and adaptability. Such an organization cannot be designed and constructed using bureaucratic style authority as a driver, it must be created through seeding, nurturing and co-evolving with the workforce and its environment via self-organization at the local level and iterative interactions with the outside world. This is not something strong, ego-driven leaders are good at, or usually willing to do.

> Leadership distributed throughout the organization aids in cohesion, alignment, rapid responsiveness and adaptability.

The key question for this chapter is: What kind of leadership can best provide the guidance and support to the workforce as they sense, interpret, respond and adjust to an uncertain and changing environment? Leadership is a quality of the organization, an institutional capacity to energize and synergize. Leadership can be described as the process of giving meaningful direction to collective effort and causing willing effort to be expended to achieve collective goals (Jacobs & Jacque, 1990). For our purposes, **collaborative leaders are those individuals *throughout the organization* who have the initiative, competency, and connections to mold, support, and guide their own part of the organization's structure, culture, and execution competency to achieve high performance.** They work collaboratively toward achieving intelligent activity. As introduced in Chapter 3, intelligent activity represents a perfect state of interaction where intent, purpose, direction, values and expected outcomes are clearly understood and communicated among all parties, reflecting wisdom and achieving a higher truth. Just as organizational intelligence must come from the structure, culture, and leadership of the organization, intelligent activity—led by collaborative leaders—comes from the knowledge, decisions and actions of every individual in the organization.

It is not surprising that the concept of collaboration is moving into the everyday language of our business leaders. As introduced in Chapter 1, concepts and terms began to emerge that tempered the hard edge of competition with elements of cooperation and collaboration as we moved into the Internet age and global connectivity.

The material provided below is the culmination of many years of study and interaction with leadership groups rich in thought and experience. However, it would be impossible to trace any specific concept back to an individual source. Thus, this section on collaborative leadership is truly a collaborative endeavor.

Senior Leadership

One part of ICAS leadership consists of senior people with top-level authority, responsibility, and accountability to determine and guide the organization's purpose, vision, and direction. These leaders have similar roles and responsibilities in all organizations, the exception being that ICAS senior leaders recognize their control limitations and are *more collaborative, servant and people oriented* than most others. This is necessary to create the flexibility, adaptability and collaboration needed to deal productively with the marketplace, customers, suppliers and other stakeholders. A bureaucratic organization that is tightly controlled will have great difficulty adapting to a rapidly changing environment. Its chain of command and bureaucratic process restrictions are simply incapable of responding quickly and flexibly. (Refer to Figure 7-1.)

In a CUCA world, no one individual or group has enough knowledge or power to control an organization, at least not for long. Because of past successes with a control-oriented approach to management (in a different world), the recognition of this limitation is extremely difficult for some senior leaders to accept. Yet knowledge worker competency, empowerment and, pro-activity are major factors in ICAS's capacity to perform. As Wiig (2004, p. 31) notes, "Improving the quality of the myriad of small problem-solving situations in every employee's daily work culminates into a significant improvement in performance for the whole enterprise." By working with their colleagues, collaborative leaders create, support and maintain an environment where employees can learn and develop the competency to create, leverage and apply knowledge. This type of relationship with employees can also be very difficult for an autocratic manager to buy into because of issues with trust and power.

ICAS performance is achieved by empowering the work force, providing a learning structure, building relationships, nurturing an action-oriented culture, and embedding and growing multiple networks that facilitate quick response. Collaboration is such an important part of creating the right environment and leveraging knowledge that we call the type of leaders described in this chapter *collaborative leaders*. It is within this context that we investigate the leadership attributes and behaviors that will move our organizations into the future.

Note that these leaders will be *found at all levels of the organization*. They can be recognized by their wide perspectives, high values, social networking efficacy and collaborative relationships with other workers. Through knowledge and a systems perspective—and taking actions that build trust, earn respect and encourage self-directed learning—these leaders are both admired and supported. By using a team/networking approach to problem solving, decision-making and implementation, they create and motivate a workforce of competent professionals.

REFLECT:

Do I openly share information?

Do I challenge the status quo to prevent stasis and the creation

of false realities?

Leadership Style

Let's explore the concept of collaborative leadership in terms of style. Drawing on a random sample of 3,871 executives selected from a database of over 20,000 leaders, it was found that those leaders with the best results **do not rely on only one style of leadership**—they use many or all of six styles which they describe as: coercive, authoritative, affiliative, democratic, pacesetting and coaching. *Coercive leaders* demand immediate compliance. *Authoritative leaders* mobilize people toward a vision. *Affiliative leaders* create emotional bonds and harmony. *Democratic leaders* build consensus through participation. *Pacesetting leaders* expect excellence and self-direction. And *coaching leaders* develop people for the future. As Goleman explains,

> These styles, taken individually appear to have a direct and unique impact on the working atmosphere of the company, division or team…the leaders with the best results do not rely on only one leadership style; they use most of them in a given week-seamlessly and in different measure—depending on the business situation. (Goleman, 2000, p. 81)

From the collaborative leader's viewpoint, it is easy to identify with each style for a given situation. In emergencies, even coercive leadership may be necessary! Authoritative leadership would likely be least applicable; rather, a collaborative leader would work with employees to understand and believe in the organization's vision and purpose. The other four styles of this model fit nicely with the concept of collaboration and leadership. By

> The collaborative leader can identify with different leadership styles for different situations.

way of summary, the descriptive elements related to these four styles are: create emotional bonds and harmony (affiliative), build consensus through participation (democratic), expect excellence and self direction (pacesetting) and develop people for the future (coaching).

Leadership evolves with the times. As the large body of work on leadership expanded, there are half a dozen forms of leadership that have come to the fore: direct leadership, servant leadership, situational leadership, collective leadership and inspirational leadership and transformational leadership, all of which can contribute to collaborative leadership. See Figure 8-1.

Figure 8-1. *Six types of leadership that can contribute to collaborative leadership.*

Related to the idea of **Direct Leadership** are authenticity, presence by example, leadership by example, role modeling, leading from the front, and setting the climate to excel. Values are directly related to authenticity; since an authentic person cannot be what they are not, values are highly visible. Presence by example and leadership by example are closely related, with presence allowing for leadership participation without necessarily involving the leader in the same activities as employees. Presence represents awareness of intent and expectation, and can be perceived as having a spiritual orientation, that is, a visible—and invisible—connection. Leadership by example and role modeling are closely related, ways of connecting with people and inspiring them to be the best they can be. Leadership by example also has a direct connect to accountability, with the leader being accountable to himself and accountable to his people.

Similarly, cognitive leadership includes "persons who, by word and/or personal example, markedly influence behaviors, thoughts and/or feelings of a significant number of their fellow human beings." (Gardner, 1995, pp. 8-9). Cognitive leadership focuses on understanding the nature of the human mind of leaders *and* followers (Collins, 2001). While leading from the front has historical precedence, with a collaborative leader *a good leader is also a good follower*. A participant in a leadership study in a military organization pointed out that the way a leader follows exhibits the leadership that *others want to follow*. Further, there has to be an understanding of the intent, not necessarily the actions that are taken, but the intent of the actions. *Why* were these actions taken? Remember that knowledge is context sensitive and situation dependent, and each part of an organization has a different focus, capability and competency. What is needed is a *connectedness of choices*, that is, different decisions and actions coming from different parts of the organization, yet moving everyone in the same direction. Understanding the why of a decision provides the opportunity for better decisions and better outcomes.

There is also an element of motivation in leading by example, since this conveys to employees that the leader knows how to act and has the confidence, skills and abilities to do so. Finally, as in all forms or styles of leadership, there are scenarios where leadership by example does not work. For example, in the everyday methodologies necessary to maintain a nuclear power plant. There are very special skills sets where only those highly qualified can accomplish them; this is the realm of the expert not of the leader.

Servant leadership describes a leader who is there to serve and not be served. Servant-leadership is an active process that involves both engagement and reflection. This is a leader who has a caring heart who has the ability to reach out and reach down, no matter how deep the organization. Leading with empathy and compassion, the servant leader takes a personal interest in each employee, drawing out what is special and showing how these special talents can contribute to the organization. Servant leadership would include affiliative behavior, the element of "create emotional bonds and harmony", and coaching behavior, the element of " develop people for the future." A servant leader helps others to help themselves. As put by Greenleaf (1977), a servant leader is servant first and only then he aspires to lead. This service orientation means that people and community take priority, above personal objectives.

As can be seen, this type of leadership is built on developing relationships, dialoging, listening and respecting the space needed by employees to be themselves and put their best foot forward. Perhaps it goes without saying that the servant leader is a nurturer who creates an environment where employees can operate as an effective team.

While servant leadership is often considered as a stand-alone approach, as with most leadership theories, there are many overlaps with other leadership approaches that put the needs of customers, employees and communities first. For example, humanistic theories place the responsibility on leaders to provide the environment (free of constraints) where employees can flourish and realize their full potential in order to serve the organizational mission. This assumes that people are naturally motivated and that organizations are by nature structured to support their development

> Servant leadership has many overlaps with other leadership approaches that put the needs of customers, employees and communities first.

(Blake & Mouton, 1994; Hershey & Blanchard, 1972). Spiritual leadership is also related to servant leadership. Fairholm (1997, p. 8) says spiritual leadership is about capturing people's souls and says that "as leaders commit to the care of the whole person, they must include spiritual care into their practice ... Leaders in the new century must consider and actively engage in making for themselves and then helping their followers make these connections."

One of the potential downfalls of servant leadership is the difficulty of instant response when a direct order must be given. Servant leadership takes time; relationships are built over time. Yet in a CUCA environment, time is not always available. Thus, we begin to understand more clearly that leadership styles and forms indeed are, and need to be, situation dependent and context sensitive. This is acknowledged by Sousa and van Dierendonck (2015), who introduce effective servant leadership as being a combination of an action driven side (stewardship, accountability and empowerment) and a moral side (humility and standing-back). Which brings us to a short discussion of situational leadership.

REFLECT:

Do I lead by example and collaboration, not by power or ego?

Am I a role model for how to lead and how to follow?

Situational leadership is common sense leadership, a natural way of sizing up a situation and using the situation to effect outcomes. Just as knowledge, leadership is situation dependent and context sensitive, offering flexibility at the point of action. Understanding the organization's strengths and weaknesses in terms of mission, values and people, and how these strengths and weaknesses shift depending on the context, structure, personnel, situation and environment, helps organize a leader's thoughts and actions towards desired outcomes.

Situational theories say that leadership is a product of demand and is dependent on the situation at hand. The specific factors of a situation determine who emerges as a leader (Hersey, 1985). Personal situational theories combine situational leadership with the belief that the leader must also have specific affective, intellectual and action traits. Affective traits bring in the element of emotional intelligence. Contingency leadership says that the *effectiveness* of the leader is dependent upon the situation. This requires the leader to understand their own orientation in terms of self and to learn how to adjust to the specific situation at hand (Fiedler, 1967).

If there is time, a leader's social network can be used to make sense of the situation before making a decision (a social form of learning). The point made here is that decision-making must be based not only on what information is available, but also on the circumstances of the situation at hand. A leader must have the ability to read the circumstances, appreciate them, make a good judgment and have the courage to take a position at the right time. Situational leadership demands choices. Effective situational leadership requires continuous learning, quick response, robustness, resiliency, flexibility, and adaptability, all sustainability characteristics that will be discussed in more detail in Chapter 12. It also requires an understanding of complexity (see Bennet & Bennet, 2013).

Collective leadership recognizes that although the leader must make the call and take responsibility, the knowledge resides within his or her team. This is quite close to the idea of collaborative leadership. In collective leadership everyone is expected to take responsibility, exercising his or her initiative to get the work done. This relates to pacesetting behavior, the element "expect excellence and self direction." That being said, there is still the need to collaborate, with leaders at all levels benefiting from listening and tapping into the different perspectives offered throughout the organization. While someone needs to make the call, the knowledge resides throughout the whole team and the team has collective ownership of the issues. This relates to the element " build consensus through participation" (democratic).

Situational leadership can also be limiting in terms of getting to the root of issues since the focus is on the current situation, and the "how" to resolve this situation and move forward, rather than understanding the "why" of the situation. In other words, while this approach can be highly effective in the instant at hand, it must be married to strategic thinking—perhaps transformational leadership—for long-term success.

Inspirational leadership is about getting a message across to people while simultaneously engaging them. While relative to a specific individual or related group and creating an emotional connection, inspirational leadership is simultaneously mission focused, painting a picture of a bright future. The living message of inspirational leaders resonates with others, building on core concepts such as believing in what you do, setting high goals, knowing your job well, learning from others, and making things happen, all circling back to an individual's purpose, motivation and commitment. This is true idea resonance. Although an entirely different approach than servant leadership, inspirational leadership relates to the coaching behavior, "develop people for the future."

To be able to influence people and get them to take the best actions to fulfill the organizational mission, the leader must first make the effort to appreciate the context of the people he or she is trying to influence. It is within this context that the inspirational leader creates an atmosphere in which people enjoy coming to work on a daily basis, an atmosphere that brings out the best in people. This is also the realm of the charismatic leader, where the influence of

> The inspirational leader creates an atmosphere in which people enjoy coming to work on a daily basis, an atmosphere that brings out the best in people.

leaders is based upon the perceptions of their followers. Also similar is aspiration and visionary leadership, which Kouzes and Posner (1995, p. 30) describe as "the art of mobilizing other to want to struggle for shared aspirations." As can be seen, this is the art of flaming the follower's desire to contribute as well as the leader's capability of mobilizing others to action.

Several words of caution with this approach. First, leaders may inspire yet not have the knowledge to deliver what is promised. There must be more than showmanship; there must be an authenticity and a sense of moral bearing to ensure using leadership skills and abilities to influence people to do the right thing. Second, it is difficult to sustain a high level of motivation all the time; to be inspired

Transformational leadership is about breaking new ground to achieve a higher level of excellence in all areas. This could involve changing mental models, mindsets, attitudes and value systems, or raising the knowledge and skills of employees to a new height of excellence. In transformational leadership we see pacesetting behavior, the element of "expect excellence and self direction."

Transformational leadership could also mean moving the organization toward commitment and engagement, winning the hearts and minds of employees. This would include affiliative behavior, the element of "create emotional bonds and harmony." In one group of leaders discussing leadership, the analogy of a dead fish emerged to convey the message that every leader must continuously try to do better, to transform. Any leader that decides to just go with the flow, not trying to achieve that bit more, is like a dead fish. Every fish that has half a life tries to struggle against the current; only dead fish go with the stream.

As with all forms of leadership, it must be recognized that values play a significant role in transformation. Not only is there the need to be able to paint a compelling and believable picture of the future, the transformational leader must gain trust and confidence through his authenticity. Further, giving employees a big idea is not sufficient to guide the process of transformation. Rather, there is much to be done, building consensus (democratic behavior), discussing issues over time, gaining more and more perspectives to help guide future decisions and employee thinking as the transformation occurs.

In a CUCA environment, change is the only constant. To break new ground amidst change you look for order, and amidst order you look for change. This is an exciting facet of the environment, providing the opportunity to create an exciting tomorrow, which in turn defines the existence of the organization today. Transformation, of course, often requires patience; change takes time if it is to be systemized and internalized and may be momentary. Cultural and holistic leadership contains elements of transformational leadership in that it focuses on the ability to step outside the culture to start change processes that are more evolutionary and adaptive in nature (Senge, 1990).

We now take another look at the six types of leadership that contribute to collaborative leadership with representative aspects that apply to each type. See Figure 8-2. As can be seen, the four styles introduced by Goleman (2000) are infolded in the six forms of leadership discussed above, all of which include basic elements of collaboration, that is, *working together with others to achieve a common goal*.

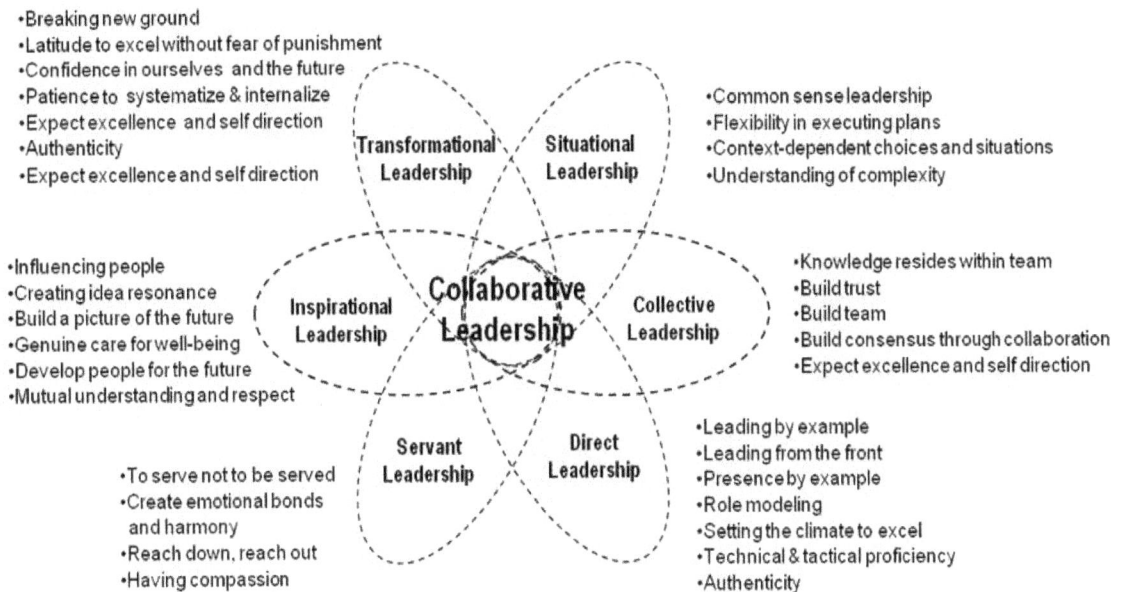

- Breaking new ground
- Latitude to excel without fear of punishment
- Confidence in ourselves and the future
- Patience to systematize & internalize
- Expect excellence and self direction
- Authenticity
- Expect excellence and self direction

Transformational Leadership **Situational Leadership**

- Common sense leadership
- Flexibility in executing plans
- Context-dependent choices and situations
- Understanding of complexity

- Influencing people
- Creating idea resonance
- Build a picture of the future
- Genuine care for well-being
- Develop people for the future
- Mutual understanding and respect

Inspirational Leadership **Collaborative Leadership** **Collective Leadership**

- Knowledge resides within team
- Build trust
- Build team
- Build consensus through collaboration
- Expect excellence and self direction

Servant Leadership **Direct Leadership**

- To serve not to be served
- Create emotional bonds and harmony
- Reach down, reach out
- Having compassion

- Leading by example
- Leading from the front
- Presence by example
- Role modeling
- Setting the climate to excel
- Technical & tactical proficiency
- Authenticity

Figure 8-2. *Six types of leadership and their aspects that contribute to collaborative leadership.*

Emerging Collaborative Leadership

Collaborative leadership *emerges*, with leadership attributes, character, and styles springing forth at all levels of the organization. This emergence occurs when there is cohesion among managers and leaders, when communication is open, and energy is focused on learning and performance, not personal gain.

Zand (1997, p. 23) believes that, "Leadership in knowledge organizations is the ability to harness, and integrate three interdependent forces—knowledge, trust, and power." We would exchange the word "power" with "influence". While power has many different definitions, in the sense of ultimate authority or control, power does not encourage collaborative relationships or processes. Even a medium use of power may quell open communication and knowledge sharing, and for any reasonable level of complexity, one mind is insufficient.

Collaborative leaders are most influential when they are distributed throughout the organization, interacting, supporting and sharing their experiences and insights with colleagues. These leaders exhibit a coherence of perspective, approach and direction that *combines purpose, values and respect for people* while encouraging creativity, diversity, risk and proactive endeavors. This is not an easy tightrope to walk. It takes a lot of communication—the sharing of understanding, not the transfer of information—and a steady build-up of trust and personal caring.

Formal staff meetings, coupled with coffee mess conversations, offer opportunities to discuss topics like success, mistakes, the contexts important to decisions, how and why decisions were made, and to provide feedback. Behaviors such as this merge management and leadership together. Managers are tasked to get things done; collaborative leaders look around and beyond the task and guide, support and integrate, moving the organization toward a connectedness of choices.[1] The two are not incompatible.

REFLECT:

Do I have a favorite leadership style?

Can I shift leadership styles when it is needed?

One caution. The mode of collaborative leadership is highly sensitive to situation and context. For example, there will undoubtedly be situations that emerge where an immediate decision is required at the point of action where the knowledge resides. Despite the lack of opportunity to handle a decision collaboratively, collaborative leadership still comes into play in this situation in terms of having provided the platform for shared understanding prior to the immediate challenge. Further, because a collaborative leader has developed an understanding of—and appreciation for—the expertise and skills of his/her coworkers, there is a knowing (in the larger sense of the term) that plays into the decision at hand, such that the immediately required decision may be part of a larger decision-chain which will be navigated through collaboration.

All qualified individuals, from the CEO to team leaders to knowledge experts, may be, or become, collaborative leaders. These individuals set standards, leverage knowledge, reinforce an action culture, interpret and explain the environment, support knowledge worker career growth, orchestrate disputes, resolve internal problems and continuously scan the environmental opportunity space.[2]

Collaborative leaders may not represent formal positions in the organization; they are individuals who have demonstrated their ability and accepted the responsibility of leadership within the context of organizational needs. They are not bosses so much as collaborators and colleagues. In a sense, they will likely be the "high potential knowledge workers" as seen by upper management. Continually reinventing themselves, their value lies in their capacity to learn, develop the key competencies, facilitate knowledge flows and create relationships and perspectives that, working in concert, will prepare and guide the ICAS into the future.

Through this complex set of interactions among the internal environment, responses from knowledge workers, the structure and culture within which they work, and their own personal needs and goals, a world view and an understanding of their purpose and who they are in the context of the workplace and the world will emerge. *During* this process, individuals change and grow in such a manner that they become respected, admired, and trusted by others. *Through* this process, collaborative leaders emerge who have earned their right of influence. These leaders are co-equals who help others get their work done, and who care about their co-workers. While they may or may not be team leaders, they are team problem solvers and facilitators.

Facilitation can be considered an advanced form of collaboration; it is clearly an important strength of leaders. An effective facilitator is a leader, a follower, a collaborator, and a servant to the group. Like collaboration, facilitation can be learned only through experience. It is both a behavior and a mental process, demanding parallel monitoring of several different processes occurring simultaneously during teamwork sessions. Experience in processing several streams of data simultaneously helps a leader monitor situations and interactions and adjust their own behavior and responses accordingly. See "Leader as Facilitator" at Appendix B.

Wherever they reside in the organization, collaborative leaders are decision-makers (see Bennet & Bennet, 2013). They develop an understanding of how and why the ICAS is what it is and does what it does, and take the time to share that understanding with their coworkers. *They develop an understanding of their organization that enables them to convey meaning, worthiness and pride to the workforce.*

A Mobilizing Force

Collaborative leaders represent a mobilizing force within the organization. It all starts with clarity and articulation of vision and creating shared expectations. By working at multiple levels and networking with each other, collaborative leaders build organizational cohesion and local flexibility. In other words, they are hierarchical level spanners, having the perspective and competency to work at multiple levels with the goal of keeping local actions coherent with top strategies. They touch people, and those people go on to different places and touch others.

As collaborative leaders learn and grow, many of them will be promoted to higher levels of management/leadership responsibility. They will also move around within their organization every three or four years, as most ICAS knowledge workers will. This mobility is part of their career growth and develops a higher-level understanding and appreciation of the needs, structure and culture of their organization. It also ensures continuous learning and selects out non-learners.

Collaborative leaders are adept at creating and using virtual and living networks. They are members of communities of practice, quick response teams and *their own personal verication network*, seeking and getting advice from knowledgeable allies. Throughout history humans have often engaged in the process of *verication*, consulting a trusted ally. For example, when we do not have explicit evidence to verify the correctness of a decision, or question the explicit evidence we do have because of our "gut" feeling, we vericate the decision. This means going to a recognized expert with whom you have a relationship (a trusted ally, often a colleague or friend) to get their opinion, i.e., grounding your decision through implicit data and information (Bennet & Bennet, 2004). This is in contrast to going to the dictionary or extant reference book to verify the correctness of your thoughts.

The process of *verication* has also expanded as social networking has become a way of life. For example, let's say a stranger provides some significant information to us, or we recall a distant memory about something that may or may not be right. We are unsure; so we go to the Internet to find out if it is right. If we use an extant source such as an expert's web site, or a validated virtual reference text, we are *verifying* the rightness or wrongness of this information through explicit data. If we go to a virtual community of practice, or a members-only chat room where experts in this domain of knowledge hang out and have a conversation, we are *vericating* the rightness or wrongness of this information through implicit knowledge, that is, knowledge triggered within the expert and made explicit through our question. Having a word for this behavior helps leaders and workers to recognize the value of expert opinion as an acceptable practice in decision-making. This process also increases the value of intellectual capital in the organization where living expertise locators can connect people to people.

Collaborative leaders serve as role models and build empowerment, collaboration and a systems perspective among knowledge workers. To meet their alignment responsibilities, they network with each other and also with operations, knowledge and learning centers within the organization (Bennet & Bennet, 2004).

They also develop other leaders through mentoring, staff meetings, and informal conversations, while continuously challenging everyone to be critical thinkers, take reasonable risks and leverage all cognitive, technical and financial resources.

Collaborative leaders will have developed competencies considerably beyond their individual discipline expertise. For example, they would expand their own learning and help others acquire and apply the integrative competencies needed to succeed in their specific markets (see Chapter 12). They continuously monitor and exercise the organization's capacity to implement actions required to meet sustainability criteria such as continuous learning, quick response, resilience, robustness, flexibility, adaptability and customer satisfaction. Each of these capabilities places certain requirements on different parts of the organization, requirements that may not come naturally. Just as the military plans for surprises during wartime and develops and practices scenarios to help prepare them for possible surprises, any organization living in a CUCA environment should consider a similar approach.

Collaborative leaders represent one resource in support of preventive planning. For example, the use of the *mesh*, a "special network" of individuals who have a deep knowledge of specific domains of knowledge and are available on short notice. These people are collaborative leaders who come to the mesh with a high level of organizational context and an understanding of the vision and purpose of the organization. Meshes are created for rapid response situations, thus the relationships among mesh members—each of them a collaborative leader in their own right with a resource network in their area of expertise already established—would have already been developed in terms of knowledge and trust.

As illustrated in Figure 8-3, members of meshes are drawn primarily out of ongoing teams and communities composed of internal and external collaborative leaders who have experience and expertise in specific areas of immediate interest to the organization. When that expertise is needed in emergencies, mesh members may need to pull from extended silent networks that could include retired employees under an "as needed" consulting contract, knowledgeable individuals from partnering organization, or experts who have had some previous relationship with the organization or with the collaborative leaders within the organization.

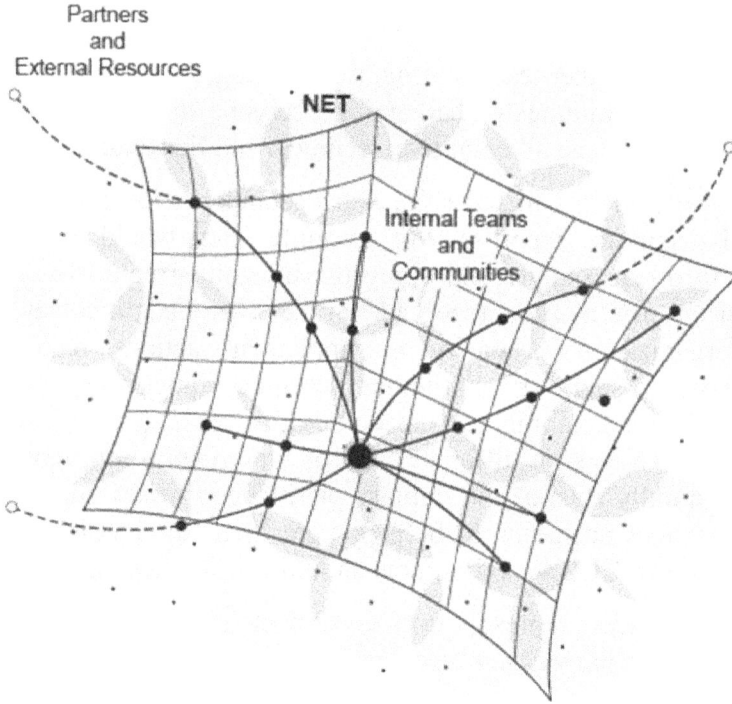

Figure 8-3: *The mesh serves as a framework for the immediate gathering of collaborative leaders from different knowledge domains to handle an immediate challenge or opportunity.*

When an event occurs, a combination virtual and face-to-face mesh meeting is called within 24 hours (or sooner). Relevant material is sent to all mesh members within six hours of such an event. After a fast exploration and development of context, and building an understanding of the problem or opportunity, the mesh self-organized, selects a leader and drafts a short charter before commencing work—all of this accomplished in a timeline of approximately four hours. Administrative procedures, resources, internal working agreements, etc. are automatically implemented, providing full support to the process. This identification of expertise, pre-organization and pre-commitment is somewhat similar to the concept used by agencies responding to national emergencies. For example, FEMA (the Federal Emergency Management Agency in the U.S.) develops formal relationships and operating responsibilities and procedures prior to the need for response. As collaborative leaders, once the emergency is over, members of the mesh are also charged with continuing interaction in their community and team settings to disseminate information and champion implementation of measures as required.

In summary, meshes are intended to be transient teams of collaborative leaders that specialize in a specific area of expertise and quick response capability. Their members know the organization, and have the trust and respect of its leaders, each other, and knowledge workers. Most of them are full-time employees, scattered through the organization and up to speed on corporate direction, vision, tactics and culture. Because they are active participants in organization communities, they have built-in relationship networks. The mesh format provides the framework for the "potential" part of actionable knowledge.

REFLECT:

Are my facilitation skills that of a collaborative leader?

How does my organization plan for future challenges or opportunities?

Collaborative Leader Actions and Values

To indicate the perspective and leadership approach, we provide a short sample of the kinds of actions, values and behaviors that collaborative leaders would exhibit. (Bennet & Bennet, 2004) As usual, actions are context sensitive and situation dependent.

*Insist that everyone be treated with respect, fairness, and equality.

*Reward sustainable high performance, not quick fixes.

*Maintain strong moral and ethical values and apply them in all areas of life.

*Treat people as professional colleagues, giving them the benefit of the doubt until proven otherwise.

*Inspire others through positive thinking, with an optimistic but not naive outlook.

*Understand and actively foster relationships and their role in ICAS operations.

*Ask how and why things happen, and how and why an action is taken.

*Challenge the status quo to prevent stasis and the creation of false realities.

*Use networks to align the organization and to leverage knowledge.

*Focus on quality, effectiveness, and organizational health.

*Lead by example and collaboration, not by power or ego.

*Build other leaders, and build leaders who build other leaders.

*Facilitate loyalty, respect, competence, synergy, and learning among the workforce.

*Do not pretend to know when you don't.

*Challenge all knowledge workers to build high standards.

*Change the structure and nurture the culture to support the workforce.

* Leverage knowledge wherever possible.

*Always share context with team members.

*Are avid social networkers.

In a session focused on knowledge and collaborative leadership and involving over a hundred senior government leaders, this group was asked how they felt they could further empower themselves. The responses to this question are included as Appendix C.

Beyond Collaboration

Another role of collaborative leaders is to guide and nurture their local workforce to *make optimum use of all of its resources*. These resources include knowledge workers, their knowledge, their ability to leverage knowledge through relationship networks (see Chapter 12), and their flexibility through empowerment and self-organization. Because knowledge workers—with their creativity, initiative, loyalty, and competency—represent a very valuable resource for ICAS, leaders support, challenge, and work with them as coequals and highly respected partners. Knowledge workers need the freedom and responsibility to decide how to organize and complete their assignments, either individually or in teams.

> A role of collaborative leaders is to guide and nurture their local workforce to make optimum use of all of its resources.

Collaborative leaders both build and leverage competency, they do not control it. They are participants, contributors, and change agents, not directors. They combine the art of collaboration, the art of leading others, and the art of alignment with appreciative inquiry, working to inspire the workforce through the leader's behavior, sensitivity, and support. As noted above, they are not only leaders *within* the ICAS, regardless of where they sit in the organization, they are *part of the leadership team* of ICAS.

Final Thoughts

In summary, collaborative leaders, rather than use power or control, use the seven "Cs" to lay the groundwork for enabling knowledge workers to learn, grow and make the difference that is the difference.

Compass—They set a direction to go, not a specific objective. In a turbulent world, the best one can do is continue pushing in the right direction.

Connecting—They make connections, know who to contact when needed, and how to help when asked.

Communicating—They do not transfer information, they share understanding with others to create and leverage knowledge and to lay the groundwork for widespread cooperation.

Collaborating—They work with others in an open and coequal basis to seed the culture where everyone contributes and helps everyone else through a continual flux of relationships.

Caring—They really care about people, listening to them, trusting in them, respecting their opinions and helping them grow.

Co-creating—They work with others to create new ideas, build new relationships, and solve problems in new ways.

Character—They demonstrate strong values, moral and ethical strength, and a high respect for their co-workers and organization.

We have discovered that collaborative leaders do not have a special style, flair, insight, personality or brilliance. What they do have is a respect for others, and an appreciation for the value of knowledge, teamwork and critical thinking. They are measured by their actions, perspectives, values and attitudes, not their positions, age or power. No individual is capable of knowing enough to make good decisions when situations turn into complex messes. However, learning to create and amplify understanding and insight by dialogue, teamwork and networking, and being able to solve problems, make decisions, and take action via collaborative efforts, may well be the keys to survival and sustainability. In the end it is all about character, intent, energy and values.

> Collaborative leaders are measured by their actions, perspectives, values and attitudes, not their positions, age or power.

As the famous Chinese philosopher Lao Tzu is credited as having said, A leader is best when people barely know he exists, when his work is done, his aim fulfilled, they will say: we did it ourselves.

Chapter 9
The Mantle of
Collaborative Leadership

We've talked a lot about collaborative leadership in Chapter 8, and hopefully you have a number of ideas now of what that might mean to you. Woven through the fabric of collaborative leadership are other threads, concepts that are foundational to successful collaboration and successful leadership.

The Golden Threads of Collaborative Leadership

Just as organizational intelligence comes from lower-level actions, processes and characteristics of the organization, so, too, does intelligent activity come from a perfect state of interaction where intent, purpose, direction, values and expected outcomes are clearly understood and communicated among all parties, reflecting wisdom and achieving a higher truth. This is the ultimate goal of collaboration.

Several threads weave through the tides of collaboration that warrant focus here: *emotional intelligence, spiritual intelligence* and *collaborative intelligence*. Let's briefly explore these threads.

In a *Harvard Business Review* article, Goleman (1998) proposed that emotional intelligence (EQ) is *twice as important as technical skills or IQ in its contribution to excellent leadership performance*. In a later article, he defines emotional intelligence as the ability to effectively manage ourselves and our relationships (Goleman, 2000). Note the close relationship to knowledge, which is defined as the capacity (potential or actual) to take effective action.

Focused on learning more about ourselves and others, Goleman identifies four components of emotional intelligence at work: self-awareness; self-management; social awareness; and social skill. Since the publication of Goleman's first book, there has been much research in this area, and today EQ is recognized as a basic requirement for effective use of the intellect, and a leadership necessity. As can be seen, emotional intelligence is both a personal tool of self and social engagement, managing ourselves and our relationships.

A power of emotions is their sensitivity to meaning. Emotions exist to alert and protect individuals from harm and to energize them to action when they have strong feelings or passions. However, emotions are concerned with the meaning of the information and not the details. This is because emotions bypass slower cognitive functions such as conscious thought. All incoming signals and information are immediately passed to the amygdala, where they are assessed for potential harm to the individual. The amygdala places a tag on the signal that gives it a level of emotional importance (Adolphs, 2004; Zull, 2002). If the incoming information is considered dangerous to the individual, the amygdala immediately starts the body's response, such as pulling a hand away from a hot stove, or an instant response to a difficult situation. In parallel, but slower than the amygdala's quick response, the incoming information is processed and cognitively interpreted as usual. Thus, the automatic reaction has occurred prior to conscious awareness or thought. From this short description it is easy to see how important self-awareness and self-management are to the collaborative leader.

An example of neuroscience learning that can support social awareness and social skill is recognition that emotional fear inhibits learning. Stress plays a strong role in arousal and attention, both of which significantly impact the motivational and cognitive aspects of learning (Bennet & Bennet, 2015b). Further, because emotional fear spreads throughout the body, high levels of emotional fear impact sensing, feeling, awareness, attention, understanding, and meaning. On the converse side, a positive attitude filled with excitement and energy would enhance all of these same characteristics.

There has been significant research—and the resultant publications—on *spiritual intelligence* (SQ), the ability to "behave with wisdom and compassion while maintaining inner and outer peace regardless of the situation" (Wigglesworth, 2014, p. 3). Recall that in Chapter 2 we forwarded that effective leadership in today's global world is, by necessity, spiritual in nature. Spiritual was defined as standing in relationship to another based on matters of the soul (*Oxford*, 2002), with soul representing the animating principle of human life in terms of thought and action, specifically focused on its moral aspects, the emotional part of human nature, and higher development of the mental

> Spiritual is defined as standing in relationship to another based on matters of the soul, with the soul representing the animating principle of human life in terms of thought and action. Thus, spiritual very much pertains to the intellect and the mind.

faculties. Thus, spiritual very much pertains to the intellect (in terms of the capacity for knowledge and understanding, and the ability to think abstractly or profoundly) and to the mind (in terms of highly refined, sensitive and not concerned with material things). Similarly, Zohar and Marshall (2012) expand SQ to describe *the intelligence we use to handle problems of meaning and value*, a necessary foundation for the effective use of the intellect and emotional intelligence.

The emotional and spiritual aspects of an individual could no sooner be separated from the whole than the mental aspects, nor would that individual be of any value to themselves or their organization if this was possible! As Zohar and Marshall (2012, Introduction) so eloquently state, "Neither IQ nor EQ, separately or in combination, is enough to explain the full complexity of human intelligence nor the vast richness of the human soul and imagination." We are holistic beings, and all our systems work together to lead, make decisions and take effective action.

In his book *Teaching an Anthill to Fetch*, Joyce (2007) suggested that the ant and the colony it belongs to are a good example of what he calls a high level of collaborative intelligence (CQ), *the capacity to harness the intelligence in networks and relationships*. Based on the concept that all things are connected—or entangled—the term CQ was coined by William Isaacs in 1999. Writing about the dialogue and the art of thinking together, Issacs (1999) described CQ as the ability to build, contribute and manage the power found in networks of people. While we applaud this effort and fully appreciate Joyce's book—well worth reading—it would be difficult for the "CQ" idea to stick since it is also out their quite heavily as Change Intelligence and Cultural Intelligence. On the other hand, both of these complement the concept of Collaborative Intelligence. So, we forward this concept as a term in the making and an idea whose time has come.

We now see that IQ, EQ, SQ and CQ are the golden threads that weave through collaborative leading, enabling the leader and the organization to dream the future together.

The Continuing Journey

In a journey towards intelligent activity, the collaborative leader: lives values, engages people, manages self, embraces learning, honors individuation, and builds organizational cohesion. Figure 9-1 shows representative characteristics, values and foundational concepts that describe how these activities play out on a day-to-day basis. All of these elements emerge from the discussion in Chapter 8 and the further explanation of foundational concepts later in this chapter.

Before we delve deeper into those foundational concepts, it is critical to understand that in collaborative leading it is not only our actions that count, but *the way we perform those actions*. Alex shared a dream she had a few years back. She was in her "basement", an analogy for the unconscious, and exploring the many "brown paper packages tied up with strings" that were in her basement. These were clearly marked as what she was taking with her from this life. Excited, she was sure she knew what was in them, all the amazing things she'd done in her life (singing on the stage of The Metropolitan Opera, being Chief Knowledge Officer of the U.S. Department of the Navy, writing and publishing books). In her dream her future self suggested she peek into the boxes. None of these things were in the boxes. As she peered into the boxes she saw clouds crossing the sky on a summer day, horses running in the field, laughing conversations with her colleagues, holding hands and walking down the driveway with David, collaborative problem solving experiences, watching her children experience and grow, the amazing joy of a new idea. These were the things of import.

- Social networking efficacy
- Team player
- Collaborative relationships
- Built on trust and respect
- Supports the new social contract
- Helps others help themselves
- Listens

- Moral courage
- Compassionate
- Authentic
- Transparency
- Respect

- Self initiated
- Thought attendance (sets intent)
- Coherence of perspectives
- Makes optimum use of all resources
- Continuously reinvent themselves

Engages People

Lives Values

Manages Self

Builds Org Cohesion

Embraces Learning

Honors Individuation

- Alignment
- Hierarchical level spanner
- Coherence of perspectives, approach and direction
- Conveys meaning, worthiness and pride to workforce

- Encourages Creativity
- Knowledge Capacities
- Continuous and Lifelong
- Develops key competencies
- Systems perspective
- Facilitates knowledge flows
- Mentors

- Build empowerment
- Respect for difference
- Distributed responsibility

Figure 9-1. *Representative characteristics, activities, values and foundational concepts that characterize the lived experience of the collaborative leader.*

The insight here is that it is the process, the experience, the journey, not necessarily the result that has long-term importance; the "how" we do it rather than the "what" we choose to do. Thus an important tool in the collaborative leader's toolbox is appreciative inquiry.

The Appreciative Mode

A collaborative leader embraces the appreciative mode as a way of life. Appreciative inquiry is an approach consistent with that mode. Appreciative inquiry (AI) was named in 1990 by Dr. David Cooperrider and his colleagues who were studying at the Weatherhead Graduate School of Management at Case Western Reserve University. In its original form, Cooperrider considered it a mode of action research, which embraces the uniqueness of the appreciative mode.

Traditional organizational interventions identify problems and hunt for solutions; the appreciative inquiry approach locates and tries to understand that which is working, learning from it and amplifying it, serving as a complement to other interventions, or, perhaps, offering a way other interventions can be approached. It is based on the simple premise that organizations (teams, communities, countries) grow in the direction of what they are repeatedly asked questions about and therefore focus their attention on (Srivastva & Cooperrider, 1990). The four principles Cooperrider and Srivastva (1990) lay down for appreciative inquiry are that action research should begin with appreciation, should be applicable, should be provocative, and should be collaborative.

Since its inception in 1990, appreciative inquiry has become a meme, that is, it has taken on a life of its own, being used as a strategic change approach and in support of knowledge sharing. The principles of AI can be translated into assumptions, the rules that a group follows when making decisions about behavior or performance (Argyris, 1993). Hammond and Hall (1996, pp. 2-3) translate the principles of AI into the following assumptions:

1. In every society, organization, or group [and in every individual] something works.

2. **What we focus on becomes our reality.**

3. **Reality is created in the moment and there are multiple realities.**

4. **The act of asking questions of an organization or group [or individual] influences the group [or individual] in some way.**

5. People have more confidence and comfort to journey to the future (the unknown) when they carry forward parts of the past (the known).

6. If we carry parts of the past forward, they should be what is best about the past.

7. It is important to value differences.

8. **The language we use creates our reality.**

What is somewhat astounding is that this set of assumptions, published in 1996, was created prior to development of measurement and excitation technology such as functional magnetic resonance imaging (fMRI), the electroencephlalograph (EEG) and transcranial magnetic stimulation (George, 2007; Kurzweil, 2005; Ward, 2006).[1] It was with the advent of these technologies that we began to see how the mind/brain works, therefore improving our understanding of learning as it relates to mind/brain processes. The mind/brain connotes the combination of the physiological brain and the patterns of neuron firings and synaptic connections (the mind) that exist in the brain.

For example, take assumption 2, 3, 4 and 8 referring to focusing, asking questions and the language we use. We now know from an understanding of Plasticity that thoughts change the structure of the brain, and the brain structure influences the creation of new thoughts (Bennet & Bennet, 2015b). There is a discussion of Plasticity in Chapter 11, "The Leader as Learner." This emphasizes the power of questions not only to trigger thought, but to actually help shape our brains. Clearly, we have a great deal to do with creating our reality!

As the focus in organizations and communities moves back to people and the knowledge they create, share and use, the empowering aspects of the appreciative inquiry approach can build self-confidence in—and receptivity to—new ideas, and accelerate behavioral change. Appreciative inquiry is the right hand of the collaborative leader, an approach embedded in every interaction, whether face-to-face or virtual.

REFLECT:

How do I engage my emotional intelligence in the workplace?

Does the appreciative inquiry approach change other's actions?

Foundational Concepts

We now consider in more detail some foundational concepts underlying successful collaborative leadership. These are: *values; trust; empowerment; alignment; vision, purpose, and direction; authenticity; risk; transparency;* and *moral courage.*

Values

Values and moral principles have historically played a strong role in the ability of leaders to lead, and keep, followers. In the ICAS they become even more significant because knowledge workers are independent thinkers, and differences in basic values can quickly lead to distrust. Collaborative leaders need to make organizational values visible, openly discussed and analyzed so they can be used as a foundation for behavior, decisions, and performance expectations.

Common values facilitate dialogue and build trust and understanding. *Strong organizational values contribute to knowledge worker empowerment.* If a worker understands and agrees with the organization's values, they have a space for empowered decision-making by knowing which decisions are acceptable and which ones are not. This also helps reduce external complexity through filtering by selecting only those opportunities consistent with the organization's values.

Collaborative leaders will improve internal communication and cooperation by talking about personal and organizational values at staff meetings, providing seminars and workshops on their importance and role in organizational performance, and through sharing stories and anecdotes from the past experiences of leaders and employees. See Chapter 16 for an in-depth treatment of thought leader values.

Trust

Trust is foundational to the ability of the ICAS to create, share, leverage, and apply knowledge anywhere and anytime it is needed. Trust is notoriously difficult to create and becomes fragile in times of stress. *Authenticity*, that is, an understanding of self and demonstrating consistent behaviors with expressed beliefs and values, is critical to trust. From the collaborative leader's perspective, *words and behaviors have to be consistent, objective, and sensitive* to coworkers. Individuals perceived to operate from power positions are easily distrusted by subordinates, who often look for sub-rosa intentions or goals. A collaborative leader with authority who uses that authority only when absolutely necessary—most of the time working with others in a collaborative, coequal way—is in a position to gain the trust and the cooperation of others.

Trust has to be mutual to be effective. Trust and confidence go both ways. A leader who does not trust his or her people will not be able to treat them as equals, openly share information and be fair in evaluations. Trust, like values, needs to be brought into the light, openly discussed and sustained, with quick actions taken when it buckles. Lack of candor, unethical behavior, a non-caring attitude relative to others, egotism, and acrimonious debate all lead down the road of distrust. Empowerment, open communication, teamwork, risk-taking and mutual respect all exist on a foundation of trust, trust among workers and between the organization and its workforce.

Empowerment

For the ICAS to have the capability to self-organize, adapt, and respond rapidly to changing events, knowledge workers must be empowered to use their knowledge and act, sometimes on their own, more often with others. Empowerment has become a touchy subject with some organizations who have attempted to use it within a classical bureaucratic structure. When push comes to shove, many managers will choose control. In fact, it is emotionally difficult in many organizations to relax the level of control. Managers who are accustomed to having authority, responsibility and accountability often find it difficult to trust others to perform well without close oversight (de Geus, 1997).

One all too common approach to empowerment is to give subordinates decision freedom without providing them the knowledge, boundaries, or context they need to make the best decisions. The result is often a series of mistakes with subordinates feeling frustrated, and even betrayed. The manager then withdraws the empowerment, convinced that it cannot work—their people are just not competent enough to be empowered. An interpretation of employee empowerment that fits the ICAS model is when Quinn and Spreitzer worked with a Fortune 50 manufacturing company that needed a turnaround, and decided to do it through employee empowerment. In interviewing the top executives, Quinn and Spreitzer found that half of them believed the above approach to empowerment was what was needed, including adequate counseling and preparation of the workers. However, the other half interpreted empowerment to mean

> …trusting people and tolerating their imperfections. When it came to rules, they believed that the existing structures often presented a barrier to "doing the right thing" for the company. They assumed that newly empowered employees would naturally make some mistakes, but that mistakes should not be punished. Empowered employees …would be entrepreneurs and risk takers, acting with a sense of ownership in the business. They would engage in creative conflict, constantly challenging each other. This group of executives saw empowerment as a process of risk taking and personal growth. (Quinn and Spreitzer, p. 37)

The implicit strategy of the second group of executives for empowerment was to (a) start at the bottom by understanding the needs of the employees; (b) model empowered behavior for the employees; (c) build teams to encourage cooperative behavior; (d) encourage intelligent risk taking; and (e) trust people to perform. From an ICAS view, this latter interpretation of empowerment is clearly most appropriate. Note the reference to enabling creative conflict, that is, creative friction through conversation (Shelley, 2016). This is the associative patterning process of our mind/brain at work.

Self-empowerment is just as critical to success. An individual must not only have the knowledge to act, that is, know what actions to take consistent with the organization, but must have the *courage and confidence to act*. This can, of course, be built up through social interactions such as dialogue, storytelling, mentoring and shadowing.

REFLECT:

Are my personal values consistent with those of my organization?

What can I do to self-empower myself?

Alignment

Alignment is the process that continually assures that the activities of workers are directly or indirectly supporting the organization's common vision and purpose. In a fluctuating environment, where the mosaic of events and tasks continually changes, there should be a network that maintains awareness and some degree of cohesion among activities. In the ICAS model there is an operations center that has the responsibility for tracking and coordinating these activities. Collaborative leaders provide inputs into this nerve center and assist in working out duplication problems or resource shifts to accommodate work goals.

Many collaborative leaders serve as team leaders and team members, and are actively involved in the day-to-day work. In a highly dynamic world, duplication may be needed to generate more ideas (optimum complexity) or keep options open (risk aversion). Alignment of work efforts is frequently a judgment call between strategic direction and variations that expand possibilities that broaden or shift that direction. This judgment requires seeing the work from the higher perspective of systems thinking and broad experience, resulting from a balance of connectedness of choices and exploration. Although the degree of responsibility for alignment may vary with the level and experience of the collaborative leader, the overall interaction of collaborative leadership helps ensure that the organization remains aligned.

One role of collaborative leadership is to ensure that the ICAS strategy, structure, culture, processes, and leadership are coherent and supportive of the intended organizational direction. Collaborative leaders do this in two ways: first, by their networks and close relationships with each other and second, by working with managers and knowledge workers to keep the culture, structure, and processes consistent with, and supportive of, the desired self-initiating, empowered and collaborative behavior needed for organizational success. Saint-Onge suggests that to meet these needs, the organization must have a "membership contract with employees, one in which their commitment creates value in exchange for an opportunity to develop their capabilities." (Saint-Onge, 2000, p. 291) This goal, from an ICAS perspective, requires collaborative leaders to work with human resource departments and with individual knowledge workers to ensure that they have, and feel, ownership of their performance and its contribution to the overall direction of the firm.

Does an individual knowledge worker serve best by following the party line or by breaking away and exploring new opportunities? We are back to the alignment, or as Birkinshaw & Gibson (2004) put it, the ambidexterity problem. They further define contextual ambidexterity as when "individual employees make choices between alignment-oriented and adaptation-oriented activities in the context of their day to day work" (Birkinshaw & Gibson, 2004, p. 49). Based on research, Birkinshaw and Gibson (2004, p. 49) identified four ambidextrous behaviors in individuals: (1) They take the initiative and are alert to opportunities [and threats] beyond the confines of their own jobs; (2) They cooperate and seek opportunities to combine their work with others; (3) They are brokers, always looking to build internal connections, and (4) They are multi-taskers who are comfortable wearing more than one hat. This is another example of one of the roles that ICAS collaborative leaders play in their support of organizational performance.

Vision, Purpose, and Direction

Senior leaders continuously communicate the ICAS vision, purpose, and direction. Vision provides workers with knowledge of what the organization is (culture, beliefs, and values), and what it should look like to a knowledgeable outsider (persona). This differs from the classical meaning of vision as a clear picture of what the organization is seeking at some point in the future. The ICAS vision is a broad description of the organization's values, beliefs, direction and underlying purpose and meaning. A phenomenon of complex enterprises is that the sum of the local visions may not add up to the overall organizational vision, yet they must be coherent with it. To be energized by vision, purpose and direction workers must be aware of them, understand their meaning and believe that they are worthy of acting upon. To take positive actions the actor must feel good about said activity, have accepted ownership for the action and be empowered to act (internal and external empowerment). This is where collaborative leaders must work with their coworkers and share significant beliefs, thoughts and feelings—a difficult challenge at best.

According to Kayser (1994), collaboration is close communication and the sharing of understanding with no hidden agendas. We broaden his interpretation to include active and effortful working together, openly and purposively, to accomplish some task or reach a common understanding. Transparency has become a powerful value in this century. Collaboration requires an open, and trusting relationship where each party contributes their capability and works with others to align and integrate the efforts of all. ICAS leaders use collaborative relationships and interactions to share understanding, get the work done, and guide development of their coworkers. It is through a collaborative approach to relationships that ICAS leaders earn their leadership rights while at the same time serving the knowledge workers.

Collaboration often includes play. As team members work a given problem they need to play with it in their minds, then share concepts and ideas and perspectives. These actions are "play" in the sense that different, and sometimes wild things are tried before conclusions are drawn. Such interactions foster mutual respect, active listening, and camaraderie—all valuable for building synergy, excitement, and feelings of accomplishment. When asked to solve a difficult problem, ICAS leaders respond by admitting: "I don't know how to solve this, but if we all work together, I know that we can figure out a good solution." This simple honesty brings others into the challenge, sets the stage for collaborative efforts, and communicates the respect and confidence the leader has in others.

Authenticity

Being genuine and true to ourselves is a commitment to identity that can play towards the strengths of our uniqueness. Authenticity that is in concert with accepted moral standards of an organization or a culture is the sometimes-hidden idea underlying integrity. As applied to collaborative leadership, this requires really knowing who we are within the context of the types of influence opportunities within the organization. Sometimes a strengths-based assessment can help us identify and embrace our strengths within a specific team role. The CoHero Institute provides a leadership assessment that aligns with the requirements of leading transformational change, which produces a strength-based profile to support an awareness of specific collaborative leadership personas.

The preferences and behaviors of some leaders are more aligned with different transformational change activities, such as identifying risks, analyzing data, inventing something new, building solutions, or running the engine. When one leader is different from most of the team, rather than remaining authentic to their strengths, without this awareness they tend to try to fit in and be a good "team fit." Not only does this negatively affect this individual leader but also the team. Just as an American football team is more than 11 players in the same role, a leadership team is also more collaborative when direct competition is replaced with role-aligned authenticity which complements other roles towards the larger goals.

In Appendix C, *authenticity* in the context of enriching relationships emerged as a characteristic of spiritual learning. It is natural for people to strive for effective interactions with their world (White, 1959). Since adults have a strong need to apply their learning to the real world, "they are motivated [to learn] when the circumstances under which they assess their competence are *authentic* to their actual lives" (Wlodkowski, 1998, p. 78) Thus, as a leader, not only the authenticity of self and of others is significant, but we also look for what is *authentic* in terms of what is consistent with our work and resonant with our thoughts.

REFLECT:

How can I help achieve alignment across the organization?

What actions do I take that reflect the authentic me?

Risk

A common interpretation of risk is the exposure to some chance event or possibility of loss. Looking from another perspective, we take risk to also mean the chance or possibility of not achieving an intended goal and the consequences associated with the outcome. In this sense, an organization always runs the risk of non-optimum performance every day. Collaborative leaders in ICAS have a great deal of freedom, and with that freedom goes the responsibility for understanding the broader ramifications, and risks, of their work.

For example, collaborative leaders are sensitive to risks that may arise within their organization, such as (a) the risk of poor decision-making and (b) the risk of poor leadership. The first category relates to the difficulty of anticipating the future impact of decisions and actions and the level of quality of decision-making. In an uncertain environment, there is no decision that guarantees the desired result. However, given good knowledge if the *quality* of the decision and the decision process is high, the probability of success may be high. Decision quality, a concern of collaborative leaders, includes factors such as: leveraging knowledge through dialogue and the diversity of team participants, the scope and timing of the decision, implementation and political ramifications, pivot points for flexibility, risk analysis and consistency with ICAS long-term objectives. The second category relates to the risk that leadership is not performing well in meeting its responsibilities *to the organization.* History has shown than it is easier to blame the workforce for poor results that to look into the mirror. By deliberately discussing the effectiveness of leadership and monitoring local and overall performance, collaborative leaders can manage themselves and help others to work toward the ideal of an energized, empowered, knowledgeable workforce.

In his book, *KNOWledge SUCCESSion,* Shelley (2016) remind us that encouraging appropriate risk taking to drive innovation and rewarding learning ensures the ideas are accelerants to the transfer and reapplication of knowledge. This is what Shelley calls knowledge recycling, which fuels creativity, invention and innovation, which he likens to cash flow fueling the economy.

Transparency

Collaborative leadership is a much deeper topic than simply trying to get along. It also requires providing transparency into our thought processes and decision making processes. Rather than combatively comparing conclusions, transparency requires openly sharing our options, choices, and reasons. In Chapter 16 we introduce transparency as a core value for the Net and Millennial generations. This is critical to establishing trusting, long-term relationships. Tapscott (2009, p. 266) forwards that true transparency "must make the processes, underlying assumptions, and political presuppositions (including supporting research) of policy explicit and subject to criticism."

There are tools that can help facilitate transparency in the decision-making process. For example, Lewis (2013) provides a visual tool called the "Option Outline" which allows others to see in one snapshot the consequential decisions as well as the options considered but rejected. For the reasons behind our choices, with his Eight Degrees of Reason, Lewis (2013) compares a "preference" (reactive) with an "error preference" (reflective). Instead of allowing organizational decisions to rest with want or preference, we are now asked to identify the tradeoffs and provide reasons that begin with "I would rather err on the side of..." in acknowledging the complexity of our choices and providing insight into our rationale.

Moral Courage

Conviction and moral courage are inextricably linked for effective leadership. Whether a leader is a good communicator, has great interpersonal skills, is an expert in his area of work, has a good grasp on what motivates people, one thing that stands out is the necessity of strong conviction toward one's goals and the moral courage to carry it out. In one of the leadership groups we worked with through the years, one participant went so far as to say that this characteristic is what distinguishes a good leader. You either have moral courage or you don't; you must stand up for what you believe.

Final Thoughts:

We started off this chapter saying that the collaborative leader lives values, engages people, manages self, embraces learning, honors individuation, and builds organizational cohesion, and in Figure 9-1 included representative characteristics, values and foundational concepts that have been part of the discussion of collaborative leadership in Chapter 8 and Chapter 9. By now it is undoubtedly clear that there is no cookie-cutter for a collaborative leader! Since people are all unique— one of a kind—and all situations different, what we are searching for is intelligent activity, and that comes from within, the choices we make as individuals and as collaborators. The next three chapters are devoted to looking within the collaborative leader and exploring those competencies and capacities needed to co-evolve with a shifting and changing complex environment.

Chapter 10
Knowledges Leaders Need

It is generally agreed in the literature that individuals who assume leadership roles in an information-rich society must develop some of the aptitudes and attitudes of a generalist (Cleveland, 2002). For example, Humphrey states, "The qualities of high-performing leaders are grounded in extensive knowledge of the general business environment; intimate understanding of their industry, company, and work group; and a strong sense of their organization's strategy, culture, and values." (Humphrey, 1997, p. 33) Further, Harris notes that there are both qualitative and quantitative dimensions to the productivity of knowledge. "Though we know very little about it, we do realize executives must be both managers of specialists and synthesizers of different fields of knowledge—really of knowledges, plural." (Harris, 1999, pp. 170-171)

Types of Knowledge[1]

There are many ways to think about different types of knowledge, all of which can come into play as leaders make day-after-day decisions. Bennet and Bennet (2007a) offer a knowledge taxonomy for understanding different types of knowledge looked at from the viewpoint of what knowledge is needed to make a particular decision, do a particular type of work, or take a particular action. These are: Kmeta, Kresearch, Kpraxis, Kaction, Kdescription, Kstrategic and Klearning. See Figure 10-1.

Meta-knowledge, **Kmeta**, represents the capacity to understand, create, assimilate, leverage, sculpt and apply various types of information and knowledge. Since most complex situations contain several disciplines and categories of knowledge, our use of Kmeta (knowledge about knowledge) also includes the ability to bring different types of knowledges together. William Whewell, in his 1840 synthesis, *The Philosophy of the Inductive Sciences*, spoke of consilience as "…a 'jumping together' of knowledge by the linking of facts and fact-based theory across disciplines to create a common groundwork of explanation" (Wilson, 1998, p. 8). E. O. Wilson also uses consilience to mean, "The explanations of different phenomena most likely to survive … those that can be connected and proved consistent with one another." (Wilson, 1998, p. 53) In making sense of complex situations, the consilience of different frames of references and knowledge categories may provide the best understanding for developing a solution.

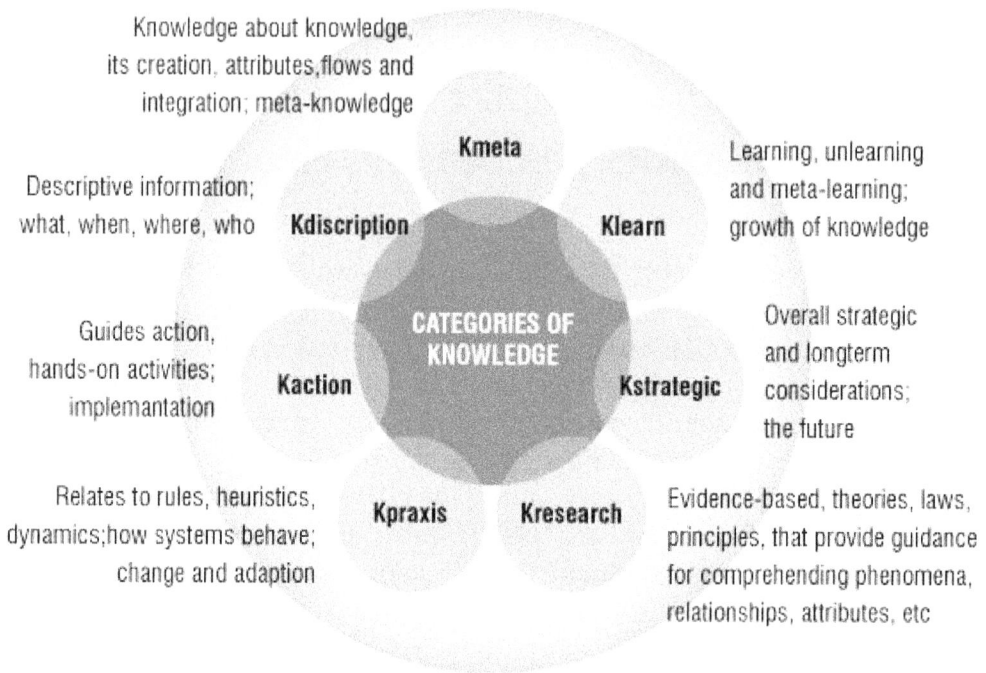

Figure 10-1. *A knowledge taxonomy for grouping types of knowledge from the viewpoint of what knowledge is needed to do a particular type of work or take a particular action (Bennet & Bennet, 2007a; 2015a).*

Evidence based knowledge, **Kresearch**, includes theoretical as well as empirical knowledge and represents the fundamental concepts that explain *why* things happen. Such knowledge serves as a guide for setting expectations and possibilities and provides the user a level of confidence.

Pragmatic knowledge, **Kpraxis**, represents the practical understanding of situations and *how* they change or *can* be changed. Much pragmatic knowledge is tacit, experiential and intuitive.

Knowledge in action, **Kaction**, represents the ability to take specific actions that achieve the desired result. It includes understanding the *local* context and situation within which the action is taken.

Descriptive knowledge, **Kdescription**, is information that informs the *what, who, when* and *where* of a situation. As can be understood from the discussion of knowledge offered by Stonier (1992), all knowledge is composed of information, but all information is *not* knowledge. Knowledge is information that, when combined in the mind (associated or *complexed)*, creates understanding, meaning and, where action is involved, the anticipation of its outcome.

The role of **Kstrategic** is to ensure that the actions taken are in consideration of their long-term impact and are consistent with the strategy, identity, and values of the organization. While this is a high-level type of knowledge (and thinking), note that this refers to the information, processes and patterns used to apply other information, processes and patterns in a strategic way. This means that many different types of knowledge can be used strategically.

The role of **Klearning** includes individual, group and organizational learning. This focus is to ensure that as a situation or process unfolds, individuals learn from each other and, when appropriate, build organizational learning into a task outcome to ensure that the organization is capable of adapting to future changes in the environment.

The above seven categories can be considered as a useful spectrum of knowledge areas, sometimes overlapping and often having gaps between them. They are selected for their usefulness in the problem solving, decision-making, execution and feedback learning processes, particularly when dealing with complex situations. An individual or members of a team or organization may have expertise in one, several, or none of these categories and the knowledge needed will depend on the content,

> The more complex a situation, the more categories of knowledge may be needed for an individual or team to be successful.

context and desired outcome of the situation/problem. The more complex the situation, the more categories of knowledge may be needed for the individual or team to be successful.

In the discussion of Kstrategic above, it was noted that this type of knowledge refers to the information, processes and patterns used to apply other information, processes and patterns in a strategic way. In other words, many different types of knowledge can be used strategically. The concepts of tactical, operational and strategic information and knowledge are often used in organizations. These three concepts can be correlated to the levels of knowledge (surface, shallow, and deep). For example, strategic knowledge would emphasize deep knowledge because of the complexity of forecasting the future environment and creating a strategy to ensure organizational sustainability into the future. A successful strategy would require creative ideas and practices with flexibility built into implementation. Operational management would require primarily surface knowledge during normal operations when the environment was stable. However, when disruptions occur in the environment or within the organization, managers and leaders with deep knowledge in the areas where the disruptions impact the organization and its future will be called upon. Tactical implementation, under stable conditions, would require mostly surface knowledge, with shallow knowledge available for equipment failures, or changes in technology or core processes. All of the above descriptions are simplifications of reality and are provided to highlight the differences and range of needs of the levels of knowledge in a typical organization.

A Variety of Knowledges

In the following paragraphs we explore a variety of "knowledges" needed by leaders as cited in a dozen (chosen for their focus from a scan of 60) leadership books, as referenced. While it is a representative set, it is undoubtedly one of many ways to organize the knowledges associated with leaders. However, these groupings provide a second frame of reference. These knowledges are: (1) tacit knowledge about managing oneself, managing others, and managing tasks; (2) vision knowledge; (3) processing knowledge; (4) specialized knowledge; (5) profound knowledge; (6) systems knowledge; (7) change knowledge (broken down into specific, systemic and generic); (8) variation knowledge; (9) knowledge about the theory of knowledge (meta-knowledge); and (10) people knowledge; (11) relationship knowledge; and (12) self-knowledge. While several of these knowledges may be part of several types of knowledge, we have included the strongest link in parentheses following the title.

(1) Tacit knowledge about managing oneself, managing others, and managing tasks (Kaction)

Wagner and Sternberg suggest that there are three types of tacit knowledge that managers must have and use to be successful. These are tacit knowledge about managing oneself, others, and tasks. (Self knowledge is discussed below.) Managing others deals with managing subordinates, peers and superiors. The example provided by Wagner and Sternberg (1990) is convincing a skeptical superior of a new idea. Topping (2002) stressed the importance of making sure there is sufficient focus on human resource development, specifically in terms of knowledge, skills and abilities (KSAs).

(2) Vision knowledge (Kstrategic)

Prahalad (1999, p. 34) points out that a "point of view about the future based on substantive knowledge is a fundamental requirement for leaders in the new millennium." Similarly, Zand (1997) calls out vision as an uncommon form of knowledge. He defines vision as *the ability to see the future and understand its meaning*, and to adapt current actions to deal with that future.

[Vision] goes beyond the simple, direct link between an action and its immediate result. Vision is a concept of longer-term relationships; it floats in imagination. Effective leaders continually communicate and interpret their visions to inspire others with a sense of prophetic urgency. Vision addresses the core of an organization's being, its sense of why it exists and what it should do. To be used effectively, vision, which is fundamentally knowledge, needs the support of legitimate power. A leader who has both legitimate power and vision combines in one person two potent sources of power. (Zand, 1997, pp. 160-161)

The concept of power has been touched upon throughout this paper, and its relationship to knowledge will be discussed further in this paper. Zand uses the term "legitimate power", which is the common ground for maintaining the imperative control proposed by Weber (Outhwaite & Bottomore, 1993).

A vision bounds the action space for decision-makers, both limiting activities and focusing and conserving energy by eliminating that which is outside those boundaries (Bennet & Bennet, 2004). Vision therefore acts as a knowledge attractor and detractor for leaders. It is an attractor because a clear vision can excite workers. By providing a direction and challenge, knowledge workers are energized and can envision a realistic scenario of their organization, and their position and participation within that scenario. A vision also identifies where the organization is not going and puts limits on workers as to what they cannot do. From a leadership perspective, a vision well inculcated into the organization can greatly assist in pulling workers together, facilitating a collaborative approach to knowledge sharing.

One final point is that a good vision can enhance the power of a leader by shifting that power from directive to collaborative, where leadership, management and the workforce are working together, with everyone knowing where the organization is going.

(3) Process knowledge (Kaction)

There are four major organizational processes: creativity, problem solving, decision-making and implementation, all of which interact with other knowledges. Process knowledge deals with the "how's": how to create new ideas, how to solve problems, how to make the best decision, and how to implement those decisions. Zand sees process knowledge as one of three dimensions in the new world with the other two dimensions building trust and using power sensitively. As Zand affirms, process knowledge is knowing how to do things: "how to access the knowledge distributed in an organization, how to build trust, how to convert knowledge into effective action, how to command, consult and consign ...." (Zand, 1997, pp. 160-161)

(4) Specialized knowledge (Kpraxis)

Specialized knowledge deals with functional and domain knowledge. Arguing that an individual's knowledge and situational assessments as well as the interaction between them are important to leadership, Stogdill (1948, p. 71) cites that "specialized knowledge and the ability to get things done are factors which contribute toward leadership status." Recall that our working definition of knowledge is the capacity (potential or actual) to take effective action. Specialized knowledge does not necessarily mean an intimate or deep knowledge. Gardner uses the term "task competence" to reference the knowledge a leader has of the task at hand.

> Obviously the knowledge required varies at different levels of leadership. The lowest levels must have intimate knowledge of the task at hand. Top-level leaders cannot hope to have competence in more than a few of the matters under their jurisdiction, but they must have knowledge of the whole system over which they preside, its mission, and the environment in which it functions. (Gardner, 1990, p.50)

(5) Profound knowledge (Kresearch)

Deming uses the term profound knowledge to describe the knowledge necessary for leaders, contending that *the quality of a company's product cannot be better than the quality of its leadership*. He calls the first step the transformation of the individual, which comes from understanding the system of profound knowledge.

> Once the individual understands the system, he or she will apply its principles in every relationship with other people. The person will perceive new meaning to life, to events, to numbers, to interactions between people. The individual will have a basis for judgment of personal decisions and for transformation of the organizations that he or she belongs to. (Demming, 1997, pp. 121-126)

From anyone other than Deming, this might sound foolish. What is profound? In the *American Heritage Dictionary* profound references extending, coming from a great depth to far-reaching, penetrating beyond what is superficial or obvious. *Profoundness is built on deep knowledge*, the knowledge of an expert, with that knowledge emerging as creativity, intuition, forecasting, pattern recognition and theories (Bennet & Bennet, 2008b). This leads to a focus on system knowledge.

REFLECT:

How can vision knowledge serve as both an attractor and a detractor?

What specialized knowledge have I developed?

(6) System knowledge (Kpraxis)

The system Deming suggests has four parts: (1) appreciation for a system, (2) knowledge of variation, (3) building an understanding of the theory of knowledge and (4) applying psychology (Demming, 1997). System knowledge leads to understanding connections, relationships, balance and tradeoffs. An intellectual aspect of leadership is considering the larger perspective, an ability to conceptualize and strategize, to see the big picture and how everything fits together.

Another aspect of considering the larger perspective is the expanding idea that there is something else out there that is more powerful than the human mind. Thinking in terms of the Earth as an ecosystem and the interconnectivity of humanity, this larger perspective might look something like the described by the French geologist/paleontologist, Pierre Teilhard de Chardin as "a human sphere, a sphere of reflection, of conscious invention, of conscious souls" (de Chardin, 1966, p. 63) The word "noosphere" is a neologism that employs "noos", the Greek word for "mind". Today more and more literature is employing the word "quantum", whether or whether not understanding anything whatsoever of the concept. Still, new words trigger new thoughts and, building on the concept of the particle/wave theory, that is, until energy is focused upon it has the potential for both, the concept of quantum bodes well for empowering people. An expression coined by one participant in our leadership discussions is command by intent. See the discussion in Chapter 7 of intent as an organizational force.

It is critical to understand the larger impact of decisions. Leaders first learn to make decisions as individuals, but as they move up to higher levels of leadership they need to learn to look at things from an organization's perspective while not losing sight of the individuals.

According to Bennet and Bennet (2004), some of the specific value of system knowledge to leaders includes:

*Expanding critical thinking skills and providing a framework for understanding and analyzing situations.

*A mechanism for identifying and adjusting parameters that play a crucial role in system performance to optimize the entire system.

*An approach for shifting frames of reference, exploring cause and effect relationships, and enabling clear perception of change.

As the environment has become increasingly complex, it has become vital to understand complex systems and know their major characteristics such as: feedback loops, time delays, tipping points, nonlinear relationships and emergent phenomena. Knowledge about causality will not work for most complex problems; it takes deeper knowledge related to intuition, heuristics and pattern recognition to successfully deal with complex issues (Bennet & Bennet, 2013).

(7) Change knowledge (Kpraxis)

A relative of system knowledge is change knowledge. Conner believes that a basic and shared knowledge about organizational change serves as a foundation for strong transition management literacy, a necessity in today's environment of change. He breaks change knowledge down into three types: specific, systemic and generic.

> Specific change knowledge comes from the lessons about an isolated aspect of a particular set of circumstances. These learnings are relevant only to the unique constellation of people issues, pressures, politics, constraints, and opportunities of a singular situation. The viability of these kinds of learnings is fragile and their shelf life is often extremely short-lived … Within any system, large or small, a single variable shifting only slightly can, within five minutes, cause a previously impeccable solution to become useless. (Conner, 1998, pp. 20-21)

So, while specific change knowledge builds upon the specific knowledge discussed earlier, it brings with it an understanding of the system.

Systemic change knowledge, then, deals with how things are connected, i.e., the impact of a particular change effort on the system. It is "extracted from the lessons from the overall impact a particular initiative has had on the various systems in and around which it occurred." (Conner, 1998, pp. 20-21) Generic change knowledge is meta-change knowledge, dealing with the process of change itself, and lessons learned from that process, "the overall transition process as it applies to any set of changing circumstances. These generic mechanisms reflect recurring patterns that form a framework for understanding how people think, feel, and behave during organizational change." (Conner, 1998, pp. 22-23)

Change knowledge clearly overlaps with people knowledge. For example, you cannot successfully tell a knowledge worker to share their knowledge, trust others, be creative, or collaborate with their peers. They will only do these things if, and when, they decide to do them, first moving through awareness, understanding, believing, feeling good, ownership, empowerment (AUBFOE), and understanding the expected impact of their actions (Bennet & Bennet, 2008c).

(8) Variation knowledge (Klearn)

Variation knowledge is the knowledge communicated through stories that tell about products and processes and the people who are involved with them. Deming introduced variation knowledge in terms of the *variation between people, as well as in terms of output, service and products* (Demming, 1997). When applied to system knowledge, it leads to an understanding of the interaction of forces as well as dependencies and interdependencies.

(9) Meta-knowledge (Kmeta)

Meta-knowledge is knowledge about knowledge. For example, knowledge about the theory of knowledge helps users understand the strength and weakness of the knowledge, increase productive capabilities, and differentiate between information and knowledge when building on experiences and observations.

Since learning is about the creation of knowledge, *meta-knowledge is about learning how to learn*. Meta-knowledge would also include knowing how to share, leverage, interpret, and apply knowledge, and the relationship between knowledge and values. It would also include the distinction between information and knowledge, and the distinction between surface, shallow and deep knowledge (Bennet & Bennet, 2015a).

Meta-knowledge is becoming more and more important as leaders have to increasingly deal with the challenges of a changing, uncertain and more complex world (Bennet & Bennet, 2004; Katzenbach & Smith, 1998; Leonard & Swap, 2004; Marion, 1999; Schwartz, 2003). Since most complex situations contain several disciplines and categories of knowledge, meta knowledge also includes the ability to bring knowledge together. William Whewell, in his 1840 synthesis, The Philosophy of the Inductive Sciences, spoke of Consilience as "...a 'jumping together' of knowledge by the linking of facts and fact-based theory across disciplines to create a common groundwork of explanation." (Wilson, 1998, p. 8) Wilson (1998, p. 53) also uses consilience to mean, "The explanations of different phenomena most likely to survive ... those that can be connected and proved consistent with one another." In making sense of complex situations, "the consilience of different frames of references and knowledge categories may provide the best understanding for developing a solution." (Bennet & Bennet, 2007a, p. 38)

(10) People knowledge (Kpraxis)

The last three, people knowledge, relationship knowledge, and self knowledge, enter the realm of knowledge of psychology. Frick and Spears (1996, p. 191) forward the term people knowledge, explaining, "To know how one is doing requires some way of getting at how people think and feel and act and grow ... A fair amount of executive competence goes into ways of knowing about people." While people knowledge has certainly been a factor of leadership in the past (in terms of understanding partners and the competition), Frick and Spears recognize it as becoming even more important in the future. "It is my hunch that it will be an even larger competitive factor in the future." (Frick & Spears, 1996, p. 191)

(11) Relationship knowledge (Kpraxis)

A remarkable shift that is occurring with the exponential increase in information is what Ury describes as a shift in the very logic of conflict. He refers to the new basic resource of knowledge: *by sharing it you can actually have more of it*. In other words, ideas build on ideas, and new ideas are largely a result of social interactions and knowledge sharing (Bennet & Bennet, 2007a). This is particularly so for shallow knowledge which requires more context than surface knowledge (Bennet, 2015a). As described in Chapter 1, the shift underway is moving the global economy from one focused on competition to a fundamental mode of cooperation and collaboration (Ury, 2002). The Bennets describe a decision-making environment built on *collaborative entanglement*, where leaders purposely and consistently develop and support approaches and processes that combine the sources of knowledge and the beneficiaries of that knowledge to move toward a common direction (Bennet & Bennet, 2007a). Thus building and sustaining relationships through relationship network management becomes critical for leaders.

Komives et al. (1998) goes so far as to describe relationship knowledge in terms of relationship leadership. The five areas of his relationship leadership model are inclusive, empowering, purposeful, ethical and process-oriented. Inclusive is in terms of both people and diverse points of view or frames of reference. Empowering deals with a leader's relationship with others, including self-esteem and the impact of power on policies and procedures. Purposeful concerns a leader's individual commitment to a goal or activity, as well as the ability to collaborate and find common ground. Ethical deals with the values and standards that drive leadership, including morality, valuing self and others, and the decision-making process. Process-oriented has to do with group, team and community processes: how a group goes about being and remaining a group and accomplishing their purpose.

REFLECT:

What systems am I part of?

Have I developed any relationship capital?

(12) Self-knowledge (Klearn)

Recognizing that self-knowledge underlies all knowledge (the capacity to take effective action), we will spend a few paragraphs exploring self-knowledge, also touching on meaning, self-confidence, and self-awareness in terms of inner sense. Shechtman states that we are moving from the age of information and communication to an era of self-knowledge.

In the Fifth Wave, the breakthroughs for both individuals and organizations are internal. The more self-knowledge we have, the better able we'll be to adapt to and capitalize on external forces ... self-knowledge is energizing. People who know what drives them are much more willing to take risks, test new ideas, and aggressively pursue opportunities. They're always looking for ways to grow and develop. For them, the frontiers are internal. They are constantly exploring who they are relative to who they've been. The knowledge they gain gives them an advantage that can no longer be gained through external means. (Shechtman, 2002, p. xiv)

In terms of leadership, Haas and Tamarkin (1992, p. 6) contend, "Leadership means self-discovery, getting a better yield out of your attributes." This is consistent with Komives et al.'s treatment of self-knowledge as the first element of the knowing-being-doing loop. "You must know yourself, how change occurs, and how others view things differently than you do." (Komives et al., 1998, p. 5) This concept has been adapted into a myriad of leadership texts. For example, Frydman sees self-knowledge as knowing yourself in the context of the journey: "One's ability to design strategy and follow one's own path seems to flow directly from self-knowledge." (Frydman et al., 2000, p. 251)

Looking from another frame of reference, *the integration of self* is the focus of Maccoby's analogy of leading with heart. Laying the groundwork for this analogy, he argues that people think qualities of the heart are opposite those of the head, with the heart meaning softness, feeling and generosity, and the head meaning realistic and tough-minded. But in pre-Cartesian traditional thought, it was the heart that was considered to be the true seat of intelligence, and the brain that did the thinking. In this approach, the head alone can certainly solve technical problems, but it cannot value or resolve emotional doubt about truth or beauty without the heart.

> Considered not as separate from but integrated with the head (and the rest of the body), the development of the heart determines not only compassion and generosity, but also one's perception-experience, the quality of knowledge, capacity for affirmation (of trust or sham, beauty or ugliness), and the will to action (courage) ... Intellect alone organizes data from and about other human beings but it does not experience them ... The head knows by inference ... The intellect may examine human problems but they are abstracted, weightless ... The more we can experience reality, inner realities as well as the external one, the more information we have to understand the world, ourselves, others. (Maccoby, 1981, pp. 85-86)

More recently, it has been discovered that *neurons are not only located in the human brain, but the heart and the gut* (Kandel, 2006). Thus neurons, their firings and their connection strengths create patterns that may influence thoughts and actions.

Reminding us that no one can teach you about yourself except yourself, Bennis (1989) observes four lessons from which to develop self-knowledge: (1) you are your own best teacher; (2) accept responsibility; (3) you can learn anything you want to learn; and (4) true understanding comes from reflecting on your own experience.

Reflecting on our own experience is what can also be called meaning-making, the "process of arranging our understanding of experience so that we can know what has happened and what is happening, and so that we can predict what will happen; it is constructing knowledge of ourselves and the world" (Drath & Palus, 1994, p. 2). Drath and Palus present two understandings of the word "meaning" that guide their thinking about the relationship of meaning and leadership.

> One use is when symbols, like words, stand for something. This process of naming and interpreting helps clarify meaning and is essential for the perspectives needed in reframing and seeing multiple realities. The second use of the word meaning involves people's values and relationships and commitments. (Drath & Palus, 1994, p. 7)

With knowledge of self comes self-confidence. Tichy forwards that self-confidence and determination—along with a healthy dose of humility—are traits of successful leaders.

> Successful entrepreneurs generally are successful because they are able to see or do things that other people can't or haven't. In order to do this, they must have the self-confidence and determination to overcome odds that others have not. But, while self-confidence and determination are valuable assets, they become detriments in the absence of a healthy dose of humility … People who think that they know it all are not only not interested in learning anything from anyone else, but they are unlikely to share power, authority or even information with their inferiors, i.e., anyone else. And, when people have no information and no opportunity to contribute, their talents are wasted. (Tichy, 2002, p. 54)

Similar to Tichy's warning to include a healthy dose of humility, Dotlich and Cairo say that self-confidence provides you with the ability to expose your vulnerabilities, to not only have a strong point of view but to be open enough to say "I don't know."

> Confidence, decisiveness, and certainty are hallmarks of leaders … Yet we have seen a number of senior executives who have made critical mistakes because they refused to admit that there was a gap in their knowledge or that they did not know how to deal with a problem … In an environment where information is vast, overwhelming, and constantly changing, it is important for leaders to … admit that their skill set or background has not prepared them to deal with a particular issue. Leaders face so much ambiguity, complexity, and uncertainty that they cannot possibly know all the answers. At times, the appropriate response is to be perplexed. (Dotlich & Cairo, 2002, pp. 17-18)

In 1995, O'Dell and Grayson titled a book: *If Only We Knew What we Know,* making the point that we know a lot more than we know we know. As Frick and Spears explain,

> The vast storehouse of knowledge in the unconscious mind is not the same stuff that is in libraries. For each of us, it is possibly the complete record of our particular

experience. Much collective wisdom may also be deposited there. Each of us apparently has a center that will process this knowledge, deal with a complexity of issues, and deliver a conclusion at a speed that makes the most elaborate electronic computer a child's toy ... compared to what the unconscious process of an ordinary person can do, it [the computer] is a relatively feeble (though nevertheless important) instrument. (Frick & Spears, 1996, pp. 54-55)

For example, Benjamin N. Cardozo (1921, pp. 167-170), U.S. Supreme Court Justice, offers the words of the French Jurist Saleilles in his treatise *De la personnalite juridique*: "One wills at the beginning the result; one finds the principle afterwards; such is the genesis of all juridical construction."

Frick and Spears caution that the new conscious knowledge can disturb this feeling of certainty about what we know, our inner sense. "If we accept the premise that most of us operate from day to day with a heavy dependence on intuitive decisions, then the intrusion of new conscious knowledge may confuse us, especially if it suggests a radical change of direction." (Frick & Spears, 1996, p. 59) As can be seen, *self knowledge may be the most important knowledge we develop*; it is the reference point for how we see and act in the world.

Final Thoughts

While this is no doubt a good set of knowledges for leaders to have, as a humanity we are learning more every day. *There are no limits except those we set upon ourselves!* For example, the term "Quantum" is being bantered around; there's Quantum learning, Quantum leadership, Quantum this and Quantum that! And the reality (or at least our reality) is, that we really don't understand Quantum! So these thought leaders may not have the understanding of what Quantum is, but *they do* recognize that Quantum is going to change we understand everything!

For example, in a recent book on Quantum biology, McFadden and Al-Khalili say that while life has built-in order at the microscopic level, there is nothing but chaos at the molecular level. This is the concept of order from disorder (Schrödinger, 1944), what lies behind the motive power of steam engines. McFadden and Al-Khalili's research suggests that "life may operate along the lines of a quantum version of the steam engine." (2014, p. 300) The ramifications are huge. We can only imagine how the next few years are going to change everyone's way of life. As we learn more, Quantum will definitely be added to our list of knowledges needed by every collaborative leader, and every citizen of the world!

Chapter 11
The Leader as Learner

In Chapter 7, we introduced the intelligent complex adaptive system (ICAS) model for organizations. While we will not redefine this concept here, recognize that people are complex adaptive systems, and that it is necessary for leaders at all levels of the organization to be *intelligent* complex adaptive systems, that is, engaging in intelligent activities. Intelligent activity represents a perfect state of interaction where intent, purpose, direction, values and expected outcomes are clearly understood and communicated among all parties,

> Intelligent activity represents a perfect state of interaction where intent, purpose, direction, values and expected outcomes are clearly understood and communicated among all parties, reflecting wisdom and achieving a higher truth.

reflecting wisdom and achieving a higher truth. Because the effectiveness of all knowledge is context sensitive and situation dependent, knowledge is shifting and changing in concert with our environment and the demands placed upon us. Intelligent activity involves engagement in the external reality. As we engage in everyday experiences, the incompleteness of knowledge that is never perfect serves as an incentive for the *continuous human journey of learning* and the exploration of new ideas.

In this chapter we will touch briefly on a conglomerate of concepts important to leaders as learners: experiential learning, the bank account of self, continuous learning, spiritual learning, plasticity and the learner, leaders as teachers, social learning, the Net and Millennial generations and the search for transcendent themes.

Experiential Learning

Life is a continuous cycle of learning experiences in a shifting and dynamic environment. Immersed in this environment, adults learn primarily through experience after their formal education. Experiential learning is the process of acquiring new skills, expertise, attitudes and ways of thinking by doing things, learning from activities, mistakes, consequences and achievements.

The Intelligent Complex Adaptive Learning System (ICALS) is essentially an expanded experiential learning model. It is a self-organizing complex adaptive system, a system in which the agents (individuals) have a high degree of freedom to organize themselves to better achieve their local objectives (Bennet & Bennet, 2004). Referring to the earlier work of Dewey, Lewin and Piaget related to experiential learning, Kolb (1984, p. 18) offered, "Common to all three traditions of experiential learning is the emphasis on development toward a life of purpose and self-direction as the organizing principle for education." As Battram (1996, p. 145) further explains, in self-organized learning, "the self organizing is taking place inside the learner's brain (which is a complex adaptive system in its own right) rather than in a networked group of individuals." Thus leaders as learners guide their own learning, heavily impacted by the individual's autobiography, motivation and beliefs about his or her learning efficacy.

Human memories are story based. One of the main jobs of consciousness is to tie our life together into a coherent story, a concept of self (LeDoux, 1996). Moving through various life experiences, the individual single out and accentuates what is significant and connects these events to historic event to

> Human memories are story based.

create a narrative unity, what Long describes as a fictionalized history (Long, 1986). This narrative is subject to selective attention and emphasis, distant memories and even forgetting, with the individual making choices about the importance of people and events and their meanings. This *autobiographical self*—the idea of who we are, the image we build up of ourselves and where we fit socially—is built up over years of experience and constantly being remodeled, a product of continuous learning.

Building on the work of Dewey (1938), Lewin, Piaget (1968), Kolb (1984) and Zull (2002), the ICALS model flows on a foundation of self, which will be explored below. The five modes of the ICALS learning model are concrete experience, reflection observation, abstract conceptualization, active experimentation and social engagement, all impacted by self-embedded in the environment, which includes the social environment. Active experimentation is intended to act upon and thereby influence the environment. Reflection creates understanding and meaning by integrating incoming experience. Meaning is the evaluation both cognitively and emotionally of the significance or importance of the incoming experience relative to the learner, or perhaps to the context of the experience. Thus reflective observation deals with the past and present, and uses these to understand and make sense of the incoming information. Abstract conceptualization, or comprehension, focuses on problem solving, decision-making, creativity, and forecasting the outcome of anticipated actions. Here the learner is focusing on the present and the future, and how to change the environment successfully by creating and applying knowledge. The understanding, meaning, problem solving, and decision-making developed during the reflection and comprehension modes contribute to the creation of the learner's knowledge. Social engagement opens up a dialogue with the environment, bringing social support and social interaction in the sphere of the self as learner. This has become increasingly important in a global world of social networking. For an in-depth treatment of the ICALS model see Bennet and Bennet (2015b).

The bottom line for the leader is understanding that *the mind is always learning*; and that *everyday experiences and interactions are impacting that learning*. Thus **choice and exposure** become critically important elements of a self-learning strategy.

The Bank Account of Self

The term self is taken from the Hindu word *Atman* (translated in English as self) and used in the Hindu teaching "Brahman is Atman and Atman is Brahman." Brahma is the Creator of the University (unknowable, infinite and transcendent) and Atman is the divine spark at the core of our being that is part of the greater whole (Brahma) (Crowley, 1999). Jung's process of individuation involves "letting go of all the false images of ourselves that we have allowed to be built up by our environment and by the projected visions of parents, teachers, friends, and lovers." (Crowley, 1999, p. 136) There is a self that is deeper, wiser and more powerful than that individual who is subject to environmental perturbations.

For purposes of this discussion, the *self* is considered to be the conscious and the unconscious mind, the brain and the body. From this perspective, self can be thought of as a self-organizing complex adaptive system—including self-referential memory, self-description, self-awareness and the personality—coevolving with its environment. American psychologist James argues that "although the self might feel like a unitary thing, it has many facets—from awareness of one's own body to memories of oneself to the sense of where one fits into society." (Zimmer, 2005, p. 51) Thus, there is no single point

> Self is a self-organizing complex adaptive system—including self-referential memory, self-description, self-awareness and the personality—coevolving with its environment.

within the mind/brain/body complex where we could situate "self". It is the interactions among all of those neuronal patterns, firings and connections that define self. And all of these interactions provide the continuously expanding foundation for experiential learning.

In the perceived external dimensions of the body that is part of self there are X, Y, Z (the height, width and breadth of three-dimensional space) and T (time). See Figure 11-1. This is true in both the external reality, and in the physical makeup of the brain structure, such as the neurons, axons, synapses and gleon cells that all exist in a four-dimensional space/time continuum. However, when we consider every chain or sequence of thoughts as a dimension and consider the variety and number of patterns continuously emerging in the mind, the thoughts that generate the persona of self are beyond our ability to count. They are also multidimensional in that these internal dimensions might be represented in vector space by geometrical relationships that are orthogonal, at right angles to each other so as to operate independently (not a subset of the other), yet with the potential to be combined. Recognizing that any model is an artificial construct, these dimensions might be grouped in many ways; for example, by autonomic systems, major sub-systems, or in relationship to the conscious and unconscious.

INTERNAL
KNOWLEDGE
DIMENSIONS

EXTERNAL
DIMENSIONS

Embodied
Affective
Intuitive
Spiritual

X

Z

Y

PERCEPTION
OF TIME
(OBJECTIVE)

PERCEPTION
OF NO TIME
(SUBJECTIVE)

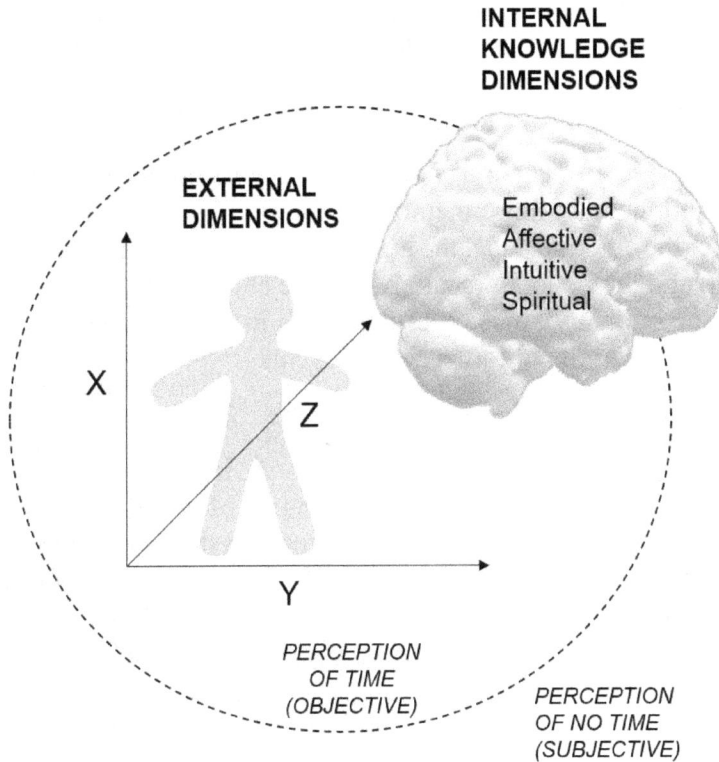

Figure 11-1. *External dimensions and internal knowledge dimensions of self.*[1]

Consciousness is comprised of a single, linear stream of thought patterns (Edelman & Tononi, 2000) and as such this mechanism of awareness can be filled with mundane facts or highly charged emotions. For a pattern to be observed and recognized (brought into consciousness) it must exist for some finite time. Thus consciousness is usually dependent on time, but not always. As Csikszentmihalyi (1990) has proposed, there are times when the mind is unaware of time. These are called autotelic experiences in which the mind is so focused and busy, and usually highly productive, that an individual simply looses track of time. In contrast, the multidimensional unconscious is not subject to a linear stream of thought (denoting time), and dreams often lack any relativity to time.

Since everything is connected within the mind/brain/body in terms of energy (through the arterial and veno systems), what becomes significant is the strength of neuronal connections, the central nervous system or what could be called the guidance system. Emotions play a large role in this process. In this context, emotions are considered signals or labels that are for the most part generated unconsciously. An emotional tag is linked to all information coming into the brain. As Lipton explains,

The evolution of the limbic system provided a unique mechanism that converted the chemical communication signals into sensations that could be experienced by all of the cells in the community. Our conscious mind experiences these *signals* as emotions. (Lipton, 2005, p. 131)

As part of the evolving learning system of self, memories and the emotional tags that gage the importance of those memories become part of an individual's everyday life. The stronger the emotional tag, the greater the strength of the neuronal connections (LeDoux, 1996) and the easier to recall. As Kluwe et al. (2003, p. 51) state, "Often we experience that emotionally arousing events result in better recollection of memories. It appears to us that we will not forget certain events in our life whenever they are accompanied by very pleasant or fearful emotions." This is true because *emotions have priority in our stream of consciousness.*

> The stronger the emotional tag, the greater the strength of the neuronal connections and the easier to recall.

Through evolution (based on survival of the fittest) our brain has been wired such that the connections from the emotional systems to the cognitive systems are much stronger than the connections from the cognitive systems to the emotional systems. As LeDoux (1996, p. 19) observes, "Emotions easily bump mundane events out of awareness, but non emotional events (like thoughts) do not so easily displace emotions from the mental spotlight." Thus we cannot "manage" self without an understanding of emotions, which can be thought of as the energetic life's blood of the learning system.

Further, we now understand that emotions are often processed unconsciously. As LeDoux (1996, p. 64) says, "It now seems undeniable that the emotional meanings of stimuli can be processed unconsciously. The emotional unconscious is where much of the emotional action is in the brain." Thus people take many actions the reason of which they are unaware.

Emotions as affective tacit knowledge are one of four areas of focus in the following discussion of tacit knowledge (see Figure 11-1). Tacit knowledge is the descriptive term for those connections among thoughts that cannot be pulled up in words, a knowing of *what* decision to make or *how* to do something that cannot be clearly voiced in a manner such that another person could extract and re-create that knowledge (understanding, meaning, etc.). An individual *may or may not* know they have tacit knowledge in relationship to something or someone. But even when it *is known*, the individual is unable to put it into words or visuals that can convey that knowledge (Bennet & Bennet, 2015a). From the viewpoint of the internal knowledge dimensions of self, we will focus on four areas of tacit knowledge: embodied, affective, intuitive, spiritual.

REFLECT:

Do I participate in rich experiential learning events?

What role do emotions play in my decision-making process?

Embodied tacit knowledge is also referred to as somatic knowledge. Both kinesthetic and sensory, it can be represented in neuronal patterns stored within the body. Kinesthetic is related to the movement of the body and, while important to every individual every day of our lives, it is a primary focus for athletes, artists, dancers, kids and assembly-line workers. A commonly used example of tacit knowledge is knowledge of riding a bicycle. Sensory, by definition, is related to the five human senses through which information enters the body (sight, smell, hearing, touch and taste). An example is the smell of burning metal from your car brakes while driving or the smell of hay in a barn. These odors can convey knowledge of whether the car brakes need replacing (get them checked immediately), or whether the hay is mildewing (dangerous to feed horses, but fine for cows). These responses would be overt, bringing to conscious awareness the need to take effective action and driving that action to occur.

Intuitive tacit knowledge is the sense of knowing coming from inside an individual that may influence decisions and actions; yet the decision-maker or actor cannot explain how or why the action taken is the right one. Damasio (1999, p. 188) calls intuition, "the mysterious mechanism by which we arrive at the solution of a problem without reasoning toward it." The unconscious works around the clock with a processing capability many times greater than that at the conscious level. This is why as the world grows more complex, decision-makers will depend more and more on their intuitive tacit knowledge. But in order to use it, decision-makers must first be able to tap into their unconscious.

Affective tacit knowledge is connected to emotions and feelings, with emotions representing the external expression of some feelings. Feelings expressed as emotions become explicit (Damasio, 1999). Feelings that are not expressed—perhaps not even recognized—are those that fall into the area of affective tacit knowledge. Feelings as a form of knowledge have different characteristics than language or ideas, but they may lead to effective action because they can influence actions by their existence and connections with consciousness. When feelings come into conscious awareness they can play an informing role in decision-making, providing insights in a non-linguistic manner and thereby influencing decisions and actions. For example, a feeling (such as fear or an upset stomach) may occur every time a particular action is started which could prevent the decision-maker from taking that action.

Spiritual tacit knowledge can be described in terms of knowledge based on matters of the soul. The soul represents the animating principles of human life in terms of thought and action, specifically focused on its moral aspects, the emotional part of human nature, and higher development of the mental faculties (Bennet & Bennet, 2007c). While there is a "knowing" related to spiritual knowledge similar to intuition, this knowing does not include the experiential base of intuition, and it may or may not have emotional tags. The current state of the evolution of our understanding of spiritual knowledge is such that there are insufficient words to relate its transcendent power, or to define the role it plays in relationship to other tacit knowledge. Nonetheless, this area represents a form of higher guidance with unknown origin. Spiritual knowledge may be the guiding purpose, vision and values behind the creation and application of tacit knowledge. It may also be the road to moving information to knowledge and knowledge to wisdom (Bennet & Bennet, 2007c). In the context of this paper, spiritual tacit knowledge represents the source of higher learning, helping decision-makers create and implement knowledge that has greater meaning and value for the common good.

Figure 11-2 is a handy guide for applying this understanding. For example, embodied tacit knowledge (at the top) requires new pattern embedding for change to occur. This could take the form of physical training or mental thinking. Examples of embodied tacit knowledge are leadership behaviors specific to an organization, physical motions on an assembly line and cultural norms such as appropriate language and subjects that can or can't be discussed. This same information is provided for intuitive tacit knowledge, affective tacit knowledge and spiritual tacit information. Print this figure out for optimum use.

Whether embodied, affective, intuitive or spiritual, tacit knowledge represents the bank account of the self. The larger our deposits, the greater the interest, the better we are prepared to co-evolve in a CUCA environment and to respond during troubled times. For a full treatment of tacit knowledge see Bennet and Bennet (2015a).

Continuous Learning

Leadership itself can be learned. As Humphrey (1997, p. 33) explains, "The ability to lead is not native talent. Some skill development is necessary, but the key is to help people understand what it means to lead and why it is important for them to be leaders if their organization is to remain competitive." Zand says that effective leaders must renew their knowledge to ensure they don't lag behind their people and obstruct progress. "Leaders know that they need to learn if they are to keep up with the learning and growth of their people." (Zand, 1997, p. 79)

This learning is continuous. For example, James Belasco, Chairman of Management Development Associates, notes that, "To keep ahead of the rapid changes, everyone, including the leader, must learn faster. We set pay and performance appraisal systems that evaluated and rewarded learning. Then, we prospered." (Belasco, 1997, p. 38) Vicere and Fulmer (1997, p. 115) describe the continuous learning process as including "new experiences and new opportunities to gain perspective and stimulate new individual learning, new linking opportunities, and ultimately new opportunities to create organizational knowledge." This continuous learning process, in turn, facilitates continuous renewal throughout the organization (Vicere & Fulmer, 1997).

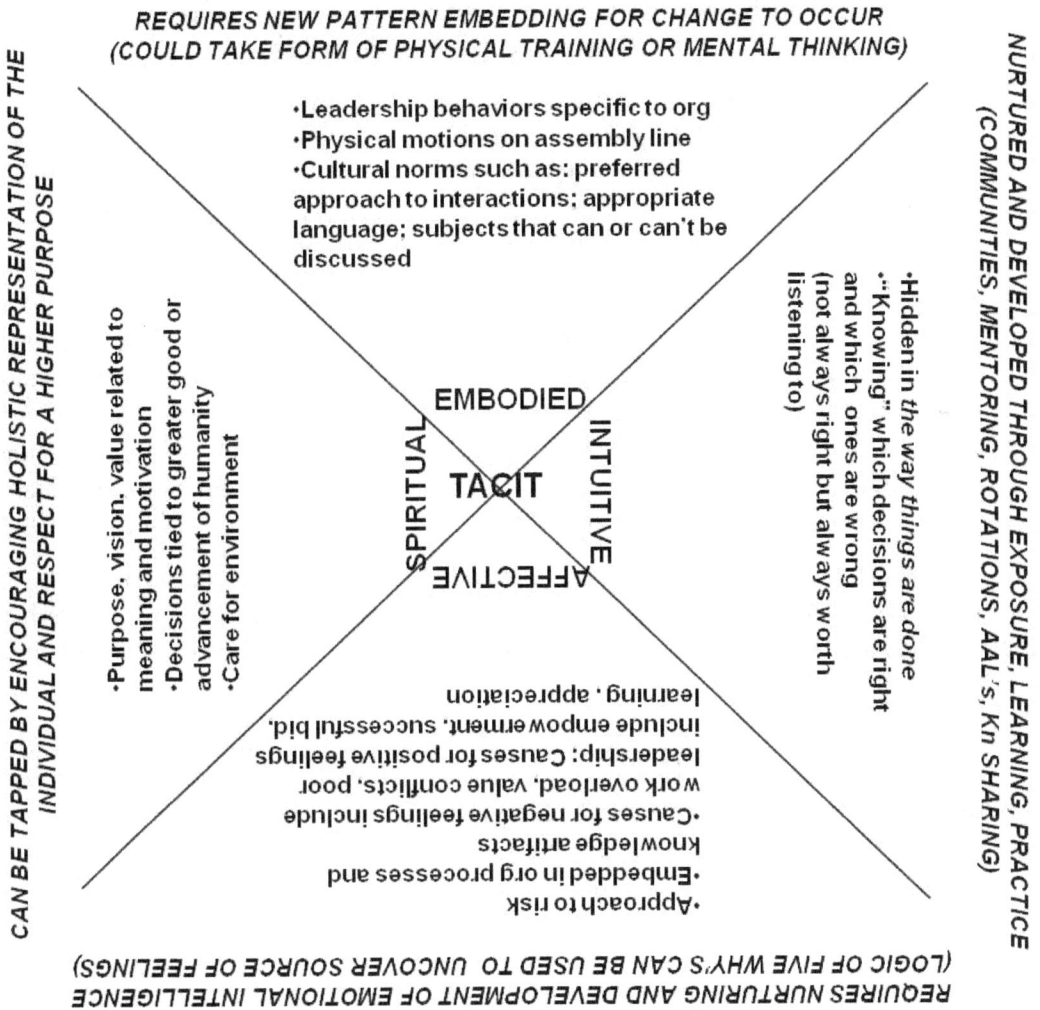

Surrounding text of the figure:

REQUIRES NEW PATTERN EMBEDDING FOR CHANGE TO OCCUR (COULD TAKE FORM OF PHYSICAL TRAINING OR MENTAL THINKING)

NURTURED AND DEVELOPED THROUGH EXPOSURE, LEARNING, PRACTICE (COMMUNITIES, MENTORING, ROTATIONS, AAL's, Kn SHARING)

CAN BE TAPPED BY ENCOURAGING HOLISTIC REPRESENTATION OF THE INDIVIDUAL AND RESPECT FOR A HIGHER PURPOSE

REQUIRES NURTURING AND DEVELOPMENT OF EMOTIONAL INTELLIGENCE (LOGIC OF FIVE WHY'S CAN BE USED TO UNCOVER SOURCE OF FEELINGS)

Top box:
- Leadership behaviors specific to org
- Physical motions on assembly line
- Cultural norms such as: preferred approach to interactions; appropriate language; subjects that can or can't be discussed

Right box:
- Hidden in the way things are done
- "Knowing" which decisions are right and which ones are wrong (not always right but always worth listening to)

Left box:
- Purpose, vision, value related to meaning and motivation
- Decisions tied to greater good or advancement of humanity
- Care for environment

Bottom box:
- Approach to risk
- Embedded in org processes and knowledge artifacts
- Causes for negative feelings include work overload, value conflicts, poor leadership; Causes for positive feelings include empowerment, successful bid, learning, appreciation

Center labels: EMBODIED, INTUITIVE, AFFECTIVE, SPIRITUAL, TACIT

Figure 11-2. *Guide for engaging tacit knowledge.*

Continuous learning refers not only to our need for knowledge, but our need for meta-knowledge, or knowledge about knowledge. Quigley contends that leaders—who must think at a theoretical and conceptual level as well as a concrete level—develop a conceptual framework of reference, or mental model, into which new information is placed. Most conceptual frameworks of today's leaders are based on past mechanistic, binary thinking, so there is a natural inclination to think of things in terms of opposites, white versus black, teacher versus student. In this mechanistic world we define ourselves by what we are not. "It is a world devoid of vision, of spiritual purpose, or even human community … machine age thinkers … think only in terms of *convergent problems*." (Quigley, 1997, p. 95) However, the processes that resolve convergent problems are not capable of resolving our fundamental human, social, and economic problems, which are *divergent* in nature. As Quigley describes,

> Convergent thinking is the method of scientifically inquiring into problems, and through hypothesis and analysis reaching a predictable solution. Divergent thinking arises from different states of consciousness and from different states of self-awareness from a multitude of experiences. These perspectives on life tend to diverge, move away, entropy. (Quigley, 1997, pp. 95-96)

Since divergent problems do not lend themselves to simple solutions, continuous learning must deal with the recognition of patterns and connections beyond that which is learned. Quigley calls this transcendent thought, or the ability to move multiple views to a level of integration. His process for leaders to bring together diverse points of view includes developing spiritual insight and understanding of life; developing moral values which recognize fundamental principles of nature; develop an intense intellectual curiosity; and developing the capacity for holistic thinking (Quigley, 1997).

Part of meta-knowledge is learning how to learn. "Learning to learn isn't easy. For sure, [leaders] do not easily open themselves to learning." (Noer, 1997, p. 235) Perhaps learning how to learn is difficult because historically it has not been an area of focus for leaders or learners.

> Because technology and the pace of change will almost surely continue accelerating, successful [leaders] … must be able to learn rapidly, continuously, and flexibly to fulfill their work responsibilities and maintain employability, as well as employment. This means that they must learn how to learn in a variety of situations and in many different ways. Rarely, if ever, do we reflect on how we learn and consciously try to expand the ways we learn. (Bennet & Bennet, 2004, p. 223)

Learning how to learn is introduced in Chapter 13 as a knowledge capacity.

Not only continuous learning, but lifelong learning is necessary, that is, continuous learning throughout every phase of life. Covey believes that leaders *must* make a commitment to lifelong learning. "People must accept the personal responsibility to upgrade their knowledge and skills, to become computer literate or gain advanced computer literacy, to read widely, and to be aware of the powerful forces that are operating in their environments." (Covey, 1997, p. 88) Managers and leaders often leap into the unknown. As Eccles and Mohria explain,

> Managers and leaders also become researchers. Most formal research conducted by business school professors is directed toward discovering general principles of

design through the rational control of narrowly defined variables. Managers, however, do not have the luxury of ignoring all but a few variables, although they do have to decide which ones are most important in a given situation ... Managers cannot defer action until enough such data points have been gathered to test for statistical significance. (Eccles & Nohria, 1992, pp. 177-8)

Certainly, business school research can serve as useful guides. But the point made here is that each leader/manager must become a researcher in their own right, formulating models of the world based on their small collection of data, and from their experience and the knowledge and experience of their colleagues.

This type of continuous learning towards formulating new models which change the basic theory and belief about how a system works is called *double-loop learning* (Argyris & Schön, 1978). This learning occurs when new thought evolves or problems are solved by changing the fundamental values and assumptions of the belief set as well as the strategy and actions driven by that belief set. Double-loop learning is difficult because it requires individuals, groups and organizations to change the understanding of their *theory of historical success*, what the individual, group or organization must do, and how it goes about doing it to achieve its

> Double-loop learning is difficult because it requires individuals, groups and organizations to change the understanding of their theory of historical success.

goals. Double-loop learning is *learning for the future* in that it changes the individual's (or organization's) frame of reference, moving beyond context sensitivity and situation dependence (Bennet & Bennet, 2007) to provide new ways of looking at similar situations.

Most continuous learning involves studying and practicing better ways of taking actions, developing new processes, tools and methods, and applying new management ideas, e.g., total quality management, business process reengineering, knowledge management, or even spirituality itself. This is *single loop learning*—learning that occurs when ideas and beliefs are reinforced, or problems are solved by changing actions or strategies for achieving a desired result, while the underlying model, theories, or assumptions about those ideas, beliefs, or actions are not changed.

Spiritual Learning

Spiritual learning is the process of elevating the mind as related to intellect and matters of the soul to increase the capacity for effective thought and action. The four primary dimensions of the human are the physical (body), mental (mind), emotional (emotions) and spiritual (soul). We can consider learning as having four types. The first, developing skills (type 1 learning), requires learning and practicing new ways of doing something. The second (type 2 learning), when developing working knowledge in a field, involves continuous learning around better ways of taking actions (see single loop learning above).

The third way to learn (type 3 learning) is to change the underlying models and governing variables from which the action strategies are based (see double loop learning above). While certainly behavior reflecting spiritual thought may be involved in both type 1 and type 2 learning, the domain of spiritual learning would reside largely in type 3 learning, that is, double-loop learning. This is because spiritual growth will undoubtedly affect or expand frames of reference more traditionally associated with bureaucratically-oriented business and government environments. Spiritual learning would also *move beyond* double-loop learning to what might be described as type 4 learning, that which has been called intuition, or the "ah ha!" experience, or what could be attributed in spiritual literature to unconscious streaming or channeling. Whatever the source, type 4 learning emerges unconsciously as a knowing, with insights often taking the form of transformative knowledge. For example, in times of warfare there are numerous recorded instances where military personnel under fire have known what movements to make without detailed knowledge of the terrain or enemy troop movement.

REFLECT:

Could I benefit from developing a life-long learning plan?

What activities might I engage in to accelerate my learning?

Appendix C shares the results of a study undertaken by the authors to explore the concept of spiritual learning and, specifically, how human characteristics that are spiritual in nature contribute to the learning process. Emergent themes in relationship to learning can be loosely described as shifting frames of reference, animating for learning, enriching relationships, priming for learning and moving toward wisdom. See Appendix C for details of the study.

There was a positive correlation between representative spiritual characteristics and human learning. This makes sense, of course, since there are overarching connections between the concepts of spirituality and learning that are embedded by virtue of the concepts themselves. For example, Teasdale explains, "Being spiritual suggests a personal commitment to a process of inner development that engages us in our totality … the spiritual person is committed to growth as an essential ongoing life goal." (Teasdale, 1999, pp. 17-18) In other words, learning (growth) is a life goal of spirituality. Therefore, it follows that human characteristics that are spiritual in nature would contribute to learning.

Plasticity and the Learner

We now know that the brain maintains a high degree of plasticity, changing itself in response to experience and learning. It has been shaped by evolution to adapt to the changes in its external environment. The sources of this ability are changes in the brain's chemistry and in its architecture (Buonomano & Merzenich, 1998, pp. 11-12). This process of neural plasticity comes from the ability of neurons to change their structure and relationships according to environmental demands or personal decisions and actions. Plasticity is increased through the production of neurotransmitters and the role of growth hormones, which facilitate neural connections and cortical organization (Cozolino & Sprokay, 2006; Cowan & Kandel, 2001; Zhu & Waite, 1998).

From a learning viewpoint, brain plasticity opens the door to the possibility of continuously learning and adapting to external environments and internal needs. This phenomenon, applying to all physiologically healthy individuals, means that everyone has the potential to improve themselves by learning and modifying the structure of their brains. It also reminds us

> In a healthy individual, plasticity means that anyone has the potential to continuously learning and adapting to external environments and internal needs.

of the importance of what and how we think, which not only drives our actions, but also influences our brains and minds that we will live and learn with in the future. Imagining and dreaming that perfect future is healthy!

Plasticity opens the door for anyone at any age to improve his or her mind/brain through learning and thinking. While many individuals may have a natural affinity for music, mathematics, or storytelling, plasticity tells us that any individual who desires can develop and improve his or her capacity in other areas of the brain's functioning. It also implies that the vast literature on different ways of thinking, creativity, competency development, analysis and so on. may be open to any individual with sufficient motivation, interest, and dedication.

Following a ten-year study of neuroscience findings connected to learning, the Mountain Quest Institute developed an expanded model of experiential learning, the ICALS model introduced above. A finding significant to this discussion is that **thoughts can change the structure of the brain, and the brain structure influences the creation of new thoughts**. This feedback loop highlights the recognition of the interdependence and self-organization of the mind and the brain in the sense that each influences the other. This also reminds us of the importance of both mental and physical health. Once conscious of this continuing cycle of learning and growth, growth and learning, we have choice.

Thinking and Learning: Fast and Slow

Recent research shows that the mind operates from two modes of thought: fast and slow (Kahneman, 2011). Thinking *fast*, aka "System 1," refers to mental operations that are frequent and automatic. Thinking *slow*, aka "System 2," refers to mental operations that are infrequent and effortful. In neuroscience experiments, we find that one stimulus will generate a fast response followed by the slow response. So it is quite natural to make a snap decision, followed by one that is more thoughtful (although as leaders we have learned to sometimes suppress our fast response). It is also quite natural to find, within some classic organizations, that the organizational chart will start with "Operations" and "R&D" in recognition that fast productivity is needed to maintain and sustain running systems, while research and development is needed to work through the trials of innovation.

Lewis (2014) provides a visualization of the change cycle which incorporates the concept of acting fast and slow. See Figure 11-3. The ADIIEA (pronounced uh-dee-uh) model of change has six phases: Automation, Disruption, Investigation, Ideation, Expectation, and Affirmation. Most of the time, we are in Automation, which simply means autopilot and *status quo*. Although we tend to think of this term in describing robotic functions, it is a state of mind that humans operate within as well. Starting from our normal routine (Automation), we encounter something out of the ordinary (Disruption) and begin to look deeper into the situation (Investigation). Then we think of some ideas (Ideation) and put a plan into action (Expectation). With a sound plan, we eventually see positive results (Affirmation), and over time, we settle into a new routine (Automation).

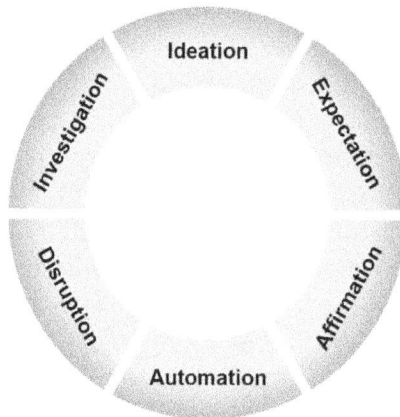

Figure 11-3. ADIIEA model of change.[2]

This path around the "full-cycle" represents thinking slow, and is related to the requirements of transformational leadership. Sometimes we want to stay in our routine (Automation), with occasionally reacting to an anomaly (Disruption) with pre-planned actions, or looking-up an authoritative answer (Affirmation). This is called staying in the "half-pipe" and is related to the requirements of transactional leadership.

When compared with methods of learning, Lewis (2014) found that experiential learning methods allowed students to travel around the "full-cycle," engaging in the questioning process and experimentation that leads to confirmation of an idea (Affirmation). Unfortunately, most contemporary education is based on "half-pipe" learning. B.F. Skinner is known for his approach to accelerate educational learning by focusing only on the desired behavior of a learner. Education provides the learning objective for what is already known (Affirmation) and training produces the desired routine (Automation), with an occasional drill (Disruption) thrown in. Half-pipe learning worked for the Industrial Age, but does not prepare students for the Knowledge Economy. As leaders are learning, and teaching, ADIIEA provides a "map" for where they have been, and where they are going.

Leaders as Teachers

Leaders must also serve as teachers. Zand (1997, p. 27) says that, "Effective leaders open the flow of information by acting as teachers, planting ideas and nurturing them." Tichy connects teacher-leaders to the success of the organization. "Ultimately, the most successful organizations are the ones that create Virtuous teaching Cycles and become Teaching Organizations from top to bottom. These are the ones in which people at all levels share information and learn from each other. Teaching and learning behaviors that permeate the environment and daily business transaction are based on mutual exchanges of valuable knowledge." (Tichy & Cardwell, 2002, p. 137)

Finally, for the leader learner, forgetting goes hand-in-hand with learning. "All leaders will be required to forget some of the old ways of competing and to invent new ones. Therefore, the components of substantive knowledge will have to include forgetting as well as learning" (Prahalad, 1999, p. 35). As Eccles and Nohria (1992, p. 178) say, "Knowing when one's knowledge is no longer useful is the beginning of wisdom." So while we may not entirely forget, we must be able to unlearn prior knowledge to make way for new learnings if we are to continue to find higher truths. From the viewpoint of the mind/brain, and consistent with the concept of *use it or lose it*, forgetting and unlearning take the form of *lack of use*, that is, no neuronal firings. This occurs when a more significant concept, thought, feeling has pre-empted an older concept, thought feeling. In other words, stronger connections are made to the more significant concept in terms of relating to and connected with a large number of other thoughts (sense-making), a higher level of emotion (passion, excitement, joy), and a conscious focus on this new concept without regard to the older concept. Note that the best mental exercise regardless of age is new learning, acquiring new understanding and knowledge, and doing things that you have never done before (Amen, 2005).

REFLECT:

Can I catch my negative thoughts early and let them go?

Do I spend sufficient time imagining and dreaming my desired future?

Learning and knowledge have become two of the three most important emergent characteristics of the future world-class organization (Bennet & Bennet, 2004). The third is leadership. This overlapping nexus not only provides the knowledge needed for decision-making, but the opportunity to nurture an environment that supports learning throughout the organization. Conner states,

> One of the great myths about humans is that repetition results in expertise. Iteration may lead to heightened proficiency, but only if new learning is associated with each interaction. Recurring episodes of change that lack the benefit of new learning produce little more than redundant experiences; no cumulative value is realized. (Conner, 1998, p. 25)

So, the job of leadership becomes the generation and dissemination of valuable knowledge, and nurturing an environment where new learning can take place. Tichy relates this process to the age-old concepts of effectiveness and efficiency.

> The twist in the knowledge era is that the gathering of raw data and the application of human intellect to turn that data into valuable knowledge must be done on a constant and cumulative basis … The challenge for leaders, therefore, is to design and build organizations where everything gets better and everyone gets smarter every day. (Tichy, 2002, pp. 32-33)

Zand agrees that the core of the leader's new role is to foster learning throughout the organization. "Leaders need to provide the conditions that foster learning if they are to build an adaptive organization." (Zand, 1997, p. 78) The conditions needed to do this include creative deviance (a tolerance for curiosity and differences); mastery of existing knowledge (avoiding useless rediscovery); unstructured time (nurturing creativity); and new perspectives (creative thinking techniques and diverse groups) (Zand, 1997).

Topping says the learning process can be managed by fostering innovation and risk taking. This is "intertwined with the managerial leader's role in creating a learning-oriented culture." (Topping, 2002, p. 71) In this rapidly changing, uncertain, and highly competitive business environment, no organization can afford to wait for everyone to learn independently. Topping describes three dimensions to handling organizational learning:

> (1) consider the myriad ways knowledge can enter the organization … [The leader's] job is to make sure you tap into as many sources of knowledge as possible that have relevance to your activities … (2) Create a systematic approach to

disseminating the knowledge gained … Knowledge that is not shared with the right people does little good. (3) Use the knowledge that has been gained to make better decisions … Encourage your associates to apply what they have learned. Reward them when they do, and hold them accountable for making mistakes they made before when they don't demonstrate learning. (Topping, 2002, p. 71)

Social Learning

At the heart of the knowledge organization and the learning organization is social networking. This term became important with the emergence of social media in order to differentiate a "social network" from a "network" used to describe a system of circuits or computers as well as a system of people or things. Networks are structures defined by nodes and connections between them. In social networks the nodes are people and the connections are the relationships they have. Networking is the process by which those online relationships are developed and strengthened. In a global world, social networking becomes a primary form of social learning, offering a diversity of thought and the opportunity to connect with that diversity in the now.

Not to be forgotten or ignored, communities of practice are incredibly effective tools for individual and organizational learning. Communities of practice and interest provide platforms for the sharing of knowledge—shallow knowledge that is context rich—building trusting relationships that offer resources for emerging issues and opportunities. Although the members of a community of practice may do similar work, their purpose is to share knowledge. The manager's responsibility is then to create such communities, support their existence and encourage the creation and exchange of information and knowledge among participants (Wenger, 1999).

Other approaches to knowledge sharing are moving people around the organization. Corbin (2000, p. 136) states, "Great leaders emphasize knowledge sharing and, in fact, structure work to require sharing." For example, Lars Ramqvist, Chairman of Ericsson, the world's leading supplier of telecommunications equipment, says, "We move executives globally to learn, using job rotations and cross-cultural training to eliminate any boundary thinking." (Rosen et al., 2000, p. 269) Access to know-how and the global transfer of knowledge have become *an Ericsson trademark.*

The speed and quality of knowledge sharing throughout an organization has become a critical factor in the capacity of the organization to respond to a changing world. As Ury (2003, p. 46) explains, "Knowledge is improved through the act of sharing … It is through … cooperation and sharing that knowledge as a resource grows more abundant for everyone. The meme used in the Department of Navy implementation was *knowledge shared is power squared* (Bennet & Bennet, 2004). Similarly, Rosen (2000, p. 269) states, "Knowledge may be

> The speed and quality of knowledge sharing throughout the organization is a critical factor in the capacity of the organization to respond to a changing world.

power in the global workplace. But knowledge must be communicated to have power." See Chapter 6 for a discussion of knowledge and power.

REFLECT:

At the last conference I attended, what did I learn from others?

Was I able to put that learning to good use?

The Connected Self

The role of nurturing and the environment have significantly more impact on individual learning than was previously thought. An enriched environment increases the formation and survival of new neurons, influencing both the nature of the experience of the learner and his or her learning efficacy. Begley (2007, p. 58) describes this phenomenon as a striking finding in neuroplasticity that "exposure to an enriched environment leads to a striking increase in new neurons, along with a substantial improvement in behavioral performance"

An enriched environment is an environment that "feels good", raises questions, offers ideas and excites the mind, combining a feeling of safety and comfort with mental excitement and stimulus. The literature suggests that there are specific changes within the brain that occur through enriched environments. Specifically, thicker cortices are created, there are larger cell bodies, and dendritic branching in the brain is more extensive. These changes have been directly connected to higher levels of intelligence and performance (Begley, 2007; Byrnes, 2001; Jensen, 1998).

The young leaders moving up in today's organizations—members of what is generally referred to as Gemeration X or the Millennials, depending upon their age—are Internet savvy, and engage heavily in social media. The term "tech savvy generations" used here describes the group of decision-makers growing up with the Internet and the World Wide Web. Their enriched environment is a virtual playground connected to a field of ideas. We live in unprecedented technologically-advanced times. "Yet new information technology merely reflects the field of intelligence that is growing upon the earth. It does not cause it." (Carey, 1996, p. 100) Let's not forget, there has been no breakthrough in technology that was not first a thought in the human mind, a thought that had to be made explicit, described in some communicable form. The creative thought occurred first, followed by its effective application (knowledge) to create the tangible innovation. Action follows thought; and action changes the world.

Of particular significance to a discussion of the new decision-makers are the characteristics of how the tech savvy generations engage the world, and *this is a generation that **does** engage*. "They organize themselves, publish themselves, inform themselves and share with their friends—without waiting for an authority to instruct them" (Tapscott, 2010), howbeit an underlying pattern of this need for immediacy is an impatience with business models and processes of the preceding generation. Similarly, Hadar (2009) describes this generation as optimistic and determined, and notes that they like public activism and Elmore (2010) points out that they are both high-performance and *high maintenance*, more likely to "rock the boat" than any prior generation (Johns, 2003). Let's dig a bit deeper and explore the values that underlie these behaviors. The research project "The Net Generation: a Strategic Investigation," which involved interviewing 9,442 young people, resulting in the publication of *Grown Up Digital*, will be used as a foundational information resource (Tapscott, 2009).

The personal values of a decision-maker, *which are also likely to represent generational values*, can exercise tremendous influence over his/her decisions regarding how to solve a problem and take the best action in a situation. Note that

> The personal values of a decision-maker—which are also likely to represent generational values—can exercise tremendous influence of decisions.

values are knowledge, and as such are situation dependent and context sensitive (Avedisian & Bennet, 2010; Bennet & Bennet, 2015a). German sociologist Karl Mannheim forwards that a person's thoughts, feelings and behaviors, including their values, are shaped by the generation to which a person belongs (Mannheim, 1980). We agree.

Values begin as principles, a rule or standard considered good behavior (American Heritage Dictionary, 2006). As these principles are repeatedly expressed (acted upon) by an individual or across an organization, they become embedded behaviors, both considered the norm and expected (Avedisian & Bennet, 2010). For example, the principles of freedom, equality, human dignity, tolerance, and the celebration of diversity have a long and storied history in the United States (Lakoff, 2006). Although today these are recognized as values core to a democracy, Knowledge (Informing), there is still disagreement among the political infrastructure when translating them into action, Knowledge (Proceeding). Knowledge (Informing) appears to be the higher-order pattern, that is, less susceptible to change.

Recognizing the new social knowledge paradigm—which supports the creation, leveraging and application of knowledge—the core and operational values linked to this generation of decision-makers include integrity, empathy, transparency, participation, collaboration, contribution, learning and creativity (Avedisian & Bennet, 2010). See Chapter 15 for an in-depth discussion of the values of thought leaders.

As an operational value **learning is integrally related to the ability to contribute**. Learning in the CUCA environment means receiving, understanding, thinking critically, and learning how to adapt and apply knowledge quickly in new and unfamiliar situations. The learning of tech savvy generations is unique. Learning in social settings locates learning "not in the head or outside it, but in the relationship between the person and the world, which for human beings is a social person in a social world." (Wenger, 2009, p. 1) The tech savvy generations are learning together, in groups and communities, through continuous interactions around the world. This new mode of learning is just-in-time, interactive, collaborative, fun, engaging, taps multiple senses (e.g., multi-media) and fosters discovery. Learning affects every other value, offering a way of practicing and applying each of the values in every aspect of work life including interactions with peers, customers, vendors, how work gets done, and how success is measured. This learning is collaborative. Demonstrating the interdependence between learning, empathy and collaboration, Tapscott says,

> It goes without saying that collaborative learning, with its emphasis on mindfulness, attunement to others, nonjudgmental interactions, acknowledgement of each person's unique contributions, and recognition of the importance of deep participation and a shared sense of meaning coming out of embedded relationships, can't help but foster greater empathic engagement. (Tapscott, 2009, p. 607)

As can be seen, learning cannot be separated from the whole of self, the experiential learner introduced above.

Final Thoughts

The human learning experience is entangled with the past and the future, and the pasts and futures of those whom we choose as our friends and colleagues. For better or worse, we have deep connections that orchestrate our learning experiences. As an emerging theme throughout this book, awareness brings with it the opportunity for choice. Now that we understand the longer-term impact of the events in our lives, we can plan activities—and relationships—that head us the direction of our dreamed future. But we're getting ahead of ourselves. This is for the next section.

Section IV
Intelligent Activity

In Chapter 3 we defined intelligent activity as a perfect state of interaction where intent, purpose, direction, values and expected outcomes are clearly understood and communicated among all parties, reflecting wisdom and achieving a higher truth. That's a long definition but every bit of it is important! We talked about the power of intent in Chapter 7 as one of the four forces in the ICAS organization, right up there with direction, knowledge and knowing. Direction tells us which way to head; knowledge is a human tool to navigate the road toward intelligent activity; and knowing represents the fog lights of the future, at least that is how knowing was introduced. Now, we're going to dig a bit deeper. Get ready for a deep dive.

Sustainability competencies are up first. We start by figuring out just what those sustainability factors are. There's a pretty good set connected to the organization: quick response, robustness, resiliency, flexibility, adaptability, and then alignment, stakeholder satisfaction and continuous learning. So how is a collaborative leader supposed to address all of that? It starts with self-efficacy, and that's just the beginning!

Chapter 13 is about knowledge capacities. These are sets of ideas and ways of acting that are more general in nature than competencies, more core to a way of thinking and being, that specifically support building capacity sustainability. The knowledge capacities include learning how to learn, shifting frames of reference, comprehending diversity, engaging tacit knowledge, symbolic representation and orchestrating drive.

Now we get a much better feel for this CUCA reality within which we are living. We were surprised you didn't want to know more about this earlier! But you didn't ask. So we first talk about complexity, and then talk about simplicity. Sounds to be like somebody is mixed up! But that's the truth of it, and then we're going to talk about two approaches or tools (whatever you'd like to call them) that can help you simplify ... (1) discernment and discretion, and (2) knowing. There, we finally reached the concept of knowing again! Recognizing that the most important factor in leadership or learning is the individual, we *purposefully push the edge* in our thinking. Unless leaders can change their thinking—and communicate that thinking—nothing will change.

Chapter 12
Sustainability Competencies

In this chapter we propose and investigate essential skills, knowledge and personal characteristics for improving our ability to deal with complex situations arising from CUCA (increasing change, uncertainty, complexity and anxiety). To fully understand the meaning and ramifications of these ideas and concepts, we build on the pragmatic and biological-based definition for information, learning and knowledge provided in Chapter 2. Since all action comes from the self—either consciously or unconsciously—our frame of reference is the self, specifically, the leader, introduced in Chapter 11 as a self-organizing intelligent complex adaptive learning system. In this chapter we introduced self as the foundation for experiential learning.

From neuroscience and learning theory we know that self-efficacy is essential for effective learning. One's actions are driven by our decisions, which are determined by our

> Self efficacy is essential for effective learning.

knowledge, which are the result of our thoughts, which arise from our beliefs. Thus, reinforcing what was stated in Chapter 11 in a little different wording, **if you believe you can learn, you can**; if you believe you cannot learn, you can't.

There are states and skills that can support sustainability in what we are going to describe as "trying times". For example, optimal arousal creates the excitement of learning without the drain from high stress. Pattern thinking, an integrative competency, makes use of what is really occurring within the mind/brain and in the environment to provide guidance on learning. Social networking utilizes the benefits of other's knowledge to broaden and enhance our own capacity for effective actions in trying times.

Trying times in a CUCA environment are learning and testing grounds, providing the opportunity and incentive for the leader to become more of what the leader is capable of being. To co-evolve with a changing, uncertain and complex environment requires speeding up our learning and expanding our knowledge bases. The sustainability competencies of Self Efficacy, Optimum Arousal, Pattern Thinking and Social Networking will prepare us to deal more effectively with whatever the future brings.

Sustainability Characteristics

In trying times, what are we trying to sustain? Physical life? Responsibility? Spiritual needs? Value sets? In an organizational setting, sustainability may mean social and economic survival. The same two things carry over to an individual. For example, survival would be maintaining the personal goals and perspectives of the individual (physical, mental, social, spiritual, etc.) However, for some people this may not be enough. They are not happy with where they are now, and want to improve themselves. This may not be possible. Trying times is another way of stating that there are going to be perturbations that have the potential to change or harm an individual's situation. The challenge is to create a survival capacity to respond and adapt to those changes while minimizing the damage to an individual's goals and objectives.

As a species—and as individuals—we survive by successfully co-evolving with our environment. This means interacting with, influencing and, as necessary, adapting to the environment. In a CUCA environment this is a continuous and difficult process because of the intensity and uncertainty of the environmental changes that occur.

The self co-evolves with its environment through the process of associative patterning, the complexing of incoming information (extrinsic signals) with internally-stored patterns (intrinsic signals). The results are not necessarily based on the amount of the extrinsic signals, but rather on neural interactions "selected and stabilized by memory through previous encounters with the environment." (Edelman & Tononi, 2000, p. 137) In other words, the more we know about a specific area that is in memory, the stronger the modulation with extrinsic signals that relate to that area. The more we know in an area the easier it is to learn in that area. The brain is continuously remodeled by the lives we lead (Begley, 2007).

> The self co-evolves with its environment through the process of associative patterning, the complexing of incoming information with internally-stored patterns.

In 2005 Mountain Quest Institute surveyed 200 senior executives in the U.S. Federal sector regarding the ability of their organizations to effectively function under the conditions of CUCA. The eight sustainability factors that emerged with a short description are as follows:

Continuous learning = having a mindset and a self-directed program to continuously learn, create and apply knowledge.

Quick response = capable of reacting/responding quickly when needed.

Robustness = the ability to respond to a broad range of tasks or problems.

Resiliency = the ability to recover from setbacks and to resume high performance.

Flexibility = keeping an open mind and attitude, willing to change positions and direction, adopt new perspectives and try new things.

Adaptability = can change habits, beliefs, and values as necessary to maintain performance in a changing environment.

Stakeholder satisfaction = providing value that satisfies stakeholders.

*Alignment = the capacity to maintain internal and personal consistency and cohesion while simultaneously staying flexible and adaptable to a changing environment.

We contend that these factors also apply to individuals.

One word of caution. Long-term sustainability in trying times often requires a trade-off. Sometimes instant decisions have to be made in response to "wicked" problems that may conflict with long-term sustainability. For example, consider the cave man. To survive over time humans statistically have to have more fat on the body than is necessarily healthy. A cave man might have to go a long time without food. An example today would be the need to have money in the bank to "live through an emergency". Therefore, you might not be able to live as well as you might desire in order to ensure long-term survivability. The focus of this paper is on sustainability of the self in a CUCA environment. As an example, sustainability of the physical body would prohibit smoking, therefore calling for a potential sacrifice in behavior for some people.

Sustainability Competencies

Competencies say you know how to do it and you can do it, which means having experience in doing it. A general definition of competence is the ability to do something well, or to a required standard (*Encarta*, 1999). This is consistent with our definition of knowledge as both the potential and actual capacity to take effective action (knowledge in action).

Figure 12-1 shows a nominal relationship between (a) the knowledge required to understand the system, and (b) the different types of systems. A system is considered a group of elements or objects, the relationships among them, their attributes, and some boundary. The five categories of systems are laid out roughly in terms of their difficulty of understanding and predictability, that is, ranging from simple to complicated to complex to complex adaptive to chaotic.

Simple systems remain the same or change very little over time, are typically non-organic, and exhibit predictable behavior. An example would be a light switch. *Complicated systems* contain a large number of interrelated parts with the connections between the parts fixed. They are non-organic and the whole is equal to the sum of its parts. Examples are an automobile and a computer. *Complex systems*, while consisting of a large number of interrelated elements, have nonlinear relationships, feedback loops and dynamic uncertainties that are very difficult or impossible to understand and predict. They have emergent properties that cannot be traced back to a specific element or interaction of these elements; thus the whole of the system is very different than the sum of its parts. Examples would be organizations and culture. Complex adaptive systems contain many elements that interact with each other that are semi-autonomous and have varying levels of self-organization. A complex adaptive system is organic and co-evolves with its environment. An example is you. Chaotic systems rarely survive because they are unpredictable and independent of their environment. Chaos is a state of limited or bounded instability (Stacey, 1996).

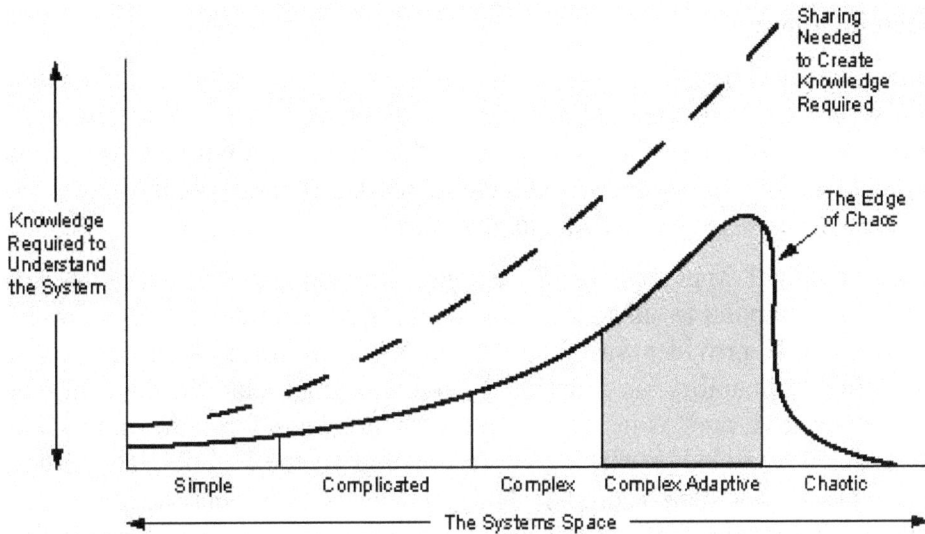

Figure 12-1. *Knowledge required to understand the system.* (Bennet & Bennet, 2004)

While the issues and situations addressed in trying times are generally complex, the people and organizations involved in those issues and situations are complex adaptive, as is the self. As can be seen, the amount of knowledge needed to understand an issue or situation would correlate with the difficulty of understanding, and predicting the future effects of, any action on the situation.

How do you learn? In trying times, it is necessary to learn quickly, accurately and be willing to take risks. If we cannot learn at least as fast as the environment changes, we are doomed to play catch-up and are tied to outmoded ideas and perhaps inadequate actions. But there are no easy answers. There is no one learning process that is optimum for different individuals. And the learning process will very much depend upon the nature of the knowledge needed, which depends upon the nature of the trying environment.

Is there specific knowledge that will help us take effective action in trying times? The knowledge needed in trying times will likely be much different than the knowledge that works for you in normal times. Under relatively stable times knowledge is developed through learning by studying, social interaction, and experience, all excellent ways to learn. Once learned it can be reused or reapplied often, perhaps with some adjustment to account for different situations. As experience is gained, this knowledge can often be pulled from memory and reused without problems. This knowledge has then become a combination of surface and shallow, with memory as the guide (see Definitions above). The "how" and "why" part of the knowledge may even have been forgotten.

During trying times, it is likely to be difficult or impossible to use memory and experience as a guide *because of the uncertainty of what will happen next*. Another difficulty is that things may change so quickly that there is little time to figure out what to do. Because of the speed of change, uncertainty and complexity, "normal" knowledge will probably be inadequate, and may even be dangerous.

A foundational approach to developing the capacity to react quickly and effectively, and respond to surprises, shocks and opportunities, is to develop the kind of knowledge that provides sustainability in its ideal form. Recalling our earlier discussion of sustainability, an individual would consider each factor from their own personal perspective and, if needed, develop their own information and knowledge base, functional knowledge capable of responding to their anticipated needs. This knowledge base would then be quickly available, that is, previously acquired and easily remembered. For example, if a focus area indicated a wide range of potential issues or problems, the individual would then develop a knowledge-based response system that was robust and capable of responding to this particular range of problems. This requires a level of forecasting which may sound forbidding, but is something every single individual participates in and does to some extent every single day. Most have just not taken the time to develop this capability at the conscious level.

There are also competencies that are integrative in nature, which are appropriately called *integrative competencies*. These competencies provide connective tissue, creating the knowledge, skills, abilities, and behaviors that support and enhance other competencies. They have a multiplier effect through their capacity to enrich the individual's cognitive abilities while enabling integration of other competencies, leading to improved understanding, performance, and decisions.

> Integrative competencies create the knowledge, skills, abilities, and behaviors that support and enhance other competencies.

Integrative competencies can be understood from two perspectives. The first is from the viewpoint of the individual. Here the competencies help the individual to deal with the larger, more complex aspects of their organization and its environment. They either integrate data, information, or knowledge to give the individual more capability, or they help the individual perceive and comprehend the complexity around them by integrating and clarifying events, patterns, and structures in their environment. From the organization's view the integrative competencies help strengthen the organization's capacity to deal with its environment by creating programs, networks, and cultures that pull together capabilities that can more effectively handle uncertainty and complexity.

While functional and operational competencies are core to an organization, integrative competencies and knowledge capacities not only expand the capability set of the individual and organization, but provide resources for sustainability. See Figure 12-2.

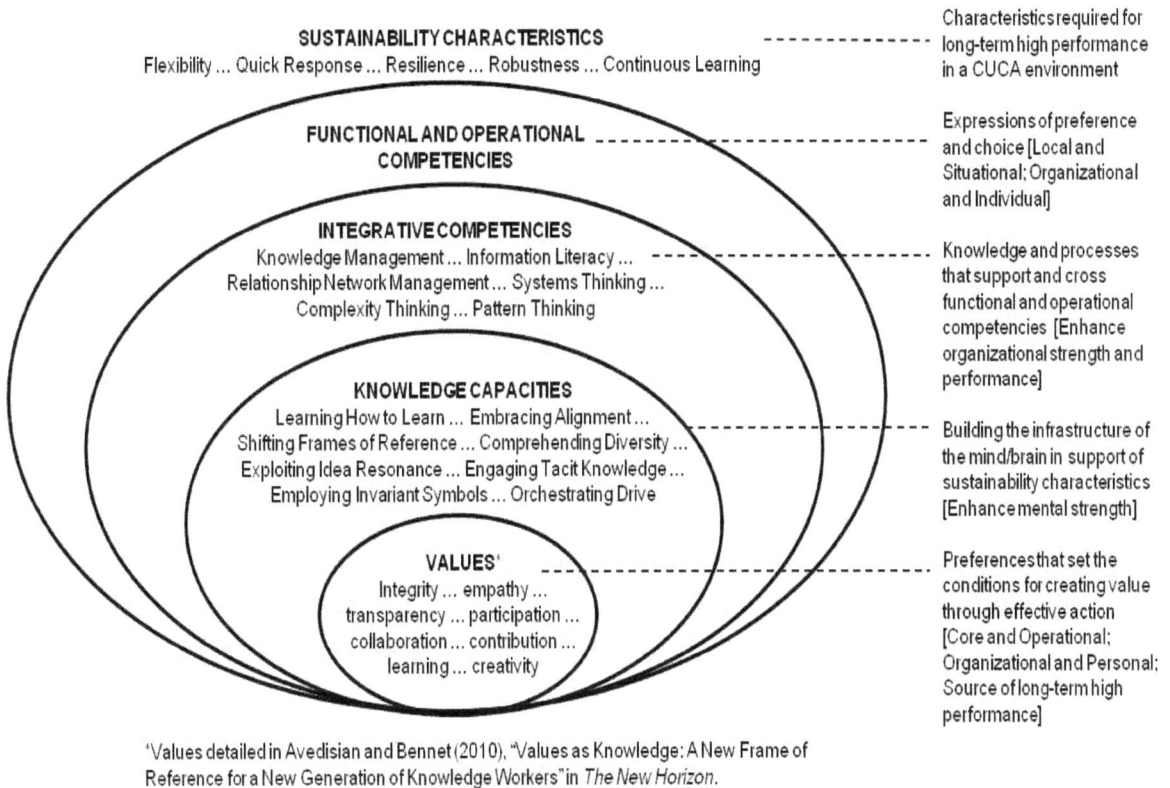

Figure 12-2: *The multidimensionality of the organization includes integrative competencies and knowledge capacities as well as functional and operational competencies.*

A number of what could be considered integrative competencies are discussed later in this chapter, specifically, Relationship Network Management and Pattern Thinking. These are also what can be described as sustainability competencies.

The leadership competencies described below focus on the internal self-organization of the mind/brain/body. The intent is to understand self in a larger way in order to embrace the power of the mind/brain/body (conscious and unconscious) to sustain us through trying times. These competencies are discussed below in terms of achieving Self Efficacy, Optimum Arousal, Pattern Thinking and Social Networking.

REFLECT:

Am I familiar with all of the sustainability factors?

What special knowledge might I need when an urgent problem arises?

Self Efficacy

We start with our feelings and what we perceive to be true about our self. The increasing anxiety that often accompanies increasing change, uncertainty and complexity may well reflect a loss of security, lack of trust, and a sense of undermining personal identity. To move through this anxiety, the individual must look within to the stability of values, integrity and ethical behavior with a clear direction, vision and purpose.

In the past a large number of beliefs have limited us. This need no longer be the case. Nature, nurture and our own choices all play a significant role in our learning and development. Bruce Lipton, a cell biologist, contends that in these exciting times science is shattering old myths and fundamentally rewriting a *belief* of human civilization. "The belief that we are frail bio-chemical machines controlled by genes is giving way to an understanding that we are powerful creators of our lives and the world in which we live." (Lipson, 2005, p. 17)

Although DNA was once thought to be destiny, this idea is changing as neuroscience and biology expand their frontiers of understanding. Epigenetics—literally meaning control above genetics—is profoundly changing our beliefs and knowledge of how life is controlled. Epigenetics, one of the most active areas of scientific research, is the study of the molecular mechanisms by which the environment influences gene activity (Lipson, 2005). Ross proposes that,

> ... biology is no longer inevitable gene expression driven unidirectionally by the DNA. Rather, genes for brain growth and development are turned on and off by the environment in a complex, rich set of feedback loops. Causality in brain development involves a dance between two partners, DNA and the environment. (Ross, 2006, p. 32)

From another perspective, it has been discovered that DNA blueprints are not set in concrete at the birth of the cell as they were once thought. Genes are not destiny (Church, 2006). Rather, it is how they are expressed. Gene expression means that the DNA information within a gene is released and influences its surrounding environment. Environmental influences such as nutrition, stress and emotions can modify those genes without changing their basic blueprint. And, in some cases, those modifications can be passed on to future generations (Reik & Walter, 2001). What we believe leads to what we think, which leads to our knowledge, which leads to what actions we take. Thus, what we believe and how we think determine what we do. It is our actions that determine our success, not our genes (Bownds, 1999).

Similarly, Lipton points out that positive and negative beliefs not only impact our health, but every aspect of our life.

> Consider the people who walk across coals without getting burned. If they wobble in the steadfastness of their belief that they can do it, they wind up with burned feet. Your beliefs act like filters on a camera, changing how you see the world. And your biology adapts to those beliefs. When we truly recognize that our beliefs are that powerful, we hold the key to freedom ... we can change our minds. (Lipton, 2005, p. 143)

In addition, environments that can and do change the actions of genes (Jensen, 1998), our feelings, attitudes, and mind-sets can actively be changed by meditation and other mental exercises (Begley, 2007). Thus our beliefs and thoughts are what will ultimately determine our ability to successfully navigate change, uncertainty and complexity in trying times.

Optimum Arousal

With our Self Efficacy intact—and recognizing that knowledge (the capacity to take effective action) is paramount to our success—how do we produce the best mental state for learning?

Amen says that physical exercise, mental exercise and social bonding are the best sources of stimulation of the brain (Amen, 2005). Complex levels of self-awareness, those that involve higher brain functions and potential changes in neural networks, cannot be accomplished when an individual feels anxious and defensive. Specifically, Cozolino says that a safe and empathic relationship can establish an emotional and neurobiological context that is conducive to neural reorganization. This relationship "… serves as a buffer and scaffolding within which [an adult] can better tolerate the stress required for neural reorganization." (Cozolino, 2002, p. 291) As Taylor explains, … adults who would create (or recreate) neural networks *associated with development of a more complex epistemology* need emotional support for the discomfort that will also certainly be part of that process" (Taylor, 2006, p. 82) [emphasis added]. In other words, the more trying the times (in terms of change, uncertainty and complexity), the more necessary it is to have a balancing emotional safety net. Johnson agrees. Referring to recent discoveries in cognitive neuroscience and social cognitive neuroscience, she says that educators and mentors of adults recognize "the neurological effects and importance of creating a trusting relationship, a holding environment, and an intersubjective space" (Johnson, 2006, p. 68) where such things as reflection and abstract thinking can occur.

The changes in the structure of the brain that need to occur in a CUCA environment are not new phenomena. This concept, called neuroplasticity, can be found not only in the history of the evolution of man, but also in the current maturation of the individual. Neuroplasticity is the ability of neurons to change their structure and relationships according to environmental demands or personal decision and action. The brain maintains a high degree of plasticity, changing in response to experience and learning. As Buonomano and Merzenich (1998, p. 21) explain, "The brain has been shaped by evolution to adapt and readapt to an ever-changing world. The ability to learn is dependent on modification of the brain's chemistry and architecture."

Learning is highly dependent on the level of arousal of the learner. Too little arousal and there is no motivation, too much and stress takes over and reduces learning. Maximum learning occurs when there is a moderate level of arousal. This initiates neural plasticity by increasing the production of neurotransmitters and

> Learning is highly dependent on the level of arousal of the learner.

neural growth hormones which in turn facilitate neural connections and cortical organization (Cozolino & Sprokay, 2001).

LeDoux (1996, p. 43) says that, "Bodily changes follow directly the PERCEPTION of the exciting fact, and that our feeling of the same changes as they occur IS the emotion." He also believes that "…once emotions occur, they become powerful indicators of future behavior." (LeDoux, 1996, p. 19) While we cannot "will" our emotions to occur—and understanding that emotions are things that happen to us rather than things we order to occur— we can set up situations where external events provide stimuli to trigger desired emotions (LeDoux, 1996). We do this regularly when we go to the movies or visit an amusement park, or even when we consume alcohol or stimulate our palate with a gourmet meal.

There is an optimum level of stress for each individual that facilitates learning. Excitement can serve as a strong motivation to drive people to learn, but not so strong that it becomes high stress moving to anxiety. For example, Merry sees adaptation not as a basic transformative change, but as having a new range of possibilities. Merry (1995) says that the natural resilience in people allows them to discover novel form of adaptation when the environment is changing. In other words, with a stressful external environment, people will naturally tend to find ways of reacting and adapting to that environment. See Figure 12-3.

Since stress is a *result of the perception of an individual of a given situation*, an individual can learn to control or minimize it. One approach is to perceive things from a different frame of reference and not judge a situation by the possibility of its outcomes. In other words, most stress is caused by anticipation of future events that offer a perceived threat of some nature. For example, imagine the amount of stress occurring in this scenario. You are a young woman in her early 20's lost in the ghettos of New York, hurrying toward the nearest subway station. Out of the corner of your eye you notice two large men dressed in black that appear to be following you. You speed up and they speed up, shortening the distance between you. You turn a corner, and now they are right behind you. You are in a near panic as one of them grabs your elbow from behind and says, "Excuse me, mam, you dropped your wallet. Here it is."

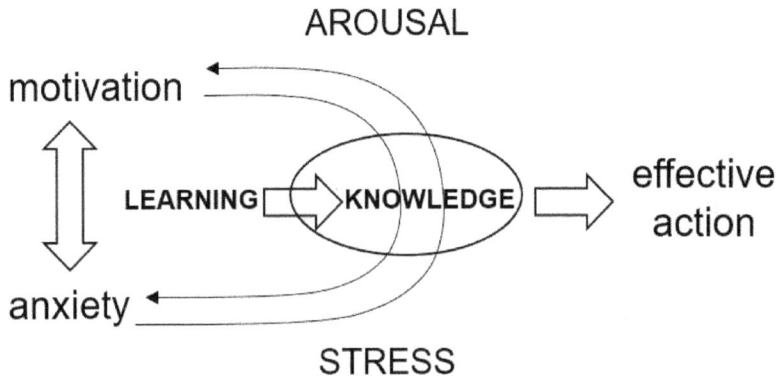

Figure 12-3. *An optimal level of stress facilitates learning.*

As another example, imagine you are the middle-aged father of a 19 year old son who is out on a late date. The phone rings. "Hello, Mr. Smith? This is Mercy Hospital. Do you have a son named John? … He's been in an accident … I'm sorry, he's been pronounced dead." As you hang of the phone your whole life spins in front of you. You are crushed; your body fails you. Two minutes later the phone rings again. "Mr. Smith? … I'm sorry, we got the wrong John Smith. This is not your son." And just then your son walks through the door smiling after a pleasant evening with that special someone in his life.

Situations occur throughout life that help us understand who we are and how well we handle stress. When these situations become closer and closer, it is paramount that we shift our frames of reference to consider them from an external viewpoint. Emotions are wonderful indicators of our preferences, and without them we would have no judgment; would not be able to make decisions. But that is just the role they need to play in a CUCA environment, when things are not in our direct control and the future is unknown.

This was driven home to the authors several years ago when we took a propjet from Washington, D.C. to New York. As what was to be a short hop dragged beyond an hour and a half, we began to wonder what was happening. We were no longer circling LaGuardia Airport (where we had been scheduled to land) but were over JFK International Airport, making a low pass with a dozen emergency vehicles (with lights flashing) following along under us. The pilots announced that while our landing gear was down and they felt everything was fine, the light didn't show that it was locked. We continued circling after that announcement, clearly getting rid of excess fuel. As panic took hold in the cabin, some people were struck silent, others couldn't stop talking, and many were praying while tightly gripping the arms of their seats. But two people on board were smiling. There was nothing they could do to change whatever was going to happen. They were in a state of wonderment, thinking excitedly "What's next?"

Pattern Thinking

Another approach is to study the trying times and the content and context of your situation to identify patterns of change and the underlying principles or drivers of the environment that generate the changes, unpredictability and apparent complexities. Much of this kind of knowledge may be in your unconscious—particularly if you have deliberately looked for these characteristics. Thus, you may not be consciously aware of them but your unconscious can, and often will, be aware of them if you observe and study the situation. Although unknown to you, you are creating knowledge in the form of understanding, meaning, insight, patterns and heuristics in your mind, albeit mostly in the unconscious part.

As we are exposed to more diverse and varying conditions, the brain creates new patterns and strengths of connections and thereby changes its physiological structure (Kandel, 2006). It is also true that the structure of the brain—containing a huge number of networks of neurons—significantly influences how incoming signals representing new thoughts (that is, patterns composed of networks of neurons) are formed. These new patterns entering the brain associate or connect with patterns already in the brain.

> Thoughts affect the patterns and strengths of connections in the physiological structure of the brain; and that structure significantly influences how new thoughts are formed.

Pattern thinking, an integrative competency, is not primarily *thinking through* patterns, although over time this will occur, rather it is *looking for* patterns in the outside world, and bringing them into your conscious awareness. The intent of Pattern Thinking is to **let the pattern emerge** as a mode of understanding a situation, purposefully thinking about external patterns in order to understand, solve problems, create new ideas and improve your capacity to forecast the outcomes of decisions.

Thinking about patterns is different than thinking with patterns. If you start with a specific pattern in mind, no doubt you will find it. This is the same phenomenon that occurs when you purchase a new car and you begin seeing similar cars every time you are on the freeway, although you'd never noticed them before. However, that being said, **pattern emergence can be stimulated by other patterns**. For example, the Systems Thinking approach developed by Peter Senge is based on matching a recurring set of relationships (archetypes) to a situation at hand. While this force-fitting can certainly help facilitate an understanding of causal relationships in simple and complicated situations, recall that complexity infers the inability to understand something due to the large number of unpredictable relationships and nonlinearity. We must then move to complexity thinking, building the ability to recognize, comprehend and learn how to influence complex systems (Bennet & Bennet, 2013). Yet once you have used the models over and over again, you begin to think systems and discover systems patterns beyond the archetypes. Pattern Thinking utilizes both systems thinking *and* complexity thinking.

REFLECT:

Is my stress level too high to facilitate learning?

Am I able to identify patterns in problems that emerge at work?

From the neuroscience perspective, Pattern Thinking involves mental exercise that stimulates the brain. The best mental exercise is new learning in multiple areas of the brain, acquiring new knowledge and doing things you've never done before (Amen, 2005). Making new connections, seeing new relationships, and bringing patterns into your conscious stream of thought does just that.

When addressing a difficult situation, there is not a cause-and-effect relationship with the amount and depth of study and the potential for discovering a solution or solution set. Individuals who are continuous learners, regardless of their focus of learning or areas of passion, will often see patterns that will suggest decision directions. Once in the middle of a situation, even the most rigorous focus and attention to detail may not present solutions. However, this type of rigor is supplying your unconscious with additional patterns to complex with all your experiences of life. While you may not have immediate answers, you are accelerating your unconscious learning (your unconscious can detect patterns that your conscious mind cannot) and increasing the potential for intuitive insights.

The above discussion brings home the fact that the mind/brain develops robustness and deep understanding derived from its capacity to use past learning and memories to complete incoming information. Instead of storing all the details, it stores only meaningful information in invariant form. This provides the ability to create and store higher-level patterns while simultaneously semantically complexing incoming information with internal memories, adapting those memories to the situation at hand. Through these processes—and many more that are not yet understood—the brain supports survival and sustainability in a complex and unpredictable world.

While there are many aspects to Pattern Thinking—including systems and complexity thinking discussed earlier—below we focus on the following: anticipating the future, hierarchy as a tool, effortful learning, symbolic representation, and shifting frames of reference. Note that these are not tools used independently of each other.

Anticipating the Future.

A significant aspect of the mind/brain is its capability to continually make sense of its environment and anticipate what's coming next. As Buzsaki states,

> ... brains are foretelling devices and their predictive powers emerge from the various rhythms they perpetually generate ... The specific physiological functions of brain rhythms vary from the obvious to the utterly impenetrable. (Buzaki, 2006, p. vii)

In other words, our behavior is closely related to our capacity to form accurate predictions. This perspective is reinforced by the neuroscientist Rudolfo Llinas who considered predicting the outcome of future events as the most important and common of all global brain functions (Llinas, 2001). The sense of movement of the body provides a simple demonstration of the need—and power—of anticipating the future. Imagine walking down a staircase and accidentally missing a step, recognizing the surprise one has when beginning to fall (Hawkins & Blakeslee, 2004). Since for thousands of years survival has depended upon humans being capable of anticipating their environment and taking the right actions to survive, perhaps it should be no surprise that that capability has come through the evolution of the brain. As Damasio explains,

> ...survival in a complex environment, that is, efficient management of life regulation, depends on taking the right action, and that, in turn, can be greatly improved by purposeful preview and manipulation of images in mind and optimal planning. Consciousness allowed the connection of the two disparate aspects of the process—inner life regulation and image making. (Damasio, 1999, p. 24)

The brain stores patterns in a hierarchical and nested fashion. Thoughts are represented by patterns of neuronal firings, their synaptic connections and the strengths between the synaptic spaces. For example, a single thought could be represented in the brain by a network of a million neurons, with each neuron connecting to anywhere from 1 to 10,000 other neurons (Ratey, 2001). Incoming external information (new information) is mixed, or associated, with internal information, creating new neuronal patterns that may represent understanding, meaning, and/or the anticipation of the consequences of actions, in other words, knowledge (Stonier, 1997). This continuous process of learning by creating new patterns in the mind and stored in the brain is called *associative patterning* (Bennet & Bennet, 2009b).

As a brief summary, our brain receives information from the outside world, stores them as memories and makes predictions by combining what it has seen before and what is happening now. In particular, the cortex is large and has a large memory capacity. It is constantly predicting what we will see, hear, and feel. This usually occurs in our unconscious. The reason we can do this is because our cortex has built a model of the world around us. Hawkins and Blakeslee (2004, p. 125) briefly described in detail the hierarchical and nested structure of the cortex and believe that this structure "stores a model of the hierarchical structure of the real world."

Hierarchy as a tool.

In a hierarchy the dominant structural element may be a central point such as in a circular structure, or have an axial symmetry. Wherever the central point (dominant structure) is located, each part is determined by where it is located in relation to the central point. While it is true that in a radial version of hierarchy the entire pattern may depend directly on an open center, most hierarchies consist of groups of subordinate hierarchies who in turn have groups of subordinate hierarchies, with each group having its own particular relation to the dominant center point (Kuntz, 1968). The core pattern stored in the brain could be described as a pattern of patterns with possibly both hierarchical and associative relationships to other patterns.

> The core pattern stored in the brain is a pattern of patterns, with possible hierarchical and associative relationships to other patterns.

Different models and theories come into play when looking at high-order patterns. The concept of heuristics is an excellent example. Heuristics are speculative formulations (or simple patterns) that serve as a guide to investigate the solution of a problem. Our personal ontology and taxonomy are another example. To consciously manage our knowledge, we must first define an organizational structure to place information into primary categories (for example, by type, use, importance, etc.) and then by terms to group like items (for example, finances, strategy, games, etc.). These concept categories are an ontology that maps the main ideas and their relationships. Once we have developed a conceptual map of our knowledge, then we can create a set of terms that will be used to label items according to the concepts described in the conceptual map. This structured set of terms is a taxonomy (Malafsky & Newman).

REFLECT:

Do I consciously exercise my predictive capabilities?

How would developing a knowledge taxonomy benefit me?

Effortful Learning and Decision-Making.

Because complex systems cannot be understood by analytical thinking or deductive reasoning, the deep knowledge created from effortful practice and the development of intuition and tacit knowledge through experience and continuous learning are essential

(Bennet & Bennet, 2008a; 2015a). Yates and Tschirhart propose that there are four ways that "deciders" make their decisions: analytic, rule-based, automatic and intuition. The analytic approach, using logic and analysis, works when the situation is not familiar, sufficient information is available and causality can be identified. In rule-based decisions the decision-maker applies previously known rules of the form if "a" then do "b". This applies in many situations that are commonly repeated. Automatic decision-making is where specific conditions arise and the decision-maker spontaneously takes a particular action "with negligible effort, control or self-insight. This mode is common in high-speed, frequently repeated situations." (Yates, J.F. and Tschirhart, 2006, p. 430) In the intuitive approach the decision-maker uses feelings and intuition based on past experience and, hopefully, effortful learning.

Effortful Learning, or what is often called deliberate practice, is critically important to achieve high levels of expertise. It consists of intense concentration, usually for only about one hour at a time, and about four hours per day. The focus is on developing meaning, insight, and judgment on

> Effortful learning is critically important to achieve high levels of expertise.

how the subject matter comes together and why it behaves the way it does. The learner continuously asks questions and seeks to find the answers. Such questions serve to test the learner's knowledge and, if possible, answers are found before moving on to the next level of learning. Creative ideas are tossed around to test learning and to look at the subject matter from several frames of reference. These often take the form of "what if" type questions that press the learner to anticipate the outcome of specific actions related to the material or situation.

Such effortful learning may also include the search for patterns, principles, relationships, sensitivities among key elements, concepts, and other aspects of the material or situation. If the objectives were to create knowledge relative to complex situations, the emphasis may also be on finding invariant patterns and fundamental drivers of the system's behavior. Examples would be linear and non-linear relationships, sources and sinks of energy or information, butterfly effects, time delays, self-organizing sub-systems, feedback loops, etc. Creating knowledge that helps to understand and make decisions on complex problems takes time, focused attention, feedback and a knowledge of how best each individual learns. Each learner must believe they can learn, be motivated to learn, have an open mind, and be willing to make mistakes.

If these ideas and practices are diligently applied, over time they will help build a knowledge base for understanding and working with challenging situations. Highly complex systems/problems such as those that can easily come up during trying times may not be comprehensible and seem unsolvable—and they may be unsolvable. However, if the individual has diligently studied and built deep knowledge related to similar situations their instincts, intuition and feelings may know more than they realize. Most of our learning rests quietly in the unconscious mind. We just have to be able to listen to it. But as a caution, Eric Kandel (2006) , warns that although the unconscious never lies, it is responding based on the information patterns (experiences) to which it has been exposed. From another point of view, it may be wrong. The self's job is to give its unconscious enough knowledge such that it won't be wrong, and to quieten the conscious mind in order to hear what the unconscious is trying to say.

Social Networking

We are social creatures. While this concept has been around for centuries, Cozolino (2006, p. 3) believes that we are just waking up to the complexity of our own brains, how they are linked together, and that "all of our biologies are interwoven". Studies in social neuroscience have affirmed that over the course of evolution physical mechanisms have developed in our brains to enable us to learn through social interactions. These physical mechanisms enable us to get the knowledge we need for survival (Johnson, 2006). People are in continuous, two-way interaction with those around them, and the brain is continuously changing in response. A great deal of this communication occurs in the unconscious (Bennet & Bennet, 2007b).

Global connectivity and the Internet are bringing about new modes of social networking. Historically, from the Total Quality perspective we learned about the power of teams and from the knowledge management perspective we learned about the value of communities, and we began to consider the importance of social capital in both cases. Teams had an action focus, a planned agenda; communities had a knowledge focus, with an emerging agenda. Both surfaced the need for developing and building on trusted relationships in order to leverage knowledge, facilitate learning from each other, and create deeper knowledge.

From a neuroscience perspective, and connected to our earlier treatment of stress in connection with Self Efficacy, trust in a relationship is very important in enhancing learning. When a secure, bonding relationship in which trust has been established occurs there is "a cascade of biochemical processes, stimulating and enhancing the growth and connectivity of neural networks throughout the brain." (Schore, 2002, p. 64; Cozolino, 2002, p. 191) This process promotes neural growth and learning. Further, Cozolino (2002) has found that social interaction and affective attunement actually contribute to the evolution and sculpting of the brain, that is, they not only stimulate the brain to grow, but facilitate organization and integration. An example of affective attunement is eye contact as expressed by the adage *the eyes are the seat of the soul*.

But what can we glean from the eyes over the Internet? The new concept of social networking—one that utilizes the Internet—demands a shift in our perceptions, and a further shift from relationship-based interactions to idea-based interactions. On first reflection, a considerable loss of context must be acknowledged and, as users flit from

> Social networking demands a shift in our perceptions, a shift from relationship-based interactions to idea-based interactions.

connection to connection, a plethora of interaction bereft of relationship building. What kind of trust does that represent?

Virtual networking primarily relies on the resonance of ideas to develop a level of trust. See Figure 3. This is quite different than the personal relationships or connections built up over time among personal and work interactions. However, those that connect continuously do build up a level of trust based on the responses of those with whom they interact (see the discussion of relationship network management below). Further, there is the concept of six degrees of separation that comes into play. If I know someone that you know who was a close colleague of someone else who owns a company that another individual is a partner in, then we have a starting place for building some level of trust. This phenomenon is particularly effective in the military. If an individual has served on the same ship at some point in their career, or experienced service in the same conflicted area of the world, there is an immediate understanding, a common platform to begin an exchange.

REFLECT:

Do I find myself continuously networking?

How might I better use this network as a learning experience?

Relationship Network Management (RNM).

Our everyday conversations lay the groundwork for the decisions we will make in the future. Therefore, since time is a scarce resource, it is critical to choose our interactions wisely.

RNM, an integrative competency, is an approach for increasing the leader's relationship capital. The relationship network is a matrix of people that consists of the sum of an individual's relationships, those individuals with whom the individual interacts, or has interacted with in the past, and has a connection or significant association (Bennet & Bennet, 2004). In short, all those with whom you have repeated interactions and comfortable conversations.

Whether virtual or face-to-face, relationships are ultimately about people and the way they interact with each other over long periods of time. There is value in connectedness and *contactivity*. The global mind described by Peter Russell (1995) compares the evolution of the telephone system and the Internet system increasing the connectedness of people and, as a result, their thought patterns. However, as one thought leader in the KMTL study noted, connectivity only has one dimension. This needs to be expanded to *contactivity*, which includes context and other senses.

The fundamental principle of success in relationships parallels Sun Tzu's fundamental principle of success in warfare, i.e., know thyself, know thy enemy (the other), and know the situation. Principles of relationship network management start with the individual (what the individual brings to a relationship in terms of values, ability to communicate, expertise and experience, ideas, and willingness to share and learn. Then, understanding the situation (virtual or face-to-face, open or guarded communication,

> Relationship Network Management begins with knowing your self, then with knowing the situation and understanding others.

content of exchange, purpose of interactions, etc.), and the other (trusted or unknown, values, communication skills, frame of reference, expertise and experience, and willingness to share and learn).

There are several critical concepts that successful relationship network management is built upon. These are:

* *Interdependency,* a state of mutual reliance, confidence, and trust.

* *Trust* based on integrity and consistency over time, saying what you mean, and following through on what you say.

* *Openness,* which is directly related to trust and a willingness to share.

* *Flow* of data, information and knowledge.

* *Equitability* in terms of fairness and reasonableness, with both sides getting something of value out of the relationship.

When we recognize the value of our relationship network, we can learn to consciously manage it. First, identify the people with whom you interact regularly; second, consciously choose to develop, expand, and actively sustain those positive relationships in terms of thought, feelings and actions; and third, stay open to sharing and learning through your relationship network.

Before identifying your relationship network, list the critical knowledge and skill areas which are needed to achieve your goals. Now, putting that aside for a short while, create a RNM Assessment Chart with the following columns: (a) Name and relationship, (b) Length of relationship, (c) Related experience and knowledge, (d) Access, (e) Willingness to share, (f) Follow-through, (g) Your feelings, and (h) Your contribution. You also need a column down the right-hand side that says "Notes and actions". Figure 12-4 will give you an idea of how this chart will look.

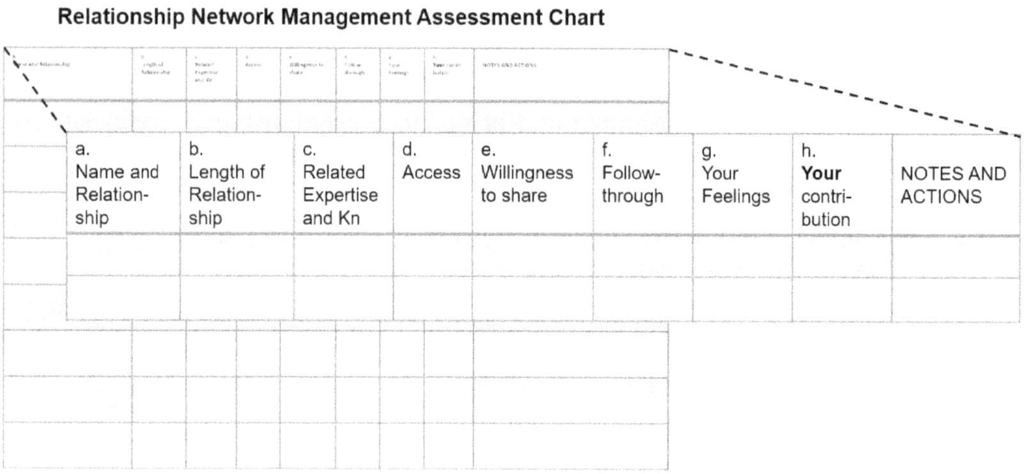

Relationship Network Management Assessment Chart

a. Name and Relationship	b. Length of Relationship	c. Related Expertise and Kn	d. Access	e. Willingness to share	f. Follow-through	g. Your Feelings	h. Your contribution	NOTES AND ACTIONS

Figure 12-4. *The Relationship Network Management Assessment Chart.*

Next, fill out columns (a) and (b), listing the individuals with whom you interact and the groups in which you participate. Examples of "relationships" would be friend, colleague, mentor, manager, etc. Assess columns (c) through (h) in terms of a strength scale from 1-10, with 1 being weak and 10 being strong. Column (g), "Your feelings", would be rated in terms of respect, trustworthiness and your ability to interact. Column (h), "Your contribution", refers to the level or value of knowledge you contribute to the relationship. Remember, one of the determinants of a good relationship network is interdependency. In columns (c) through (h), positive learning relationships would be those rated above the midpoint (5). Under "Notes and actions" write anything you think may be important to the relationship; for example, "Need to interact more.

From this simple chart, assess your gaps, that is, circle any number less than "5". Now, comparing your chart with your list of knowledge and skill areas, determine the relationships that need to be expanded or areas where you need to find individuals with whom you can interact. For example, if your numbers are low and a specific individual or team is important to accomplishing your goals, then action must be taken to build/expand that relationship and increase the assessment numbers (refer to the RNM key success factors). Add the actions you plan to take under "Notes and actions". It is necessary to periodically revisit this process as your knowledge needs—and relationships—change.

Final Thoughts:

The first time we thought about ourselves as social creatures was a bit of a shock. I guess if we'd thought about. Our brains actually need to seek out an affectively attuned other for learning. Affective attunement involves a mentor, coach or another significant individual who is trusted and capable of resonance with the learner. When this happens, a dialogue with such an individual can greatly help the sharing of understanding, developing meaning, anticipating the future with respect to actions, and receiving sensory feedback. As Johnson (2006) explains, affective attunement reduces fear, and creates a positive environment and motivation to learn.

Choose your network wisely and stay open to learning. At some point in the future you will make a decision based on a conversation you had today or last week, although you might not remember the conversation.

Chapter 13
Knowledge Capacities

Knowledge itself is a capacity. Recall that we define knowledge as a capacity, the capacity (potential or actual) to take effective action. Capacity is defined as the ability to receive, hold or absorb, a *potential for accomplishment* (*American Heritage Dictionary, 2006*). Capability is a subset of capacity, that is, a specific ability—a capacity to be used, treated or developed for a *specific purpose* (*American Heritage Dictionary*, 2006). Take the simple analogy of a bucket (capacity) which sits in the locker of a speedboat among various ropes and floats until needed for bailing water or holding your daily catch (capabilities). In a changing, uncertain and complex environment where surprises emerge and must be quickly handled, capacity is more important than capability for sustainability over time.

Our thoughts affect our mind and body. Thoughts in the mind are patterns of neuronal firings, which in turn change the physical structure of the brain. Simultaneously, the emotional tags connected to those thoughts affect the release of chemicals, which impact the neuronal junctions (synapses), which influence thoughts. This is at the core of the mind/brain/body system. This has only been understood the last decade. In 2000, Eric Kandel won the Nobel Prize for showing that when individuals learn, the wiring (neuronal patterns, connections, and synapse strengths) in their brain changes. He showed that when even simple information came into the brain it created a physical alteration of the *structure of neurons* that participate in the process. Thus, we are all continuously altering the patterns and structure of the connections in our brains. The conclusion is significant; thoughts change the physiological structure of our brains. This plasticity results from the connection between the mind (patterns in the brain) and the physical world (atoms and molecules of the brain). What and how we think and believe impacts our physical bodies (Medina, 2008; Kandel, 2007).

Thus, the knowledge worker has the capacity to shape and influence their future thinking and behaviors through current thoughts and behaviors. The knowledge capacities we present here are sets of ideas and ways of acting that are more general in nature than competencies, more core to a way of thinking and being, that specifically support building capacity for sustainability. The analogy here would be the building of an infrastructure of sorts relating to the mind/brain (information, knowledge and the structure and connection strengths of neurons within the brain).

Knowledge capacities complement six different ways that humans operate in the world. These are looking and seeing, feeling and touching, perceiving and representing, knowing and sensing, hearing and listening, and acting and being. Each of these sets has two concepts introduced because while they are related, there is clarity added by coupling the two concepts. Each area will be briefly addressed. See Figure 13-1.

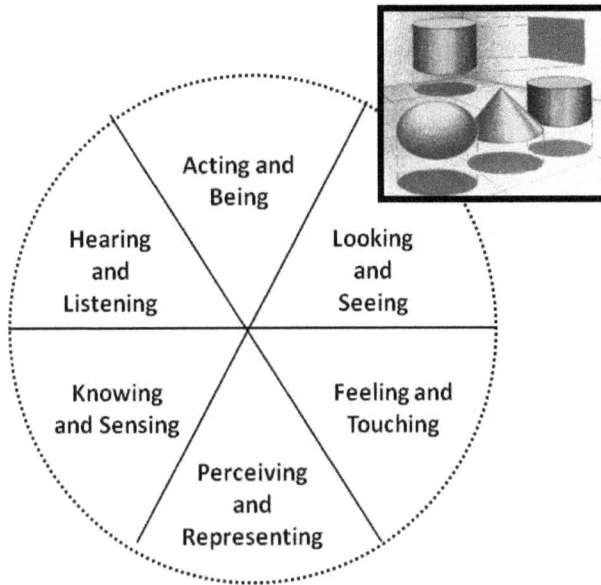

Figure 13-1. *Ways humans operate in the world.*

With our compliments (and apologies) to *Encarta World English Dictionary* (1999), we attach specific meanings to these six ways humans operate in the world, meanings that suggest ways of observing and processing the events that occur in our lives. Knowledge capacities are all about expanding the way we see those events in order to raise our awareness and, in the case of problem solving and decision-making, offering new ideas and an expanded set of potential solutions.

Looking and Seeing: To direct attention toward something in order to consider it; to have a clear understanding of something.

Feeling and Touching: The sensation felt when touching something; to have an effect or influence on somebody or something; to consider the response of others being touched.

Perceiving and Representing: To acquire information about the surrounding environment or situation; mentally interpreting information; an impression or attitude; ability to notice or discern.

Knowing and Sensing: Showing intelligence; understanding something intuitively; detecting and identifying a change in something.

Hearing and Listening: To be informed of something, especially being told about it; making a conscious effort to hear, to concentrate on somebody or something; to pay attention and take it into account.

Acting and Being: To do something to change a situation; to serve a particular purpose; to provide information (identity, nature, attributes, position or value); to have presence, to live; to happen or take place; to have a particular quality or attribute.

We suggest that one set of what we call knowledge capacities would include: Learning How to Learn (perceiving and representing), Shifting Frames of Reference (looking and seeing), Comprehending Diversity (perceiving and representing), Engaging Tacit Knowledge (knowing and sensing), Symbolic Representation (perceiving and representing) and Orchestrating Drive (acting and being). While this set is certainly not complete, each of these capacities will be briefly introduced below as example of knowledge capacities.

Learning How to Learn (perceiving and representing)

Every individual is unique. Each person has a unique DNA, unique early development history, and adult life experiences and challenges different from all other humans. This uniqueness means that each of us learns differently and, to maximize that learning, we must understand ourselves, how we think and feel about specific subjects and situations, and how we best learn. For example, people who are more visual learners would prefer learning through books, movies or databases; those who are more auditory would prefer learning through stories and dialogue; those who are kinesthetic would prefer learning through hands-on approaches such as role-playing.

A first step is to observe ourselves as we learn and assess our efficacy in different learning situations, noting what works well and what doesn't work well. We can also try adding different techniques that aid learning such as journaling, creating songs and stories, or asking others (and ourselves) key questions, then trying to answer those questions, recognizing the importance of emotions and repetitiveness in remembering and understanding. For skills that require body movements, then similar body movements must be included in the learning process. For skills that require mental agility, then mental games or simulations might be involved. In other words, the best way to learn is to understand your preferences and ensure that the learning process is consistent with the skill or knowledge you want to learn.

Undoubtedly, *the most important factor in learning is the desire to learn*, to understand the meaning, ramifications and potential impact of ideas, situations or events (Bennet & Bennet, 2008d). In the present and future CUCA world, learning—

that is, the creation and application of knowledge, the capacity to take effective action—is no longer just an advantage. It is a necessity. Because of their uniqueness, each knowledge worker must learn how they learn best; they cannot be taught by others.

There is a relationship between your own learning style preferences and the way you share. Effective facilitation and communication requires tailoring learning techniques to the preferred learning styles of your target audience. Applying multiple learning and communication styles enables you to reach target audiences with multiple preferences. Further, exposing multiple learning styles to the larger audience helps expand individual learning capacities, enriching their learning experience.

REFLECT:

Can I fill the capacity I have within to learn?

How do I best learn?

Shifting Frames of Reference (looking and seeing)

When we find ourselves in confusing situations, ambiguities or paradoxes where we don't know or understand what's happening, it is wise to recognize the limited mental capacity of a single viewpoint or frame of reference. Confusion, paradoxes and riddles are not made by external reality or the situation; they are created by our own limitations in thinking, language and perspective or viewpoint.

The patterns in the mind have strong associations built up through both experience and the developmental structure of the brain. For example, as children we learn to recognize the visual image of a "dog" and with experience associate that visual image with the word "dog". As our experience grows, we identify and learn to recognize attributes of the visual image of "dog" such as large, small, black, brown, head, tail, poodle, Akita, etc. The way we store those in the brain are as associations with the pattern known as "dog" to us, perhaps connected to the particular characteristics of a beloved childhood pet. Thus, when we think of a dog, we immediately associate other attributes to that thought.

Shifting Frames of Reference is the ability to see/perceive situations and their context through different lenses; for example, understanding an organization from the viewpoints of its executives, workforce, customers, banker, etc. The ability to shift frames of reference is enhanced by a diversity of experiences available to networked and interactive knowledge workers. Individuals who are subjected to a wide range of ideas and perspectives through social media are going to be much more attuned to difference, while at the same time becoming involved through dialogue. This participation with lots of people and interaction with differences helps develop a healthy self-image, and comfortable connections with different situations and people that build a feeling of "capability." Through these interactions, knowledge workers are actively doing things, which in and of themselves demonstrate their capability of interacting with the world. Through this broad set of reference experiences individuals can identify those disciplines or dimensions that they are excited about, and capable and competent to develop and grow from. This process can result in better decisions and choices that match their personal needs.

Frames of reference can be both expanding (as introduced above), and focusing and/or limiting, allowing the individual to go deeper in a bounded direction. Learning to consciously shift our frames of reference offers the self the opportunity to take a multidimensional approach in exploring the world around us. One approach is by looking at an issue from the viewpoint of different stakeholders. For example,

> Learning to consciously shift our frames of reference offers us the opportunity to take a multidimensional approach in exploring the world around us.

if you are looking at an organization problem, you might ask the following questions: How would our customers see this problem? How would other employees see this problem? How would senior management see this problem? How would the bank see this problem? As another example, when exploring a system's issue you might look at it from the inside out as well as the outside in, and then try to understand how you might see it differently from looking at it from the boundaries. Another example is learning to debate both sides of an issue. Still another approach is to look at an issue first as simple, then as complicated, then as complex and then as chaotic, each yielding a different potential decision set. A unique capability that develops as the self becomes proficient at shifting frames of reference is the ability to extend our visual and auditory sensing perception capabilities by analogy to other dimensions. For example, having the ability to "see" and "hear" some point in the future that is the result of a decision that is made today.

Dihedral Group Theory is a process that helps shift frames of reference. Thought processes of entrepreneurs like Steve Jobs follow six distinct shifts in perspective which directly correspond to the six permutations of what is known in mathematics as a Dihedral (3) Group. Each of the six models changes the relationship of subject/verb/object, offering the opportunity to discover hidden connections and unique insights, giving rise to faster innovation and potentially more significant breakthroughs (McCabe, 2012). This meaning-making approach also helps individuals understand their personal focus, that is, where their awareness is centered.

Comprehending Diversity (perceiving and representing)

From an internal perspective, quick responses require a diversity of responses from which to draw. Since there is not much time to effectively respond in a CUCA environment, it makes sense to explore and develop a variety of potential responses prior to their need. An example is the use of scenario building, a foresight methodology that has been well-developed and tested in government, business and education.

Scenarios are a form of story that can be used to consider possible, plausible, probable and preferable outcomes. Possible outcomes (what might happen) are based on future knowledge; plausible outcomes (what could happen) are based on current knowledge; probably outcomes (what will most likely happen) are based on current trends; and preferable outcomes (what you want to happen) are based on value judgments. For a well-connected knowledge worker, building scenarios can be both fruitful and fun. When facing surprises, scenarios can help in understanding new situations or at least foster a faster response by comparing the surprise with a related scenario.

From an external perspective, Comprehending Diversity means developing a competency in identifying and comprehending a wide variety of situations. For example, if you know nothing about complexity you won't be able to differentiate a complex system from a complicated system, each of which requires different sets of decisions and actions to achieve goals.

A first step is to recognize what you are looking at: the existence of diversity, the situation, and its context. Key questions: Is it diverse? Does it have many aspects that are in play or that may come into play? A second step is to comprehend it. *Vericate,* that is, consult a trusted ally, someone who understands the systems at play (introduced in Chapter 8). Develop knowledge about a situation to comprehend it within the context of the situation. Move through the knowledge chain to develop knowledge about the diversity, that is, awareness, understanding, meaning, insight, intuition, judgment, creativity, and anticipating the outcome of your decisions and actions.

Engaging Tacit Knowledge (knowing and sensing)

Knowledge starts as tacit knowledge, that is, the initial movement of knowledge is from its origins within individuals (in the unconscious) to an outward expression (driving effective action). Michael Polanyi, a professor of both chemistry and the social sciences, wrote in The Tacit Dimension that, "We start from the fact that we can know more than we can tell" (Polanyi, 1967, p. 108). He called this pre-logical phase of knowing tacit knowledge, that is, knowledge that cannot be articulated (Polanyi, 1958). Tacit knowledge can be thought of in terms of embodied, intuitive, affective, and spiritual, with each of these aspects representing different sources of tacit knowledge whose applicability, reliability and efficacy may vary greatly depending on the individual, the situation and the knowledge needed to take effective action. See Bennet and Bennet (2008a; 2015a).

The challenge is to build capacity (extraordinary consciousness) through creating greater connections with the unconscious, building and expanding the resources stored in the unconscious, deepening areas of

> Ways to engage tacit knowledge include surfacing, embedding, sharing and inducing resonance.

resonance, and sharing tacit resources among individuals. The Bennets developed a four-fold action model with nominal curves for building extraordinary consciousness within individuals that includes surfacing tacit knowledge, embedding tacit knowledge, sharing tacit knowledge, and inducing resonance. See Figure 13-2.

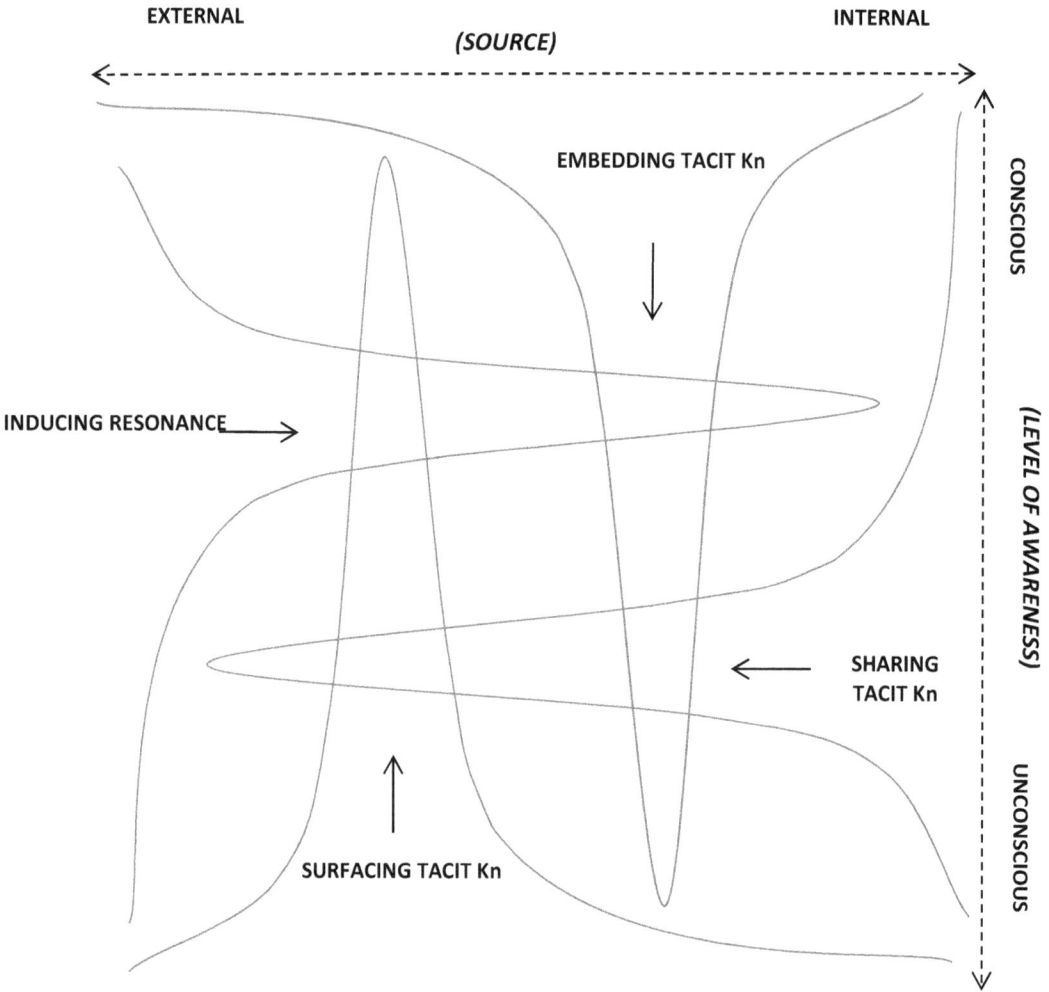

Figure 13-2. *Building extraordinary consciousness (Bennet & Bennet, 2008a; 2015a).*

Three ways to ***surface tacit knowledge*** are external triggering, self-collaboration and nurturing. Triggering can occur through conversations, dialogue and questions. Although collaboration is generally thought about as interactions among individuals and/or groups, there is another collaboration that is less understood. This is the process of individuals consciously collaborating with themselves. What this means is the conscious mind learning to communicate with, listen to, and trust its own unconscious. In order to build this trust, it is necessary for individuals to first recognize where their tacit knowledge is coming from. Since tacit knowledge is created from the continuous mixing of external information with internal information, this means that when you trust your unconscious you are trusting yourself! Your unconscious holds the results of the semantic complexing of all the experiences, learning, thoughts and feelings that occurred throughout your life. Thus, the process of associating (learning) in your unconscious is related to life-long conscious learning experiences (see the section below on embedding tacit knowledge).

One way to collaborate with yourself is through an internal dialogue. For example, accepting the authenticity of and listening deeply to a continuous stream of conscious thought while following the tenets of dialogue. Those tenets would include: withholding quick judgment, not demanding quick answers, and exploring underlying

> There are a number of ways to purposefully collaborate with yourself, including developing an internal dialogue and asking questions of yourself.

assumptions (Ellinor & Gerard, 1998), then looking for collaborative meaning between what you consciously think and what you feel. A second approach is to ask yourself a lot of questions related to the task at hand. Even if you don't think you know the answers, reflect carefully on the questions, and be patient. Sleeping on a question will often yield an answer the following morning. Your unconscious mind processes information 24/7 and exists to help you survive. It is not a figment of your imagination, or your enemy. Self-collaboration and nurturing can also be achieved through meditation, inner tasking, lucid dreaming, or hemispheric ssynchronization.[1]

Embedding tacit knowledge can be accomplished through purposeful learning, mimicry, practice, competence development or visual imagery coupled with practice. It can also be accomplished by placing yourself in an environment conducive to learning what you choose to learn. In the late 1990's, neuroscience research identified what are referred to as mirror neurons. As Dobb's explains,

> These neurons are scattered throughout key parts of the brain—the premotor cortex and centers for language, empathy and pain—and fire not only as we perform a certain action, but also when we watch someone else perform that action. (Dobbs, 2006, p. 22).

Watching a video is a cognitive form of mimicry that transfers actions, behaviors and most likely other cultural norms. Thus, when we see something being enacted, our mind creates the same patterns that we would use to enact that "something" ourselves (Gazzaniga, 2004). It would appear that they represent a mechanism for the direct transfer of tacit knowledge between individuals or throughout a culture.

The power (and difficulty) of ***sharing tacit knowledge*** has been recognized in organizations for years, and tapped into through the use of mentoring and shadowing programs to facilitate imitation and mimicry. More recently, it has become the focus of group learning, where communities and teams engage in dialogue focused on specific issues and, over time, develop a common frame of reference that results in language and understanding that can create solutions to complex problems.

Inducing resonance is a result of external stimuli resonating with internal information that brings it into conscious awareness. For example, through exposure to diverse, and often opposing, concepts that are well-grounded (such as occurs in a debate), it is possible to create a resonance within the mind that amplifies the meaning of the incoming information, increasing its emotional content and receptivity.

An example of inducing resonance can be seen in the recent movie, The Debaters. We would even go so far as to say that the purpose of a debate is to transfer tacit knowledge. Well-researched and well-grounded external information is communicated (explicit knowledge) tied to emotional tags (explicitly expressed). The beauty of this process is that this occurs on both sides of the debate question such that the active listener who has an interest in the area of the debate is pulled into one side or another. An eloquent speaker will try to speak from the audience's frame of reference to tap into their intuition. She will come across as confident, likeable and positive to transfer embodied tacit knowledge, and may well refer to higher order purpose, etc. to connect with the listener's spiritual tacit knowledge. A strong example of this occurs in the US Presidential debates. This also occurs in litigation, particularly in the closing arguments, where for opposing sides of an issue emotional tags are tied to a specific frame of reference regarding what has been presented.

Symbolic Representation (perceiving and representing)

Representations in terms of words and visuals are the tools of trade for facilitating common understanding. The mind/brain does not store exact replicas of past events or memories. Rather, it stores invariant representations that color the meaning or essence of incoming information (Hawkins, 2004). There is a hierarchy of information where hierarchy represents "an order of some complexity, in which the elements are distributed along the gradient of importance" (Kuntz, 1968, p. 162). This hierarchy of information is analogous to the physical design of the neocortex, "a sheet of cells the size of a dinner napkin as thick as six business cards, where the connections between various regions give the whole thing a hierarchical structure" (Hawkins, 2004, p. 109). There are six layers of hierarchical patterns in the architecture of the cortex. While only documented for the sense of vision, it appears that the patterns at the lowest level of the cortex are fast changing and spatially specific (highly situation dependent and context sensitive) while the patterns at the highest level are slow changing and spatially invariant (Hawkins, 2004). For example, values, theories, beliefs and assumptions created (over and over again) through past learning processes represent a higher level of invariant form, one that does not easily change, compared to lower level patterns (Bennet & Bennet, 2013).

Thus, once learned, the mind/brain can quickly associate with symbols which can represent large amounts of context yet be immediately understood and interpreted. As self, symbols are everywhere we look. Mathematics build upon hypotheses and relationships, that is, patterns, assumptions and relationships. Letters represent sounds, notes represent tones, pictures represent thoughts and beliefs, shapes of signs on the highway represent the context of rules, and so on. We use symbols to organize our thoughts.

> Once learned, the mind/brain can quickly associate with symbols which can represent large amounts of context yet be immediately understood and interpreted.

For example, in human face-to-face interactions it has long been recognized that non-verbals and voicing (tone, emphasis) can play a larger role in communication than the words that are exchanged. New patterns are emerging in social media that represent and convey these aspects of communication, helping provide the context and "feeling" for what is being said. For example, whether on Twitter on eMail, :) immediately conveys a smiley face, so much so that when these keystrokes are entered in MSWord followed by a space, they are immediately translated into ☺. As social media has matured, these symbols have become patterns of patterns, well understood by practicing social networkers and quickly conveying the message they are sending.

Then there are patterns over time: trends, cycles, spikes, curves, sinks, sources, and so on. Forecasters use scenario planning: setting up patterns, creating self-consistent patterns over time and looking at what happens. Scenario development can be used to create applicable knowledge by starting with the recent past and developing several possible scenarios for the future. Here you may have to identify trends by averaging over time, considering the most desirable, acceptable and least desirable possible outcomes. Knowledge can be developed from creating, studying and playing with the possible results of these scenarios. Other ways to think about forecasting is in terms of laying out a trail (a pattern) with milestones (symbols), and, of course, through dynamic modeling.

There is an important role that symmetry and parsimony play in patterns and in the physical world. Symmetry is the exact correspondence of form on opposite sides of a centerline or point (*American Heritage Dictionary*, 2006). Parsimony is the principle of least action or energy and conservation. Nature is fond of doing things in the most economical and efficient way. Since symbols are short forms of larger patterns, they help facilitate thinking about symmetry, and can help us recognize simpler solutions to issues and situations.

REFLECT:

Do I have special ways to tap into my tacit resources?

What symbols do I regularly use in messaging to convey feelings?

Orchestrating Drive (acting and being)

There are many wives' tales and beliefs about our personal energy. One is that we just have so much in a life, and we just sit down and die when it is spent. Another says the more you give away the more you have. Regardless of whether we refer to this energy as spark, subtle energy (metaphysics), prana (Hindu), chi (Chinese), libido (Freud), orgon energy (Reich), or any other of the numerous other descriptive terms, every individual possesses a life force or, as described by Henri Bergson,2 the élan vital, a source of efficient causation and evolution in nature. What we have learned about this energy—both by observation, and confirmed more recently through neuroscience findings—is its relationship to feelings. As Candace Pert, a research professor of physiology and biophysics at Georgetown University Medical Center, describes, "… this mysterious energy is actually the free-flow of information carried by the biochemicals of emotion, the neuropeptides and their receptors" (Pert, 1997, p. 276.).

While the expression of any strong emotion requires an energy output, the expression of negative emotions generally represents an expenditure of energy, and the expression of positive emotions generally represents a generator of energy. For example, consider the crowds following a close-tied football game. While all may be physically tired from the experience, those who supported the loosing team are generally depressed and drag home; those who supported the winning team are generally buoyant, and may well go out and celebrate.

By understanding—and using—the emotions as a personal guidance system and motivator, knowledge workers can orchestrate their energy output. For example, by interacting, working with, and writing about ideas that have personal resonance, a knowledge worker is generating energy while expending energy, thus extending their ability to contribute and influence. For many of the reasons already discussed earlier in this book, we would contend that this is naturally occurring in leaders emerging out of the tech savvy generations.

Final Thoughts

As situations become more complex, the nature of learning, knowledge, and action shifts. Building capacity lays the groundwork for those shifts. Six areas were introduced that are general in nature, but core to a way of being, and specifically support developing capacity for sustainability. These Capacities are: Learning How to Learn, Embracing Alignment, Shifting Frames of Reference, Comprehending Diversity, Exploiting Idea Resonance, Engaging Tacit Knowledge, Employing Invariant Symbols, and Orchestrating Drive.

How close are we to the point of singularity?[3] While our technology systems are not yet implanted, they are near at hand and have extended and expanded our sensory capabilities in terms of space and time. As our neurons fire and connect and our brain restructures in a continuous loop of learning and changing, we are beginning to understand how important our choices and the way we think and act upon the world are to us as individuals and to the connected reality in which we function.

If we think we can or can't, we're right.[4] Now, all we need to do is make the best choices.

Chapter 14
Complexity Driven Simplicity

We have spent so many years trying to understand complexity and how to influence complex adaptive systems, people and organizations (see Bennet & Bennet, 2004; 2013). Yet, here we present a leadership phenomenon, the need for complexity driven simplicity, with the recognition of how easy it is to get caught down in the midst of a complex situation and how difficult it is to see the way ahead from that position. It is reminiscent of an age-old wisdom phrase: *flow above the drama*. Perhaps we can sum this chapter up by saying: *flow above the complexity*.

To build the necessary resonance, or drama, needed to fully understand this phenomenon, we first expand on the description of the current environment introduced in Chapter 1 as CUCA.

The New Reality[1]

Today there's a lot that is new, different, challenging, and hard to understand. There is the change of the pace of change and there are ever-changing ideas, products, processes, desires and needs of customers, rules, laws and regulations. There is change in the way we communicate and the speed of communication, change in our jobs and careers, and what we need to know and do. There is the change in weather patterns, travel processes, speed of products to market, expectations of workers, and the complexity of the problems we are asked to solve daily. There is change as we grow older, move our household, and see our children grow up and get married, all occurring in the fog of a changing threat and reality of global terrorism and weapons of mass destruction.

Amidst this change there is the heavy weight of **uncertainty**. With all of the economic, social, political and technological change there comes a creeping uncertainty about what to expect in the future. We say "creeping" because we easily create explanations of history and then, using our analytical insights, extrapolate the past into the future. This sometimes works, and when it is wrong, we shrug it off by saying "well no one can predict what is going to happen." *Then we repeat the same process the next time we make a decision, with the same results*. Back to Einstein, if you want things different in the future you can't keep doing things the way you have in the past.

In our organizations when there is a very important decision to make, we may use the Delphi technique or go for advice to futurists, experts who spend their lives studying the future. While these approaches can certainly provide some answers and good ideas to think about, there are no warrants on future predictions. *As our society speeds up, there is less time to make decisions, often more information available than we want, and so many choices and possibilities* that we either simplify by fiat or con ourselves into thinking that we are smart enough to make the right decision based on our past record (as we remember it). For a deep treatment of decision-making in this new reality, see Bennet and Bennet (2013).

However—and it is a major however—if the decision environment is changing in a substantial way that is unpredictable and unforeseeable, all of the planning and forecasting in the world will never allow us to consistently set and achieve clear targets and objectives, or to create a successful strategic path to continue from here to there. The entire world is becoming more tightly connected and smaller; technology provides instant communication and our symbols (money, data, information, and timing triggers for coordinated actions) move with the speed of light.

Evolution has clearly shown that complexity begets more complexity; this is how we have arrived as a species from a simple single celled amoeba to where we are now. As our systems continue to increase in **complexity** with the Internet, world GPS tracking, products, power grids, medical support, water supply, big data, distribution, etc., they *become more vulnerable to failure*, either from natural causes or from intentional sabotage. There are a number of reasons this is true. First, as systems become more complex, they have more internal connections and networks, making them more susceptible to possible failures. Second, these same systems are—or can easily become—unpredictable because they no longer operate via identifiable cause-and-effect relationships. This is the essence of complexity. While each connection may or may not be causal, the number of connections, the possible feedback loops (or sneak circuits), the time delays and nonlinear relationships, plus the sensitivity to input values and the effect of their local environment, create a situation of non-predictability.

> Evolution has clearly shown that complexity begets more complexity.

The more complex the more difficult to understand the outcome of many of our decisions by relying on Newtonian deterministic assumptions and the application of Aristotelian logic to understand our world. In other words, we may become victims of our past successes unless we admit the tremendous ability of Homo sapiens for self-delusion. Both unfortunately and fortunately, determined mostly by our own actions, we have entered a time in evolution where our reality has transformed itself from simplicity and slow change (hunter gatherer era) to medium change and complexity (farming, rise of civilizations, the Renaissance and the age of Reason) to an exponential rise in change and complexity starting with the industrial revolution to the unknown future of 2020-2050.

In short, our world is *accelerating toward greater complexity and increasing levels of entanglement*. This depth and breadth of change is leaving the Industrial Age in the dust. The end of the 20th century brought with it email, the Internet, computer viruses and spam killers. Today revolutionary technologies such as nanotechnology, biotechnology, quantum computers and neuroscientific instruments, coupled with dynamic economic shifts and culture clashes, are all interacting to produce a new emergent phenomenon—the new reality (TNR). Unless some terrible disaster such as a nuclear holocaust puts the world on a different timeline, this is the world in which we now live.

REFLECT:

As a leader, am I flowing above the complexity or drowning in it?

How are the shifts and changes in the world affecting me?

Simplicity as a Strategy

Our entire life is spent prioritizing, then interacting with the environment, and re-prioritizing. We are caught up in complexity, we seek structure, we simplify, we act, and repeat this cycle over and over again. Simplification reduces our own uncertainty, makes decisions easier, and allows logical explanations of those decisions. Simplicity captivates the mind. Complexity confuses, and forces us to use intuition and judgment, both difficult to explain to others. As humans we tend to continuously simplify to avoid being overwhelmed, to hide our confusion, and to become more focused and efficient.

In a simple, predictable world, this is rational and generally works well, although it is easy to ignore many incoming signals when we feel that they are not important. Unfortunately, in a complex situation and environment this approach can become dangerous, perhaps even disastrous. As Murray Gell-Mann (1995) states,

> One of the most important characteristics of complex non-linear systems is that they cannot, in general, be successfully analyzed by determining in advance a set of properties or aspects that are studied separately and then combining those partial approaches in an attempt to form a picture of the whole. Instead, it is necessary to look at the whole system, even if that means taking a crude look, and then allowing possible simplifications to emerge from the work. (Battram, 1996, p. 12)

We agree. Using a systems framework, understand the complexity of a system before you attempt to simplify it. As Covey (2004, p. 103) says, "We must *earn* a comprehension of the *nature* and root of the problems we face in organizations and likewise earn our learnings about the principles that govern the solutions by incorporating the new mind-set and skill-set they represent into our character." This calls for a combination of knowledge, attitude and skill.

This is not easy. Where complexity lives it is hard to separate the unimportant from the critical information, events, or signals. As Oliver Wendell Holmes is quoted as saying, "The only simplicity for which I would give a straw is that which is on the other side of the complex—not that which never has divined it." (Holmes & Pollock, 1971, p. 109)

The question becomes, *how to get to the other side of the complex?* What aspects of a complex situation *can* be simplified, and *how does* simplification benefit the overall solution set?

Discernment and Discretion

Two words that quickly come to the fore are discernment and discretion (D^2). Taken together, these terms address the concept of selection, valuing, and laying aside, i.e., the ability to identify and choose what is of value, and the equally difficult ability to toss aside that which is not of value. With the continuous increase of available information comes the need to quickly discern what information is of value to the organization, and what information can be considered "noise," and of no consequence to the organization (Bennet & Bennet, 2004).

D^2 can focus learning in the right directions to reduce error signals, confusion, and wasted effort. Recall that knowledge is the capacity to take effective action. The word

> Discernment and discretion can focus learning in the right directions to reduce error signals, confusion, and wasted effort.

effective is significant because of the inundation of possibilities and the chaotic nature of events in the environment of many extant firms. To learn to take effective action means to learn the relevant things, to unlearn those things that hide the right actions, and not fall prey to educated incapacity or information overload.

There is an optimum complexity for leading in a complex environment. In this context, complexity is taken to be a measure of the number of meaningful states that a system can have. Meaningful refers to those states that make a difference to the leader and their organization, that is, those states that influence the organization's ability to meet its goals and objectives.

D^2 can strongly contribute to achieving the optimum complexity for organizational success. Discrimination will significantly lower the number of states and hence the complexity of a system. It also injects the subjective interpretation of meaningfulness into the description, looking at the world from the leader's perspective, ideally aligned with the objectives, vision, history and culture of the organization. While evolving in a hyper-complex environment, the organization must optimize its own internal complexity and minimize external complexity by whatever means possible. Using its own criteria of meaningfulness, the organization must hunt for the strange attractors—the leverage points that count. Embracing discernment and discretion, the organization will ignore, or filter, external states that are unimportant to the organization's purpose, and internally—through collaborative leadership—generate new ways of taking advantage of opportunities or rebutting threats.

Another way to approach complexity using D^2 is from the discernment of *trust*. Recall that trust was listed as a foundational concept of collaborative leadership in Chapter 8. As the number of meaningful states increases, and after disregarding the "noise," trust of a system's operational readiness can be assigned to another collaborative leader. But Lewis (2013) points out that trusting is more than simply "citing" an expert or knowledge base—we always cede before we cite. Each leader is responsible for their decision to cede (concede) authority to another source as a credible source for that knowledge within that context. For example, we can cite a law and trust it as the authoritative answer, but we are responsible for knowing if we are citing a state law when there may be an overriding federal law. Or we could cite our manager as the requester of some action, but we would also be held responsible if that action was unlawful. And, some teachers disallow students to cite Wikipedia as an authoritative reference, in actuality due to not knowing the credibility of the material and to whom they are ceding their reasoning. Listing our qualifications and providing recent status provide others reason to cede to our authority and cite us from trust.

REFLECT:

Do I look at the whole complex system before trying to simplify it?

How do I use discernment and discretion (D^2) for selecting, valuing, and laying aside?

Tapping into Knowing

Similar to complexity, *knowledge begets knowledge*. In a global interactive environment, the more that is understood, the more there is to understand. All knowledge is not only situation dependent and context sensitive, but it can be considered imperfect and incomplete. This is because the world is continually shifting and changing and what we think we understand today may be a thing of the past tomorrow. Have no doubt, knowledge, at the core of what it is to be human, is a very real tool for navigating our world.

As part of a larger ecosystem there is another core tool that is in relationship to knowledge, that of knowing, tapping into our internal resources. *Knowledge enables knowing, and knowing inspires the creation of knowledge.* We have previously alluded to the concept of "knowing" but have not defined it; nor is this easy to do, since the word and concept are used in so many different ways. We consider knowing, connected at the center of the collaborative leader, as a *sense* that is supported by tacit knowledge, a cognizance, a conscious state of being aware or informed (Oxford, 2002, p. 1510). Poetically, it can best be described as: *seeing beyond images, hearing beyond words, sensing beyond appearances, and feeling beyond emotions.*

There are many ways to perceive the world. There is an innate way of knowing that makes it possible to know the right thing to do at every point without deep reflection or forward planning, but it often only occurs *after many years* of deep reflection and forward planning. This knowing begins with expanding our five external senses and increasing our ability to consciously integrate these sensory inputs with our tacit knowledge (embodied, intuitive and affective), that knowledge created by past learning experiences residing in the unconscious. This internal resource is *entangled with* the flow of spiritual tacit knowledge continuously available to each of us. Recall that spiritual alludes to standing in relationship to another in terms of the soul, the animating principle of human life, specifically focused on its moral aspects, the emotional part of human nature, and higher development of the mental faculties. In other words, knowing is the *sense* gained from experience that resides in the *subconscious* part of the mind *and* the energetic connection our mind enjoys with the *superconscious*.

The subconscious and superconscious are both part of our unconscious resources, with the subconscious directly supporting the embodied mind/brain and the superconscious focused on tacit resources involving larger moral aspects, the emotional part of human nature and the higher development of our mental faculties (our definition of spiritual). When engaged by a collaborative leader who recognizes the connectedness and interdependence of humanity, these resources are immeasurable.

> The subconscious directly supports the embodied mind/rain and the superconscious focuses on tacit resources involving larger moral aspects, the emotional part of human nature and the higher development of our mental faculties.

In Figure 14-1 below, the superconscious is described with the terms spiritual learning, higher guidance, values and morality, and love, all connected to the concept of the greater good. For example, love represents the concept of *agape*, explained by Thomas Aquinas (2015) as willing the good of another. It is also characterized as "pre-personality" to emphasize that there are no personal translators such as beliefs and mental models attached to this form of knowing. The flow of information from the superconscious is very much focused on the moment at hand and does not bring with it any awareness patterns that could cloud the individual's full field of perception.

In contrast, the memories stored in the subconscious are very much a part of the individual, and may be heavily influenced by an individual's perceptions and feelings at the time they were originally formed. Embodied tacit knowledge, also referred to as somatic knowledge, would be based on repeated physical patterns and preferences of personality expression while affective tacit knowledge, connected to emotions and feelings, would be based on the feelings connected with the personality of the leader. For example, if there was a traumatic event that occurred in childhood that produced a feeling of "helplessness," later in life there might be neuronal patterns that are triggered that reproduce this feeling when the adult encounters a similar situation. While these feelings may have been appropriate for the child, they would rarely be of service to an adult.

Intuitive tacit knowledge is what Damasio calls "the mysterious mechanism by which we arrive at the solution of a problem without reasoning toward it" (Damasio, 1994, p. 188). The unconscious works around the clock with a processing capability many times greater than that at the conscious level. This is why as the world grows more complex, decision-makers will depend more and more on their intuitive tacit knowledge. A form of knowing, deep tacit knowledge is created within our minds (or hearts or guts) over time through experience, contemplation, and unconscious processing such that it becomes a natural part of our being—not just something consciously learned, stored, and retrieved (Bennet & Bennet, 2007e). In other words, intuitive tacit knowledge is the result of continuous learning through experience!

> The unconscious works around the clock with a processing capability many times greater than that at the conscious level.

In Figure 14-1, the descriptive terms for the subconscious include life learning, memory, associative patterning, and material intellect. The subconscious is an autonomic system serving a life-support function. We all must realize that as part of the self, **the human *subconscious* is in service to the conscious mind**. It is not intended to dominate an individual's decision-making; rather, to serve as an information resource and a guidance system. The subconscious expands as it integrates and connects (complexes) all that we put into it through our five external senses. *It is at the conscious mind level that we develop our intellect and make choices that serve as the framework for our subconscious processing.*

REFLECT:

Am I able to tap into my resources of inner knowing?

Which tacit knowledges are the greatest service to me?

Figure 14-1 is a nominal graphic showing the continuous feedback loops between knowledge and knowing. Thinking about (potential) and experiencing (actual) effective action (knowledge) supports development of embodied, intuitive and affective tacit knowledges. When we recognize and use our sense of knowing—regardless of its origin—we are tapping into our tacit knowledge to inform our decisions and actions. These decisions and actions, and the feedback from taking those actions, in turn expand our knowledge base, much of which over time will become future tacit resources. Since our internal sense of knowing draws collectively from all areas of our tacit knowledge, the more we open to this inner sense, respond accordingly, and observe and reflect on feedback (reflective observation), the more our inner resources move beyond limited perceptions which may be connected to embedded childhood memories. An in-depth treatment of engaging tacit knowledge can be found in Bennet and Bennet (2015a).

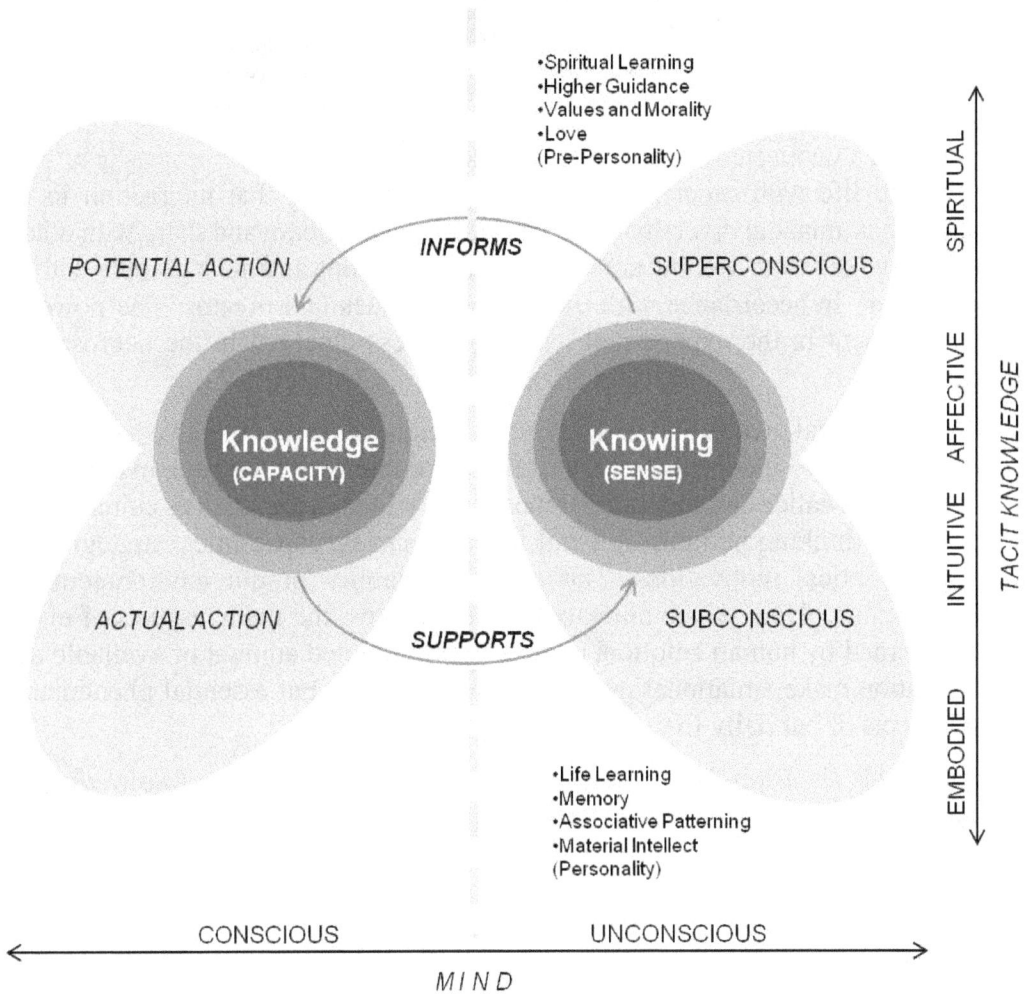

Figure 14-1. *The eternal loop of knowledge and knowing (Bennet & Bennet, 2013).*

Critical Areas of Knowing

The Knowing Framework encompasses three critical areas: knowing our self, knowing the other, and knowing the situation (the context of the environment).

Knowing our self includes learning to love and trust our self; all growth starts with an understanding of self. This includes deep reflection on our self in terms of beliefs, values, dreams and purpose for being, and appreciation for the unique beings that we are. It includes understanding of our goals, objectives, strengths and weaknesses in thought and action, and internal defenses and limitations. By knowing our self we learn to work within and around our limitations and to support our strengths, thus ensuring that the data, information, knowledge and wisdom informing our system is properly identified and interpreted. Further, knowing our self means recognizing that we are a social being, part of the large ecosystem we call Gaia and inextricably connected to other social beings around the world, which brings us to the second critical element: *knowing the other*.

> We are social beings, part of the large ecosystem we call Gaia and inextricably connected to other social beings around the world.

We live in a connected world, spending most of our waking life with other people, and often continuing that interaction in our dreams! There is amazing diversity in the world, so much to learn and share with others. Whether in love or at war, people are always in relationships and must grapple with the sense of "other" in accordance with their beliefs, values and dreams. The power of social engagement in the experiential learning process emerged in the neuroscience findings.

The third critical area is that of *knowing the situation* in as objective and realistic a manner as possible, understanding the situation, problem, or challenge in context. In the military this is called situational awareness and includes areas such as culture, goals and objectives, thinking patterns, internal inconsistencies, capabilities, strategies and tactics, and political motivations. The current dynamics of our environment, the multiple forces involved, the complexity of relationships, the many aspects of events that are governed by human emotion, and the unprecedented amount of available data and information make situational awareness a challenging but essential phenomenon in many aspects of our daily lives.

In our book *Decision-Making in The New Reality: Complexity, Knowledge and Knowing* (MQIPress, 2013), we discuss complex decision-making in terms of the complexity of situations, the complexity of decisions and the complexity of actions. It is easy to understand why we describe the collaborative leader of today as an intelligent complex adaptive system, that is, a leader who can co-evolve with a changing, uncertain and increasingly complex environment.

As we move away from predictable patterns susceptible to logic, leaders must become increasingly reliant on their "gut" instinct, that internal sense of knowing combined with high situational awareness and the tools of discernment and discretion. Knowing then becomes key to decision-making at all levels. The mental skills honed in knowing help leaders identify, interpret, make decisions, and take appropriate action in response to current situational assessments.

By exploring our sense of knowing we expand our understanding of our self, improve our awareness of the external world, learn how to tap into internal resources, and increase our learning skills to affect internal and external change. The concept of knowing focuses on the cognitive capabilities of observing and perceiving a situation; the cognitive processing that must occur to understand the external world and make maximum use of our internal cognitive capabilities; and the mechanism for creating deep knowledge and acting on that knowledge via the self as an agent of change. The Knowing Framework provides ideas for developing deep knowledge within the leader and sharing that knowledge with others to create new perceptions and levels of understanding. The full Knowing Framework is detailed in Bennet and Bennet (2013; 2015a).

It's a New World

We all have been touched by the current climate of increasing change, uncertainty and complexity. As we co-evolve with our environment, new characteristics and ways of thinking and being are emerging both in seasoned learners and in our younger generations. One of these characteristics could be described by the expression *knowing*, being open to the fullness of who we are. The global network providing connectivity and communication between the collaborative leader and the world provides greater access to our sense of knowing and expanded opportunity for learning. We, indeed, have entered a new way of being—amongst the complexity, a simpler way of being—in a new world.

[Intentionally left blank]

Section V
Thought Leadership

With the Internet came global connectivity such that leaders at all levels had greater access to an exponentially expanding amount of information. And thought that had been vibrating around the word collided with the expanding minds of leaders at all levels of the organization and society. Out of this melee patterns appear and new thought emerges, and our threshold for learning[1] rises higher and higher, with our knowledge coming ever closer to intelligent activity.

This section is about how thought leaders feel about thought leading. Through the years we've had the opportunity to work with thought leaders around the globe. One group was comprised of over 100 senior leaders from more than 20 U.S. government organizations; another the senior leadership of a military organization; and dozens of leadership groups from not-for-profits and different sectors of private industry. One expansive study (the KMTL study) involved thought leaders in the field of knowledge management from four continents. Although the focus of this study was on passion and the field of knowledge management, what emerged from those interactions in terms of thought leading and values was spectacular. This is the first time this rich material has been organized and made available to the general public. Thus, you will find this section quite different than the previous four sections in this book. Since each of these thought leaders released this material at the time of the study, we will include stories and names that undoubtedly many of you will recognize. There is so much learning for all of us from this material!

In Chapter 15 we first explore the concept of thought leader, taking a closer look at various characteristics before delving into the effects of being a thought leader. The Leader Within, the title of Chapter 16, refers to the belief and value sets of thought leaders. We take an extensive look at the material emerging from the KMTL study and provide a deeper look in Appendix D, supporting this chapter. As we come to the end of the chapter, we present several higher-order beliefs for your reflection.

Chapter 17 deals with ideas, the offspring of thought leaders. Did you know your mind is an associative patterner? Yep, all of this stuff applies to you as well as the thought leaders we're talking about in the book. We asked them how they get their inspiration, and how they feel about their ideas when they leave home. Where do you get your inspiration?

We're going to end on a high note. With lots of passion. In the course of this work we developed a passion model, that is, all the types of things that excite our passion. This will be found in Chapter 18. We challenge you to look closely at this model. These are the very same things that excite your passion! And we know if you've hung in this long with us in this book that you've got a lot of thoughts floating around banging themselves to the inside of your skull. Okay, let them out. It's okay. It's time to come out into the light. We know who you are, and so do you.

We hope you enjoy this section as much as we enjoyed pulling it together.

Chapter 15
The Thought Leader

The term *thought leader* is one that emerged just before the turn of the century. In 1998, Booz, Allen & Hamilton, working with the world's largest companies and those that lead them, interviewed top executives, authors and academicians between 1995 and 1997. These interviews addressed the big concerns such as defining values and vision, managing people and risk, adapting to changed markets and new technology, and assessing performance and portfolio mix. When the results were in, Brian N. Dickie, the President and COO of Booz-Allen & Hamilton, stated:

> [These issues] have only become more important as competition intensifies, the speed of computers multiplies, and the economy becomes increasingly global. At the same time, because of external pressures and changing management approaches, new ways of thinking about those concerns have swept through boardrooms and across factory floors with remarkable synchronicity, as shown by this collection of interviews . . . . We call this cutting-edge group 'Thought Leaders'. (Kurtzman, 1998, p. xi).

The 2003 publication of *The Ultimate Book of Business Thinking* cites thought leadership as an idea that has delivered (or has the potential of delivering) significant and lasting benefits. As we moved solidly into the new century, Des Dearlove stated that the "top consulting firms now invest millions on thought leadership as a brand-building strategy. In an ideas business, it is a competitive advantage to have more and better ideas. The battle for thought leadership is incredibly intense" (Dearlove, 2003, p. 230). We would shift this focus to collaborative advantage.

In 2005 we published a study of thought leaders in the field of knowledge management (KM) (hereinafter referred to as the KMTL study).[1] In the field of KM, Mary Durham with the Genzyme Corporation found that there were three individual roles central to successful KM initiatives: line management, moderator, and thought leaders (Durham, 2004). Thought leader—as much a social role as the command of knowledge—goes beyond subject matter expertise, implying leadership and a willingness to assert direction. In her words,

> The social role of thought leadership goes beyond subject matter expertise, implying leadership and a willingness to assert direction.

> Thought leaders can articulate vision . . . and hone in on the core issues. They possess social capital . . . influence . . . actively mentor others . . . generate novel ideas and connections. Further, they have earned the respect of their colleagues, and their leadership is not only asserted but acknowledged. (Durham, 2004, p. 306)

In contrast, in mid-2003, Tom Davenport and Larry Prusak published a book entitled *What's the Big Idea? Creating and Capitalizing on the Best Management Thinking*. The book was a result of interviewing gurus and what they call "idea practitioners". Idea practitioners are defined as individuals who use business improvement ideas to bring about change in organizations. They were identified through interactions with the authors or their network of associates. Gurus must do three things: "interact with companies, think and write, and present their ideas at meetings and conferences" (Davenport & Prusak, 2003, p. 74). In this context, "idea" is synonymous with "thought"; i.e., these idea practitioners take on the role of thought leaders within their organizations or networks.

In other words, there are thought leaders who are highly visible and those who take on local roles. This drives us to consider thought leaders in terms of tiers, noting that there are (1) giants in related fields who have contributed to knowledge strategies but hold their focus in their primary field, (2) the widely-recognized thought leaders of any field (those who publish, speak, teach, share, consult widely, etc.), and (3) individuals who are less visible, working behind the public scenes, serving as leaders in associations and/or organizational implementation. Another way of looking at this third group is as *those who are enormously gifted and talented, and whose ideas are actually permeating everyone else's work, but who are not recognized*. As one of the participants in the KMTL study stated, "These people are the ones who have helped all of us in moving forward, sometimes not by what they wrote or their speaking, but maybe the questions they ask. To me, these are the people who are the real thought leaders, the ones asking and tackling the really hard questions."

In this context, everyone who is out there thinking and contributing to new thought (and action, i.e., knowledge is actionable) is a thought leader! This is similar to Boden's (1991) breakdown of creativity into P-creative (psychological or personal) and H-creative (historical). P-thought leading would be fundamentally novel with respect to the individual mind and to those in the local environment (home, workplace, church, small community organizations, etc.). H-thought leading would be historically grounded, fundamentally novel with respect to the whole of recorded human history. By definition, H-thought leaders—the ones that are socially recognized as thought leaders—are also P-thought leaders, and P-thought leading is possible in every human being.

Global connectivity, access to an exponentially increasing amount of data and information, and expanding virtual relationship networks provide the opportunity for collaborative leaders to build on others' ideas and to contribute their own insights to the network. It follows that this common virtual availability of ideas combined with P-creativity supports the continual emergence of new ideas (P-thought leading) with the potential for similar ideas simultaneously emerging throughout the world. In this environment it is not just the creation of new ideas, but how quickly the organization can comprehend, select, and act on these new ideas that will mark them as leaders in their field (H-thought leading).

Other terms for a thought leader that emerged from our various research efforts include: thought inspirer (the joy of someone else getting an "ah ha!"), boundary spanner, new lens grinder, and envelope pusher. Thought inspirer refers to the joy of someone else getting an "ah ha!" when a thought leader is sharing words or reflections in response to questions. Boundary spanning is the ability to bridge, that is, opening the eyes and bringing new concepts to your part of the world that are already developed world-wide. The art of grinding conceptual lenses has two sides: how the thought leader does it for

> Boundary spanning is the ability to bridge, opening the eyes and bringing new concepts to your part of the world.

himself and, then, once it is done, how to communicate that new point of view. It's not a question of giving someone new lenses, *it's a question of letting them experience something so that they start to chew away and grind their own new lenses* or point of view. The term envelope pusher has been around a long time; that's all about getting the word out.

The Emergence of Thought

As we take a closer look at the concept of thought leadership, our focus will be from the viewpoint of business organizations, although many of the concepts can be extrapolated across to other fields of endeavor. This material, taken primarily from the KMTL study, represents the free flow of response triggered by specific questions. Answering questions is quite often a self-discovery process, triggering that which was tacit to surface and play with our conscious thought.

In his Symbiotic Table of Knowledge, Lewis (2013) forwards that questions come from two forces, curiosity and conviction. For example, when engaged in a dialogue questions are generally asked out of curiosity. In contrast, in a groupthink, participants ask collaborative questions from conviction, and in a debate participants ask competitive questions from conviction.

Further, each of these areas of force can be considered from three operations: conception, choice and certainty. Most of the questions asked of our thought leaders are driven by curiosity and produce conceptual responses. What are the characteristics of a thought leader? Do thought leaders interact? What are the effects of being a thought leader? These are the questions that start our conversation on thought leaders. What you choose to learn from them, of course, is a choice.

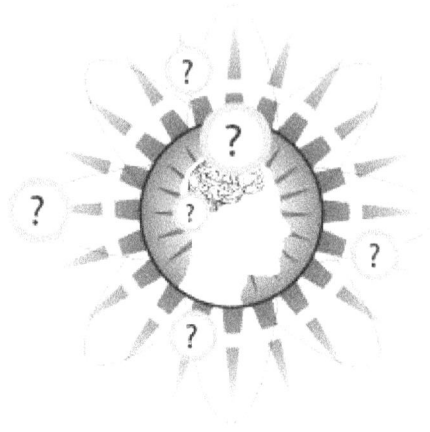

Before moving further into this chapter, we encourage you to consider yourself as a thought leader, which is true because, whether an H-thought leader or a P-thought leader, you have new thoughts emerge every day. This is what we describe as learning and, consider this, if you stop learning, you stop living. The responses below are broken down into the following focus areas: thought leader characteristics, pass it on, the circle of thought, and the effects of being a thought leader. As we move through these responses, we challenge you, as a thought leader, to stop and reflect wherever we have inserted a marker next to a characteristic, and ask the questions of yourself: Is this a characteristic that I have exhibited in some situation? Is this a characteristic I enjoyed? If the answer is yes to these two questions, then you are already on the road toward intelligent activity.

Thought Leader Characteristics

Thought leaders are people who have a *deep understanding of their field of focus*. From this framework, this would be a deep understanding of the business world. They have been in their field long enough, and have dealt with enough diversity, that they recognize patterns (moving toward deep knowledge) and are continuously developing themes in their thinking. Given an openness to learning and a comfort with systems, this may very well have moved into wisdom, that is, the ability to extrapolate the patterns from one domain of knowledge to another for the greater good (Bennet & Bennet, 2015a).

Thought leaders are clearly *learners*, a theme that appears throughout their response. One responder explained this in terms of: "Knowledge is not static. Knowledge is like water, when it stops flowing, it stinks. So to really know, you really have to be learning. When you stop learning, you stop knowing as well." This is consistent with our definition and use of knowledge, and also consistent with what it is to be human, that is, we are a verb, not a noun (Bennet & Bennet, 2015a.) What this means is that we are continuously processing incoming information, mixing it with that which we know, connecting the dots, creating knowledge for the situation at hand, and acting on that knowledge. Through learning, we can choose to co-evolve with our environment; indeed, collectively *creating* that environment based on our choices!

REFLECT:

Do I have a deep understanding of my field?

Am I a learner?

Now thought leaders are all very different people. In essence, no two people have ever been, or ever will be, alike! Each thought leader has different interests, diverse educations, varied professional experience, divergent passions, individuated thought patterns and connections, and a unique social network. Because of this, each brings the potential for uncommon contributions to collaborative leadership.

> Each thought leader brings the potential for uncommon contributions to collaborative leadership.

Appreciating this diversity, at the same time there are a number of traits that can be grouped, or categorized, which is what we do as conscious thinkers. For example, thought leaders *recognize in a textured and nuanced way the complexities of human behavior*. This is necessary to connect ideas and people. While leaders are generally thought of as being out in front with their ideas, they also have a following, which means that their ideas are understood by and resonate with others such that they are shaping other people's behaviors and activity. Thought leaders have credibility in terms of delivering contributions to real organizations. So, this means both being early in the marketplace of ideas and having the ability to communicate these ideas and influence others to act on these ideas, facilitating innovation.

There was general agreement that TLs are "addressing the unknown and able to develop the taxonomy and *language for the unknown* as well as apply it to develop something that has an impact on society." As one TL described, "These are people who are trying to attack the foundation of the goals of the field, trying to attack the foundation of the triad (people/process/technology) that is required to really address issues in any meaningful way."

Shifting perspectives, which was included in Chapter 13 as a knowledge capacity, is another theme. Thought leaders shape the thinking in a field, pushing the boundaries, giving fresh ideas in such a way that people walk away with a different perspective, which drives their decisions and actions. One TL says, "it's the originality of what they are trying to articulate, even though much of it might be considered common sense, it's the way they frame the apparent common sense." Another TL calls this conceptual blending, that is, the human capability of taking a concept with some relevance into a new concept or mental model that has the potential to provide a better approach, a better solution, an improvement. In this concept deep knowledge is not something that previously exists. Rather, people have to perform these conceptual blendings to fit the new context, the new challenges. "Therefore, you will never have deep understanding of things yet to come, you will get that deep understanding when the situation emerges, but a priori you would not have it. We're on a raft going down a white river and the actions respond when you get around the next corner and see the big rock in the middle." This is a wonderful example of the associative patterning power of the mind/brain and the need to co-evolve with your environment.

REFLECT:

Do you notice and honor diversity?

Can you look at challenges from different perspectives?

Abilities

Thought leaders are intelligent, creative in their thoughts, and relatively humble. They have the ability to articulate ideas very clearly; the ability to listen, and to be challenged and questioned; and the ability to think originally and come up with new fundamental ideas that challenge conventional wisdom.

Another common theme is *research*. Clearly all thought leaders have done some research, and are fairly grounded in research. They have the ability to integrate information, come up with ideas, create a vision for where these ideas can take us, and aren't afraid to act on their ideas to achieve that vision. This takes a form of courage. One TL tried to put into words what she was calling *courage*. "Some thought leaders have certainly done a great deal of research and the research reveals something we haven't quite understood so clearly before, and to some extent the research is also providing something that we all knew, but it's a little bit on the edge because it's presenting a new way of looking at something, and sometimes it goes a little against the grain, so it takes some courage to write some of those things that push the system."

Several TLs consider themselves martyrs. As one TL describes, "I'm one of those people who is prepared to try a new idea, to take the risk, and I'm prepared to lose my job over it if it comes to it. You often have to have a martyr before people will listen to something. What happens is the system starts to change as a result of the behavior, so the two interact with each other." Similarly, another TL shares, "There's a lot of fresh new ideas that are still applied to our work. So I believe that there are many things within economic sciences that are totally false.' An example is the idea of rational decision-making, and a lot of those basic such as the idea that competition is the best means to get efficiency. That's not the way nature works. *Nature works through collaboration being the best means toward effectiveness and efficiency.* As one TL concludes, "I think that many things are going to be seen through new eyes in the very, very near future."

REFLECT:

Do you come up with creative ideas?

Are you able to articulate these ideas and brave enough to put them into action?

Intangibles

Several responders specifically stated that thought leaders were *intrinsically motivated*. For example, one responder stated, "I don't think one of the people I know is motivated much, much more than intrinsically. This is what they do." Another responder described thought leaders as very giving and very generous of both their time and their ideas; and another responder said that thought leaders were idealists and dissatisfied with the status quo.

As Laurence Prusak sums up this intrinsic quality, "I've known many people who really spend a lot of time and energy writing books on management and they don't have to. They have plenty of money, they have plenty of status, they are senior executives at a consulting firm or business, but they do it anyway because obviously they're intrinsically motivated. They're playing to a different audience besides the masses or the people in their firm. They are playing to the gods." From this rhetoric and reflective thought, we can see why Larry Prusak was—and still is—a thought leader in the field of knowledge management.

Making a difference is a common theme. Dozens of thought leaders have confided that knowing they made a difference is the most important thing in their lives. We agree. The highest level of reward is a thought leader's ability to *make a difference*. Not surprisingly, this emerged as one of the rewards connected with thought leading (see the heading Effects of Being a Thought Leader below) and "making some sort of a difference for other people" was cited in Chapter 16 as a thought leader value.

There is also a degree of *altruism* involved in being a thought leader. For example, one responder said, "There's a degree of altruism because if you believe in this then it's natural to say I want other people to use it and benefit from it. And I think all these leaders do feel that way." Another TL brought up the natural leaning toward altruism when you put your ideas out there and let them go on to have a life of their own and hopefully help someone. As he explains, "I've basically given everyone the right to them. It excites me when I see people using them, independent of whether they know where they came from or not." In Chapter 17 we dig deeper into the relationship of thought leaders with their ideas.

Another aspect of this altruism is *moving the ball forward*. As one TL explains, "It's moving the ball forward in many different fronts for the next generation to grab hooks. It's putting out all these hooks for people to grab and build on." An analogy was provided by way of explication. Take someone who's a natural hitter but then goes and plays in a team with a Mickey Mantle. All of a sudden you start seeing how there is a certain copying, modeling of the grip of the bat. In some cases, it's not like Mickey Mantle was necessarily coaching, but there was a certain aspect of mentoring, and you can then start to trace those influences. This is where tacit knowledge is so important. This is the positive role thought leaders have on their field.

In general terms of *intangibles*, thought leaders have: a sense of mission; integrity, consistency and persistence; the courage to stand in what you believe; the humility to realize that it may not be right; an openness for listening and seeing new signals; a sincere desire to help people in organizations; passion of one sort or another; an expanded set of sensibilities; a true interest in improving the system; a social dynamic, a more full-blooded understanding of what it means to be human, what it means to be a worker or employee, and what learning really means in these complex settings; and an openness for listening and seeing new signals, but also *balancing that with personal wisdom and a very humble approach to moving along that, the rhythm related to applying the wisdom.* They also "become endlessly prolific." We can certainly attest to that attribute!

REFLECT:

Do you have a passion to make a difference in the world?

Do you get joy out of working with others?

Arrogance?

Several responders described thought leaders in terms of *more,* or *what they were not.* As an example of the more, one responder stated that the criteria for leadership was *more* than just a flash in the pan, but an on-going stream of visible contribution. From the what they were not point of view, a half dozen participants in the KMTL study said thought leaders are *not* arrogant. For example, one TL said, "I have a really hard time with individuals who appear to exhibit arrogance. Now these people [the TLs he was describing] are not necessarily humble; they are very confident of themselves, but this is not arrogance."

In contrast to this reference and in disagreement with the necessary quality of being humble introduced earlier, one TL felt that arrogance was important. Describing a specific individual, this contributor stated: "He's never going to make it because he's too nice about it; he doesn't have something distinctive. If you listen to their speeches, most of the thought leaders do a lot of negative stuff. They knock things down, bang, bang, bang, then they put their wonderful idea in place. Of course, there's nothing left but your idea, so it's a sort of arrogance creating inspiration space where people want to go, creating a willingness for people to go over the barricades." He provides the example of pioneers, who get shot in the back, not in the front, because people are behind them. "It's useful to have them break in the trail, but now they've broken the trail, so get them out of the way."

Clearly, the jury is out on whether arrogance is a necessary trait of thought leading. Certainly, the approach cited above is consistent with Kurt Lewin's by now almost classic three-stage model of change: unfreeze, change and refreeze, or in more blunt terms, break it, change it, fix it. While this approach may have been consistent with past practices, its value in today's environment has been reappraised (Burnes, 2004). The question is posed: Is it necessary to break something down in order to change it? Is it necessary to put down a current approach in order to have receptivity for a new approach? Is it necessary to junk another idea in order to have yours accepted? Is this collaborative leadership? We think not.

Affirming what emerged from the participants in the KMTL study, Debra Amidon offered ten characteristics she attributes to thought leaders (shared from a summary chapter of "Creating the Knowledge Based Business Research Report" which is on her website). "They are people of substance, of value, they value and they should be valued. They have vision, they are not afraid to put their vision into motion with their actions. They have a holistic perspective and are systematic in what it is they do, and they don't do it necessarily themselves, but usually in collaboration with others. They are effective communicators. They are effective in their interactions with purposeful conversations. They learn from these conversations. They tend to be open, transparent. They have integrity. They have convictions, and some of their convictions may not necessarily be aligned with my own, but I respect people who have convictions. And basically, I think thought leaders are learners."

What a wonderful diversity of opinion! Of course, this has been the historical approach of learning based on duality. We as humans need to know *what we don't like* in order to understand *what we do like*. Fortunately, with enough experience under the belt, this experiencing of duality is no longer required. With appreciation of the journey, we are able to rise above the lessons of duality and move into expression of our dreams and imagination. As you will see in Chapter 18, this is consistent with the passions of the dynamic thought leader group involved in the KMTL study.

Pass it On

Thought leaders live by the legacy of "pass it on", not only igniting action in the first tier of their relationships, but incentivizing the passing on of these ideas and the actions they drive. In short (and there is really no "short" for an intelligent complex adaptive system), collaborative thought leaders serve as catalysts to bring about conditions under which advances can be made.

Thought leaders have looked at their new ideas and treated them seriously, exploring their nuances and possibilities, and then communicating them well in ways that have succeeded *in influencing people's behavior*. In another thought leader's words, "Basically a thought leader, either through writing or through speaking or through both, *changes the way that people think about the world.*"

Again, openness and the free flow of ideas became a focus. As one TL stresses,

"It's very difficult, for example, to have freedom and democracy unless you have an open marketplace of ideas, ideas of course linked to knowledge. I think you cannot just absolutely stiff-arm and obliterate an idea just because you don't like it. You need to let it play out. *Ideas, by the way, are going to in some way have the marketplace vote on them, and more often than not you'll find that society will move in directions that are for the common good.* So openness is really, really important."

One thought leader went so far as to say that *the knowledge quality of a system is valued on its connectedness*. If knowledge functionally or basically is connectedness, then how important or unimportant they are is how they are related or not related to each other. This is similar to the understanding that knowledge is situation dependent and context sensitive, and also related to the incompleteness of all knowledge (Bennet & Bennet, 2015a).

The generic dimension is *consistency and authenticity*. An example is our biological wiring for knowledge, our neuro-system, which is basically a structure for building connectedness. At the upper most level, social network analysis portrays the same basic phenomenon, the extent to which significant elements react to each other and develop provocative interaction. Provocative does not just mean generating an economic or pragmatic value, rather it means generic in any form of value that is recognized as such by relevant agents. So, the fundamental dimension in terms of knowledge taking place is consistency or coherence or authenticity of the transactions between the elements in a system.

REFLECT:

Do you have the ability to influence others?

Do you have a wide network of friends and colleagues?

In terms of their ideas, thought leaders: break new ground; shape the discourse of the field; open your eyes on the subject; are out of the box when most people are in the box; are primarily theoretical but also with a lean toward the practical; have interesting thoughts that someone listens to; discuss things that other people don't discuss; challenge your assumptions; and help people make sense out of their ideas. This is *the ability to turn ideas into reality, not just theory.*

In terms of the delivery of those ideas, thought leaders: tend to engender trust; articulate ideas very clearly; share their thoughts freely; say something unexpected; can articulate their vision; listen very well (willing to suspend disbelief); excite people and show what's possible; and guide the thought processes in your head. The ability to articulate was stressed by one TL. "In order to be a thought leader, I guess you have to not only have some ideas but you also have to be able to express them in such a way that people use them

> Thought leaders have the ability to turn ideas into reality, not just theory.

so that *you have an impact*." Another noted that thought leaders could catch onto something that's already there, then "amplify it and cause us to see it more clearly and begin to make it so that we can use it and focus on it. They *legitimize it* in some sense." The question, of course, is whether you can get traction on your ideas, not whether you that this novel, breathtaking insight.

One responder who was successfully implementing a collaboration process for harvesting and restructuring relevant knowledge that could be reused, said that people seemed to be able to identify with this process very easily and recognize value in it. It was rewarding to him that a large number of people as well a management in this large organization were really demonstrating some passion around this approach. As he reflected, "I haven't quite figured out why, other than I think they really believe it's the right thing to do. Somehow I've matched up a large group of people's value systems with a process." This is clearly *the resonance of the field with the best of what it is to be human*. (Thought leader values are discussed in Chapter 16 and thought leader passion is discussed in Chapter 18.)

Thought leaders operate at the intersection of self and humanity, the internal and the external, in such a way as to offer the potential to make a difference for individuals and organizations. These thought leaders learn, share, teach, lead, and generally make sense of the world in their domain of expertise, moving toward what some of them refer to as a state of wisdom. Wisdom infers acting for the greater good. This intersection is briefly visualized in Figure 15-1.

In today's interconnected work, thought leaders are not alone. *You're never a thought leader by yourself.* As one TL expressed, "It's not this grand thing all by yourself somewhere. It's just putting that little piece of the puzzle in that lets you see the broader picture." This leads us to a short discussion of the influence thought leaders have on each other.

SHARING   TEACHING

STATE OF
WISDOM

LEARNING   LEADING

Thought
Leader

KM   KM

SELF   Passion   HUMANITY
              Creativity
              Integrity
              Courage

GROUNDED ON

-Sense of   -Holistic
  mission   perspective
-Expanded set   RESEARCH   -New view of
  of sensibilities   EXPERIENCE   reality
-Continuous   RELATIONSHIPS   -World problems
  thought   NETWORKING
                       VALUES

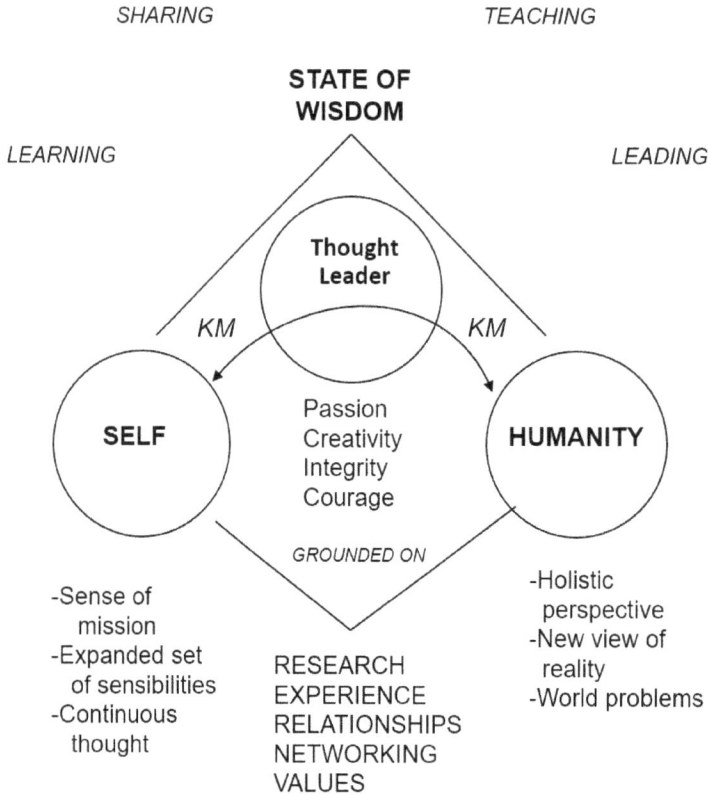

Figure 15-1. *Thought leaders operating at the edge of self and humanity.*

The Circle of Thought

The power of relationship network management (introduced in Chapter 12) is the recognition that the conversations you have today serve the decisions you make tomorrow. This is the power of the multidimensional unconscious, which observes, processes and associates all that it is exposed to through your choices. While we may not remember from whence comes our knowledge, through our experiences it does come, often in the form of intuition. Ideas spark ideas. Thought leaders spark thought leaders.

While agreeing that he was influenced by other thought leaders, one TL explained it's a *complex system*. "I don't know what words or articles that I read or presentations that I saw were decisive, or how each of those has influenced me. It's like a constant mixture of what I hear, learn, see, observe, do and think. So this is, I guess, the constant turbulence you have in your head. You have an idea, then all those thought leaders bring you input, which either explains something or challenges what you already know, and puts the whole system into turbulence again." The unconscious is working for you day and night, 24/7, processing and connecting ideas. Consistent with the complex adaptive systems that we are, it becomes difficult to trace the root of an idea, if, indeed, there is a root.

Another TL cited a similar effect: "I look at a variety of references and synthesize and integrate them, and then it becomes *hard to pinpoint one source from another*." This brings up questions that are at the very core of our global economic structure. Do ideas really belong to an individual or a company or a nation? CAN ideas be owned? In a changing, uncertain and complex world, WHY would we want to own them? If an individual is a verb, a continuous learner and creator of knowledge, what is the value— and danger—when we own/become our knowledge and cease learning?

Another TL shared a story about spending some time with a major thought leader in international politics, who was very humble in a way, a good listener and a quiet speaker. Suddenly he was spending more time talking to other people about this thought leader's ideas than his own ideas. He had not only begun to enculturate those ideas into his own intellectual space, but had also started to appropriate some of the thought leaders demure. This, of course, is who we are, the experiential learner. We can call this concept second-loop thought leading, where we think so highly of another thought leader's ideas that we embed them in ourselves and share those ideas outwardly.

Two other thought leaders noted the importance of *being a part of the conversation*. For example, Debra Amidon says, "People write books to share their experience and observations with others, but they are instruments for a conversation, that's what they are." Hubert Saint-Onge adds another viewpoint, "I was included in many conversations, and this is really in many ways the key. It's how you get included in many conversations that are really important. It becomes a privilege; you get exposed to ideas that you wouldn't have seen."

REFLECT:

Do you expose yourself to, and listen to, other's ideas?

Are you a part of the conversation?

Thought leaders provide a framework of ideas off of which others bounce *their* ideas. John Seely Brown describes, "Category of the future, the category of the human condition. *They provide us a vision that compels*, they help us envision what our organizations and societies could be like." Esko Kilpi shares, "If I see that there's something that I haven't been able to see before and I see a new approach, in a way I see *a new view of reality*. Then, of course, what I try to do is combine this new view of reality with my earlier experience, which means that I get new approaches to who I am and what I do." Very eloquently stated, this is the human process of associative patterning.

Each individual brings different perspectives to thought leading, from history, from science, from the arts. And among thought leaders in the same field, a shared language emerges. As one TL noted, "The language I've introduced has gotten picked up and is very commonly used. I know that people reference my work. It really isn't so much the content as it is the way people are with the questions, and how people model a way of being in the world." In contrast, another TL noted that other thought leaders didn't feel the need to do a citation.

> Each individual brings different perspectives to thought leading, from history, from science, from the arts.

"So, it's become a part of their lingo, and that's great!" This goes back to our earlier conversation regarding language and concepts picked up by the unconscious without conscious awareness from whence they came.

This *cross-pollinating of ideas* is not a simple process. As one TL says, "I like what I write to be connected to my own and other's research. So, you take other's ideas and blend them with yours, or push them forward, or use them as a support for the way you're thinking." TLs don't just take other's ideas, they try to adapt and adjust them to their own schema, creating a cohesive world view which belongs to them. Recall that each individual has an upper and lower threshold within which they operate. Ideas that are above the upper threshold but close enough to be accessible, that is, understood, or reached for and, by definition, the threshold adjusts upward. This incoming idea (information) is now associated with all that is known and brought into the situation and context of the moment, that is, creating a cohesive world view from the learner's point of view. Similarly, Ramon Barquin reflects, "The contribution that has been made to me by some of these folks is that it has *brought it all together*. Two plus two equals seven! It takes awhile to get there, and not everyone gets it, but when you have it all coming together it is very, very powerful!"

Some TLs reach purposefully out to other TLs, engaging in open exchanges that lead to new ideas, and some are affected, unconsciously, over time. For example, three TLs have mentoring relationships with other thought leaders. As one TL states, "People who have been through this process were able to provide context and perspective to me at times when I needed it to think about how I want to shape my own activities and initiatives." As an example, Karl Wiig shared two points he had learned from another TL: "One thing was that *things are never as they appear to be*, and the second thing is *for you to do something about anything, you have to delve deeply into it*."

Other TLs serve as sounding boards. An example of an open exchange is the response, "I had a conversation in the 80's actually sitting in an office tower in San Francisco. We called it mindcrafting, crafting our minds for doing something along the road. It's like crafting on a piece of wood but crafting on minds." And finally, there is the idea of *presencing*. "I try to be alive in my network and to be present to them and to be there when things aren't going so well." This is the penultimate value of networks (and families), a living presencing, a being there when they are needed.

REFLECT:

Are you able to imagine and vision an exciting future?

Do you sustain a living presence in your network?

The Effects of Being a Thought Leader

There are both tangible and intangible effects that result from being a thought leader. From a mental and emotional point of view, thought leaders perceive this role as ego-boosting, energizing, enjoyable, fascinating, fun, gratifying, happy, interesting, invigorating, joyful, motivating, pleasing, rewarding, satisfying, and stimulating. Being asked for your opinion is an incentive to keep thinking and writing, and inspires thought leaders to put energy into trying to do more. There is a satisfaction not only in the sharing but from seeing people get value out of sharing with each other; the satisfaction of "passing it on" discussed above. As one TL in the KMTL study shared, "Where a lot of reward was based on hierarchy, it is now based your own merit, your own original ideas, your own collaborative work. Your knowledge contribution takes you forward."

Because thought leaders generally resonate with the ideas emerging in the field upon which they focus, there is an excitement, or *passion*, around these ideas. This passion itself is part of the reward system; as one TL described, "giving wind to my sails". With passion, ideas glow white hot as opposed to being an ember, adding richness to life. Passion is explored more fully in Chapter 18.

Being a recognized thought leader increases effectiveness in *networking*. Because they are interested in what thought leaders have to say, people reach out to them, resulting in a large number of interactive relationships with many people around the world. These relationships, in turn, expand the thought leader's intellectual capital; a two-way gifting. This interactive networking spreads over to other recognized thought leaders, It is not uncommon to have leading thought leaders in a specific domain of knowledge interacting regularly. There is a sense of community as they learn from each other, and bounce ideas back and forth. Because they are engaging in enough different things, these ideas start to clash in really interesting ways. This is, of course, the stuff of creative abrasion.

One TL talked about *receiving a warm welcome by the community*. "I really wanted to be a part of this because people were far more interested in learning from each other and building off of each other's ideas than tearing each other down." This cohesiveness and connectedness of the field was expressed in several different ways. For example, one TL, describing a major conference he had promoted and attended, said a management guru in attendance could not believe the cohesiveness of the group. In the responder's words, "He watched our group for two days and said it was the most connected professional group he had ever seen."

Negative Effects of Thought Leading

There are potential negative effects in dealing with the demands of being a thought leader. One central theme is loneliness. It's tough being out there on the edge, knowing what needs to be done or what could be done, yet other can't see it. At any single point in time no one can see beyond their threshold of perception (based on a lifetime of living and learning). Thus, the challenge of the thought leader is to be able to express leading edge ideas at a level understandable to their potential followers, to demonstrate the usefulness of these ideas. See Chapter 17.

At first, I felt a little bit lonely, a lonely quest … It was very, very hard to find anyone to at least spend time in a relevant dialogue. And now I feel [I'm part of a] very, very active and enthusiastic community, a lot of **young people**, who are extremely motivated and fascinated and passionate about KM!"

Another issue is *demand and competition*. As one TL says, "It's just generated a surge of demand on my time, and there are a lot of decisions suddenly around what to focus on." A second TL says, "This is hard work, quite stressful because people want more from you."

Another TL forwards this is a more negative way, "The reality is that *this has become a very political and very competitive profession and some people are really ruthless and unfair to position themselves*." This second feeling was only expressed by one individual, while the other TLs interviewed talked about the high level of collaboration in the field.

Another is the difficulty of *staying ahead, but not too far ahead*. This is consistent with our understanding of the upper and lower thresholds of attention and learning. This can be a double-edged sword. "If you're a thought leader, you can be too far ahead of where people are, and completely lose them, so it's really forced me to *listen to people*. It's part of the philosophy of Disraeli who said, there they go, I must hurry and follow because I'm their leader. And that's exactly how I feel. I've got to *hurry and catch up because I'm supposed to be a leader*." Sometimes this takes patience and self confidence. "You can't just say here's the thought, and here's where it came from, and then let the audience do with it whatever they will." ***You can't argue someone into a new ide***a.

There is also the difficulty of *not slipping backwards*. As one TL explains, "The art is to *hold the line* with the ideas and principles so that we're not sucked right back into that old way of working. Sometimes I'll reach for an analogy, and the heads will start nodding, and I think great, we communicated, then I'll realize they just fell back into the old thinking." And then there is the fear of people not thinking their own thoughts, "One of the things that I'm very, very careful of is giving my opinion when someone asks it. Not that I'm scared to, I'm just cautious that I want to have enough time to understand the potential implications of what I might have to say before I say it." Perhaps this is also the recognition that knowledge in one context is not necessarily knowledge in another context. "The anxiety around that is not that I might come up with some bad opinions or wrong opinions; the thing that scares me is that if people rely upon my perspective of the world enough then they won't develop their own."

And, finally, a WARNING: **Thought leading is addictive!** One TL says, "It's a drug. You get big audiences and they feed you." And as another TL shares, "If the nutritious-ness of recognition becomes an addiction for your little ego, then, if you pursue this, your creativity is almost like the goose with the golden egg. It goes away. You can only get it if you don't pursue it! You just feed it. You feed the goose, but if you try to open that stomach to get the gold, you're not going to find gold."

Final Thoughts

One way to think of thought leaders is as T-shaped people, with the T representing the ability to connect people to people and ideas to ideas. as one TL describes, "That is one of our characteristics. Most of us, if not all of us, are not people you are going to find sitting in your average cube. Never. They're the people on the wagons heading west." There was agreement that thought leaders don't sit in a room and think about thought leading. THEY ARE ACTION ORIENTED. They write. They publish. They speak. "And that is one of the most important things about a leader. You've got to get out there!" They become part of the larger community of the field. "Because so much of this field is tied to communities and knowledge sharing, thought leaders voluntarily chat and speak and participate and become members of the community." In other words, thought leaders are also *practitioners operating in the community*. This proved to be the case for 33 of the 34 (97%) participants in the KMTL study; each considered themselves practitioners in some sense of the word as well as thought leaders.

As one thought leader concluded, "What we're doing, it's *in a way my life's work*, and if people find it valuable, it's a tremendous boost. If it works for them, then of course I'm extremely happy." Thought leaders share a feeling of being *pulled forward*. "I'm not pushing myself anymore. I feel as if I've come into a space which has a life of its own. And it just feels right. It feels right down to my core that I'm on the right track." And so it is.

Chapter 16
The Leader Within

As within, so without. Whether this is completely true or not, we have absolutely no idea! What we do know is that the way the mind/brain/body works has much to teach us about being a successful leader in a shifting, changing, complex environment. "Within"—the self—is where all our thoughts and feelings originate, with each moment of our lives dependent on *the current situation at hand complexed with everything we've ever experienced and learned*. Thus, there is a storehouse of information available to leaders at all levels. From the deepest levels of this storehouse—with many connections throughout the mind/brain—our beliefs reside and our values emerge, ever guiding us.

We cannot address collaborative leadership or thought leadership without a deeper discussion of *the leader within*, the patterns of synapse firings that are our beliefs and values, fueled by our emotions and feelings and shaping the very thoughts we think. We begin with revisiting the self.

The Self is in the Driver's Seat

Our genes do not control us. Epigenetics, the study of mechanisms by which the environment influences gene activity, provides strong indication that we as individuals may significantly influence our destiny through our own decisions and our ability to influence gene expression (Lipton, 2005). Epigenetics refers to processes that alter gene activity but do not change the DNA sequence, although these processes may lead to modifications that can be transmitted to daughter cells.

Genes can be considered as molecular blueprints, guidance documents if you will, for the construction of cells, tissues and organs. As Lipton (2005, p. 15) posits, "The environment serves as a 'contractor' who reads and engages those genetic blueprints and is ultimately responsible for the character of a cell's life." Thus, it is the awareness of the environment by a single cell, not the genes, that "sets into motion the mechanisms of life" (Lipton, 2005, p. 15).

This means that the genome is more fluid and responsive to its environment than was previously thought (Zull, 2002).

Further, the neural organization of our brain is not set in stone at birth (Byrnes, 2001). There is no doubt that in some areas genes play a significant role in our development. However, this neuroscience finding provides evidence that learners have the opportunity and challenge to make independent decisions and take actions to significantly influence and direct their learning and personal development (Bennet &

Bennet, 2015b). The myth that genes control destiny is no longer valid, and therefore this myth should no longer inhibit individuals from developing themselves to the maximum extent possible.

What epigenetics suggests is that the self is in control. For example, if the learner chooses positive and relevant beliefs toward learning, that individual will indeed be able to learn (Begley, 2007; Bownds, 1999; Lipton, 2005; Rose, 2005). **The power of the will and the choice of beliefs are in the hands of the individual.** It is no longer reasonable to sidestep personal responsibility under the guise that genes control destiny.

Beliefs and Values as Knowledge

The concepts of values, morality, ethics and truth appeared repeatedly throughout the KMTL study. Beliefs and values, often embedded with strong emotional tags, are context sensitive and situation dependent. If I have a decision to make, or am in a situation where I need to act, my response is driven by my basic beliefs and values, often through a feeling called to the surface—called to action—based on how they pertain to a certain situation at a particular time. So, I may have different values that are *pertinent to different situations at different times*, i.e., not necessarily a specific value that carries all the way through. As one TL in the KMTL study explained, our reactions to situations, meaning the way we handle situations, is essentially evoked through priming, and primed by our basic beliefs and values, and essentially called to the surface, called to interaction, based on recognition of how they apply to a certain situation as well as how well they deal with our basic values.

Even our deepest beliefs and values are context sensitive and situation dependent. For example, consider the slaughter of children in a school, a situation that has happened far too many times in recent history. Even with the strongest belief against killing, given the opportunity to protect these children by

> Even our deepest beliefs and values are context sensitive and situation dependent.

killing the perpetrator of this evil would you do so? Yes, of course, if there was any other way you would certainly attempt it first; but if there was no other way would you kill this perpetrator? As can clearly be seen, your choices are highly context sensitive and situation dependent. A strong value in one situation might be a weaker one in another situation, taking a life to defend life. As Henderson and Thompson (2003, p. 15) explain, "A value can be described as a preference, multiplied by its priority." Values provide guidelines around what is important and not important, and how to get things done to meet performance objectives and cope with the environment.

Consistent with Knowledge (Informing) and Knowledge (Proceeding), there is both an *information* (or content) part of values, and a *process* or *action* part of values, that is, Values (Informing) and Values (Proceeding). Values (Informing) is that which is highly regarded, perceived as worthy or desirable, and Values (Proceeding) is the way values are put together and acted upon in a specific situation or context.

Values (Informing) provide a central core of meanings and feelings which influence what people see, think, and feel, providing the meanings they subscribe to what they see and feel, and guiding how they evaluate alternatives, make decisions, and take actions, Values (Proceeding). Values (Informing) also influence how people see, think, feel about and interact with dimensions such as time, change, activity, human nature, and relationships, and artifacts and tools such as technology.

Shared values mean that the personal values of a group of individuals are congruent with each other and, in an organizational setting, consistent with their organization's values. Shared values provide a common context for understanding and interpreting the rapid proliferation of information from the environment and using that information to create knowledge that leads to quality decisions and the capacity to take effective action.

The personal values of a decision-maker—and by decision-maker we infer each and every individual who walks this Earth—are also likely to *represent generational values*, and can exercise tremendous influence over decisions regarding how to solve a problem and take the best action in a situation. German sociologist Karl Mannheim forwards that a person's thoughts, feelings and behaviors, including their values, are shaped by the generation to which a person belongs (Mannheim, 1980).

Recognizing the new social knowledge paradigm—which supports the creation, leveraging and application of knowledge—the core and operational values linked to this generation of decision-makers include integrity, empathy, transparency, participation, collaboration, contribution, learning and creativity (Avedisian & Bennet, 2010; Bennet & Bennet, 2015a). Collaboration is a core value embraced by tech savvy generations, involving engagement and participation. "Collaboration as Net Geners know it, is achieving something *with* other people, experiencing power through other people, not by ordering a gaggle of followers to do your bidding" (Tapscott, 2009, p. 163). As noted by a student researcher, "Collaboration and communication are second nature for the Millennial generation" (Panetta, 2013, p. 51). This bodes well for collaborative leadership.

Values are an emergent phenomena. This idea of emergence has only recently come into the mainstream of businesses. Through most of the last century we were still living blindly in a cause-and-effect world, where we honestly believed that certain behaviors and actions would cause certain results. Emergence, and the concept it represents, helps provide us a way of thinking beyond a cause and effect relationship. Something that emerges comes from the interactions of many different things, moving beyond the sum of those things and producing something different. And what emerges doesn't just come from those things, but from the interactions and relationships among those things in a particular context.

REFLECT:

Knowing that you choose your beliefs, what might you change?

What generational values have you brought from the past?

The Power of Belief

We introduced Henry Ford earlier in the book. He was an entrepreneur. He dreamed the Ford automobile, and recognized the efficiency of assembly lines to increase his production, and profits. He was also right about the power of mind. Recall his powerful words, *If you believe you can or if you believe you can't, you're right.* Note that these words were said long before development in the late 1990's in

> If you believe you can or you believe you can't, you're right.

computer technology and measurement techniques that enabled us to significantly increase our understanding of what goes on in the mind/brain. We now know that positive and negative beliefs not only impact our health, but every aspect of our life. As Lipton describes, "Your beliefs act like filters on a camera, changing how you see the world. And your biology adapts to those beliefs. When we truly recognize that our beliefs are that powerful, we hold the key to freedom ... we can change our minds." (Lipton, 2005, p. 143)

In 2000 Eric Kandel won the Nobel Prize for showing that when individuals learn, the wiring in their brains changes. He showed that when even simple information came into the brain it created a physical alteration of the structure of neurons that participate in the process. Thus, we all are continuously altering the patterns and structure of neuronal connections in our brains. The conclusion is significant; thoughts change the physiological structure of our brains. This plasticity results from the connection between the mind (neuronal patterns) and the physical brain. The implications are significant: What and how we think and believe impacts our physical bodies (Medina, 2008; Kandel, 2006).

The bottom line is that **what we believe leads to what we think leads to our knowledge base which leads to our actions, which determines success** (Bownds, 1999; Lipton, 2005; Rose, 2005; Begley, 2007; Bennet & Bennet, 2015b)**.** If we believe that we cannot do something, our thoughts, feelings, and actions will be such that, at best, it will be much more difficult to accomplish the objective. If we believe we can accomplish something, we are much more likely to be successful, and this results from choice, not genes.

This statement is derived from the following chain of logic that ties our beliefs to our actions and our successes—or failures. Our beliefs heavily influence our mindset or frame of reference—the direction from which we perceive, reflect, and comprehend an external experience or situation. Thus, beliefs influence how we interpret and feel about the information that comes into our senses, what insights we develop, what ideas we create and what parts of the incoming information we focus on. From these reflective observation and abstract conceptualization processes (Kolb, 1984; Bennet & Bennet, 2015b), we create our understanding and meaning of the external world how we see the external world and how we emotionally feel about external events drives our actions and reactions. How we act and react to our external environment influences whether we are successful or not, that is, whether we achieve our goals or not.

Believing happens in the unconscious, that is, not residing in and not available to conscious awareness. This includes most of the stuff the brain does, "from standard body maintenance like regulating heart rate, breathing rhythms, stomach contractions, and posture to controlling many aspects of seeing, smelling, behaving, feeling, speaking, thinking, evaluating, judging, believing and imagining." (LeDoux, 2002, p. 11) Thus the individual often does not have a conscious awareness of his/her beliefs until they are triggered (see the discussion of engaging tacit knowledge in Chapter 13). The first step to becoming the master of your self is to become aware of your beliefs and values. Conscious choice can only occur from a level of conscious awareness.

The Ethics of Thought Leading

Values and ethics are entangled throughout the thinking and actions of thought leaders. In this context, ethics is considered a framework of how you approach leading your life

> Values and ethics are entangled throughout the thinking and actions of thought leaders.

and taking action in regards to the greater community. As a thought leader you're trying to perform at a level which is alive with best practices, laws, regulations and, in some sense, aligned with a moral framework. For something to be knowledge requires trust and verification, and for people to have confidence and trust in the information informing that knowledge, that it is correct and blessed by the formal standards body or the proper chain of command, and that it can be used effectively in this particular context. In other words, ethics is an underpinning of the trust framework among people. Moral ethics involve and affect our organizations, our systems, the procedures we use, the practices we adopt, etc. For a thought leader, building new knowledge through research to improve behaviors of people and organizations is a moral ethic.

REFLECT:

Can you connect your beliefs, values and actions?

What might you do if you had no limits?

There is also the dilemma of proxy values brought up a number of years ago in a conversation with Karl Wiig, an early thought leader in the field of knowledge management. Proxy values essentially deal with such things as the tendency of a person—given a certain situation and certain condition about which the person would want to have an opinion—to project their personal understanding and beliefs onto a situation. These beliefs, and personal value set, become the embodiment of how this particular situation would evolve, and the outcome of what would take place. As a result, it becomes a *proxy value* for what the person's real values are as influenced by their understanding of how this particular condition would evolve. Proxy values touch. The example Wiig cited dealt with pollution. We all want to have clean water and clean air, and the reason we disagree (apart from the political motivation that we might have people we want to pay back because they have invested in us) is that a projection of our basic values (which might be identical) are influenced in different ways by our understanding of the evolution that we project; our values become a function of *what we believe the physical system will do*. And since we all have imperfect and partial knowledge, a bad understanding of the dynamics of how things propagate in an open system such as the ecology, there is a great deal of room for disagreement and misunderstandings, not because we have different basic values, but because we end up with different proxy values.

Another potential ethical dilemma emerges with the realization that more knowledge does not necessarily mean better knowledge, and that both the thought leading and the receptivity of that thought operate within boundaries, highly dependent on the people involved. People put their bounds around what they wish to know about, and they can grow a great deal of knowledge within that boundary,

> More knowledge does not necessarily mean better knowledge.

but there's a fence around the field of knowledge. One TL gave the example of being a mom in Iraq. The only relationship that the growth of knowledge has to this mom is the growth of knowledge about a particular part of Islam; that's all she cares about, all she recognizes and brings into her awareness. This is consistent with the upper and lower focus and learning thresholds of each individual. So, for this mom in Iraq, her "learning" has nothing to do with relationships except within those bounds. There is no outreach, no additional connectedness; rather, her learning is narrowly framed and bounded, so her gathering of knowledge has bounds beyond which she can go. This tends to be true for a lot of religious-based knowledge systems. So knowledge gathering and sharing does not inevitably lead to tolerance, or larger connectivity, unless it's involved in experience where there is a permeable and porous boundary, that is, an openness to new ideas.

Further, as knowledge *outside the bounds of our value system* becomes more familiar. there is a potential for that knowledge to become more acceptable. This problem emerges as we become more and more familiar with a situation, even if it was the type of situation that was at odds with our basic values and issues. The more familiar it becomes, the more acceptable, until it actually changes the perspective that we have. An example of this would be kids who are exposed to violence who suddenly find it less objectionable to them to do bad things.

Values Espoused by Thought Leaders

The 34 thought leaders in the KMTL study identified 53 personal beliefs or values. While primarily working in the field of knowledge management and organizational learning, this group stretches across four continents with tremendous diversity in focus, education and skill sets. Since our focus in this book is on knowledge and leadership, it is quite appropriate that the thought leaders in the KMTL study were engaged in helping organizations manage knowledge!

The groupings fall loosely into the following eight areas: honoring the world, valuing others, nurturing self, honoring relationships, valuing learning, staying open, living values and work ethic and organizations, and rules for living. See Figure 16-1. In exploring these values, we asked thought leaders to describe these values and how they applied to their work. While we will explore a few of these values below, the full set is Appendix D.

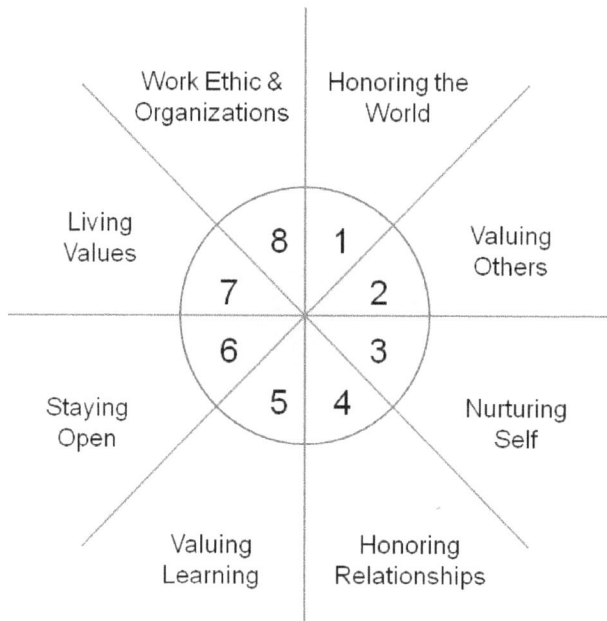

Figure 16-1. *Loosely grouped, thought leader values fall into eight areas.*

Honoring the World (group 1) deals with the larger perspectives of life, the concepts of honoring the world and working together to make it a better place and, more focused on humanity, the value of life, living with love and compassion, and making a difference. While these perspectives were largely outside the self, the self is also connected to this larger perspective. For example, one value was that of trying to understand the world intellectually and one belief was simultaneously a recognition of connectedness and an acknowledgement of the power of the thought leader's mind/brain: *There is a creator in my mind of this universe.*

Valuing Others (group 2) brings the focus to people and other living entities, specifically dealing with beliefs about the goodness in all people and values related to social life. For example, the belief that people know a lot, can contribute, and everybody wants to learn and do their best. It was pointed out that o*rdinary people can create extraordinary results.* As one TL says, "Ordinary people have capacities that we can't even imagine when they're given the context to contribute." This fundamental principle led him to create a form of dialogue and knowledge sharing that is evolving under his stewardship. A second core belief is *the power of individuals and teams to lead others.* This belief leads organizations to value relationships, networks and communities.

Nurturing Self (group 3) is about building, developing and nourishing our own identity, being close to our own livingness. This is the counterpart to the other. In looking outward towards discovering and responding to others, we capitalize on the very significant cultural process by which personal identity or group identity or organization identity or national identity have been built over the past, and the elements that we have to understand and make rationale and emotional sense of in identity are very strong and powerful. , traveling makes you a wiser person, self-initiation and ownership, the whole idea of self-worth.

Livingness is both individual and social. As one TL explains, in Africa there is this saying, *I exist through you.* So, our livingness is the ability to be aware, and this is a sociological construction as well as a biological construction. An example is community as a fundamental principle of humanness, something that is experienced profoundly personally, but also profoundly social, with the "me" as part of a network of relationships. This grouping also includes the idea of self worth, both as thought leader in valuing self knowledge, and in terms of other, that is, giving people a sense that what they are doing is worthwhile and important, and giving them full respect in whatever we do.

Honoring Relationships (group 4) is referred to as both a belief and a value, with family right at the core. One TL correlates building relationships with empathic design and creative abrasion concepts. *Empathic design is an attempt to understand someone else's thinking, and it's a generosity of spirit that allows you to take another person's point of view. That relates to creative abrasion in that you respect other people's points of view, and that allows you to have many people contribute to a project or process.*

Valuing Learning (group 5) focuses on the joy of learning, the value of sharing and the power of continuous learning. Learning is, of course, an absolute key to knowledge and underpins the organizational philosophy to collect, organize, share and disseminate knowledge. One expression of this value was the belief that *experts should be teachers*. When leaders realize that they have developed an expertise in an area, there is a moral obligation to become a teacher and share that expertise and know-how. One approach to implementing this belief in an organization is to create the role of a knowledge asset manager for each area of identified expertise. The intent is that organizational learning around these areas will be understood, embraced within the organization, and taken forward to the organization's customers.

Thought leaders believe in *the joy of learning*. "It's what gets me up in the morning, and it's what makes me tired in the nighttime. I mean it's the sense of the world. always afresh and something new happening." Along with this comes the belief that *tomorrow is going to be a better day than yesterday*. Of course, this belief comes with a hitch. Tomorrow is only going to be a better day than yesterday, it's only possible, if learning takes place. "This is what makes knowledge competencies and learning such tremendously interesting things, because this is what actually makes tomorrow a better day than yesterday."

Staying Open (group 6) includes the characteristics of curiosity, perspective and openness and receptivity to new ideas and perspective. Thought leaders are not only intellectual, but are naturally curious about most things. Curiosity and receptivity to new ideas are core values. We are reminded that knowledge cannot exist in a vacuum, nor should it. Consistent with curiosity is the ability to shift perspectives, to look at and explore things from multiple viewpoints. What is the context in which this exists? What are others ways of approaching this? Thought leaders explore the "*why?*", not only the "*what?*".

Living Values (group 7) deal with the way thought leaders live in the world, the personal values they convey through their beingness and interactions. These include kindness, honesty, integrity, caring, tolerance, being genuine and telling the truth. This group also includes the beliefs in equity and justice, and respect for and love of others. These provide the subtext for the way thought leaders live. All of these values play out in community settings and are fully reflected in listening to others and their ideas. To be in relationship, the human being has to be true to themselves and to other people.

Truth is important in terms of building credibility and authenticity and in terms of getting things done. and to other people. If you stray from those paths you may make some short-run gains for some time but you will lose the main game. As one TL describes, "You're not going to be able to change the organization, you're not going to be able to convince others to do things differently, you're not going to be able to get people to share their knowledge if people no longer trust you. I make a major point of in my own life embodying those principles and encourage others to do likewise." One of the ways to convey these values is through organizational storytelling. "It's a matter of telling a true story that is factually accurate. Most corporate communications paint a rosy picture of some scene just around the corner, then there is backlash. So, it shouldn't be a surprise to anyone that trust levels are low." Note that integrity not only involves integrity as a person, but the integrity of knowledge.

Respect and equity go hand in hand in honoring the potential capacity of people. One TL points out, "Often people's opportunity to make a contribution does not exist in equal measure by no fault of their own. Our work creates the context for every voice to contribute across all of these hierarchies and imagined boundaries." One way to help people gain more perspective over their environment, through creating constructive and productive conversations

> Respect and equity go hand in hand in honoring the potential capacity of people.

around issues that are relevant to them and the people around them. In one TL's words, "It is fundamentally that simple. If you want a good organization, you create good conversations and you allow people to get access to conversation vessels and environments where they can be who they are in confidence, and where they can make sense of what surrounds them so they can deal with it."

Work ethic and organizations (group 8) includes a rich set of beliefs and values that can be in service to leaders at all levels. For this reason, we will provide a bit more detail in this grouping. There is a very strong belief in *working cooperatively toward common goals*. Both collaborative leading and thought leading require an environment where people share their information, knowledge and ideas, which could be described as a collaborative or cooperative ethic with a team and community orientation. As one TL shares, "We're living in an environment that is full of change and knowledge provides the medium of flexibility. Continuity and transformation need to be in balance."

A related core value is that working collaboratively is not about winning or losing. While people love to be acknowledged for their contributions, and deserve to be acknowledged for them, it is about seeing if you can get something done together. As one TL says, *"It's amazing how much you can get done, if you don't care who gets the credit for it."* A related belief is that *what goes around comes around*. The more knowledge is shared the more it comes back to you, and the more new ideas emerge from the sharing

Thought leaders try to *apply their best efforts on whatever they are working on*. This includes going the extra mile, making the extra effort, to ensure presenting your thoughts from as many different perspectives as possible and with enough detail. There is a *sense of rigor and discipline* that comes into play in the way they approach problems solving and decision-making right alongside bringing other people into the solution. [See Bennet & Bennet, 2013.] Ultimately, the solutions need to be useable. That is what knowledge is all about, taking effective action.

Finally, thought leaders that *organizations should be seen as living entities*. Organizations are not mechanisms or machines, they live and die. A long lifespan means co-evolving with the environment in which they live. The ICAS model for organizations introduced in Chapter 7 is a model for creating an organization that can co-evolve with a CUCA environment (Bennet & Bennet, 2004).

REFLECT:

Do you identify with any of the values and beliefs of these TLs?

What additional value or belief would you add?

Higher Order Beliefs

Because the concept of spirituality appears across the response, we will take a closer look at its relationship to thought leaders in terms of the response. Other TLs referred to the spiritual concept in terms of "living in the light", and while they talk freely of these concepts, each made a point to share that they DO NOT talk about spirituality from the podium. However, these ideas emerge in their writing. Five of these higher order beliefs—representative of the larger response—are shared below.

BELIEF: *Knowledge and the field of knowledge management have inherent value in terms of spirituality*. For individual workers to continue learning and gaining knowledge, it's essential that they learn how to learn and understand themselves. This is particularly important when it comes to the phenomena of knowing and developing intuition and judgment, necessary for leaders to make decisions in a changing, uncertain and complex environment. As individuals in organizations pursue learning, the development of knowledge and the sharing of that knowledge, as well as the application in organizational context, they not only learn more about themselves, but they learn how they learn, and through this process have the possibility of developing a higher sense of the self and the relationship of the self to the external environment.

This relationship is as much the Eastern perception of spiritual understanding—including meditation and self-awareness and mindfulness—as it is the Western perception of the acquisition of knowledge about the external world. Thus, while perhaps not a direct intention of the fields of knowledge management and organizational learning, thought leaders who work in these fields have the intuitive feeling that the acquisition of knowledge (and particularly self-knowledge, intuition, judgment and heuristics) will move the individual beyond the Western perception of developing knowledge about the external world and include developing knowledge about the individual person and the worthiness and usefulness of that knowledge relative to both organizational performance and personal and collegial human worth and intention.

BELIEF: *I do believe that the human being is of full dimensionality*. This TL added that a mentor of his spoke a lot about spirituality and the need for the human being to be fully recognized in all of those dimensions. Another TL explains, "From the spiritual point of view, I think there's a strong drive to grow, to expand. I forget who said it, but to *release the imprisoned splendor* as it's called, not only from within each person as an individual, which I think is something we individually work at, but also collectively in terms of the human race. One might say knowledge is the life blood of doing that." Another TL says that when you get into definitional issues around what knowledge really is, all we as human can see tangible proof of is the knowledge limited to the physical head or the physical body. He then asks, "What is this knowledge that comes to us from seemingly nowhere? The nowhere is, of course, somewhere. Then it's a matter of what we define as the borders of our knowledge. I believe we should search outside the traditional lines, the traditional tangible realm, to get closer to the real source of knowledge. Unless we do this, or are prepared to do this, we are incredibly poor compared to if we actually embrace it and work with it." [See the brief discussion of knowing in Chapter 14.]

BELIEF: *One of the few things that outlasts us human beings after our death is the knowledge that we leave behind.* "Some people think the field of knowledge management is about converting knowledge into action and then using this to define products, patents and copyrights. Other people think knowledge networking is great because you can share this knowledge with other people and make the world a better place—you accept people, who share their knowledge with you just as you share yours with them. Embedded in the knowledge movement is a spiritual wonder of what this world is about. That's the connection, in the creation and application of knowledge."

BELIEF: *The sharing of knowledge and perception across connections built on relationships can provide value in a larger sense.* "I mean I don't know how else it can work. Absolutely. We're going to be held together by new types of social fabrics, and I think we're beginning to see this even in our ability to change the use of information technology to support the emergent as opposed to the authorized, support the social rather than the formal." One TL tells the story of an 18-year-old illiterate girl in Viet Name who, up until she had the opportunity to learn, thought she was life's failure. "All of a sudden she was competent in the world, had confidence in herself, self-esteem." A TL who is an academic says, ""As an academic, that's what we're all about here, the discovery and distribution of knowledge [as value], so it's something I almost take for granted as part of my job." While he likes to consider what he is doing as of basic, far-reaching value, there are a lot of tentacles. "You never can tell where and how this is going to influence somebody. One hopes always positively, but yes, the ramifications of what's done can be extremely far-reaching, so I think the whole idea is that you throw a pebble into a pond and every molecule is going to be affected ... sometimes we make a big splash and other times small ripples come out from what happens. It all ties back into this notion of making a difference and, in general, I don't put any boundaries on that."

There is also an ethical dimension, a concern that people have to have a sound set of values and moral foundation in order for these things to be used properly. As one TL explains, "Knowledge is sort of like nuclear power, it could be used for constructive purposes or destructive purposes, and it's up to us living in the world on the constructive side to do what we can to defeat the forces on the destructive side." However, he also sees an opportunity for those who are touched by the new ideas to divert their path in life toward one that's more constructive. Ultimately, it goes back to the core family notion of *the importance of relationships* where a set of values is initially established that allows new knowledge developments to be used properly for the greater good.

BELIEF: *There is hidden knowledge, knowledge that seems to have a significant impact on the way we live and act regardless of religious preferences*. This hidden knowledge is often passed on from master to student with a set of techniques and it's often codified. For example, if you look at the Zen side it's in terms of koans; it's codified in the Confucian approach so far as parables; and in the Judeo-Christian context as far as the Torah, the Old Testament and stories. Even the Alchemical concept of turning lead into gold had nothing to do with lead or gold. Those were both symbols of a **transformative process within the individual to bring certain qualities of the mind and heart under control** to supposedly enable that individual to grow spiritually and develop. They were symbol systems, knowledge systems.

As one TL in the KTML study explained, "Within this hidden knowledge is an incredible capability to convey very abstract feelings, concepts, ideas, affection through a reasonable rigorous set of exercises. This is fourth world knowledge, what Jung would call the superconsciousness, which is a world of spiritual entities and spiritual abstractions that are available to people if they can exercise their mind appropriately and keep their physical form in a certain level of balance. Knowledge management is at the level of changing the core of individuals who have decided to develop more; there is a lot to study and research in the more esoteric realm as well.

Symbols and metaphors contain a huge amount of meaning for those that are in the know, and they are incredibly powerful for those who are initiated in their meaning and in their use. For example, symbols used for spiritual and energy healing are amazingly powerful if you are attuned to their energies. This is part of the concept of hidden knowledge explicated above. The Internet serves as an example of an outward or material manifestation of what is beginning to happen worldwide in a non-material, inner way. One TL felt that perhaps knowledge is the key. "That's what flows and connects it all." As forwarded in Chapter 2, the understanding of spiritual, which used to be relegated in the past to structured religions or groups, today is more pervasive as connectivity among all things.

Chapter 17
Thought Leader Offspring

IDEAS. IDEAS. IDEAS. Without ideas, there would be no thought leaders. Where do these ideas come from? What is the inspiration for these ideas? The simple answer to these two questions is "life".

The mind/brain is an associative patterner. While we've previously introduced this idea, we have not provided an explanation in this book as to what exactly that means. Associative patterning means that new ideas are a result of the complexing of all past experiences and learning with incoming sensory input. In the brain, thoughts are represented by patterns of neuronal firings of 70 milivolt pulses and the strength of their synapse connections. The brain stores information (thoughts, images, beliefs, theories, emotions, etc.) in the form of patterns of neurons, their connections, and the strength of those connections. Although the patterns themselves are nonphysical, their existence as represented by neurons and their connections *are* physical, that is, composed of atoms, molecules and cells. Incoming signals to the body (images, sounds, smells, sensations of the body) are transformed into internal patterns in the mind/brain that represent (to varying degrees of fidelity) corresponding associations in the external world. The intermixing of these sets of information (patterns), what is referred to as semantic mixing (Stonier, 1997) or complexing, creates new neural patterns that represent understanding, meaning, and the anticipation of the consequences of actions (knowledge). Because the human being is a complex system, the associative patterning process can take unusual and unexpected "leaps" as a long-forgotten (at least in conscious memory) pattern associates with the situation at hand.

> Associative patterning means that new ideas are a result of the complexing of all past experiences and learning with incoming sensory input.

Inspiration for New Ideas

How appropriate to begin this conversation with Newton's concept of building on the shoulders of giants; in this case, earlier thought leaders. When we have new ideas they have undoubtedly been influenced in many ways by things we've read and seen, and all the things happening around us. Thought leaders are reasonably adept at spring-boarding off the experiences in their lives. One TL calls this a random mixture of intellectual atoms bumping into one another and making molecules and encounters in elevators, things you see crossing the street, deep dives into history.

Another TL expresses this mixing in terms of **interactions with the world**, letting reality hit you in the face, and listening to the backtalk of the situation instead of trying to inject or superimpose your past thoughts. Most people who attend management and leadership conferences are familiar with Einstein's famous words that if we want something different, we can't keep doing things as we have in the past. *Letting reality hit you in the face and listening to the backtalk of the situation instead of trying to inject or superimpose your past thoughts* is guidance for how to change future outcomes.

This, however, can be difficult. While there are many reasons this is true, there are several that are paramount. First, we are not our bodies, nor our minds, nor our emotions, nor our souls. We are bodies, minds, emotions AND souls, entangled in so many ways. So, when there is an emotional event in our lives, even when the event is over, the emotional tags that have been created often remain. Because our minds are associative patterners, whenever something connected to the previous traumatic event, or a similar event, comes into our minds, emotions come to the fore and we are unable to think clearly. Therefore, the advice to not inject or superimpose your past thoughts enables the mind and body to think and feel clearly in order to address the situation at hand.

> We are not our bodies, nor our minds, nor our emotions, nor our souls. We are bodies, minds, emotions AND souls, entangled in so many ways.

Second, as introduced earlier in this book, at the conscious level we all operate within an attention space that has an upper and lower threshold. So even if reality is hitting us in the face, we still must translate that through our personal lens. The TL's words provide a clue on how to help that process along when he says to listen to the back talk of the situation. Recall that all knowledge is situation dependent and context sensitive. *The back talk of the situation* refers to both the situation and the context, that is, shifting your framework to look from the point of view of the situation, taking into account the people, relationships, networks, events, culture and structure. In systems language you would identify the system in trouble and its subsystems, exploring the relationships among these systems and the state of boundary conditions, etc. In complexity language, you might look for and explore feedback loops, emergent properties, nonlinearities, time delays, trends and patterns, events and processes, sinks and sources, and so forth. (See Bennet & Bennet, 2013, for an in-depth treatment of decision-making in the new reality.) No matter what language best makes sense to you, the idea generator, the decision-maker, the bottom line is to look at (and listen to) the current situation at hand, not to rely on the way things have been done in the past. This is a rethinking of the way to look at the world emerging from the ability to listen with humility. If you can't see the world from the perspective of others, you cannot understand others; *if you can't see the world, it's very hard to know how to cope with it.*

Facing problems is itself a strong motivator for creating new ideas. This source of inspiration was described by thought leaders as encountering issues, engaging a real problem, addressing major problems and solving day-to-day problems. As an example, Hubert Saint-Onge says he is inspired when there are *very demanding kinds of situations to resolve.* As he explains, "Situations that are difficult make me more creative, pressing me to apply my knowledge in different ways and interact with people in such a way as to bring their knowledge in to complement mine." He adds after a pause, "So facing important challenges, that's what makes me *the most creative* and *provides more leverage* in terms of my own knowledge and the knowledge of those that surround me." Since most thought leaders would rather try to solve a hard problem and not make it than solve a simple problem and get through with it, they are continuously looking at harder problems to try to solve or new areas to understand.

There are pragmatic ways of thinking and behaving that encourage the creation of new ideas. For example, the concept introduced in Chapter 14, that is, trying to strip things off, keeping it simple and looking for the essence. A second approach is being well-prepared, that is, appreciating the work that has been done in the field and other related fields, being reasonably well-read and up to date, trying to gain appreciation of the problems that practitioners are facing, and understanding research methodologies. A third approach is active involvement across disciplines. For example, Geoff Malafsky says, "If you have an awareness of a broad array of technical disciplines, you'll see that there is a great deal of commonality, even though they're called different things. So, you can see that there's a foundation there that is really the same problem that is being tackled in different ways."

REFLECT:

How do you interact with the world?

When facing a problem, are you excited by possible solutions?

As can be seen, much of the inspiration for new ideas comes from interactions with the world, what Dorothy Leonard describes as creative abrasion. Books—from pulp fiction to business books to Ph.D. treatises—and movies, plays and music are a part of these interactions, as well as people ... and nature. A source of inspiration to all of us at some point in

> Much of the inspiration for new ideas comes from interactions with the world, what is called creative abrasion.

our lives is Mother Nature, and certainly many of us have, in some way, had the opportunity to develop a close connection with nature. For example, Larry Prusak attributes his source of inspiration to his genetic framework. "I'm just built that way. I have to say I'm intrinsically motivated. I can't offer any explanation, but since I was a little boy, ideas interested me very much and talking about them, learning new things. I'm very curious how the world works and why it works the way it does. Again, I just think that's who I am."

Juanita Brown says that nature is her source of inspiration. "I am mesmerized by the natural world and our part in it." She finds patterns in the water, the quality of air, the relationship between the fishing birds and the fish in the water that they dive down and pick up in their claws, and watching the seals play off the end of a tiny boat. This is where the ideas come from. "On a spiritual level I would say it's being in conversation with the natural world, and in the co-creative sense with people, it happens in conversation."

Interactions with people, that is, getting out and moving around can be described in terms of collaboration, conversations, brainstorming, talking, interviewing, networking and listening. Ross Dawson believe in engaging people. "When I was young, I became excited with this idea that things come out of us—**what comes into us is our experience, and what comes out is what we create**—and in some form what you create is also what you experience." Dawson's whole philosophy in life is to create as much as possible in order to be able to experience, and that's where his network comes in. "Being able to engage with people in the world has always been my dream, and that's what I'm able to do."

Every individual and group in the thought leader's relationship network can participate in the emergence of a new idea! (Relationship network management is described in Chapter 12.) This might include your spouse, your colleagues, your kids, your customers, your parents, your teachers, the neighbor, a doctoral student or the person in a chat room with whom you have idea resonance. And this person could be an 80-year-old, 3 PhD professor in India, or a 16 year old Chinese student. The idea is that age, culture, race, sex, education and experience take a backseat to idea resonance!

Idea Resonance

Consistent with the increased availability of information (primarily surface knowledge as Knowledge (Informing)), and the resultant coupling of knowledge and creativity, an emergent quality of our new paradigm is idea resonance. With the rise of bureaucracy in the 1900's, idea resonance was primarily built on relationships, that is, the valuing of ideas based on attunement with trusted and respected others who were personally known to the decision-maker. As organizations grew more powerful, there was an expansion to include value built on respect and trust of structure, that is, work associates in "my" organization, and external " experts" (Fortune 500, etc.) who were identified as successful by "my work associates" and the world in general, and recognized as experts in "my" domain of knowledge (many belonging to companies which have now failed). While this resonance still often included an attunement with specific people, there was a larger resonance with purpose and ideas beginning to occur.

In the global social networks of the past several years—and consistent with an expanding focus on innovation—we have moved fully into the venue of idea resonance, that is, value built on relationship of, respect for and resonance with ideas. As we increasingly become aware, "Exposure to a greater

> In the global social networks of the past several years, we have moved fully into the venue of idea resonance, value built on relationship of, respect for and resonance with ideas.

diversity of perspectives and knowledge increases the quality of ideas, leading to better innovation results." (Carpenter, 2009) See Figure 17-1.

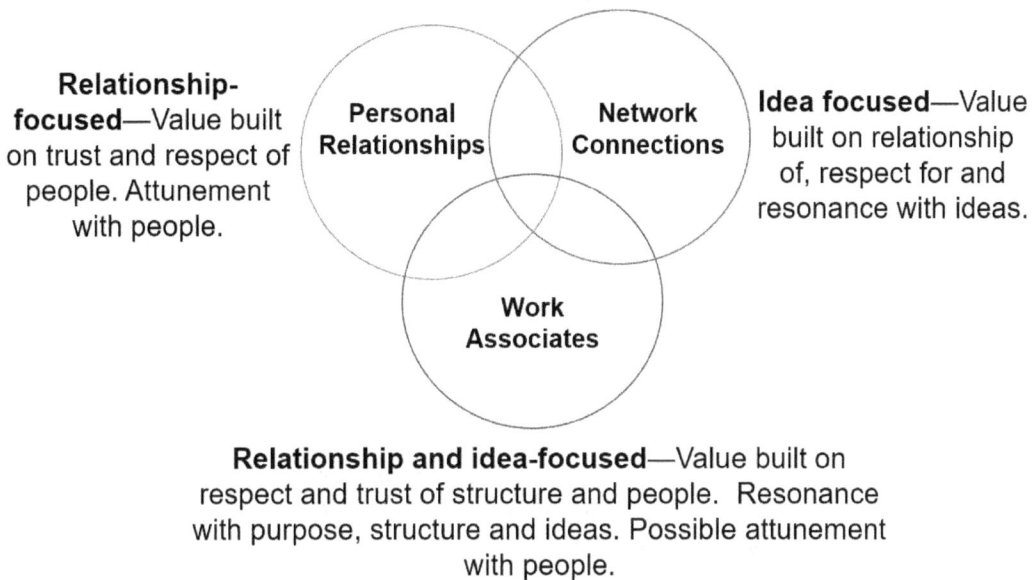

Relationship-focused—Value built on trust and respect of people. Attunement with people.

Personal Relationships

Network Connections

Idea focused—Value built on relationship of, respect for and resonance with ideas.

Work Associates

Relationship and idea-focused—Value built on respect and trust of structure and people. Resonance with purpose, structure and ideas. Possible attunement with people.

Figure 17-1. *The movement from a focus on value built on trust and respect of people to value built on the relationships of, respect for and resonance with ideas.*

This global shift toward expansion of, and dependency on, social knowledge is clearly demonstrated by the new generation of decision-makers. Through continuous connectivity and engagement in conversation and dialogue (a search for meaning), the tech savvy generations have developed—and continue to develop—a wide array of shallow knowledge. Recall the discussion of the levels of knowledge in Chapter 2 and our earlier descriptions of surface, shallow and deep knowledge. Surface knowledge is predominantly but not exclusively simple information (used to take effective action), answering the question of what, when, where and who, and generally explicit. Shallow knowledge includes information that has some depth of understanding, meaning and sense-making such that it requires context. This is the realm of social knowledge, with conversations offering the opportunity for creating a shared understanding of context and meaning.

Until the end of the last century, conversations for most employees were largely limited by organizational relationships and geographical location. Today, the Internet and travel options provide the opportunity for a diversity of conversations which facilitate the cross-crossing of ideas around the globe. In Figure 17-2, to the left is a nominal graph illustrating the historical levels of knowledge needed/used in an organization on any given day. These levels are consistent with the level of decisions made in an organization (tactical, operational, strategic/ontological) (Bennet & Bennet, 2010; 2013). To the right is a nominal graph illustrating the current levels of knowledge needed/used in an organization on any given day. The increase in shallow knowledge is a result of consistent expanded interactions via social media (Tapscott, 2010).

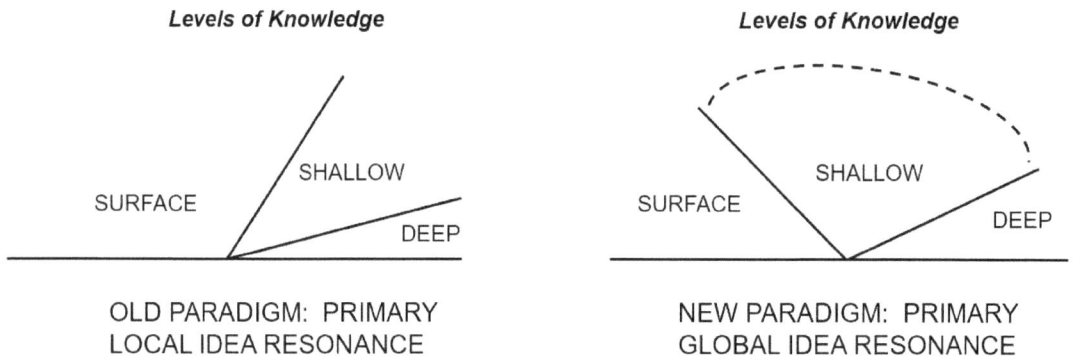

Levels of Knowledge

SHALLOW

SURFACE

DEEP

OLD PARADIGM: PRIMARY
LOCAL IDEA RESONANCE

Levels of Knowledge

SHALLOW

SURFACE

DEEP

NEW PARADIGM: PRIMARY
GLOBAL IDEA RESONANCE

Figure 17-2. *(Left) A nominal graph illustrating the historical (2000) levels of knowledge used in an organization on any given day. (Right) A nominal graph illustrating the current (2015) levels used in an organization on any given day. (Adapted from Bennet & Bennet, 2010)*

What does this mean? First, we are moving toward a transparent world. Little is held back in the everyday tweeting of younger generations. More formally, this transparency is supported in global organizational protocols and government directives around the world. For example, in 2009 the U.S. Government issued an Open Government Directive in support of the President's Memorandum that set forth three principles for government: transparency, participation and collaboration. Government organizations—and by extension the private, educational and nonprofit sectors that support these government organizations—were provided general and specific directions for achieving behavior changes in support of these principles. Per the Directive, a starting place was expanding access to information by making it available online in open formats, and developing policy frameworks supporting the use of emerging technologies. Concurrent with this Directive, the U.S. attorney General issued new guidelines under the Freedom of Information Act (FOIA) reinforcing the principle that openness is the federal government's default position.

Second, knowledge as a primary facet of power through control is a thing of the past. Knowledge as an idea generator, the currency of creativity and innovation, is the future of organizations. As information flows freely and is generally available to all— and as people recognize the power of and creative potential in the mind/brain and learn to tap into that power and creativity—each individual indeed has the ability to be a thought leader, taking effective action in their domain of focus.

REFLECT:

Can you think of a new idea with which you resonate?

How might you apply this idea in your everyday life?

Further, in an increasingly complex environment with a free-flow of data and information, no single individual has enough knowledge to move through the complex decision-making process (Bennet & Bennet, 2013). Success rests in social knowledge creation, the same informal process naturally engaged by tech savvy generations and, now, their children. Social knowledge is at the core of collaborative leadership.

How might we exploit idea resonance? Idea resonance can occur from opening yourself to thoughts in your environmental opportunity space (Bennet and Bennet, 2004), coupling these thoughts with your own thoughts to create knowledge, and recognizing that which is of value to you. Recall from Chapter 7 that the environmental opportunity space is a window of opportunity in terms of space and time, when within a specific domain of knowledge a gap is identified just waiting for the right expertise, the right entrepreneur, to fill.

As large numbers of people talk to large numbers of people, kicking out a variety of information and ideas crossing knowledge domains and responding to those ideas, it "feels good" to be part of the group. Our feelings are a personal guidance system. When emerging ideas begin to "feel good" and are important to a desired outcome, you have idea resonance.

The Art and Science of Questioning

The pressure of a group of people produces inspiration. For example, Dave Snowden says that most of his ideas come from a stage in front of an audience. "The pressure of the group means that suddenly something clicks in your head and you articulate it, and you understand it for the first time. I need an audience to do that." A large part of this is in the questions asked.

Leif Edvinsson speaks to the power of Quisics, the art and science of questioning, in inspiring new ideas. Since our minds are associative patterners, a question serves as the trigger for the emergence of a thought pattern. And while all minds are associative patterns, you must ask the right question to get the right answer. Lewis (2013) proposes a "Framework-Question" Theory from which—given the frameworks and mental models we think from—four levels of questions can be generated. Questions like "How are our numbers looking?" are Level 1 questions that are just confirming a location within a predetermined spectrum (framework). In contrast, Level 4 questions originate from curiosity about or beyond the current framework. Rather than just saying that someone is "creative", this approach requires that we identify that a Level 4 question has been asked. For example, most people would agree that Albert Einstein was creative in formulating his theory of relativity. Yes, he was, since this theory started with Einstein's Level 4 question: "What would I see if I could ride on a beam of light?" Unfortunately, our minds are usually asking Level 1 questions instead of Level 4 questions. Framework-Question Theory requires that we *think about the frameworks from which our questions have been generated*, so that we gain awareness of our mental models, begin to ask questions "about" them and not just "within" them, and move towards innovation.

The Field of Ideas

System knowledge is one of the knowledges required by leaders in a CUCA world. In Chapter 10 we forwarded that system knowledge leads to understanding connections, relationships, balance and tradeoffs, and that an intellectual aspect of leadership is considering the larger perspective. This is the ability to conceptualize and strategize, to see the big picture and how everything fits together. The example we provided was of Pere Pierre Theilhard de Chardin's

> An intellectual aspect of leadership is considering the larger perspective, to see the big picture and how everything fits together.

noosphere, "a human sphere, a sphere of reflection, of conscious invention, of conscious souls" (de Chardin, 1966, p. 63). This is a similar concept to the idea of Quantum, a field of potential and possibilities. The concept of Quantum leadership has emerged in the business field and as an offering from various transformational leadership gurus.

For our purposes, let's think of this field in terms of WiFi and the Internet. Thoughts, in the form of electromagnetic energy, are floating through the air, picked up by a grid that surrounds the world, float through the air again, and are brought to the screen for our consideration and potential use. Note that they are not brought to any screen, but to the place they are directed, a place where they will, at least most of the time, be welcomed. This analogy is similar to the idea of the Noosphere. Thoughts are energy patterns floating around the world waiting to be brought to the awareness of individuals who welcome them, those individuals who have expanding their threshold of focus and learning in a specific domain such that these thoughts are understandable and/or can trigger other thoughts in their mind/brain.

This is the concept that several of the thought leaders in the KMTL study expressed. "The **ideas are already out there, just waiting to be recognized**, and we just need to be open to recognize them and catch hold of them. For example, Etienne Wenger, the first to develop the community of practice idea for organizations, says that ideas are, "In the air ... you know what I mean? It's not like you invented things, you just sit and they're in the air. And you say, oh yes, that's right, but it was already in the air, you know?"

Another TL refers to this field in terms of the Akashic records. He says that along the way to becoming a thought leader he developed a holographic method to record interactions among people, and between people and computers in organizations, from spiritual models such as the Akashic records. The Akashic records represent the membrane of a higher frequency upon which every thought and every action is written such that the past and history can be read as a series of streams. By visioning this capability, this thought leader was able to birth a new process.

Diving within to our sense of knowing, another TL says he listens to his inner voice. Knowledge and knowing (see Chapter 14) are the source of this inner voice. In Chapter 13 we introduced Engaging Tacit Knowledge as a knowledge capacity. Tacit knowledge is within the storehouse of self, expanding and connecting within from the time each of us is in the womb. Intuitive tacit knowledge is the sense of knowing coming from inside an individual that may influence decisions and actions, what Damasio (1994, p. 188) calls "the mysterious mechanism by which we arrive at the solution of a problem without reasoning toward it." The unconscious works around the clock with a processing capability many times greater than that at the conscious level. This is why as the world grows more complex, leaders depend more and more on their intuitive tacit knowledge.

One of the ways to surface tacit knowledge is through inner tasking and lucid dreaming. One TL touts this as his pathway to ideas. "It has been his experience from the beginning, as far back as he can remember, being able to state a problem in his head and then within a short period of time, definitely overnight, having a variety of solutions available." Several of the authors have had a similar experience.

Ideas Emerging

By definition thought leaders are part of a social network and they have both formal and informal, visible and invisible, networks with whom they exchange viewpoints, engage in discussions and use as sounding boards. This network can be described as partners, co-authors, spouses, friends, mentors, colleagues, associates, thought partners, people we trust, and other people who work in the field.

During the process of developing new ideas, these networks provide the opportunity to validate these ideas with other people who can help sharpen them so you can proceed with confidence. As Hubert Saint-Onge shares, "Very little of that can take place in complete isolation," "So relationships are what help you compliment your own capabilities with those of others, and help you see things that you couldn't see yourself." By seeing more completely what you're talking about, your ideas are more valid, more accurate, and of higher quality. "This is why I think the people you see being leaders in this field [KM] are people that are not only thoughtful

> During the process of developing new ideas, networks provide the opportunity to validate these ideas with other people who can help sharpen them.

on their own—because that's also very important—but people who have self-knowledge, people who understand their own limits and in fact celebrate their own limits and don't get taken by their own press clipping, people who can interact with other people with humility and can learn from anyone with whom they're interacting because they're part of a reality that surrounds them."

REFLECT:

When is the last time you shared an idea with others?

Did the idea improve with the sharing?

So this ability to have relationships is absolutely essential to the ability not only to craft ideas and concepts and tools and principles, but also to be able to convey them in a way that people will see the message and understand its intent. These interactions are also called relationship capital. Two other thought leaders shared, in separate responses, that when developing new ideas they were engaged with the world, with every conversation and interaction contributing in some way. For example, Rob Cross says that what he gets enthused about are the ways in which the work that's been done to this point helps him engage with others. This creates an enthusiasm around possibilities in the work. Thus these exchanges can be credited with moving ideas forward. As another example, Nancy Dixon says that for her, "It has been nearly always the exchange I have with others about this set of ideas that moves it forward. The skill I have is the seeing of a pattern, saying what I'm seeing out loud, talking about it, hearing their ideas, hearing their questions." It's in conversation that often the knowledge moves from an undifferentiated sort of a thought into something that might actually be coherent that you can do something with.

There is a feedback loop in the creation and application of new ideas. First, part of getting ideas out there is the feedback that provides fodder for additional thinking. "Ideas are very close to biological entities, and much like sexual reproduction where genes are combined and new things are formed." Second, the reception of new ideas, and seeing them applied, is an inspiration for thought leaders to create more new ideas. For example, Tomasz Rudolf says that, "If you can see your ideas put to action, either by yourself or by the team you're in, then this makes you really energized."

The Relationship Among Thought Leaders and Their Ideas

The ideas build into some kind of new theory, pattern or approach and are published. While clearly choosing to share their ideas, once birthed most thought leaders remain attached to those ideas in a relationship similar to what several thought leaders term that of a parent and child. They feel absolutely thrilled, enthusiastic, excited, grateful, proud, very positive and, well, good. Most not only enjoy their ideas, but genuinely like them. And then, like children, they grow up and leave home, and you only hope they won't embarrass you and they might even do some good in the world! And when they are successful, you're happy to see them successful. The way these ideas are received, however, is out of your control.

Now that they are out there, how are they received? Often thought leaders are "blown out of the water" as they begin to be referenced, received invitations to conferences and after a time delay become heavily Googled and quoted! And from another, ""I had no idea it would have such an effect on people." Of course, from the first time their ideas are released out into the world and read or heard, there is a time delay before they are out there in the larger field of ideas! And along the way, their idea might be simplified or expanded, or become part of a larger idea, or become a meme, never reach the field of ideas exactly as it was intended. As one TL expressed: "I always get a little sad when an idea that's very complex gets sort of transferred into a simplified way that doesn't carry the power of the whole idea." See Figure 17-3.

When those ideas are misinterpreted and/or misapplied, some thought leaders turn this into a learning experience and to provide energy for new thinking. For example, John Seely Brown shares, "The way these ideas are being misinterpreted often turns out to be insightful." This insight can take several forms. Because knowledge is context sensitive and situation dependent, the interpretation may be exactly right for the situation in which it is being applied. On the other hand, the thought leader now has the opportunity to ask the question: Why did these things get heard one way when I meant them another way? So putting things out and having them either accepted, slightly transformed or rejected all leads to additional signals that turn out to offer learning opportunities. Through this process, the thought leader discovers how these fundamental constructs can be used in new ways.

Memes may or may not reflect the intent of the original idea. A meme is an idea, behavior pattern, or piece of information that is passed on, again and again, through the process of imitation such that it takes on a life of its own (Blackmore, 1999). The role that memes play in learning comes from their capability to retain the memory because of their sound and meaning. Memes become stronger (more memorable) when they are delivered in connection with an emotional event that engages the listener's/participant's feelings. This is the same importance of an emotional response (enthusiastic reception, hostility, total confusion) shown in Figure 17-3.

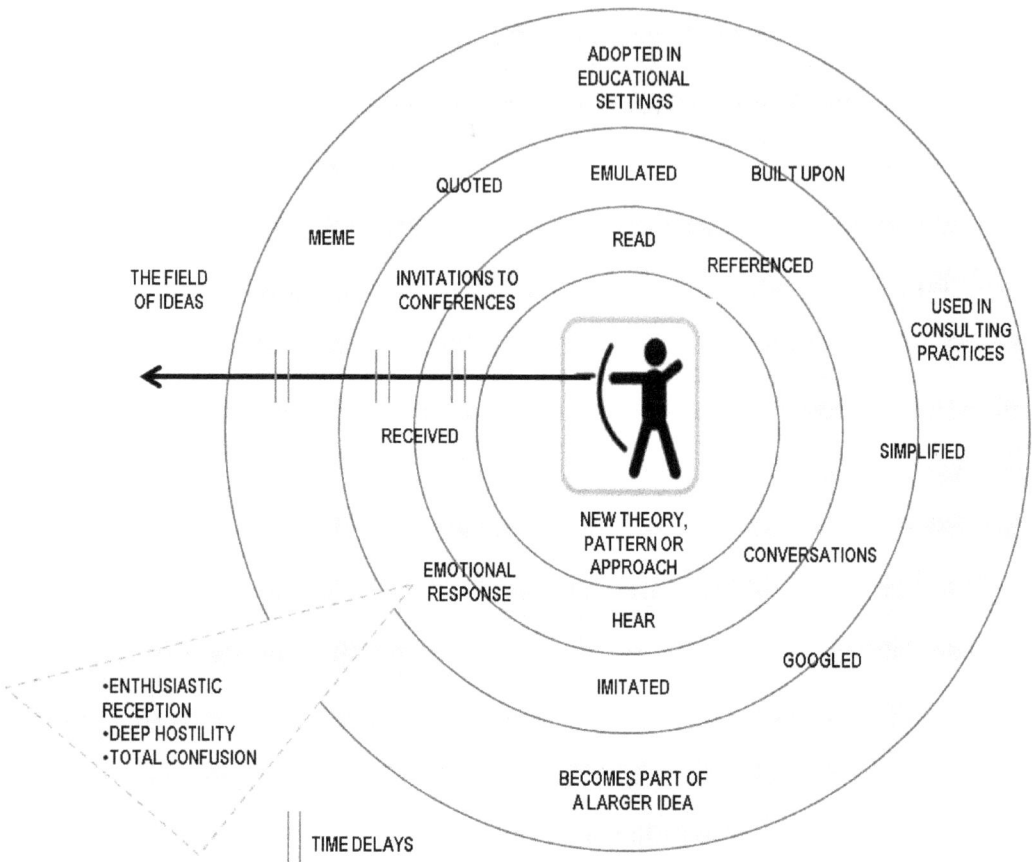

Figure 17-3. *Once an idea is released out into the world, there are many potential responses.*

A role that memes play is to act as replicators of information (that may become knowledge) as they spread throughout groups of individuals. Of course, learning only occurs if their meaning and relevance is understood by individuals within the group. This means that for memes to spread they need to relate to the culture, attitudes, expectations and interests of the group. Learning can be greatly enhanced by the effective choice and use of memes throughout the communication process. People using similar memes, together with common syntax and semantics, can understand each other much more effectively and rapidly, there by more easily creating social networks which facilitate the transmission of information and the creation of knowledge (Bennet & Bennet, 2007). A well-known example of a meme is the U.S. Army's slogan for many years: Be all you can be!

While they may or may not be referenced, may or may not be quoted—and their originator may or may not be acknowledged—having the ideas out there and being applied is what is most important to a thought leader. As one TL explains, "The interesting thing is that I don't see a tremendous amount of reference to them, which is kind of interesting, so I think it's something that works on people at a deeper level. Some people get picked up and others don't. It doesn't matter. It's all pebbles in the pond. It's what I'm called to do. It's just what I do." These ideas are painting in some of the white spaces.

For those who choose to do so, there are a number of ways that thought leaders use to determine how their ideas are being received. These include such things as how many times they are asked to speak at conferences, how many times they are quoted, whether their book is adopted for use in a university course, how many articles are accepted for publication, how many people talk to you at conferences and email you with questions, how many hits you and your ideas get on Google's search engine, and how good a living you are making. Dave Snowden works to push the edge of people's thinking, and expects a strong response, whether negative or positive. "Enthusiastic reception, deep hostility, total confusion, and if ever I get something that isn't in that category, I know I'm not doing the right thing. If you don't have all of those three groups present, then you've not pushing the boundaries. If I'm not upsetting people I'm not innovating!"

In contrast, the impact of ideas is not always immediately discernible. As a TL recalls, "One professional found this interview that I did and he was telling me this is really great, and I couldn't even remember what was in it. You think that things don't have an impact, but sometimes later on you find that they do." Whether immediately or after a period of time, these ideas become part of a foundation for other ideas to build upon.

Final Thoughts: *The challenge of dreaming the world together.*

Verna Allee said that when she was doing some research on how we learn together as a whole group, she looked at serious studies about how people change from understanding things one way to collectively understanding them differently. Basically, there was no body of literature. As she exclaimed, "We do not know how we really dream the world together!"

That's exactly what we do. We imagine and we dream. We set our intent and we act. Everything that we touch, everything that we create, begins with an idea, and it's an idea or a dream, if you will, that we had together. What is the process of dreaming together, or thinking together, or evolving our ideas together? Verna Allee says that, "It's the question of how everything comes in and out of being and how are we as humans, through our thought magic, through our thought talent, how are we co-creators to manifest different things into the world." She then asks the hard questions that face us as a humanity. How do we really create the society that we're all a part of, and what is that process for how that emerges through our thoughts, and our shared beliefs, and our shared understanding? If we can't drill down to that level of assumptions and beliefs and *work together, collectively and collaboratively*, at that very fundamental place of creation, then how can we create a more hopeful future? How can we dream a different kind of future together if we don't even know how to do that?"

How indeed?

Chapter 18
With Passion, I Lead

Looking at the term in a historical context, the term "passions" (in the plural) was used in the work of early Western philosophers to represent what we now call emotions. For example, early analysis of emotions using the term passions appears in dialogues of Plato and in Aristotle's Rhetoric; as well as in the Greek discussions of virtue and vice. As an aside, according to Lou Marinoff, ancient Greek philosophers had a propensity to indulge both their reason and passions alike, in the hopes of perfecting the former and outgrowing the latter (Marinoff, 2003).

Passions also appears in the moral theology of Thomas Aquinas and in Benedict Spinoza's Ethics; and in books of political theory, such as Niccolo Machiavelli's The Prince and Thomas Hobbes's Leviathan (Adler, 1992, p. 185). Rene Descartes' "six 'primitive' passions—wonder, love, hatred, desire, joy, and sadness—are not meaningless agitations of the animal spirits, but ingredients in the good life" (Frijda, 2000, p. 6). David Hume insisted that, "What motivates us to right (and wrong) behavior . . . were our passions, and rather than being relegated to the margins of ethics and philosophy, the passions deserve central respect and consideration" (Frijda, 2000, p. 6). Hume also believed that moral distinctions are derived from passion rather than from reason. "Morals excite passions, and produce or prevent actions." By contrast reason is "perfectly inert" and can never produce or prevent an action (Honderich, 1999, p. 110). The philosopher Georg Hegal affirmed, "Nothing great in the world has been accomplished without passion." In like manner, the term "passions" appears in many historic works of poetry and history (Adler, 1992, p. 185).

Although the use of the word passion to specifically represent a strong emotion or desire is first recorded around 1250 AD, "the generalized meaning of a strong liking, enthusiasm (as in a passion for horses) is first recorded in 1638" (Barnhart, 1988, p. 761). The Oxford English Dictionary (updated in 2002) cited 12 different perspectives on the concept of passion, first presenting the use of the term representing the suffering of pain, specifically the suffering connected to Jesus' Crucifixion in Christian theology. Among these dictionary listings, the specific meanings that help build context for this research are:

passion/noun (5a) A strong barely controllable emotion; (5b) A fit or outburst of such an emotion; (5c) A literary composition or passage marked by strong emotion; an emotional speech. A strong enthusiasm for (specified) thing; an aim or object pursued with strong enthusiasm.

passion/verb: Excite or imbue with (a) passion. Express or be affected by passion or a strong emotion. (Oxford English Dictionary, 2002)

As an operational definition—building on the earlier chapters—*passion is considered a term to indicate those desires, behaviors, and thoughts that suggest urges with considerable force* (Frijda, 2000). Characteristics of those urges specifically include the assertion that positive passions affirm that something is precious, and that passion can be used as a determinant of what is of higher interest and great (Polanyi, 1958, p.135). Considering these characteristics, positive passion is used to indicate value (something precious) and passion, whether positive or negative, is used as a determinant of what is of higher interest and great.

Psychologist Nico Frijda saw passions as often extending to desires, thoughts, plans, and behaviors that persist over time. "They may lead to performing behaviors regardless of costs, external obstacles, and moral objections. These are the characteristics of passion in the more modern sense—the desires, behaviors, and thoughts that suggest urges with considerable force" (Frijda, 2000, p. 59).

REFLECT:

How do you feel when you listen to a passionate thought leader?

Do you think passion is important in living and leading?

A Quick Review of the Literature

We begin with a quick review of the content of Appendix E. The intent of this review is to pull together the core concepts so that we can develop a framework for understanding the various aspects of passion and their relationship. This framework provides a model to explore thought leader passion. These core concepts are also expressed in the prose at the end of this chapter.

For those who wish to delve down a bit deeper into this fascinating topic, a more substantial literature review is available as Appendix E.

From a biological viewpoint, passion (both the emotion that is externally observed and the feeling that is internally experienced) can be induced by external events and circumstances, which become part of a set of stimuli that includes considerable variation in the type of stimuli both across individuals and cultures (Damasio, 1999, pp. 52-53). Further, morals excite passion and even that moral distinctions are derived from passion. (Honderich, 1999, p. 110)

Passion is considered an important leadership attribute, and the most passionate people are described as those that have a purpose beyond themselves. It is considered contagious, and "by caring, loving, and showing compassion we can release a spirit in people that is unequaled" (Kouzes & Posner, 1993, p. 235). Passion and trust are linked directly to leadership, defined as unleashing energy, building, freeing and growing (Peters & Austin, 1985, p. xix). Servant-leadership is specifically described as a passion to serve (Batten, 1998), and approaches to servant-leadership encourage passionate commitment, action, and a sense of urgency (Lad & Luechauer, 1998, p. 60). Further, passion is the counterpart of doing the right things right (Neff & Citrin, 1999, pp. 379-380).

Love and passion are directly linked to thought leaders (Leonard & Swap, 1999, p. 182) and both passion and enthusiasm are found to thrive in an atmosphere of optimism and confidence in the future (Leonard & Swap, 1999, p. 191). Whether communities thrive or not is directly linked to the ability to have the "goals and needs of an organization intersect with the passions and aspirations of participants" (Wenger et al, 2002, p. 32). Here goals represent the values of the organization.

Passion, driving the intensity of flow, elevates values and engages reality at all levels in its search for "what it means to be alive" (Csikszentmihalyi, 2003, p. 60). This is also reflected in the spiritual context of passion as a strong vehicle for awakening (Gyatso, 1992; Walsh & Shapiro, 1983; Watts, 2002) and energy that helps people speak from the heart, and draw out other people and engage them (Rockwell, 2002. p. 52).

To help understand the meaning of *intellectual passions*, Polanyi identified science itself as an intellectual passion.

Passions charge objects with emotions, making them repulsive or attractive; positive passions affirm that something is precious. The excitement of the scientist making a discovery is an intellectual passion, telling that something is intellectually precious ... The function which I attribute here to scientific passion is that of distinguishing between demonstrable facts which are of scientific interest, and those which are not ... scientific passion serves . . . as a guide in the assessment of what is of higher and what of lesser interest; what is great in science, and what relatively slight. (Polanyi, 1958, p. 135)

Several points in Polayni's work are significant to this chapter. First, his **close linking of joy with intellectual passion**. Second, his assertion that positive passions affirm that something is precious. Third, that *passion can be used as a determinant of what is of higher interest and great.*

Passion is also that *gift of emotion* that causes individuals to take a precise interest in and pay keen attention to (Bennett-Goleman, 2001, p. 312); to open us up to a larger picture (Belitz & Ludstrom, 1997, p. 57); and to promote the greater good (Melendez, 1996, p. 299). As Senge so eloquently stated above, passion is directly connected to the "deep longing of human beings to make a difference," to contribute (Senge, 1999, p. 62). Passion, then, has potential as an indicator of value to the individual, and is directly linked to those larger things the individual (self) feels are important.

Passion is *a source of energy for the leader*. The question presented by Marinoff is how to bring the mind and the heart, reason and passion, into a peaceful coexistence. He believes that almost everyone can transform their passionate energies into the art of living reasonably, with the goal of using reason to channel passion into beneficial forms of expression. Going even further, Marinoff stated that it is possible for the "passion for one's own life . . . [to take] a backseat to principles of duty toward others, or other causes." This is a "victory of a passion for serving others over a passion for preserving the self. It can even be interpreted as a way of making one's life meaningful" (Marinoff, 2003). This is the higher passion for the greater good called out by Belitz, Goleman, Teerlink, Neff and Citrin, Czikszentmihalyi, Melendez, Senge and in other discussions above. This context sets the stage for recognizing passion as a determinant or indicator of what, in Polanyi's words, is of higher interest or great.

It is now clear that passion is not just a part of the thought leader, but that it is triggered by both internal and external inducers and that there is a continuous connection with externally observed and internally felt elements and self correlates. This is graphically expressed in Figure 18-1.

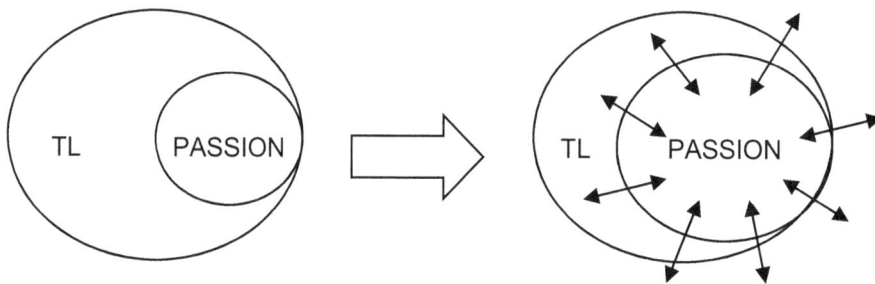

Figure 18-1. *Relationship of Thought Leaders and their Passion.*

Appendix E provides additional detail to further explore this relationship between thought leaders and passion.

REFLECT:

Do you feel passion around other's ideas?

When you have a passionate idea, do you feel joy?

Developing a Working Framework

From a literature review, a framework was developed to explore the aspects that contribute to the passion expressed by thought leaders in the KMTL study. Underlying this framework is the biological viewpoint forwarded by Damasio that passion can be induced by external events and circumstances, which become part of a set of stimuli. Further, that this set of stimuli includes considerable variation in the type of stimuli (across individuals and cultures).

Passion is an emergent phenomenon. External and internal inducers make up a set of stimuli that result in passion. This passion is both externally observed and internally felt in a variety of ways, and is also correlated to the larger aspects of Self. The definition of passion, the internal inducers, lists of elements externally observed and internally felt, and a list of correlates to the larger self are all developed from the characteristics of passion discussed in Appendix E and summarized above.

Because this construction is based on a biological model, passion is considered in terms of an autopoetic system, that is, a system that evolves through continuous exchange and interaction with its environment (both adapting to and influencing its environment). In the framework, feedback loops have been drawn from externally observed elements to passion as well as from internally felt elements to passion, indicating that—as an autopoetic system—the things we feel and the ways we act influence ourselves as well as our environment.

There is also a feedback loop from the larger elements of self correlated to passion back to passion, indicating that these elements have the quality of sustaining or increasing passion. This idea of larger elements of self-sustaining or increasing passion is based on the references cited above. For example, Kouzes and Posner asserted that the most passionate people are those who have a purpose beyond themselves; Melendez said effective leaders are passionate because of their commitment to the greater or public good; Senge said passion comes from what you contribute not what you get, etc. This framework serves as a template for clustering and exploring the passion of thought leaders. See Figure 18-2.

Thought Leader Passion

Thought leaders all have a passion of one sort or another. It is apparent when you meet them, in the tone of their voice and their excitement, and it's contagious. It fuels continuous thought and the desire for clarity.

Validating our passion model, thought leader responses in the KMTL study spanned the entire sphere of the framework. It is notable that not only did the aspects expressed by the thought leaders interviewed closely match the meaning of the descriptive terms in the passion framework, but also many of the words used to describe them are the same. This mapping helps demonstrate the validity of the framework in terms of thought leader perceptions of what excites their passions. Note that the question of passion was related directly to the work they do, in this context as thought leaders in the field of Knowledge Management. It is assumed that thought leaders in other fields have the same level of passion related to their domain of knowledge.

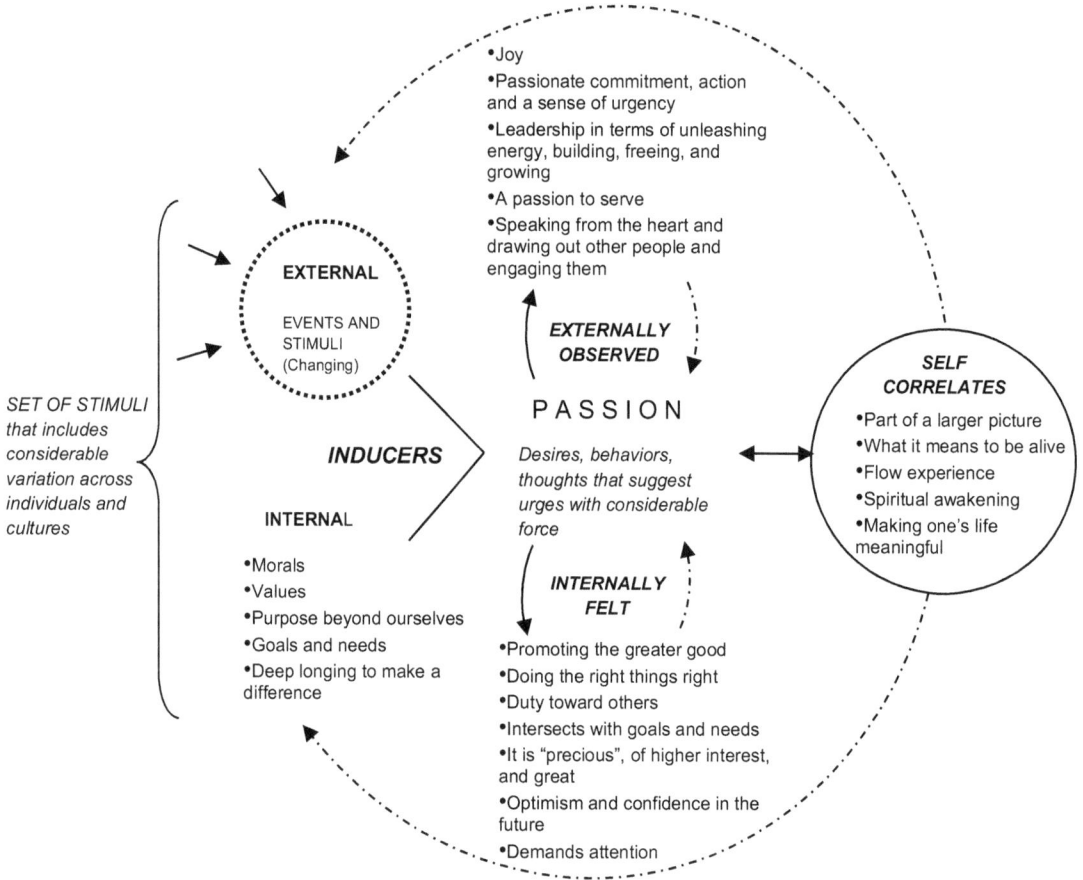

The figure contains the following text elements:

- Joy
- Passionate commitment, action and a sense of urgency
- Leadership in terms of unleashing energy, building, freeing, and growing
- A passion to serve
- Speaking from the heart and drawing out other people and engaging them

EXTERNAL EVENTS AND STIMULI (Changing)

EXTERNALLY OBSERVED

SELF CORRELATES
- Part of a larger picture
- What it means to be alive
- Flow experience
- Spiritual awakening
- Making one's life meaningful

SET OF STIMULI that includes considerable variation across individuals and cultures

INDUCERS

INTERNAL

PASSION

Desires, behaviors, thoughts that suggest urges with considerable force

- Morals
- Values
- Purpose beyond ourselves
- Goals and needs
- Deep longing to make a difference

INTERNALLY FELT

- Promoting the greater good
- Doing the right things right
- Duty toward others
- Intersects with goals and needs
- It is "precious", of higher interest, and great
- Optimism and confidence in the future
- Demands attention

Figure 18-2. *Framework to explore aspects of passion.*

Specific external events and stimuli that trigger thought leader passions include the field itself (breakthroughs, the nature of knowledge), the breadth of the field (richness of multidimensionality of experience), the changing nature of the field, the value (growing collaborative advantage of knowledge in the world), the transfer and reuse of knowledge (improving organizational memory, not repeating mistakes), new thinking (intellectually exciting, new way of looking at things) and challenges and opportunities (incredible challenge, confronting moral and political dilemmas very openly). The rich response related to the externally observed, correlation to larger picture, internally felt and internal inducers dimensions of the passion model are Appendix F.

Overall, this response is about the work thought leaders do: their thinking, their feelings, their actions. The passion around their field of choice is evident in both their words and the way they talk about the field. The bottom line is that ALL of these elements of passion are represented in thought leader response. We now have a better understanding of the passion with which thought leaders lead.

REFLECT:

What area of your life ignites your passion?

Do elements of the passion model resonate with you?

Adding Context to These Responses

While it's nice to simplify responses and use highlights of the fuller responses for the mapping process in exploring and understanding overall patterns, it is difficult to fully appreciate and understand the significance or intent outside the context of the thought leader's wording and phrasing. So here are a few examples of that phrasing.

One TL explains this passion as a *missionary zeal*. It runs through the community and its thought leaders "and I think it's somewhat a missionary zeal because I carry it too." The questions being surfaced by the field are *important questions for our society and for the planet*, not just business questions. This theme emerged again and again, with the role of thought leader considered in terms of a mission, even close to a religion, a feeling that "you have here a mission to achieve and that you need to open the eyes of the people." This concept of being on a mission and "passing it forward" (introduced in Chapter 16) is cited as the reason why so many people in this field are involved in educational projects or supporting knowledge cities at the societal level.

There are many reasons for this passion. First, passion for *the exciting emergence of new ideas*. There is a drive to contribute to the exploration of this frontier, and to encourage others to strike off in directions that they might not have otherwise seen. Second, thought leaders find passion in finding solutions to things people didn't think they could pursue. The highest level of reward is a thought leader's ability to *make a difference*. This emerged in Chapter 15 as one of the rewards connected with thought leading and cited in Chapter 16 as a TL value.

One viewpoint of the CUCA world is that during this period of history humanity is so highly polarized that there is the potential that our collective intelligence is failing us as a species. Thus, thought leaders carrying positive messages about how to do things better can be life affirming. This is the passion around *empowering people*, that is, helping people realize the amazing knowledge they have amassed through the experience of life—the bank account of self—and helping them build the confidence and courage to act on what they know.

Third, thought leaders find passion in doing something they love to do. When this occurs, it's not work. Many years ago a colleague shared that when she was young she had envisioned a life of traveling around the world, seeing interesting places, doing interesting things, and hanging out with really interesting people. While all of her dreams have come true, what she didn't understand as a child is that the really great thing is to be able to *live a life of passion*.

Another theme that emerged through the KMTL study is the concept of being a *revolutionary*. As one participant described, "One of the peculiar things about this field [knowledge management] is that people who get into it develop passion for it. I think if you develop a passion you are at heart a revolutionary. You're just a little too late for the French and American revolutions, so you join this one." What she considered revolutionary about knowledge strategies was that you're *challenging the establishment*. This reference goes back to Drucker (1998). Humanity has moved into the knowledge era, some unwittingly, and for those who are being pulled along, trying to *wake up to the new reality* is extraordinarily difficult.

This passion is catching. Many thought leaders are also educators ranging from professors to lecturers. As one thought leader describes, "I'm changing my students. It's positive for them in their own life. I think they're catching the passion." *Recognizing passion in their instructors increases student acceptance of and belief in the material being presented.* This is the same with leaders and managers in organizations. And, as one thought leader stresses, "If you don't have the passion how are you going to spark the passion in these folks?"

Thought leader passion for their work even changed their ontology. For example, in thought leader words: "It's kind of like building a whole new set of dispositions on how we see the world"; "suddenly we see the world differently"; and "our passion for this work changes aspects of who we are." To these thought leaders, their passion was considerably more than energy. *It crept into their being, their basic existence, and influenced how they say themselves in the world.*

And More Passion ...

Many of the thought leaders with whom we have had the opportunity to interact are not tied to a single field of endeavor; indeed, a focus on knowledge, context sensitive and situation dependent, demands a level of expertise in many related fields. For example, knowledge management practitioners emerge from various disciplines, and most of the theories applied in the field of knowledge management originate from other domains such as psychology, neuroscience, sociology, economics, behavioral science, neuroscience, systems and complexity, learning theory, and political theory, among others (Bennet & Bennet, 2014).

Below are short scenarios describing areas of passion for several of the thought leaders who participated in the KMTL study. The elements of the model shown in

Figure 18-2 that relate to each area of passion are in brackets at the beginning of each paragraph.

[Externally Observed: *A passion to serve*]

One participant in the KMTL study, who has a passion around the use of stories, noted that this passion shifted his focus from spending no time thinking about story or knowledge to spending 24 hours a day doing just that. *He admits to dreaming in story.* Steve Denning *tells* a story to express his passion. "When I was director of knowledge management at the World Bank, this was the central focus of my working life so I was quite passionate about it, and I'm certainly passionate about it for any organization that is facing challenges for which this is a central issue. For instance, when I was in Paris talking to the Nuclear Energy Agencies of the world. They are facing massive knowledge problems. They have a large number of nuclear facilities, many of which are being decommissioned. The number of nukes coming into the sector is in very sharp decline since in Europe and the U.S. there are no new facilities being built, and there are major problems being faced about how to run and maintain these facilities and the waste deposits, which will last for another 10,000 years at least. This is a massive knowledge problem which may well affect the future of the planet. I was passionate about helping them see **how important it is for them to share their knowledge**."

[Inducers: *External events and stimuli*]

Kent Greenes is passionate just about every time he's on a real project using KM for real business. He shares a story. "In Algeria we were asked to go out to the Sahara Desert where a company was building its first drilling in what's called a brown field site. This is an oil field that has lain dormant for a while, and then you restart it, which means you have all these old maintenance problems. It's a real sort of macho environment. So there was the company man, the drilling guy, and now we're out at the rig and this is where he's boss. I listen. When he's done, I'm explaining what we can do, and as we're talking there's this big explosion. A lot of the people working there are nomads who wander the desert like gypsies. Well, the supervisor had told this guy, this nomad, go cut one of those oil barrels in half so we can use it to put this waste in. What he didn't tell him was make sure there was no vapor or fumes in the barrel before you get out the welding torch. So this nomad fires up that torch and puts it on the container, and boom, it blows up right in his face. Now, he's not badly hurt. So I said, let's talk about what just happened. So we used that opportunity right then and there—and here's where my passion is. I said man, why don't we do an action review right now. Instead of me telling you what this is about, let's do it. So it's being able to actually impact performance in the moment."

[**Externally Observed**: *Leadership in terms of unleashing energy, building, freeing, and growing*]

Karl-Erik Sveiby is excited by anything that has to do with tacitness, the ability to transfer knowledge without having to make it explicit. "Just by seeing another person you learn a lot about that person. How can we improve this type of transfer? How can we create environments conducive to tacit knowledge transfer without having to make it through computers? And how can computers help us to generate tacit knowledge?" Sveiby looked at ancient aboriginal knowledge creation and the tools and methods they had to store and retrieve tacit knowledge, to make it trade from one generation to another over thousands and thousands of years through storytelling. "This is not just any storytelling, it is aboriginal storytelling, which is quite a complex art. And this is what excites me at the moment."

[**Internally Felt**: *Demands attention*]

Tom Davenport says the attention work affected him. "In terms of attention, I did become much more conscious of the emails that I send, the letters that I write, and the presentations that I give. I ask myself, am I getting the attention of the people this is targeted at? What can I do to make it more engaging for them, to get their attention? Am I allocating my own attention effectively?" This focus on attention changed his behavior, as has his passion around the work he is doing on personal information and knowledge management. He explains, "It's how individuals manage their own personal information and knowledge environments, and that has changed my behavior, too. How could it not?"

[**Self Correlates**: *Making one's life meaningful*]

John Seely Brown says his passion for this knowledge work creates meaning. The telling of his story is full of his passion. "It was so fun, for example, we had this book all figured out but we hadn't started writing it in detail and my co-author and I flew to Asia and we experienced things that we only vaguely understood intellectually. We started experiencing things with texture, which was amazing to us, and we started seeing things that we never thought existed." He laughs. "There was a sense of suddenly being a participant in some incredibly, rapidly evolving, passionate ecologies, knowledge ecologies. It just changed our lives. We went in with one set of eyeglasses, and we honestly came out with another set of eyeglasses." The effect? "It's sort of changing my whole sense of what globalization is about. It's changing my whole sense of where value gets created, and somehow there were a lot of precursors. A lot of things I've been experiencing in the last four or five years got all twisted in a very interesting way such that suddenly I see the world differently." Still energetic, he continues after a pause, "So half of my life is seeing the world differently having to do with rethinking globalization and what this is going to mean to business architectures, learning architectures, knowledge sharing and so on and so forth. And the other half is understanding kids that grow up digital and what digital culture is about, which I'm equally passionate about and spend equally as much time doing. But both of these activities have involved me grinding my lenses. So it's not a question of learning, it's a question of learning to see completely differently. My ontologies themselves have had to shift. It's kind of like building a whole new set of dispositions on how to see the world."

[**Externally Observed**: *Joy*]

Leif Edvinsson is passionate about the nourishment and cultivation of the future. "Initially it was probably to measure it, and the second part was to cultivate it. Today it's been more to the joy dimension of it, energy, and the energy comes when you have fun actually. What is leading up to that is what I'm very much trying to learn more about, the neuroscience dimension of it. If you get a good story, a good narrative, you activate at least three parts of your brain, and that's where the energy is emerging and you could, for example, look into a hippocampus and see how the hippocampus is your intelligence center and that is leading to either adrenaline or serotonin, and if it's serotonin, it's the chemical of joy of life."

[**Internal Inducers**: *Purpose beyond ourselves*]

Passion drives action. As one thought leader summed up, "We're still organizing those meetings, rewriting articles, trying to promote this topic, and not just from the business perspective but to show the people the potential that is there. If you believe it, you try to show it to others. These are the words you use when you talk about religions ... *the believing and the passing the good word,* and so on."

The Nature of Thought Leader Passion

The passion felt by these thought leaders is very positive, and helps fuel their personal energy, their personal satisfaction, and the love for their work, and that passion includes values and aspirations of a higher order of meaning. For example, thought leaders refer to this passion in terms of nourishment and cultivation of the future, the richness of multidimensionality of experience, work really worthy, and the value of knowledge and what it can do for society, for individuals, for interactions among individuals. Such responses as these—and many others—indicate that thought leader passion is not just for their work but also for the higher good to which their work contributes. This overall response would indicate *that thought leader passion is derived from a higher order*.

Another aspect of the nature of thought leader passion is the energy level changes that occur over the years thought leaders work in their field. As Figure 18-3 indicates,

31% of the TLs interviewed thought their energy had steadily increased over the years, while 54% saw it as varying up and down during their tenure in the field. One thought leader who clearly felt an increase in energy explained, "I think I've just sort of become more who I am. It's kind of always been there, but it's getting more and more comfortable in the messages that I carry. There are some deep principles about working with other people and collaboration that I live and breathe down to my toes." Another TL who felt a continuous increase in energy said, "I find it an enormous source of energy being able to work with someone that has the same passion, the same drive, and the creativity. I love it, absolutely love it."

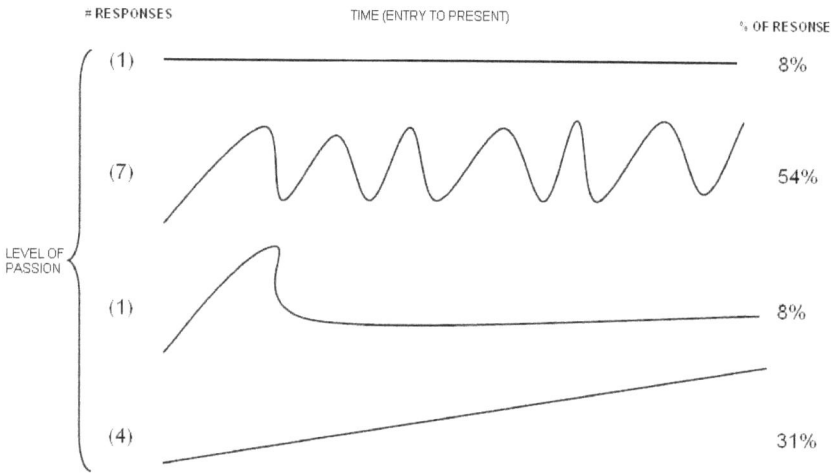

Figure 18-3. *Patterns of passion levels described by thought leaders.*

The "up and down" movement cited by the largest number of responders (54%) is similar to the pattern described by Csikszentmihalyi linking passion and creativity, that is, the energy generated by the conflict between attachment and detachment, a yin-yang alternation between passion and objectivity. Specifically, Csikszentmihalyi (1996, p. 316) states, "Their creativity unfolded organically from idea to action, then through the evaluation of the outcomes of action back to ideas—a cycle that repeated itself again and again. Linking our thought leaders' description of this changing energy and these findings, we discover a model that looks something like Figure 18-4, a dance between passion and objectivity, action and reflection.

PASSION (Action)
Without the passion, we soon
loose interest in a difficult task[*]

LEARNING AND ADJUSTING TO NEW SITUATIONS

OBJECTIVITY (Reflection)
Without being objective about
it, our work is not very good
and lacks credibility[*]

[*](Csikszentmihalyi, 1996, p. 72)

ENERGY

Figure 18-4. *The changing energy of thought leaders.*

The descriptions of energy fluctuations provided by the thought leaders certainly support this model. As one thought leader in this grouping says of their passion, "It rises and falls like circadian rhythms and all that." *Circadian rhythms* is the term given to the daily rhythmic activity cycle (24 hour interval) of many biological organisms, similar to the rise and fall of tides. Another responder actually describes this process in words similar to our model:

> Well, there was a period of high passion when I was actually implementing theory in action, you could say ... Then my interest waned, then caught a renewed push when the interest in KM made people also show an interest in my early work, and I got more enthusiastic toward the end of the 90s when I could see a shift in the trend away from IT and technology and more towards people.

And the shift continues as we begin to value the passion of our thought leaders, the diversity of thought emerging in expanding domains of knowledge around the world, and the collaborative nature of how that thought is being acted upon.

Final Thoughts

Desire wells up with thought, forcing us forward,

    contagious urges that excite our actions.

We unleash it, set it free to serve,

    optimistic, and confident in the future.

Goals and needs intersect with passions and aspirations,

    ever pulsing in circadian rhythm,

elevating values and engaging reality.

Still, the thoughts rise with our consciousness,

> awakening our hearts, engaging the masses,

> soothing the deep longings within,

> which only just now we begin to understand.

This passion expresses our Selves,

> and moves beyond, expanding into commitment,

> enthusiasm, action, a sense of urgency.

And in the midst of the flow we reach out to others,

> awakening to an incluessent future,[2]

> moving from lessons into expression.

With *passion*, we lead.

Afterward

There is always an Afterward. It goes on forever. Nonetheless, our *Afterward* begins with a *Beforeward* occurring several years ago, specifically, on December 18, 2012.

Beforeward

We were gathered around the conference table at the center of Mountain Quest surrounded by the Allegheny Mountains of West Virginia. This was the first gathering of what would come to be laughingly called the Universal Knowledge Guild.

The gathering was originally scheduled for two days, but at the last minute one of the participants shot an email to the group suggesting extending the visit an extra day. And here is what John responded,

> *After some deep thought, I agree with Franc's wisdom on staying over to another day. I just reread the Institute's mission statement. If there was ever a time for a meeting of the minds, it would be now. Our ability to articulate the central importance that learning and knowledge and innovation management play in the productivity and survival of an organization, even a nation, as a collective mind share is more important than any one of our individual efforts. I want to have the time to learn, share, and then move from the interesting aspects to the productive aspects.*

The challenge posed to the group: With all this CUCA activity, how are we going to develop learning aids for the future when we don't know what the future looks like? An age-old question, really, one asked by any futurist with our little twist on learning! And from a larger frame of reference, how can we help humanity move to the next level, whatever that means?

Sitting around the table was a scientist, a philosopher, a professor, a mathematician, an engineer, an educator and a psychologist. Disjointed thoughts emerged from the ensuing conversation, becoming ideas and coalescing into a connected whole. Of course, first came agreement on the assumptions, which in itself was an enlightening experience!

*We were currently operating in a knowledge economy, sharing a deep appreciation for the collaborative entanglement of people and their communities, of organizations and their competitors.

*We fully appreciated the values of transparency, participation and collaboration rapidly becoming embraced throughout the developed world.

*We recognized the human as holistic (physical, mental, emotional, spiritual) and the power of the mind/brain; that each person was sovereign, and had choice.

Next we focused on the critical elements, little pieces of understanding that would drive our modeling of the future. Out of the conversation seven elements emerged:

* *First*, the sense of, "We are here." I recall standing out under the country sky situated here on the edge of the Milky Way and thinking the thought, "I am here." Other places were no longer important; I didn't require difference to have appreciation, no lessons to dampen my full expression. So, this "We are here" is a presencing that does not require the duality of black and white, good and bad. An awareness, a consciousness of being present.

* *Second*, that creativity is based on Unk Unks (that's short for unknown unknowns). This is all the stuff that's going on within us of which most people are unaware! So much knowledge and knowing stored up in our minds and in our bodies. This is an honoring of our Selves.

* *Third*, the idea of a memory shift underway. Things are so complex that we no longer can afford to hold on to all the unfruitful thought and emotion from the past. Rather, ideas were floating in and out continuously, and we want to grab hold of the ones that resonate, connect with others who resonate, and explore those ideas!

Fourth, the concept of simple elegance. We don't have to be burdened down by the things we own, tethered by overwhelming burdens and commitments. Time to simplify, discovering the elegance of a simpler way of living.

Fifth, the value of diversity. We've had our lessons in this as a humanity. Diversity is the spark for ideas, the action power for intelligent activity. This means honoring each and every individual for the unique person they are.

Sixth, the idea of the singularity. We've reached a tipping point, and things are changing. Our job is not to try and hold it back, but to stay open to the amazing energy patterns of thought emerging from our expanding social engagement. We are all connected. We are one world.

Seventh, the human drive for—and deserving of—physical, mental, emotional and spiritual freedom. Ultimately this brings us full circle to choice. "We are here and we have choice."

Since leaping from these assumptions and critical elements to the world of the future seemed impossible we took incremental steps. The world of 2010? Still very much caught up in duality, WIFM (what's in it for me?), control and separateness, although much headway had occurred from the early domination and bureaucratic models. And, admittedly, there was an emerging focus on participation, collaboration and transparency.

So, what might 2012 hold for us? We agreed this meant letting go the 2010 status quo, breaking the bonds of the past to live in the NOW, although there was no doubt that participation, collaboration and transparency were laying the groundwork for this shift. In fact, as boundaries are released between nations and connectivity continues to expand, transparency plays an even larger role. With this comes a need for authenticity, a greater freedom for all, and the desire and opportunity for choice. And with a feeling of oneness riding on the coattails of connection, compassion emerges. See Figure Aft-1 below.

Figure Aft-1: *The shift of humanity underway.*

With the maturing focus on knowledge in a global world, comes the understanding that people are at the core of our organizations and communities, bringing with them the power of diversity and individuation as they join hands to dream the future. Raising of awareness is coupled with knowledge resonance, that is, the free flow of ideas around the world, offering a bouquet of choices for each person. Coupled with an openness to new ideas, and openness to learning, is thought attendance, that is, a rising awareness that form follows thought, a consciousness of our own consciousness and the thoughts and feelings emerging from Self. And empathy emerges, a stronger, more intimate, form of feeling with the other. And in the larger population there is a resonance with new ideas precognating the coming Renaissance, the Golden Age of Humanity.

And these thought leaders continued to paint the future with their words. See Figure Aft-1. And then they asked, what resources can we provide to help people move through this shift?

Now the Afterward

It's strange how our unconscious works. Beautiful thoughts seep their way into our awareness, then pop up again and again, connecting themselves to other thoughts. And so it is as we look at this model it is clear that it is woven throughout this text! Perhaps that's not so surprising. More and more we are meeting leaders around the world with whose thoughts we resonate.

Then the idea for this book emerged. Quickly. In 2014, Alex did a keynote at the Information & Knowledge Society Conference in Singapore, and was eagerly looking forward to returning for the 2015 conference. Life had other plans. The date of the conference collided with her commitment to teach the Systems and Complexity course in Rotterdam Management School's global ONEMba program. As spring sprang its way into being, she began pulling together materials on collaborative leadership and thought leadership that had always been intended for a book. Then, as the date of the conference loomed closer, she committed to the book, a way of supporting the expanding connectivity of this program.

Simultaneously, the Bennets finally released *The Course of Knowledge: A 21st Century Theory*, a culmination of many years of focus on knowledge. This, of course, was forwarded to participants in the Universal Knowledge Guild, along with a line about an upcoming book focused on knowledge and leadership. There was an immediate response from John Lewis, saying that he had also focused on collaborative leadership and thought leadership, and that sometime in the future it would be fun to work together on this topic. The immediate response from the Bennets was, how soon in the future did you see that happening? Now? "Game on" came back the response.

So, what fun to actually *put everything we're writing about into action in the process of writing*, howbeit a book is a small project in comparison to changing the world! Certainly, collaborative leadership and thought leadership are keys to the future. Can these keys help us dream the future together? Game on!

Yours in Learning, Alex, David and John

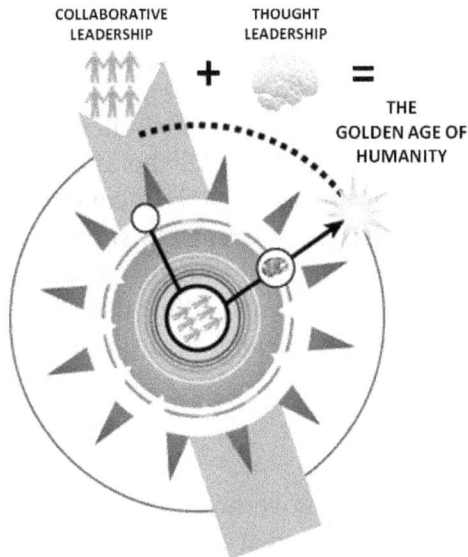

Together we dream the future ...

Appendix A
Leader as Facilitator

Facilitation might be considered an advanced form of collaboration; it is clearly an important strength of leaders. An effective facilitator is a leader, a follower, a collaborator, and a servant to the group. Like collaboration, facilitation can be learned only through experience. It is both a behavior and a mental process, demanding parallel monitoring of several different processes occurring simultaneously during teamwork sessions. Experience in processing several streams of data simultaneously helps a leader monitor situations and interactions and adjust their own behavior and responses accordingly. To expand on this, consider the following story.

Thoughts of a Facilitator[1]

John had been facilitating a group of government executives all morning but had not been able to get them to communicate very well. They faced a challenging and complex issue that was hard to understand, confusing, and had potentially very serious consequences to their organization. Everyone took the issue seriously and most of the group had their own quick solutions, but they all seemed to be talking at cross-purposes. There had been many heated discussions and arguments with little listening; some personal animosities had burst forth. Even when they *did* seem to listen they did not get the deeper meaning behind the words. It was a classic case of everyone feeling that they knew the right answer. In frustration, John begged away from lunch and went to his office to think about what he should do. He was a good, proven facilitator, yet nothing he had done seemed to be working that morning. In desperation, he picked up an old sheet of questions he had kept from a seminar years ago. It read:

1. What are "you" doing to make the problem worse?

2. Are you enforcing the ground rules?

3. Did you prepare the group for dialogue and inquiry?

4. Is the process appropriate for the objective?

5. Is the problem due to diversity of personalities, language problems because of different disciplines, levels of seniority, competing objectives, inexperienced participants, organizational loyalties, personal arrogance, or misguided faith in their own knowledge?

John read over the questions carefully and began to realize that the essence behind all of the questions was to prepare the individuals in the group so they were open to *learning and knowing*. Such preparation would help the participants question their own beliefs and knowledge and look carefully at other ideas—and how they were delivered and responded to—in order to see beyond images, hear beyond words, and sense beyond appearances. This was essential to get to the heart of the matter and create an understanding and consensus for the road ahead.

Regarding the first question, John realized that he had become involved in several of the discussions and, although he always tried to be objective, there were probably individuals in the group who felt he was biased. In thinking about his behavior, he recalled the trick of taking himself out of himself and looking at himself from the upper corner of the room. When he reflected on this, he became aware that he had been giving some participants more attention than others and that his mannerisms had shown some of his personal bias.

Regarding the second question, several times John had not enforced the ground rules and allowed some individuals to ramble and talk too long. This had undoubtedly irritated other participants. He recalled the first rule of management, "If you're not getting what you want the first thing that has to change is you."

Regarding the third question, he realized that although he had originally intended to talk about the question "How do we know what we know?" and to do a systems review of the topic, he had let several of the senior participants talk him out of it because they thought it would waste time and they wanted to have more time to resolve the issues. He now realized this had been a serious mistake on his part.

Thinking about the fourth question, John felt certain that all participants were extremely well-qualified, dedicated, and loyal, and trying to do their best in coming up with a good solution. Certainly there were personality differences. The language problem was not too serious, although he knew it would probably have been better had he helped them develop a common perception of the problem. Looking at the other possible problems he concluded that the major issue was that, even though all participants were well intended, they each had a strong belief in their own knowledge and were certain that their answer was the right one. They came from a culture of hierarchy and combativeness. They had proven themselves through their careers, had demonstrated good decision-making capabilities, and firmly believed that their understanding and solution was the best.

Reviewing the last question he concluded that although the group had shown some signs of every possibility in the question, none of their behavior was enough to be the cause of the current problem.

As a final thought, John reviewed in his mind how well he had been able to keep up with the four processes that unfold simultaneously during every teamwork session. He felt good about being able to follow the flow of content of the group and to understand the significance of some of the ideas. Monitoring the quality of interpersonal relationships among members and taking early action to prevent disruptions had been straightforward. The third process, the movement of the group toward its objective, is what got stymied and he had not handled it well. He also knew that he had not monitored his own behavior—how he came across to the group—very well. Learning to track all four of these processes in real time while standing in front of a group of well-educated, proactive knowledge workers had not been easy for him. But through experience and the school of hard knocks he had come to feel confident about his abilities as a facilitator.

Reviewing all of these thoughts in his mind, John realized that he had not given enough attention to preparing the group to question their own knowledge, and thereby open to other ideas and perspectives. He knew this was a critical step in guiding the group through the overall path. Once it is brought to their attention that there is no solid answer to the question, "How do I know what I know?" almost everyone is willing to consider other answers and try to keep an open mind.

Since it was too late to drastically change the planned process, John decided the best action was to get everyone to step back from the situation and spend time looking at their own belief sets, recognizing and respecting the belief sets of others, and exploring the context within which the task needed to be accomplished. In addition, he wanted to explore the possibility there were no right or wrong answers, only possibilities and probabilities. He really wanted to spend time on complexity thinking to get the group to appreciate the challenges and possibilities of piercing their unknown world of the future. "But there was no time for that," he quietly muttered under his breath as he walked back into the lunchroom.

When lunch was over, John began the afternoon session feeling much better about the way ahead. John's experience, here described as a formal facilitation responsibility, is very close to what collaborative leaders do in their interactions with knowledge workers. During their conversations, they continuously monitor and support the content flow, the process and direction of the discussion, the interpersonal relationships being developed, and their own behavior as seen by others—always done within the framework of honesty, openness, values, and integrity. This is how collaborative leaders lead, learn, and build their own character.

Appendix B
Collaborative Leaders
Actions to Further Empower Self

These actions were proposed by senior government leaders to help empower themselves.

Be willing to accept other's ideas over your own; ask others for assistance; be more open to divergent opinions; keep my temper and realize I don't know all of the answers; be receptive to suggestions/recommendations; be open to learning and appreciating different perspectives.

Listen to others more; listen and learn; ask questions.

Practice conscious reflection periods; take walks-allow think time; reflect more; take time to reflect on my actions and what I observe; reflect on what you know and don't know; think about what I've read or heard; picture a better self with more knowledge; pray/meditate; meditate and understand self better; practice focused/deliberate attention.

Engage continuous training; more training; continuing education; finish graduate school; get another degree; study; study new things; school; continuous learning; more learning; develop new skills; apply learning; personal learning and growth planning.

Collaborate; collaborate with experts; network; improve networking; network "what makes sense"; network with co-workers; network with others; network to expand circle of knowledge access and knowledge sharing and exchange; broaden personal networks and nurture those networks; participate in communities of practice.

Share; share information; share knowledge; share with others; instill in others the need to share information/ teach; share (sharing begets sharing)

Communicate; more communication; learn from communications; communicate with your colleagues more; talk to someone; start blogging with colleagues

Maintain health; healthy living; yoga; more sleep; get more sleep; increased sleep; good night's sleep; get more sleep; sleep more-give mind a rest; eat right; eat less food.

Read more; read something; read many different things; read about new ideas; read more non-fiction

Know your subject; establish yourself as an SME (subject matter expert); be conscious of being a knowledge professional; document personal knowledge; use opportunities to apply newly acquired knowledge; research; organize information/research; be aware of information sources; do a skills assessment; engage in journaling

Adapt to change; plan change; stay open to new ideas, change and growth; be more sensitive and responsive to external changes.

Align yourself with management; stay on top of leadership to provide vision and goals; tactfully work with supervisors so they understand they don't have all the answers either.

Establish relationship/trust; get to know your associates and let them get to know you to foster trust and ownership; understand the culture of the organization

Place yourself outside of your comfort zone to force practiced responses to uncertainties; open up to ideas; look for new ideas; seek answers to the unknown

Play with the IT solution to see what it can do; research new technologies constantly; integrate technologies into work; walk away from the computer more often.

Learn more about yourself; take decision-making to the next level of intuitiveness and actualization; conceptualize and "connect" to inner self intuition; use sleep to break through tough problems by enabling the subconscious to work the problem; arrange tacit knowledge

More compassion/understanding; be passionate; be authentic; be honest with yourself.

Appendix C
The Knowledge and Knowing
of Spiritual Learning

The question that we ask is: Do human characteristics that are spiritual in nature contribute to the learning process? To explore the answer to this question, we will take the following approach: (1) carefully define our terms and the intent of those terms in the context of this article; (2) utilize a variety of disciplines as resources to investigate the nature of spirituality in terms of human characteristics; (3) surface the assumptions underlying our engagement with this question; (4) provide a baseline discussion of ways of learning; and (5) map the themes emerging from identified spiritual characteristics to the learning process.

Further, it is forwarded that since this study (and these co-authors) could not fully accomplish (1) through (5) above in the space available covering the entire scope of diverse points of view regarding spirituality and learning (assuming it *could* be accomplished), representative thought will be used. For example, consider number (2) above. Even within a single discipline, the concept of spirituality could not be agreed upon, yet there is what we might call a direction to that thought. Therefore we will use characteristics representative of this direction, characteristics that lie somewhere at the midpoint of the spectrum of thought within each field.

While relationships to specific disciplines are not necessarily called out, this cross-discipline study emerges out of research in learning, spirituality, psychology and knowledge management. Also note that the intent of this article is to focus on *spirituality as it contributes to learning, not the learning of spirituality*, although there may inevitably be some overlap.

Definitions

Spiritual is taken to mean pertaining to the soul, or "standing in relationship to another based on matters of the soul" (Oxford, 2002, p. 2963). Soul represents the animating principle of human life in terms of thought and action, specifically focused on its moral aspects, the emotional part of human nature, and higher development of the mental faculties. From the philosophical aspect, it is the vital, sensitive or rational principle in human beings (Oxford, 2002, p., 2928). Csikszentmihalyi says that "an enduring vision in both work and life derives its power from soul—the energy a person or organization devotes to purposes beyond itself." (Csikszentmihalyi, 2003, p. 19)   As a point of reference, in a 1990-1993 World Values Survey, 93 percent of U.S. responders, 85 percent of Canadian responders, 81 percent of Swiss responders and 75 percent of West German responders expressed belief in a soul. Only 6 nations of the 38 nations surveyed had less than 50 percent of responders express a belief in the soul (Inglehart, et al., 1998, p. 168).

It is also noted that an alternative definition of spiritual is of or pertaining to the intellect (intellectual, the capacity for knowledge and understanding, the ability to think abstractly or profoundly) (American Heritage, 2000, p. 910) and of the mind (in terms of highly refined, sensitive and not concerned with material things) (Oxford, 2002, p. 2963). The term spiritualism is taken as a spiritual nature or quality, so that to spiritualize is to give a spiritual character to, or to elevate (Oxford, 2002, p. 2963). In this paper, then, **spirituality is the elevation of the mind as related to intellect and matters of the soul reflected in thought and action**.

As introduced in Chapter 2, *knowledge is considered the capacity (potential or actual) to take effective action in varied and uncertain situations* (Bennet & Bennet, 2004). In considering the concept of spiritual knowledge, it would be useful to more fully understand the source or spirit of life. Unfortunately, while progress is being made toward this understanding, to the authors' knowledge we are not there yet (Capra, et al, 2007; Bortoft, 1996). To date this connection would represent an individual or group belief set.

Knowing is a sense, a cognizance, a conscious state of being aware or informed [having knowledge] (Oxford, 2002, p. 1510) beyond that which is perceived through the five senses, although it does not exclude incoming signals from the five senses. Knowing was introduced in Chapter 13. Knowing is created at the unconscious level, and then perceived as it emerges through our intuition, feeling or awareness. In other words, through associative patterning the mind creates feelings and a linear set of words or images based on what has been known such that there is conscious recognition and understanding (Bennet & Bennet, 2006). Understanding, in Bortoft's view, is: "Seeing something in the context in which it belongs … the experience of seeing it more fully, or itself. Instead of seeing it as instance of something else, it becomes more fully itself through being seen in its context." (Bortoft, 1996, p. 291) Knowing could be thought of as deep knowledge (see Chapter 2), knowledge created within our minds (or hearts or guts) over time through experience, contemplation, and unconscious processing such that it becomes a natural part of our being—not something learned and stored in the mind. An old adage is that one must "live" with complex subjects so that knowledge can soak into the mind until it becomes a part of who we are, not just something we know.

Learning is an increase in the capacity for effective action and was introduced in Chapter 2. This definition emphasizes the importance of taking actions and achieving results vice intellectual knowledge without communication or application. Further, we emphasize the continuous nature of learning, recognizing that no thing is ever in the state of learnedness (possessing profound or systematic knowledge) in a changing, uncertain, complex world. Therefore, **spiritual learning would be defined as the**

process of elevating the mind as related to intellect and matters of the soul to increase the capacity for effective thought and action.

Models and Assumptions

To provide context to this exploration—and focus the field of shared understanding—the thoughts presented in this study are shored up by a number of assumptions. First, it is assumed that consistent with human learning, the focus of this exploration, learning occurs by and within complex adaptive systems.

Second, it is assumed that spiritual learning as a way of learning is involved with the sevenfold spectrum of knowledge: information, sense-making, understanding, meaning, anticipating the future, intelligence and wisdom. Further, that the domain of spiritual learning (1) is neither dependent upon nor independent of the learner, but interconnected with the learner; (2) deals with the non-material and through the non-material affects the material; and (3) is primarily concerned with long-term learning (type 4 learning explicated below). By non-material we mean patterns, either patterns represented by configurations of material entities such as neurons in the brain, intestines or heart, or perhaps patterns represented by non-material entities such as photons.

Third, it is assumed that the human mind has some degree of access (through the five senses and beyond the five senses, whether originating consciously or unconsciously) to both that which is material (in terms of the physical world) and that which is non-material. Oversimplified, this access is represented in Figure C-1.

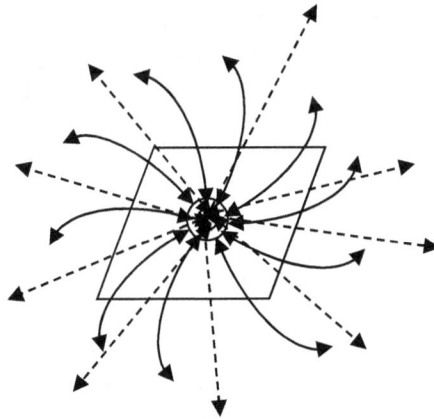

Figure C-1: *Individual interactions with the material and non-material.*

Individuals can influence the material and the non-material aspects of reality. The solid lines represent our interactions with the material world and the dotted lines are those interactions continuously underway in the non-material domain. The slanted box represents our material frame of reference, or how the "I" perceives the reality within which we live (our personal reality). Note that the "I" recognizes and interacts with a material reality beyond the personal reality, whether consciously or through the auspices of the unconscious, i.e., the division in interactions is not that of the conscious and unconscious, but rather that of the material and non-material. Further, there is continuous feedback, providing learning or learning opportunities, that occurs in interactions with the material and non-material, both consciously and unconsciously.

Enter the Human Learning Process

In the ICAS model (Chapter 7; Bennet & Bennet, 2004), we forwarded that there are three types of learning. The first, developing skills (type 1 learning), requires learning and practicing new ways of doing something. The second (type 2 learning), developing knowledge in a field, requires studying and practicing better ways of taking actions, developing new processes, tools and methods, and applying new management ideas, e.g., total quality management, business process reengineering, knowledge management, or even spirituality itself. This is *single loop learning* (Argyris & Schön, 1978)—learning that occurs when ideas and beliefs are reinforced, or problems are solved by changing actions or strategies for achieving a desired result, while the underlying theories or assumptions about those ideas, beliefs, or actions are not changed.

The third way to learn (type 3 learning) is to change the basic theory and belief about how a system works. This might mean developing new thoughts and ideas that change your beliefs or even your value set; or, in an organization when problems arise and never seem to be solved, changing the underlying theory of how the system works; or, making changes in the system to co-evolve with a changing environment. When any of these occur, an entirely new understanding of the system's structure and what makes it behave the way it does comes into being, and a new frame of reference is developed. This is *double-loop learning*—learning that occurs when new thought evolves or problems are solved by changing the fundamental values and assumptions of the belief set as well as the strategy and actions driven by that belief set. Double-loop learning is difficult because it requires individuals, groups and organizations to change the understanding of their *theory of historical success*, what the individual, group or organization must do and how it goes about doing it to achieve its goals. Double-loop learning is learning for the future in that it changes the individual's (or organization's) frame of reference, moving beyond context sensitivity and situation dependence (Bennet & Bennet, 2007) to provide new ways of looking at similar situations.

While certainly behavior reflecting spiritual thought may be involved in both type 1 and type 2 learning, the domain of spiritual learning would reside largely in type 3 learning, that is, double-loop learning, in that spiritual growth will undoubtedly affect or expand frames of reference more traditionally associated with bureaucratically-oriented business and government environments. spiritual learning would also *move beyond* double-loop learning to what might be described as type 4 learning, that which has been called intuition, or the "ah ha!" experience, or what could be attributed in spiritual literature to unconscious streaming or channeling. Whatever the source, type 4 learning emerges unconsciously as a form of knowing, with insights often taking the form of transformative knowledge. For example, in times of warfare there are numerous recorded instances where military personnel under fire have known what movements to make without detailed knowledge of the terrain or enemy troop movement.

If "thinking and emotions [are] inseparable from each other and from the social context in which the activity takes place" (Wlodkowski, 1998, p. 68), another way of exploring the concept of spiritual learning is in terms of human capital, social capital and spiritual capital, all of which may contribute to individual—and subsequently organizational—learning (Bennet, 2006). Human capital is an individual's knowledge, competency and future potential, including a unique set of characteristics and values from the past such as expertise, education and experience. Social capital is built from the interactions across human relationship networks (Bennet & Bennet, 2004). It is also considered by some economists and sociologists as "the social benefit gained by a society that has low crime, low divorce and illegitimacy rates, low litigation figures, higher literacy, and a high degree of trust" (Zohar & Marshall, 2003, p. 26). Beyond material worth, then, social capital involves a "raised quality of life in a society" (Zohar & Marshall, 2003, p. 26), a wider sense of connectedness and social responsibility. Further, learning is directly connected to an individual's everyday life *and* the community in which an individual lives, the social context. "To view the learning experience in isolation from everyday experience is to miss some valuable aspects of the learning process. The spiritual dimension is best seen through an understanding of the whole person in a social context." (Wickett, 2000, p. 45)

While spiritual capital could be considered in terms of the *amount* of spiritual knowledge and expertise available to an individual (Zohar & Marshall, 2003, p. 27), in our model spiritual capital is both an amount (in terms of subject/object feelings and feeling activities) and an internal state-of-being (in terms of a condition, nature or essence), or a quality. Considering capital in terms of stock, spiritual capital would represent an individual's (or organization's, or country's, or world's) investment in the process of spiritual growth. In its entangled learning role with human and social capital, spiritual capital expands the individual's threshold of awareness, the functioning space within which knowledge and events make sense (Bennet & Bennet, 2006).

Learning itself can be a state of being, carried over time, that contains, accepts and nurtures a process of becoming that continues throughout a lifetime. In this regard it is similar to spiritual capital: learning capital is the capacity to learn, both the potential and actual ability to implement learning processes and create knowledge. When the process is spiritual learning, the outcome is likely to be, or be associated with, human development, growth and becoming. While the word "becoming" begs the question:

"Becoming what?" we defer here to our previous discussion of being as a condition, state or essence—with a continuous existence and influenced by a higher order of the possibilities open to the expanded aspects of being human. Our answer is, becoming more of what it is to be a higher-order human. An analogy in the organizational frame would be continuous learning. Human capital, social capital and spiritual capital, then, are entangled forms of learning capital.

Representative Human Characteristics that are Spiritual in Nature

While there is a bevy of information written on what it is to be spiritual, we have chosen to use two primary sources: (1) text reference materials: several dictionaries (American Heritage, 2000; Oxford, 2002); multiple-author reference books focused on the great ideas, modern thought and human thought (Adler, 1992; Rohmann, 1999); and (2) a bevy of randomly-collected books in the spiritual section of our 27,000 volume research library (Almass, 2004; Ardagh, 2005; Brussat & Brussat, 2000; Dyer, 2001; Elbert, 2000; Hendricks, 2000; Lerner, 2000; Rasha, 2003). Beyond identifying repetitions, we add to the mix our own intuition and speculation on which of the multiple repetitive concepts introduced in the various reference texts represent the highest order of human evolution. These characteristics are not forwarded as an exclusive set, but rather as indicators of the nature of the spiritual human.

As characteristics began to emerge through our research, we explored those characteristics considered emotional in nature in a subject/object relationship, denoting feelings or feeling activity directed toward a specific event, person or thing. The "subject" is "I" (the individual human as learner) who is in relationship with some object as denoted by the blanks in Table C-1. In alphabetical order representative characteristics include the following: *aliveness, caring, compassion, eagerness, empathy, expectancy, harmony, joy, love, respect, sensitivity, tolerance* and *willingness*. As shown in Table 1, these characteristics can generally be considered context-dependent and time-sensitive. This categorizing is discussed further below. Context is the set of circumstances surrounding the subject "I" (Bennet & Bennet, 2007b) and time-sensitive means occurrence of a feeling or feeling activity at a particular time or for a bounded period of time.

aliveness	"I feel alive" in response to surroundings or a stimulating event or series of events
caring	"I care about _____"
compassion	"I have compassion towards _____"
eagerness	"I am eager to _____"
empathy	"I have empathy towards _____"
expectancy	"I expect _____ to happen/to come"
harmony	"I am in harmony with _____"
joy	"I feel joy about/because _____"
love	"I love _____"
respect	"I respect _____"
sensitivity	"I am sensitive about/to _____"
tolerance	"I am tolerant of _____"
willingness	"I am willing to _____"

Table C-1: *Subject("I") in relationship with object (event, person or thing)*

Each of the characteristics in this subject/object group can become a condition as the object moves beyond an event, person or thing to holistic concepts embracing humanity and the world, as well as domains of the spirit. An example would be moving beyond love of a person or thing to living life fully in the condition of love (although love still denotes some form of generative activity—emotional involvement—even when addressed toward the world in general). This condition of love would be the higher order of love that is framed in Latin as *agapé*. A second example would be putting "conscious energy into developing a compassionate attitude toward all of being, all animals, and all human beings, including yourself" (Lerner, 2000, p. 291), what we would call the higher order of compassion.

The second group of characteristics that are spiritual in nature represent a **state-of-being**. For this usage, being is considered a condition, nature, or essence (Oxford, 2002, p. 212) of existence, specifically, immaterial aspects of human existence. These characteristics are descriptive in nature. In alphabetical order, characteristics representative of this group are: *abundance, authenticity, awareness, connectedness, consistency, grace, morality, openness, presence, readiness, unfoldment* and *wonder*. When considered as a condition or nature of an individual, these characteristics are continuous or a "mark of character," that is, not a temporal phenomena but a long-term or possibly life characteristic.

There is often pre-history to a state-of-being. This pre-history might include events, people and things that move an individual towards a state-of-being, or bring to the surface an essence or nature of the person. For example, Buddhist monks can undergo years of training, reflection and contemplation prior to achieving states of expanded awareness. While events and interactions occurring during the preparation period may be reflected in subject/object terms, over time they blend into a larger state-of-being. There is a fuzzy continuum between the subject/object characteristics and the state-of-being characteristics, with those characteristics described above as having a subject/object relationship having the potential—when repeated over and over again in different situations—to serve as conditioning for a way of being. We might even go so far as to say this progression represents spiritual growth. For example, Catherine Ingram presents aliveness, listed above in the subject/object category, as a state-of-being,

> [A]nyone who has been rendered speechless in the presence of beauty, genius, love, birth, or death, anyone who simply observes the most mundane of this fantastic existence and marvels at the stunning intelligence that informs it, lives in a sense of aliveness that no religion or belief can provide. (Ingram, 2003, p. 192)

Does this mean that those characteristics presented in the state-of-being group could be reduced in scope to a subject-object relationship? While certainly they *could* be considered in terms of a subject/object relationship, a state-of-being infers a higher order such that there is no subject or object. For example, while authenticity could also be considered a subject/object characteristic that is situation-dependent and time-sensitive (that man is an authentic Indian), in the higher-order context of a spiritual life it is considered an authenticity of self, a condition or nature, finding the whole in the parts. As Bartoft writes,

> The meaning of a sentence has the unity of a whole. We reach the meaning of the sentence through the meaning of the words, yet the meaning of the words in that sentence is determined by the meaning of the sentence as a whole. (Bortoft, 1996, p. 8)

Further, while being authentic may mean that what you see is what you get, the expanded state of authenticity strives "for an authenticity that is kind, caring, and socially responsible." (Chickering, et al, 2006, p. 8)

Within our organizations—heavily embedded in the historical precedence of an economy of lack and competition—an economy of *abundance* is difficult to imagine. Knowledge and learning provide good examples for understanding abundance. The only limits to learning are those imposed by the individual (and the organization); and the more you learn, the more you realize there is to learn. Similarly, since knowledge is a product of learning, and knowledge begets knowledge, there is *potentially no end in sight*. Lerner says the lived experience of spirituality includes "a deep trust that there is enough for all and that every human being deserves to share equally in the planet's abundance and is equally responsible for shaping our future" (Lerner, 2000, p. 5). The recently-released book/movie titled *Secret* is built on a theme of abundance using what is termed the law of attraction, "See yourself living in *abundance* and you will attract it. It works every time, with every person." (Byrne, 2006, p. 12)

Awareness is being conscious, having knowledge and being cognizant of current conditions and developments (Oxford, 2002, p. 160). "Spirituality means waking up" (De Mello, 1990, p. 5), being aware within the reality framework within which we live as well as within the larger framework of connectedness. This is consistent with the definition of knowing introduced above. Awareness does not necessarily mean that knowledge is at the forefront in every single moment, although when we speak we are generally aware of the meaning of what we are saying after we have said it. Recall that knowledge is the capacity (potential and actual) to take effective action. Awareness (in close relationship with knowing) carries with it an internal conviction that subtly, beneath the waters of consciousness, guides our actions. Take for example a situation where you are an invited speaker at a strategic conference in your area of expertise. As Dummett explains,

> [Y]our confidence that you understand an utterance, like your assurance that you know the identity of an individual you encounter or perceive, carries with it a conviction that you can do various relevant things—not merely that you could explain it if asked, but that you can react to it appropriately, comment on it, raise objections to it, act on it now or later, and so on—in short, that you *know* [emphasis added] what to do with it. (Dummett, 1991, p. 99)

Connectedness refers to a connectedness of all things, a oneness not necessarily a subject-object mechanistic connection. Rather, it is closer to being immersed in an energy field (light or heat, for example) where everyone is giving off and receiving energy; where sinks, sources, resonances and interdependencies may occur between, among and throughout the entire space. The concept of connectedness is so prevalent in spirituality that English and Gillen define spirituality itself as awareness of connectedness, an "awareness of something greater than ourselves, a sense that we are connected to all human beings and to all of creation." (English & Gillen, 2000, p. 1) In a learning group, connectedness is perceived as "a sense of belonging for each individual and an awareness that each one cares for the others and is cared for ... a shared understanding ...." (Wlodkowski, 1998, p. 70). The connectedness or oneness as a state-of-being would then manifest in a life of service, which concept is also forwarded as spiritual in nature. In its highest order, connectedness would include an understanding and appreciation for the autopoietic aspects of an individual's framework of reality as well as expanded states of consciousness. Autopoiesis is the property of complex living systems that structurally adapt and co-evolve with their external environment while maintaining their organization.

Consistency is a life consistency, where beliefs, values, feelings, thoughts and actions are integrated into a life-long cohesive approach to living and learning. *Grace* represents a credible, virtuous aspect that is in favor. In spiritual terms it is considered a regenerating, inspiriting and strengthening influence (Oxford, 2002, p. 1132). Directly related to discussion of connectedness, Williamson says that a state of grace exists "when we have remembered at last who we are to one another. That we *are* one another." (Williamson, 2002, p. 252).

While *morality* is generally used in a subject/object manner, with some specific qualifier, our usage is larger, supporting the belief that there can be/should be/will be a universal morality. The philosopher Hobbes recognized that moral virtues were praised because of the calamities avoided if people act morally (Gert, 1998). The point made here is that morality is concerned with *how behaviors affect others*. Further, Gert states that any definition of morality includes two necessary features: that anyone about whom a moral judgment is made know what morality is, and that the individual making moral judgment use that same morality as a guide for their own conduct (Gert, 1998, p. 9). Herein lies a paradox between the understanding of morality in the material world and an interpretation that would be consistent with other characteristics of spirituality. Often-repeated guidance appearing in spiritual literature is to suspend judgment, judgment of oneself and judgment of others. Recognizing that judgment is a faculty for operating in the material world, Dyer states, "Hold no one or no thing in judgment … In the world of spirit there is no right side and wrong side. There is only a field of infinite harmony that we are calling spiritual." (Dyer, 2001, p. 133) Conversely, as Gert forwards, our historical understanding of morality implies moral judgment. Compounding this paradox is the accepted terminology used earlier (see Definitions) that describe the soul as the animating principle of human life in terms of thought and action, specifically focused on its moral aspects (Oxford, 2002, p. 2928). Before we spend too much thought in this quagmire, let us recognize that this paradox may only exist because of our inability to perceive morality without judgment, a morality that might well usher in an advanced social state of existence.

Openness is directly related to trust, which is only possible when we relinquish control of our day-to-day lives to some greater order. In an organizational setting, this might be defined as a cumulative belief that another individual will live up to our expectations. As De Furia (1997) notes, "Interpersonal trust is present in a situation in which one individual places his or her interests under the control of another individual, with the expectation of gaining a desired outcome for which the potential negative consequences of violated trust are greater than the value of the potential desired outcome" (p. 5). This example, of course, represents a subject/object relationship. The higher-order of openness included in the state-of-being group of spiritual characteristics describes a *trusting nature*, what might be referred to as trusting the universe. Note that this does *not* insinuate naivety.

Presence builds upon this openness. It is the capacity for accessing the field of the future, a letting go and letting come, a "deep listening, of being open beyond one's preconceptions and historical ways of making sense" (Senge, et al., 2004, p. 11). In a more rhetorical sense, Jaworski sees presence as, "A profound opening of the heart, carried into action" (Senge, et al, 2004, p. 240). Presencing, then, can be considered opening to a shift of awareness, recognizing a changing environment and embracing new ways of learning, thinking and acting (Bennet, 2006), or what Scharmer refers to as "waking up together—waking up to who we really are by linking with and acting from our highest future self …." (Senge et al., 2004, p. 240).

Readiness goes beyond a state of preparedness to include an embedded capacity for quick response and a general openness and willingness toward future growth and learning. Again, note the expansion of the term willingness which is referenced above in a subject/object relationship. This usage is larger, insinuating a continuous willingness as an element of the nature of readiness. In like manner, while *unfoldment* represents a process over time as we know it, unfoldment is a continuous process throughout a life of growth and learning. The spiritual context to unfoldment includes an *allowing* in terms of space and time somewhat similar to the well-worn adage, everything in its own time. *Wonder* occurs at that intersection of one's boundary of youth, knowledge and spiritual maturity. Wonder is an element of what could be called awakened awareness. In a state of wonder, there may be no need for answers to the higher-level questions; we may be content to *live with* the questions. Lerner states that, "In a spiritually oriented society, the people most highly regarded will be those whose skills are concerned with nurturing others, helping them to develop their own capacities to be loving, conscious, self-determining, wise, playful, joyous, and *filled with awe and wonder.*" (Lerner, 2000, p. 269-270).

Finally, considering our tendency to interpret the materialistic world as dualistic (black/white; good/bad; negative/positive; soft/hard; male/female), we can look at spiritual characteristics in terms of those barriers that must be overcome in order to fully engage the spiritual state. In alphabetical order, representatives of these barriers are: ego, fear, judging (discussed above) and worry. While clearly all negativity can interfere with higher states of spirituality, it is also acknowledged that our wide range of feelings and experiences often serve as the process of learning, propelling us towards higher states of thought and being. A deeper discussion of this nature is beyond the scope of this paper.

While by definition ego is individualistic and self-centric, concerned with self-esteem or self-importance, in a larger sense it can be viewed as "a set of thoughts that define an individual's universe" (Dass, 1980, p. 138). Ego represents the "I" of the subject/object relationship, which must be moved beyond individual confinement to engage oneness, or being in a state of connectedness. The spiritual concept is to move beyond our ego (again, a faculty for engaging the material world), detaching from our old habits and freeing our awareness and thoughts. As Dass explains,

> We need the matrix of thoughts, feelings, and sensations we call the ego for our physical and psychological survival … [but] as long as the ego calls the shots, we can never become other than what it says …We can learn to venture beyond it, though … [then the] ego is there, as our servant." (Dass, 1980, p. 138)

In the context of spiritual learning, we are concerned with releasing the ego to inner development, to learning.

Facing and overcoming fear has been a close companion of man's conversations throughout recorded history. We draw quotes from a multi-discipline group of historical figures to comment on the value of overcoming fear:

> "Your greatest gift lies beyond the door named fear ...." (Sufi saying); "If we have respect for all created things and treat all human beings with love and respect ... we are spared the need to live in fear or tension ...." (Babaji); "Nothing in life is to be feared, only understood ...." (Marie Curie); "Fear is the main source of superstition, and one of the main sources of cruelty. To conquer fear is the beginning of wisdom ...." (Bertrand Russell); "The only thing we have to fear is fear itself ...." (Franklin D. Roosevelt); "Of all the liars in the world, sometimes the worst are your own fears .... (Rudyard Kipling); "Fear is fatal ...." (Harry Houdini); [and so forth] (Zubko, 1996, pp. 164-165).

Worry can be considered a form of fear, anxiety in terms of uncertainty about the future (or perhaps a fear of failure). The spiritual response to worry is mindful living, the concept of living life moment by moment, or in the now. Part of the "overcoming" is embracing the fear and letting it go. As Lesser explains, "Everything that occurs is not only usable and workable but it is actually the path itself. We can use everything that happens to us as the means for waking up" (Lesser, 1999, p. 126), what could be called spiritual learning.

Finally, a discussion of representative characteristics of spiritual learning cannot ignore the larger context of meaning and values. Wlodkowski forwards that, "One way to understand meaning is to see it as an increase in the complexity of an experience or idea that relates to people's values or purposes. This meaning may be beyond articulation, as in the realm of the creative or spiritual." (Wlodkowski, 1998, p. 75) Similarly, Van Ness contends that spirituality is the expression of an individual's quest for meaning (Van Ness, 1996). In presenting their case for what they call spiritual intelligence, Zohar and Marshall argue that,

> Human beings are essentially spiritual creatures because we are driven by a need to ask 'fundamental' or 'ultimate' questions ... We have a longing for something that takes us beyond ourselves and the present moment, for something that gives us and our actions a sense of worth." (Zohar & Marshall, 2000, p. 4)

We agree that meaning and values are that which provide context to life. It is this longing to find meaning that propels the human forward along the path of learning. In the largest sense, Lerner sees this as "a deep inner knowing that our lives have meaning through our innermost being as manifestations of the ultimate goodness of the universe" (Lerner, 2000, p. 5).

Connecting the Dots

An exploration of the relationship of those human characteristics that are spiritual in nature and human learning begs the questions: Do these spiritual characteristics contribute to learning? Is there a subset of these spiritual characteristics that contribute to deep learning or knowing? If we combine these spiritual characteristics, do any patterns emerge that will help us further understand this concept of spiritual learning?

We will explore the answers to these questions collectively by beginning with the last question. See Figure C-2 for a graphical display of these characteristics. Recognizing that the spiritual characteristics presented in this paper are representative only, there still appear to be a number of emergent themes in relationship to learning. These themes are loosely described as: shifting frames of reference, moving toward wisdom, priming for learning, enriching relationships, and animating for learning.

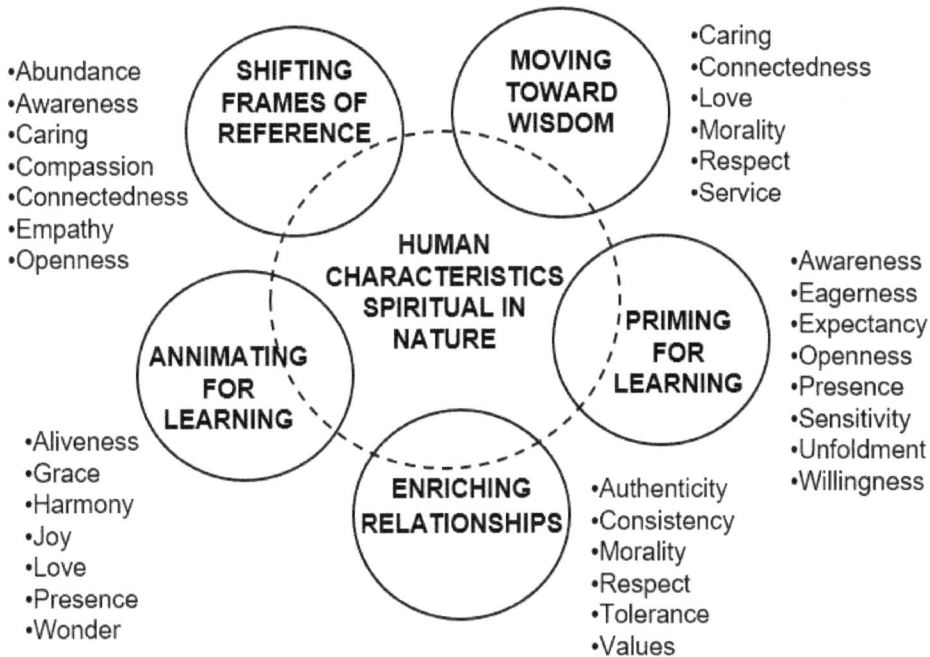

Figure C-2: Spiritual characteristics and spiritual learning.

Shifting Frames of Reference are intertwined with learning, thinking and acting (Bennet, 2006), and can be the result of type 3 and type 4 learning. There are two categories that shifting frames of references fall into: (1) looking from a different perspective (the external approach), and (2) taking an empathetic perspective (the internal approach), which moves the viewpoint from the objective to the subjective. The internal approach is one step beyond a hermeneutic approach (the thing in itself, the observed). It is not merely embedding yourself into the object but becoming part of the object and observing (and feeling) from within the object. Spiritual characteristics introduced above that support shifting frames of reference include: *abundance,* *awareness, caring, compassion, connectedness, empathy* and *openness*. As Senge et al (2004, p. 10) state, "The key to the deeper levels of learning is that the larger living wholes of which we are an active part are not inherently static … When we become more *aware* of the dynamic whole, we also become more *aware* of what is emerging." Note that Shifting Frames of Reference has been developed as a Knowledge Capacity (see Chapter 13).

We have introduced wisdom as a part of the knowledge spectrum and taken Sternberg's definition which forwards the goal of achieving the common good (Sternberg, 2003). See Bennet and Bennet (2015a) for an in-depth treatment of Wisdom. While spiritual terminology forwards the term "greater good," for purposes of this paper the common good is taken to mean the greater good. Spiritual characteristics that support **Moving Toward Wisdom**—contributing to a common good—include: *caring, connectedness, love, morality, respect* and *service*. If you think from the perspective of wisdom—looking above and beyond the subject and object—you learn about the system in which the subject and object interact. Further, the content and context of that interaction may change from that viewpoint, facilitating a higher order of understanding both in terms of the system and what is being communicated. For example, Chickering, et al, said that grappling with a personal understanding of the concepts of wisdom, *compassion*, integrity, *values*, *morality* and character will determine if individuals "will use the knowledge and skills they have acquired … for the betterment of the individual, their communities, and the larger society." (Chickering, et al, 2006, p. 2) Wisdom can be directly linked to knowing. For example, the inventor of the polio vaccine, Jonas Salk, rejected common wisdom and tapped into what he called the *continually unfolding dynamism of the universe*, "an active process that … I can guide by the choices I make" (*The New York Times*, 1993, p. 1, 9). This is what we would define as type 4 learning. As a second example, Senge, et al, state that this inward-bound journey is what lies at the heart of all creativity. They quote W. Brian Arthur, a noted economist of the Santa Fe Institute, as saying: "Every profound innovation is based on an inward-bound journey, on going to a deeper place where knowing comes to the surface." (Senge, et al, 2004, p. 11)

Priming for Learning concerns attributes that facilitate the condition of learning. Priming is used in the sense of preparing, but an active preparing, a moving *toward* learning. Spiritual characteristics that support a priming for learning are: *awareness, eagerness, expectancy, openness, presence, sensitivity, unfoldment* and *willingness*. These characteristics also operate at the fringe of knowing, operating between that of which we are consciously aware and that of which we are less aware. The psychologist William James suggests that thoughts and feelings move in and out of *awareness* (James, 1890). As we move about our lives, what is on the fringe is the context, the entangled associations and feelings that give meaning to the content (Bennet & Bennet, 2007). Frager and Fadiman describe this fringe as the feeling of *almost knowing*, the feeling of being on the right track, and the intention to act before you know exactly how you are going to act (Frager & Fadiman, 1998) Similarly, *expectancy, presence* and *unfoldment* are focused on future experiences.

The spiritual characteristics in the category of **Enriching Relationships** contribute to building social capital. These are: *authenticity, consistency, morality, respect, tolerance* and *values*. Competence theory (White, 1959) assumes that it is natural for people to strive for effective interactions with their world. Further, Nouwen (1975) contends that it is through the two dimensions of spirituality that exist beyond ourselves—with others and beyond the human—that we can truly learn to grow in understanding. English & Gillen state that "*authentic* spirituality moves one outward to others as an expression of one's spiritual experiences." (English & Gillen, 2000, p. 1) Wlodkowski says that since adults have a strong need to apply their learning to the real world, "they are more motivated [to learn] when the circumstances under which they assess their competence are *authentic* to their actual lives" (Wlodkowski, 1998, p. 78) From a learning motivational viewpoint, Wlodkowski would add the word inclusion, which he defines as "awareness of learners that they are part of an environment in which they and their instructor are respected by and connected to one another" (Wlodkowski, 1998, p. 69).

Respect is a condition of being esteemed or honored. It carries with it a sense of worth, of value. Respect is central to a spiritually-based relationship (Orr, 2000; Vogel, 2000). It is at the core of the Native American medicine wheel, often referred to as the circle of life, as teaching and learning is passed from elder to child in a continuous process of what Orr calls the spirituality of relationships: teaching through sharing and respect (Orr, 2000). Similarly, Csikszentmihalyi says, "We have to learn [values], as we learn the language our parents speak … *Values* are memes, units of information passed down from one generation to another that shape our ways of thinking and our actions." (Csikszentmihalyi, 2003, p. 209) From these examples it appears that this group of spiritual characteristics might also be thought of as guiding and perpetuating the process of learning.

Animating for Learning speaks to the fundamental source of life—learning, energy used for survival and growth. Spiritual characteristics that fall into this area include: *aliveness, grace, harmony, joy, love, presence and wonder*. Csikszentmihalyi's flow state—the positive aspects of human experience (*joy*, creativity, *total involvement with life*)—enables people to "experience the remarkable potential of the body and mind fully functioning in *harmony*" (Csikszentmihalyi, 2003, p. 63). Studying adult learning, Wlodkowski concludes that, "more positive emotions, such as *wonder* and *joy*, are often more likely to deepen interest and nurture involvement" (Wlodkowski, 1998, p. 76) While focusing on adult educators, Vogel "honors the experience of each person and leaves room for mystery [that] can lead to transformative teaching and learning" (English & Gillen, 2000, p. 3). Vogel's ideas include not only exploring our inner lives to discover insights that can inform our questions, but tapping into our spiritual lives in *life-giving ways*, open to difference and accepting of others (Vogel, 2000). *Presence* might also support this animating for learning category in terms of moving toward an emerging whole.

> In talking with entrepreneurs, we found extraordinary clarity regarding what it means to act in the service of what is emerging … We came to realize that both groups are really talking about the same process—the process whereby we learn to "presence" an emerging whole, to become what George Bernard Shaw called "a force of nature". (Senge, et al, 2004, p. 10)

Responding to our first and second questions, the characteristics surfaced that represent those human characteristics spiritual in nature clearly support learning, both in terms of knowledge and knowing. Further, all those characteristics that support type 3 and type 4 learning would be strong contributors to deep learning or knowing. By definition, type 4 learning *is* knowing. Through our grouping we have surfaced themes that would appear to contribute to understanding the evolving concept of spiritual learning. However, this is only the beginning. Spiritual characteristics could also be related to a multitude of conditions and processes that contribute to good business; for example, the direct relationship of openness and respect to successful communications—and successful communities of practice—in organizations. We invite the reader to follow these logical relationships.

A Final Reflection

We believe there is a positive correlation between these representative spiritual characteristics and human learning. This makes sense, of course, since there are overarching connections between the concepts of spirituality and learning that are embedded by virtue of the concepts themselves. For example, Teasdale explains, "Being spiritual suggests a personal commitment to a process of inner development that engages us in our totality … the spiritual person is committed to growth as an essential ongoing life goal." (Teasdale & Dali Lama, 1999, pp. 17-18) In other words, learning (growth) is a life goal of spirituality. Therefore, it follows that human characteristics that are spiritual in nature would contribute to learning.

Further, from the above discussion, we would agree that spiritual learning supports personal growth, helps us understand reality, helps others, and contributes to the greater good. There are indicators that recognition of the relationship of spirituality to these values is spreading. For example, as we entered the new millennium a World Commission on Spirituality was inaugurated whose commissioners included Nobel Prize winner Elie Wiesel and Bishop Desmond Tutu (Cousins, 1999; Shafer, 1999). In the field of adult education, English and Gillen conclude that "a more holistic approach of learning, which includes a spiritual dimension, is what is needed in the field of adult education in the years ahead." (English & Gillen, 2000, p. 5) The authors recognize this movement. But how can we engage this spiritual learning to solve problems, make decisions, take actions and survive in our everyday lives and organizations? Historically, at least on paper, there has been a separation of state and religion. Whether that separation is, ever has been, or could exist is highly debatable (that is another paper for a different journal). However, regardless of one's position on that debate, what we have dealt with in this paper is *not* religion, but the concept of spirituality, which by its definition—taken from two major dictionaries of the English Language—is impossible for the human mind to disengage. For better or worse, the material and non-material—if they exist—are married in the conscious and unconscious learning of the human mind.

As Posner informs us, "The workplace spirituality movement is … beginning to penetrate the consciences of the world's corporations." (Posner, 1999, p. 72) While the idea of embracing spirituality in the workplace is just beginning to appear in organizational literature, as can be recognized by the discussion above, wherever the human mind exists so too does spirituality, and so too does spiritual learning. The implications of these finding to organizations may be profound. While more rigorous research is required, by recognizing the presence and value of Spiritual Learning in our lives and in our organizations, we can open our minds to new frames of reference. Through these new frames of reference, we can build organizational environments that not only honor diversity of thought and belief, but diversity of learning, capitalizing on new ways of learning and the higher values of the human soul.

Appendix D
Thought Leader Values

This appendix includes the 53 personal beliefs or values identified by the 34 thought leaders in the KMTL study. While primarily working in the field of knowledge management and organizational learning, this group stretches across four continents with tremendous diversity in focus, education and skill sets. Since our focus in this book is on knowledge and leadership, it is quite appropriate that the thought leaders in the KMTL study were engaged in helping organizations manage knowledge.

The groupings fall loosely into the following nine areas: philosophical issues, the other, self, relationships, learning, characteristics, personal values, work ethic and organizations, and rules for living. For each grouping we will first provide an overview of the beliefs and values, followed first by the explication and then the extrapolation to the KM field provided by the thought leader. This is this format: TL Value / Explication of Value / Extrapolation to KM Field.

Grouping 1: Honoring the World:

positive energy, honoring the world, living in the light, living with love and compassion, making some sort of a difference for other people, working with people together to change the world to be a better place, wanting to make a difference, working for a larger good than yourself, trying to understand the world intellectually, the inviability of humanity, the value of life, life, there is a creator in my mind of this universe

Positive energy / It's very **important that there's positive energy flowing**, because some people are energy destroyers and I stay away from them. / The energy around KM is warm and peaceful. It's positive due to the building of relationships and trust that support sharing.

Honoring the world / The way to make the world a slightly better place is to figure out what is the productive way that honors the world. I think it's a good feeling to say, hey, the world might be slightly better off because we have a more realistic understanding of it at this moment and we have honored it. / **Knowledge sharing honors the world**. It tries to say listen to the backtalk of the world. When we do not listen there are unintended consequences. We've created a multibillion dollar market in heroin now with what we did in Afghanistan that's feeding terrorism. That's the world talking back. When you listen you can ask, what can we do about it?

Living in the light / People are at the core. / **I share as much as possible** of my knowledge free of charge. I have uploaded everything I've written on my web site for free download.

Living with love and compassion / Adapted from the Yoga philosophy: "Love everybody, do your meditation, all the rest is entertainment." What it really means to me is that **everything is here for my learning**, everything that we're going through collectively is for our learning, and to bring us joy, to bring us insight, to bring us compassion. / Now that KM's evolved into the questions of knowledge networks and relationship, it's getting a lot closer. When we talk relationship and honoring relationship we're talking about *Philos* at least, brotherly love. We also know that knowledge will not multiply or be shared where there is no trust, where there's no respect. So we're evolving into a way of coming at that knowledge question that is a very human-focused question. **Our knowledge is very deeply linked to our identity**, because in a very real sense we're sharing who we are when we talk about the things that we know, understand, care about and believe in.

Making some sort of a difference for other people / When I was a teen, this just struck me as to do what needed to be done, so I've adhered to that ever since. Interestingly, by doing so, the fun or feelings of goodness, or whatever one might want to call it, is the result as opposed to the business-oriented goals that some people would have, which often tend to be the byproduct. / I guess there are two things. One is that **now there's more of a foundation to stand on**. There are many more kindred spirits out there, and that helps to increase visibility and the interest in the work and the feedback mechanisms that flow through all of that help buttress the work and encourage it. And from that base, looking ahead how to make a further difference, taking it more to the micro level and more to the macro level.

Working with people together to change the world to be a better place / This is one thing I aspire to which is really important to me, to do this by somehow inspiring people and **leading through inspiration** not through power, creating an environment where the better idea wins, and people will somehow learn to collaborate better. / I think it's a great challenge for the knowledge economy to help people learn how to work together and understand each other, and it's a huge KM challenge to teach people how to collaborate, how to value one another's capabilities and aspirations. We need to somehow learn to **see organizations as environments for people to create great things together**.

Wanting to make a difference / It has always seemed to me that there's something incredibly selfish doing work that just benefits self and doesn't benefit others. I don't have words for it, it's just that I know I feel a kind of a joy when I think that I may have made a difference, and in some small way there's such a wonderful feeling about that. / If people could **speak their own truth** we wouldn't have the kinds of anguish and problems that we have in many organizations, where many people come to work every day pretending to be something they are not, leaving a good part of their self and soul at home because they know they just can't bring it to work. So I think knowledge serves that end. I think for me there's something close to, I don't even know what word to use for knowledge, it is so precious … it's close to being sacred or holy in some sense. It has that set of characteristics in terms of the highest good kind of thing … like **knowing or understanding is one of the higher goods**. It almost has an end in of itself.

Working for a larger good than yourself / It is the need for making sense and not just doing a job, but **contributing to the larger good**. I think that is a very important dimension. This is the larger good of humanity and the world. / KM and knowledge navigation contribute in the way that you see with the genome project. We learned about the gene structures and it plays out in the research in the health sector, it plays out in exploring the unknown for the larger good, actually. That's why knowledge navigation has a very important role to play versus just sorting what we know that we know. Knowledge navigation is **exploring the opportunity space or the unknown**, what you don't know that you don't know, and why. KM is actually administering what you know that you know, therefore you get the kind of balance between developing new intelligence versus handling what you already know.

Trying to understand the world intellectually / I try to understand the world by an approach that's probably analytical and intellectual. **I like ideas so I like trying to apply ideas to the world**. I don't think that's necessarily a better way to live than people who approach it primarily aesthetically or morally, but it's just who I am. / KM is a set of ideas

The inviability of humanity / I don't think this word exists. I mean that **we must never harm another person** either physically or psychically in all its fragility and the importance of human beings. / All the tools that I develop, all the texts I write, have this aim to improve connectedness, to improve people's ability to share, to improve people's ability to link and learn from each other irrespective of technology.

The value of life / And not expending incredible amounts of effort in war. I believe we've got to find a way to be expending the energies on this planet toward peace instead of toward armaments and war. / Intelligence systems to track terrorist movements.

Life / Tension between love and beauty, and **finding a balance** in all that … Tension between knowing and doing. There are times when you want to do exactly what you want to do, but something else is pulling at you and wants a certain response from you … Balance. / A lot of people believe that KM is just to become a smarter person, but I think the important thing is to both **become smart and do something with that smartness**. So, a lot of people that I meet tend to say, Oh, I know all this stuff, but my next question to them is, So what? So, what are you going to do with it? Or some people say, "I don't like the way this organization is going." So what are you going to do about it? Are you going to change something? Are you going to become an activist? Are you going to write about it? Are you going to become a heckler, a lobbyist? What are you going to do with it? So, I think to **take the passion of doing something and then converting it into responsibility**.

There is a creator in my mind of this universe / There's no doubt in my mind. / This legalizes the search for underlying principles, the fact that **things are not totally arbitrary**. There are principles, or mechanisms if you will, in other words, there are mechanisms of how one works, how one interacts, how physics hangs together if you will, and that **it is appropriate for us to try to learn** about these mechanisms and apply the principles of these as best we can to shore up these buildings that we build on top .. maybe I should say card houses.

Grouping 2: Valuing Others

the other, a sense of other, everyone is fundamentally good and nice and peaceful, everybody wants to learn, everybody truly wants to do their best, real contributions come from people, people know a lot, people have a fundamentally good side, everybody thinks that they are basically better than everybody else and more ethical and more compassionate, supporting people, ordinary people can create extraordinary results, the power of individuals and teams to lead others

The other / The other is any other entity **beginning with all other human beings and all other life creatures**. Right at the core of this transition from modernity into alternative societies is development of an entire new set of values and competencies that actually make social life viable, a social life that is tolerant of differences, that is creative in analysis, and so on. It is not bounded by the mere indigenous, but it is basically potentialized by the quality and quantity, but above all the quality of interactions with others. / If we manage to understand more from the mental, the mechanisms that contribute to create, to make connectedness efficient, maximizing value for every constituent part; if we manage to understand and propitiate, then we are really doing KM. We are getting to the point where in our organizations we have a dialogue amongst the parts, and in the end that connectedness makes sense to all in its own terms.

A sense of other / Part of that is my spiritual belief or at least the sense that **there's something outside of us**. But it's more in terms of interaction with others and the quality of interaction with other people. / **It's happening**. It's happening faster than I can even keep up with it. And I think there are things we can do toward increasing the contactivity related to that. We could build incentives to do that, and the conditions to do that. There are certain conditions for building an innovation culture to put those ideas into action.

Everyone is fundamentally good and nice and peaceful. Everybody wants to learn. Everybody truly wants to do their best. / People are often displaced, either because they were brought up to believe that they shouldn't be doing something, or that **their careers have taken them in one way and their hearts in another**. Whatever it may be, the more people can learn about different disciplines, the more people will be able to find their niche and really, really be happy. / Organizations need to give their people opportunities to learn and find out what they do best. **Value differences and knowledge**.

Real contributions come from people / It's great that we have all this technology, but let's not forget that **the real contribution comes from people**. / I'd like to think that if people look at my work on KM as well as other things, they would say this guy never really forgot the importance of people and was always kind of talking about the importance of people.

People know a lot / I really believe that other people know a lot, and try to respect that and not to assume they have no knowledge on a subject. We all only know what we know internally, and yet you have to operate from the point of view that everybody else also has that enormous reservoir of knowledge and information. If we can **give them the right space, ask questions in the right way, give them the right opportunity to blossom** … so it's respecting that other people have the same interior life you do, have the same rich set of experiences, different but just as rich. / KM basically comes from the point of view that people have a lot of knowledge and in most cases we have to set up the circumstances around them so that it can be effectively shared or used. You know I just hate it when somebody makes a mistake or does a lot of extra work, and I could have said to them, you know that we did that already, go here and just use it, or, oh don't do that, let me tell you what happened last time we did that. I'm always going around saying, "You know somebody already has a template for that." I think that's one of the reasons it made so much sense for me to gravitate to KM.

People have a fundamentally good side / I also think there's the beast within and the dark side, and that both of those are there. Assuming that your chemistry is not screwed up and your wiring is not congenitally messed up, then **it's the circumstances around us that creates us and a lot of our behaviors**. / I like the collaborative aspects of KM so much that I think people, given the right, can work together and decide what their common mission and goal is. In most cases, if people have the support of other people and are working together toward what I call positive goals, a lot of knowledge sharing takes place. That creates the context.

Everybody thinks that they are basically better than everybody else and more ethical and more compassionate / If you do a survey, 90 percent of the people—and I'm not exaggerating—will say they are more compassionate and ethical than other people are. People do things for their reasons, not for your reasons. You have to tap into what it is that is really driving other people if you want them to in any way get on board with what you're doing. **Only you can change you**. If you get on their side then there isn't any other side. / We're all connected but we don't know it, and **it's the knowing that we're all connected that empowers a whole different set of actions**. I may be connected, you know, six degrees of separation, to somebody in Germany who's working on some drug that I don't know about, but if I had a need to know it and now the world gives me all these ways to make that connection, then it would be possible.

Supporting people / How others are being treated, not only in terms of what society deems appropriate. / What I can see there is this whole notion of societal KM as well as KM in the small that allows us to **behave in ways where we share understanding**, share knowledge, to help other people build value to them in pursuing their own goals; all of the aspects of how to deal with situations in ways that are more supportive of the type of life that you'd like to live.

Ordinary people can create extraordinary results / Ordinary people have capacities that we can't even imagine when they're given the context to contribute. / A form of dialogue and knowledge sharing and collective intelligence that has evolved under our stewardship is based on that fundamental principle. It's that **people collectively have within them the wisdom to confront even the most difficult of challenges** if they are provided a context and support for doing so. That's really what it's all about. As simple as that.

The power of individuals and teams to lead others / This opens up the potential in organizations to be more receptive to people with ideas, and the ideas. So we still need to learn *how we can value ourselves, not so much by how much we are better than others but by how much we have learned, how much we have grown ourselves, and how much we are helping others grow.* / Relationships, networks and communities. Valuing intellectual capital.

Grouping 3: Nurturing Self

building and developing and nourishing our own identity, being close to my own livingness, traveling makes you a wiser person, self initiation and ownership, the whole idea of self-worth

Building and developing and nourishing our own identity / This is the counterpart to the other. In looking outward towards discovering and responding to others, we capitalize on the very significant cultural process by which personal, group, or organizational or national identity has been built over the past. And the elements that we have to understand and make rationale and emotional sense of in identity are very strong and powerful. So I think it is very significant, and not to be diminished when looking towards the other, but something that actually makes it possible to build a constructive and assertive dialogue. / Example: Capital systems is an attempt to formally specify two requirements and conditions: **completeness and consistency**. Basically, it includes all of the significant elements and has no contradiction among any of these. So in terms of KM, one of the fundamental questions that still has not been really, really substantially addressed is the theory of the firm. What makes the business be a business or a productive organization to be a productive organization? And so what I have attempted is first to establish this specification for a capital system, namely, one has to have management systems that involve all the necessary and sufficient value elements for any given organization. And the response to that is capital systems.

Being close to my own livingness / My own **livingness is both individual and social**. In Africa they have this saying, I exist through you. So when I say my own livingness I mean my ability to be aware, and this is very sociological constructed as well as biological. / To accept community is a fundamental principle of identity, of humanness. It is to recognize that my livingness is not just my own, and that my core value, even if it is something that I experience profoundly personally, it is also profoundly social … not shared, because nobody knows what it's like to be me, but to be me is part of a network of relationship, it's not just me.

Travel makes you a wiser person / Traveling to different countries, especially when you have to fend for yourself for a couple of weeks. / If you look at how human beings have evolved over the millennium, there was a time when gypsies were the carriers of knowledge. They would travel around with stories from different parts of the world; they would carry with them information about what is happening in different parts of the world. Today. I think some of **the best innovations come from people who can juggle perspectives**, people who are one with nature, and can work in technology for some time, then in humanities, then management, and feed off each of these very different subjects.

Self-initiation and ownership / The fundamental belief that I don't work in an organization because it represents a shelter. I'm not entitled to anything, and fundamentally I'm a business of one. My role is to create value for the organization I happen to be working for in exchange for the ability to continuously develop my capabilities. **I own my performance**. I own my contribution and the extent to which it is creating value. **I own my learning** because this is what allows me to meet increasing challenges. I'm fulfilling the talents that I've been given to the greatest extent that this is one of my fundamental responsibilities. / Self-knowledge. KM increases self worth.

The whole idea of self-worth / Giving people a sense that what they are doing is worthwhile and important, and always giving them full respect in whatever we do, even when we're about to fire them because they no longer fit in the organization. / In terms of KM, it has a lot to do with the ability of people to share what they know, to share what they are finding, to explore without feeling undue risk or undue vulnerability, to be in confidence that **when they share it's in a win-win environment**. By helping their colleagues and the organization succeed, they actually help themselves succeed.

Grouping 4: Honoring Relationships

family belief in family, building relationships, relationships with other people, community or relationship

Family / That's kind of the core. It seems one has to first of all have health, then there's the family (so relationships), and I'd say extremely important. / Well, I suppose the work I do is very collegial in nature, that is, it involves doctoral students and in some sense they are like an extended family, maybe a scholarly family in a sense. They are almost like children in a way, and I continue to work with them and encourage them in their own efforts. Then the person who was my major professor is almost like a father figure, I suppose, so my students are almost like his grandchildren in some sense, in **sharing the thought and growing it and passing it on**. A larger network gives the opportunity to make a larger difference. Building the analogy, in some sense it's almost like family and country, so to speak. There are those with whom I've worked, and we have some sort of joint fruits from our labors in a direct sense, that's the family aspect. But then there's the entire community of researchers that are interested in the same topic but with whom there may not have been a direct a relationship in the past, and that's almost like one's country, so to speak.

Belief in family / Belief in relationship. / Work looks at relationship; they look at more than just instrument aspects of relationships.

Building relationships / With my family, in particular. / Correlates with empathic design and creative abrasion concepts. Empathic design is really an attempt to understand someone else's thinking, and **it's a generosity of spirit that allows you to take another person's point of view**. That relates to creative abrasion in that you respect other people's points of view and that allows you to have many people contribute to a project or process.

Relationships with other people / Family and colleagues as well as other citizens. To honor the relationship actually. / I'm trying to act as a kind of example, so **I'm sharing with delight**. I'm trying to inspire other people. And relationships play out in writing, or in trying to proselytize to the next generation.

Community or relationship / It seems to me that all of us have two warring forces within us. One of those forces is for self-sufficiency, and the ability to sort of prove what we can do and that we can. This is the competitive side that wants to be independent and stable, and do amazingly well. The other part of us wants to be in community, with others, the "we" rather than "I"; wants the relationship and values. So, **we simultaneously want to be in relationship and independent**. So the whole issue of how we function in community or how we function independently, and what that balance is and how to live within that balance, is a lifelong struggle. / I've written a lot about relationships and community.

Grouping 5: Valuing Learning

everybody wants to learn, experts should be teachers, continuous learning (twice), the joy of learning, the value of sharing, and "Tomorrow is going to be a better day than yesterday."

Everybody wants to learn / [See Grouping 2.]

Experts should be teachers / When you realize that you have developed an expertise in an area, at that point **you should become a teacher and share that expertise and know-how** regardless of what the topic is or area. / An example: We've identified 30 centers of expertise in the company and we've created a role called knowledge asset manager, and then as we expand into the global company each of them will also have a knowledge asset manager. The intent is that the things that we've learned around the discipline of KM will be understood and embraced and then that message will be taken forward.

Continuous learning / If that's not going on, then what's the reason for being around? Learning can make a positive difference in the advance of something, of anything. / **Learning is an absolute key to knowledge**.

Continuous learning / This is critical. / Plays out in multiple ways. One way is that KM is still an immature field. We're still striving for how to really implement it and find procedures and tools and everything else to make it a reality in a framework that is affordable for organizations. And so we need to learn how to do that, and **we can only solve the critical problems by being aware of what is current and trying to improve it at all times**. It also underpins the organizational philosophy to collect, share, organize, disseminate knowledge.

The joy of learning / It's what gets me up in the morning, and it's what makes me tired in the nighttime. I mean it's the sense of the world always afresh and something new happening and I can look with great excitement when I look out the door or get the newspaper. There's going to be another kind of micro discovery made by me today! / I always ask myself, **how is the audience going to see the world differently after my talks**. So, I think about it as seeing differently, and having a different mental model in their heads, maybe. I get a great kick out of learning something new, understanding it, and then, if it's really neat, having other people appreciate it as well. I have a rich social life, a very broad set of interactions. If people are doing this knowledge sharing in a very positive way and learning from each other and affecting their work and their organization and learning themselves as individuals, then there's joy in that for them.

The value of sharing / I've, with few exceptions, generally experienced positive effects from giving away ideas and knowledge. / Knowledge sharing.

"Tomorrow is going to be a better day than yesterday." / There's a hitch. / Tomorrow is only going to be a better day than yesterday, it's only possible, if learning takes place. This is why knowledge competencies and learning are so tremendously interesting things, because **learning is what makes actually tomorrow a better day than yesterday**.

Grouping 6: Staying Open

curiosity, openness and receptivity to new ideas, and perspective

Curiosity / I'm very curious. Not only intellectual. I'm curious about most things. For example, **when I meet someone, I ask questions because it might be that they have something to tell me**. / Innovation and new ideas.

Curiosity, openness and receptivity to new ideas / I think curiosity and receptivity to new ideas are absolutely core values to me, and I think that it's a core value to err on the side of sharing ideas rather than the side of withholding ideas. **Knowledge does not exist in a vacuum** and should not exist in a vacuum but should be shared broadly and put to work is sort of a central message. / Knowledge sharing and use.

Perspective / I don't trust narrow perspectives. I've always been concerned with in which context does the situation exist, and not only the context itself, but **what are the guiding objectives of the context? The why, not only the what, and how can we possibly find different ways of approaching it?** / This is why I see KM as such an integral part of integrative management whether a society, organization or person., it requires the integration of everything that has happened. **Everything is connected**, but then, of course, you would go into a total tailspin if you tried to connect everything. You'd go into analysis paralysis if you were to do that, so you have to set priorities, but I think that setting a single dimension is wrong.

Grouping 7: Living Values

kindness, honesty (twice), honesty is the best policy, being genuine, doing one's best to tell the truth, tolerance, integrity (twice), sense of justice, equity or justice, respect, respect and caring, respect others beliefs, and love of your fellow

Kindness / I really feel very strongly about kindness. I think people should really make a tremendous effort to be as kind as they can to all people, all living things, as best they can. I try to live that way. It doesn't always succeed, but I try to. / I would say that's one of the subtexts of a lot of the KM literature, that **we should value people for what they know and that all people know things. The nature of hierarchy that people in charge know much more than those who are not in charge is just**

bologna. I don't believe it. And I think believing in kindness, I think we should all respect the knowledge of everyone we work with in organizations.

Honesty / It's the grounding principle of my life. And it's interesting; it has negative implications. There are times when telling the truth is not the right thing. / Relationships. Plays out in community efforts, because in order to be open you have to have trust, so a core value of knowledge sharing.

Honesty / Other things are not easily capsulated and labeled. I don't' think people really think in labels. I do believe in caring for other people, I believe in listening what their thoughts are. I believe in being kind to people. / Those kinds of value are not common features of a strongly-hierarchal style of management, so KM certainly created opportunities to push approaches to management that more fully reflected those kinds of things: **listening in to other people, listening to their ideas**, understanding where they're coming from and being careful of how one treats people. These things become much more central once you try to share knowledge because if you don't do those kinds of things you quickly run into problems.

Honesty is the best policy / - / We try to be consistent. We've established some terms of practice, so part of it is maintaining that line of consistency, and therefore you're not always being politically correct. Then I think it's developing some guiding principles and maintaining those.

Speaking honestly and openly / If we could **understand each other more fully** tan we could solve many of the problems that we all deal with. / In KM we create the conditions in which those kinds of conversations can take place.

Being genuine / It's important being yourself, being genuine. / Knowledge innovation is people intensive; the knowledge is inside people, and innovation doesn't usually happen by yourself. So that's the focus on interactions and conversations and relationship building and social capital. **To be in relationship, the human being has to be true to themselves and to other people.**

Doing one's best to tell the truth / I stress how important the truth is in terms of building credibility, **building authenticity**, and in terms of getting things done in this area. If you stray from those paths you may make some short-run gains for some time but you will lose the main game. You're not going to be able to change the organization, you're not going to be able to convince others to do things differently, you're not going to be able to get people to share their knowledge, because people no longer trust you. So I make a major point of in my own life embodying those principles and encourage others to do likewise. / Storytelling has this nuance in some uses of the word, so it's quite important for me in terms of establishing the credibility to say that, in organizational storytelling, telling true stories is basically the name of the game. It's not simply a matter of telling the truth, being factually accurate as far as it goes, but **truth in context**. Most corporate communications paint a rosy picture of some scene just around the corner, just below some details which become known in due course, if they are not already known, then the backlash on the story and the storyteller is immense. So, it shouldn't be a surprise to anyone that trust levels are low.

Tolerance / I believe in the importance of individuals and respect for individuals. I believe everybody is equal. I believe in people being able to achieve their potential. / This plays out in building open and responsive relationships across large networks. **KM environments and learning promote achieving potential**.

Integrity / I never tried to publish something that I didn't feel was true. / This related to my sense of providing a framework, being sure of those ideas, that they were substantiated, that I could stand behind them and a manager could rely on them. So, **integrity of knowledge**.

Integrity / When people don't have integrity, I'm very unforgiving about it. / **Nobody will share anything with anybody unless they feel they have credibility and integrity**. KM is all about knowledge sharing, and when ideas are shared other people build on those ideas.

Sense of justice / Something fundamental, very basic about me. It has to do with when people aren't treated with integrity or respect. What we do is injure people and their self pride and worth and the way in which they perceive themselves doing something worthwhile. We shut them down and force them into distrustful and sometimes dysfunctional behavior. / **In order to have good conductive networks, the organization has to have a relatively high level of trust**. And the level of trust in an organization would be in large part related to the integrity that it witnesses about itself and bout its relationship with its environment.

Equity or justice / When ordinary people have the capacity, often the opportunity to make that contribution does not exist in equal measure, by no fault of their own. / **Our work creates the context for every voice to contribute** across all of these hierarchies and imagined boundaries.

Respect / The ability to listen to one another, and to free one another up by the way in which we interact. I believe that you can help people gain more perspective over their environment. / By **creating constructive and productive conversations around issues that are relevant to them and to people around them.** It's fundamentally that simple. Like if you want a good organization, you create good conversations and you allow people to get access to conversation vessels and environments where they can be who they are in confidence and where they can make sense of what surrounds them so they can deal with it with relative confidence, and with a sense that whatever is going to happen they're going to be supported

Respect and caring / Respect, because I fell that **what the world needs today in order to meet the demands of more complexity is more diversity**. There often needs to be understanding based on dialogue, understanding of diverse views, and that cannot be done without respect. / **Knowledge is a social phenomenon** and because of that, in order to have the free flow of understanding that is required to respond to an increasingly complex world, it takes respect and caring in the sense of listening and understanding different perceptions and caring enough to try and understand those perceptions. I cannot do anything alone anymore, so I desperately need, in knowledge-based work, others. I need the experiences of others; I need the ideas of others; I need the advice of others. This is why the work needs to be based on these values.

Respect other people's beliefs / I feel as if my life has been negatively affected on occasion by intolerance of belief by people. I find that arrogance very unappealing, so I guess the opposite of that is an **openness to other people's belief systems**. / Value systems are a theme you see going through all my work, and relationships with other people is a theme that goes through it as well. Opening of options is the simplest connection.

Love of your fellow / I believe in relating it to self interests and so on, but ultimately you have to believe in these involvements, like the person who runs a "super service", which is sort of a program that helps connect people. / We can actually network and talk about different aspects of the way knowledge flows. You create connections out of the knowledge flows in a broader sense, and map anything out at a whole human transactional level. So, it can assist us in making our lives richer.

Grouping 8: Work Ethic and Organizations

very strong belief in attempting to be cooperative in working toward common goals, sense of rigor and discipline, trying to apply my best effort whatever I'm working on, things should be useable, people should behave within the organization toward the goal of the organization, what goes around comes around, organizations should be seen as living entities and "It's amazing how much you can get done if you don't care who gets the credit for it."

Very strong belief in attempting to be cooperative in working toward common goals / I feel I am this way because of the influence of some of my high school teachers in life, and the influence of even my training as a Jesuit. We didn't call it KM. / In almost all of the business environments and other environments I've had a chance to work in, I've attempted to build a **collaborative or cooperative ethic** to try to get people to share their ideas and share the information and knowledge they have. Then there's communities of practice and communities of interest.

Sense of rigor and discipline / … in the way I approach problem solving and decision-making. [See Bennet & Bennet, 2013.] / With my understanding of different aspects of KM, I know that the decision-making side is very important in order to instantiate certain actions. The problem-solving side is manifested generally in terms of different codified knowledge bases that we work through to be able to solve a problem/ Then we bring the raw material home from one's brain and experience to the problem to be able to come up with a solution. Then we document that solution and give the team you're with enough information about it that they can deploy it and take ownership of it.

Trying to apply my best effort whatever I'm working on / For example, it's taking the extra effort to make sure when you're presenting something that **you've thought of as many different perspectives as possible and that you've got enough detail**. / Knowing your audience, and put the knowledge you are trying to share and direct in the right context.

Things should be useable / I have a strong work ethic. I'm sure that has contributed or affected me in the way these ideas have developed, with a consistent pushing and pushing and pushing in various incremental areas as opposed to a grand oversight. / The whole academic community is largely built around building knowledge instead of using it. KM is drawing attention to the use of knowledge. I contribute at the intersection of scholarship and practice.

People should behave within the organization toward the goal of the organization / There should be a team orientation for organizations. / We're living in an environment that is full of change and knowledge provides the medium of flexibility. **Continuity and transformation need to be in balance**.

What goes around comes around / The more you spread knowledge, the more it comes back to you; the more you spread music, the more people come back to you. / There's a limit to how much you can continue to patronage the old, use the same knowledge; but there's always more, and the more I give away freely and use for others, the more I give away in the form of books and presentations, etc.., **the more it keeps coming back to me**. The more I talk about the importance of knowledge management, the knowledge economy, the more I hear other people say, ah ha! That's right. I want to be a part of this.

The power of individuals and teams to lead others / This opens up the potential in organizations to be more receptive to the people with ideas. So we still need to learn how we could **value ourselves**, not so much by how much better we are than others, but **by how much we have learned, how much we have grown ourselves, and how much we are helping others grow**. / Relationships, networks and communities. Valuing intellectual capital.

Organizations should be seen as living entities / Organizations should not be seen as mechanisms or machines, which means that all living entities that do not change die. It means continuous involvement in everything we do, and that changes the norm, and the most interesting thing is what should not change. / We're living in an environment that is full of change and **knowledge provides the medium of flexibility**. Continuity and transformation need to be in balance. [The ICAS model for organizations introduced in Chapter 7 is a model for creating an organization that can co-evolve with a CUCA environment.]

"It's amazing how much you can get done if you don't care who gets the credit for it." / Core value about life. / It goes back to that idea that getting things done and **working collaboratively with other people is not about winning and losing, it's about seeing if you can get something done together**, and people love to be acknowledged for their contribution, and deserve to be acknowledged from them.

Appendix E
Expanded Literature Review
on Passion

Recall our operational definition that *passion is considered a term to indicate those desires, behaviors, and thoughts that suggest urges with considerable force* (Frijda, 2000). Characteristics of those urges specifically include the assertion that positive passions affirm that something is precious, and that passion can be used as a determinant of what is of higher interest and great (Polanyi, 1958, p. 135). Considering these characteristics, positive passion is used to indicate value (something precious) and passion, whether positive or negative, is used as a determinant of what is of higher interest and great.

Psychologist Nico Frijda saw passions as often extending to desires, thoughts, plans, and behaviors that persist over time. "They may lead to performing behaviors regardless of costs, external obstacles, and moral objections. These are the characteristics of passion in the more modern sense—the desires, behaviors, and thoughts that suggest urges with considerable force" (Frijda, 2000, p. 59).

In support of the passion model presented in Chapter 18, we now provide a more extensive literature review in the following areas: the biological context, intellectual passions, passions and leadership, passion and creativity, in the workplace, passion and flow, and the spiritual context.

The Biological Context

In a biological context, passion is an emotion (externally observed) or feeling (internally experienced), a biologically determined process that can be induced by internal or external events and circumstances. This induction process may be either conscious or subconscious to the individual. "The brain induces emotions from a small number of brain sites, most of them located below the cerebral cortex and are known as subcorticals" (Damasio, 1999, p. 60). Cognitive changes are induced through emotions via the secretion of certain chemicals that cause significant alterations in brain function. Such alterations may change the mode of cognitive processing, such as the sensitivity of auditory and visual sensors (Damasio, 1999).

Further, Damasio talked about a range of stimuli that constitute inducers for certain classes of emotions, allowing for a considerable variation in the type of stimuli that can induce an emotion (both across individuals and cultures). But all the stimuli are considered part of the set of inducers (Damasio, 1999, pp. 52-53). These concepts are used to provide the foundation of a passion framework through which we will take a quick look at thought leaders.

In *How the Mind Works*, Steven Pinker presented a theory that passions are "no vestige of an animal past, no wellspring of creativity, no enemy of the intellect" but that the intellect is "designed to relinquish control to the passions so that they may serve as guarantors of its offers, promises, and threats" (Pinker, 1997, p. 412). To illustrate, Pinker presented examples from *The Maltese Falcon*, *The Godfather*, *Dr. Strangelove* and other movies that demonstrate sacrifices of will and reason as effective tactics in the bargains, promises, and threats that are part of social relations. In *The Maltese Falcon*, the character played by Humphrey Bogart dares the henchmen to kill him, knowing he is needed alive in order for them to retrieve the falcon. The Godfather tells the heads of other crime families that he is a superstitious man, that if an unlucky accident befalls his son, he will blame them. Dr. Strangelove, a top nuclear strategist, carries the news that the doomsday machine is triggered automatically and cannot be reversed. These, then, are acting as guarantors.

In like manner, if you were buying a car from (for example) Mother Teresa, her passion and reputation for doing good would serve as the guarantor that you were not being cheated. Pinker concluded that "the apparent firewall between passion and reason is not an ineluctable part of the architecture of the brain; it has been programmed in deliberately, because only if the passions are in control can they be credible guarantors" (Pinker, 1997, p. 412-413).

The latest scientific findings reviewed by Norman Rosenthal suggest that we "endorse the existence of unconscious emotional processes and their powerful influence on preferences and actions" (Rosenthal, 2002, p. 29). While he admits emotions do not always work as they should, Rosenthal argues in favor of the emotions as intelligent and necessary for proper decision-making. He stated,

> It is clear now that the two great domains, reason and passion, are both critical to our ability to make proper decisions. Emotion unchecked by reason can lead to disaster, but without emotion, a person is unable to plan properly or form and sustain social bonds, even in the presence of adequate reasoning ability. . . . When passion and reason work well together, like the partners in a successful marriage, the outcome is a happy one. When they are at war, like hostile spouses, the result is no end of grief." (Rosenthal, 2002, p. 31)

Citing recent studies in neuropsychology, Damasio reported that human beings actually require emotions in order to reason effectively (Damasio, 1994). Similarly, Marinoff reminded us that, "People are not machines, nor should we behave like machines" (Marinoff, 2003, p. 62).

Intellectual Passions

To help understand the meaning of intellectual passions, Polanyi referenced a study done with chimpanzees, stating that the researcher demonstrated that chimpanzees "derive pleasure from the discovery of a new ingenious manipulation, quite apart from the practical benefit they derive from it . . . they will repeat the performance for its own sake, as a kind of play." He likened these intellectual tastes of the animal to those of a child, and said that these "prefigure, no doubt, the joys of discovery which our articulate powers can attain for man" (Polanyi, 1958, p. 133). Polanyi went on to identify science itself as an intellectual passion.

> Passions charge objects with emotions, making them repulsive or attractive; positive passions affirm that something is precious. The excitement of the scientist making a discovery is an intellectual passion, telling that something is intellectually precious ... The function which I attribute here to scientific passion is that of distinguishing between demonstrable facts which are of scientific interest, and those which are not . . . scientific passion serves . . . as a guide in the assessment of what is of higher and what of lesser interest; what is great in science, and what is relatively slight. (Polanyi, 1958, p. 135)

Several points in Polanyi's work are significant to this chapter. First, his **close linking of joy with intellectual passion**. Second, his assertion that positive passions affirm that something is precious. Third, that *passion can be used as a determinant of what is of higher interest and great.*

Passion and Leadership

In their work on leadership credibility, James Kouzes and Barry Posner (1993) discussed both exhibiting and encouraging passion as an important leadership attribute.

> "When we talk about what we love to do, gain a deeper understanding of others, share more intimately, and truly enjoy the interaction, our energy and passion are contagious. By caring, loving, and showing compassion, we can release a spirit in people that is unequaled. This is something that we can do in business every day" (Kouzes & Posner, 1993, p. 235).

Interestingly, Kouzes and Posner related leadership passion to suffering in their discussion of credibility. They believed that the most passionate people are those who have suffered the most, those who have "risked their independence, their fortunes, their health, and sometimes their lives for people and a purpose beyond themselves. Passion earned from suffering is inspiring. Leaders who are truly inspirational, who demonstrate courage and passion, are the first to suffer" (Kouzes & Posner, 1993, p. 232). While this study may not take the concept of passion to this extreme, in a highly competitive and potentially crisis-oriented world there is certainly risk in creating and forwarding new ideas.

Peters and Austin (1985, p. xix) said that leadership connotes "unleashing energy, building, freeing, and growing." They further stated, "We must cultivate passion and trust, and at virtually the same moment we must delve unmercifully into the details. How do we do it, or at least make a beginning? That's what *A Passion for Excellence* is all about" (Peters & Austin, 1985, p. xx). Joe Batten called his leadership article based on go-givers instead of go-getters as, "Servant-Leadership: A Passion to Serve." Lad and Luechauer (1998, p. 60) discussed five pathways to achieve servant-leadership (cognitive, experiential, spiritual, organizational and community) stating that, "Each of the approaches encourages passionate commitment, action, and a sense of urgency on behalf of the leader" See the discussion of servant leadership in Chapter 8.

The relationship between leadership and passion is not new to the literature. John Maxwell cited passion as one of the 21 indispensable qualities of a leader, becoming the person others will want to follow. He saw passion as the first step to achievement and stated that passion increases your willpower, changes you and makes the impossible possible. In summary, "Nothing can take the place of passion in a leader's life" (Maxwell, 1999, p. 83).

In answering the question of whether leaders are born or made, Charles Handy responded that **if you find some thing you're passionate about, then you have got one of the three elements of being a true leader** (Handy, 1999, p. 131). Neff and Citrin interviewed 50 business leaders who have achieved what they term as extraordinary success. While these leaders demonstrated a wide range of personalities and styles and represented a cross section of the population, they identified 10 traits that these leaders appeared to have in common. No trait appeared more noticeable than that of passion for their people and companies. "Quite simply, they love what they do. In many ways, passion is the counterpart of ... Doing the Right Things Right, inspiring employees to achieve greatness" (Neff & Citrin, 1999, pp. 379-380). For example, Dole states, "Having a passion for what you do, a sense of mission that comes from the heart, gives you the energy, drive and enthusiasm that's contagious and essential for leading an organization" (Neff & Citrin, 1999, p. 380).

Passionate leadership is a term used by Chip Bell, who believes that the reason some leaders are embraced while others are rejected has little to do with reason, but everything to do with passion. Bell asserted that *passion is more honest than reason.* Passion "makes us feel free, alive, and somehow 'a real, whole person' and, when leaders surface that feeling in us, we are somehow more energized, more like a knight ready for battle" (Bell, 1997, p. 196). Philosopher/psychologist Rollo May believes there is an energy field between humans, and that when a person reaches out in passion, others answer with passion (May, 1953). Bell sums this up, "Passionate connections provoke passionate responses. Leadership is fundamentally about influencing" (Bell, 1997, p. 197). Anita Roddick, The Body Shop founder, agreed, "We communicate with passion—and passion persuades" (Kouzes, 1998, p. 324). Bell went on to say:

> People may be instructed by reason, but they are inspired by passion ... Why are you here, in this role, at this time? What difference will you being here make?

What legacy will you leave behind? Will you be forgotten for what you maintained or remembered for what you added? Imposing mountains are climbed, culture-changing movements are started, and breakthrough miracles are sparked by leaders who took the governors off rationalism and prudence, letting their spirit ascent from within. (Bell, 1997, p. 198)

Sara Melendez stated that, "Effective leaders are passionate about the cause they are promoting and about their commitment to the greater or public good" (Melendez, 1996, p. 299). We have noticed this expression of passion related to commitment beyond the self in references cited earlier. Peter Senge said that people's passions flow naturally into creating something that truly excites them. "The passion at the heart of every great undertaking comes from the deep longing of human beings to make a difference, to have an impact. It comes from what you contribute rather than from what you get" (Senge, 1990, p. 62).

And so forth ... As can be seen passion and effective leadership go hand in hand. *You can't have one without the other.*

Passion and Creativity

In the Public Broadcasting Station (PBS) television series on "The Creative Spirit," Daniel Goleman, Paul Kaufman and Michael Ray revealed what they called the hidden anatomy of the creative process. They stated: "Finally, the element that really cooks the creative stew is passion. The psychological term is intrinsic motivation, the urge to do something for the sheer pleasure of doing it rather than for any prize or compensation" (Goleman et al., 1992, p. 30). This quality surfaced in the discussion of effects in Chapter 15 and in the discussion of thought leader values in Chapter 16.

The Nobel Prize-winning physicist T. Amabile, when asked what he thought made a difference between creative and uncreative scientists, stated that the most successful, groundbreaking scientists were not always the most gifted ones, but those that were driven. "To some degree a strong passion can make up for a lack of raw talent. Passion 'is like the fire underneath the soup pot,' Amabile says. 'It really heats everything up, blends the flavors, and makes those spices mix with the basic ingredients to produce something that tastes wonderful'" (Goleman et al., 1992, p. 31).

Mihalyi Csikszentmihalyi also relates passion directly to the attribute of creativity. From 1990 to 1995, Csikszentmihalyi and his students at the University of Chicago videotaped interviews with a group of 91 people who they termed as exceptional individuals, people who (a) had made a difference to a major domain of culture (sciences, arts, business, government, or human well-being in general), (b) were still actively involved, and (c) were over 60 years old. From these interviews, Csikszentmihalyi developed the 10 dimensions of complexity—what he called the real characteristics of creative persons. His ninth dimension states, "most creative persons are very passionate about their work, yet they can be extremely objective about it as well" (Csikszentmihalyi, 1996, p. 72).

The research identified an energy generated by this conflict between attachment and detachment, an energy that was mentioned by many of the respondents as being an important part of their work. Csikszentmihalyi believed that the reason for this was relatively clear. "Without the passion, we soon lose interest in a difficult task. Yet without being objective about it, our work is not very good and lacks credibility. So the creative process tends to be what some respondents called a yin-yang alternation between these two extremes" (Csikszentmihalyi, 1996, p. 72). This movement from passion to objectivity, from action to reflection, was called out by respondents as what allowed them to keep learning and adjusting to new situations. "Their creativity unfolded organically from idea to action, then through the evaluation of the outcomes of action back to ideas—a cycle that repeated itself again and again" (Csikszentmihalyi, 1996, p. 316). This tension is also part of the experiential learning model (see Bennet & Bennet, 2015b).

Dorothy Leonard and Walter Swap noted the movement from Taylorism (where people were hired for their muscle) through total quality (where people were hired for their muscle and brains) to knowledge work (where people are hired for their muscle, brains and passion). "This passion is what gets people up in the morning . . . and it can come in the form of passion for the job, for innovation, or for the organization" (Leonard & Swap, 1999, p. 178). Built on intrinsic and extrinsic motivators, Leonard and Swap noted that it is passion that "fuels creativity," then presented dozens of examples that support their statements. For example, a former Harley-Davidson CEO, Richard Teerlink, explained:

> We didn't want people who just come to work. We wanted people to be excited about what they do, to have an emotional attachment to our company. It was the excitement they got when they were standing in line in the supermarket wearing a Harley T-shirt and someone said, "Do you work at Harley? Wow!' We got people who wanted to work for this kind of company, who wanted to make a difference. (Leonard & Swap, 1999, pp. 182-183)

Leonard and Swap believed that real enthusiasm is contagious. They quoted Fisher-Price's Lisa Mancuso: "I love the product; I feel passion for what I do … I couldn't champion something I didn't love" (Leonard & Swap, 1999, p. 182). Before leaving these authors, we cite one more finding, "Passion and enthusiasm thrive in an atmosphere of optimism and confidence in the future" (Leonard & Swap, 1999, p.191).

Amabile and Polanyi have also, separately, presented significant evidence of the importance of passion alongside personal investment to spur creativity and engage the persistent effort required to develop expertise or create significant innovations in a domain (Amabile, 1997; Polanyi, 1966).

In the Workplace

With the emergence of knowledge management came a new understanding of the importance of relationships in the workplace, and interest in communities of practice as a practical way to manage knowledge. The authors of the definitive text on communities of practice found three criteria that help to define the scope of the domain. First, was to focus on dimensions of the domain important to the business. Second, was to focus on "aspects of the domain community members will be passionate about. This assures that the community will be attractive enough to members to grow and develop" (Wenger et al., 2002, p. 75). Third was to define the scope wide enough to bring in new people but narrow enough that most people in the group would be interested in the topics discussed.

Later in the text, the authors stated that "Informal phenomena—professional passion, relationships, and identity—are now the frontier of management" (Wenger et al., 2002, p. 217). In Tom Stewart's work, the value of the firm's knowledge earnings can be calculated as the difference between the earnings from the financial plus physical assets and the total earnings (Stewart, 2001, p. 319). This new approach to managing in the knowledge economy recognizes the importance of intangible assets—passions, relationships and skills—on the balance sheet. Etienne Wenger concluded that, "The most successful communities of practice thrive where the goals and needs of an organization intersect with the passions and aspirations of participants" (Wenger et al., 2002, p. 32).

Passion and Flow

Charles Belitz and Meg Lundstrom identify passion as one of the nine attributes that create the power of flow (Belitz & Lundstrom, 1997, p. 47). Flow is a concept described by Csikszentmihalyi in the early 1990s and the subject of considerable research and study since that time. In the early work of Csikszentmihalyi, flow is defined as "the state in which people are so involved in an activity that nothing else seems to matter; the experience itself is so enjoyable that people will do it even at great cost, for the sheer sake of doing it" (Csikszentmihalyi, 1990, p. 4). This is the optimal experience, "when a person's body or mind is stretched to its limits in a voluntary effort to accomplish something difficult and worthwhile" (Csikszentmihalyi, 1990, p. 3).

Using Csikszentmihalyi's concepts of flow, the eight conditions that combine to create the flow experience are: Clear goals; quick feedback; a balance between opportunity and capacity; deepened concentration; being in the present; being in control; an altered sense of time; and the loss of ego. As Csikszentmihalyi noted, "I have given the name 'flow' to this common experience, because so many people have used the analogy of being carried away by an outside force, of moving effortlessly with a current of energy, at the moments of highest enjoyment" (Csikszentmihalyi, 2003, p. 39).

In discussing the origins of flow, Csikszentmihaly found elements of the flow experience in a number of religions—Christianity, Buddhism and Taoism, for example. He then quoted the anthropologist Mel Konner, who when asked if every culture produced a religion, why every culture sought God, answered: "It's not God—they are seeking the rapture of life, to understand what it means to be alive" (Csikszentmihaly, 2003, p. 60). Similarly, Belitz and Lundstrom state:

> Flow is engendered by passion—passion for life, for knowledge, for a cause, for a relationship, for truth. Passion means caring deeply about something beyond ourselves. It means engaging with it at intense levels. It means letting go of self-protective caution to involve ourselves wholeheartedly with what we love. (Belitz & Lundstrom, 1997, p. 57)

This passion "opens us up to a larger picture" (Belitz & Lundstrom, 1997, p. 57). Passion is the intensity of flow, the intense desire to be "active and engaged in the course of events" and the intense drive to know truth, "to answer the basic questions of existence: why we're here, what we're supposed to be doing, what it all means. Not satisfied with surface explanations, we use every moment as an opportunity to break through to something new, to learn. We fully engage with what comes our way" (Belitz & Lundstrom, 1997, p. 57). In a discussion of people skills, Goleman cited focus and passion as an important element of achieving group flow. "The demands of meeting a great goal inherently provide focus; the rest of life can seem not just mundane, but trivial by comparison. For the duration, the details of life are on hold" (Goleman, 1998, p. 228).

The Spiritual Context

The concept of passion also plays a significant role in the Five Buddha Families of Vajrayana Buddhism. This teaching describes processes for the transmutation of the five major energies (anger, pride, passion, jealousy and apathy) and the emotions connected to these energies. The Vajrayana approach looks at these energies as part of the spiritual path—the stronger an emotion, the more useful it can be as a vehicle for awakening. Awakening is the aim of consciousness, the Buddha's state of mind, the only state in which even pain and suffering are borne with ease (Walsh & Shapiro, 1983). Alan Watts described awakening in this manner, "If you were awake, you would understand that you and the whole universe are pretending: projecting yourself at the point called here and now in the form of a human organism" (Watts, 2002, p. 57). The Dali Lama, certainly a definitive source on Buddhism, defined the verbal root of Buddhism as, "to waken from the sleep of ignorance and spread one's intelligence to everything that can be known" (Gyatso, 1992). Passion, then, is viewed as a strong vehicle for awakening.

Each of the five major energies has both negative and positive potential for the individual, and it is part of the individual's growth process to work through the negative and transform these energies into positive forces in their lives. Of the negative aspect of passion, Tara Bennett-Goleman stated that,

> Passion, in the sense of neurotic clinging, grasping, and craving, can manifest itself as a hysteric's shallow seductiveness, or as the hypnotic charisma of a manipulative con artist. It manifests as an alluring, pleasing and always seductive pursuit of objects of desire. (Bennett-Goleman, 2001, p. 312)

This energy, when transmuted, takes the form of discriminating awareness, "taking a precise interest in, and paying keen attention to, whatever presents itself. This ever-inquisitive awareness opens up communication: other people are seen and understood in their full distinctiveness, and related to with empathy and a warm compassion" (Bennett-Goleman, 2001, p. 312).

Irina Rockwell went so far as to state that we create our reality based on passion. Passion is referred to as "padma energy," energy that helps people speak from the heart and "draw out other people and engage them ... This sense of pleasure and promise magnetizes others" (Rockwell, 2002, p. 52). On the negative side, Rockwell said that people have to "engage their passion without losing sight of the danger of getting caught up in or intoxicated by it . . . we don't want to eliminate their passion; we want to cultivate it, refine it." (Rockwell, 2002, p. 184) Similarly, to the religions of India who draw their fundamental teachings from the Bhagavad Gita and Upanishads,

> The most basic human struggle is not the external quest for food, shelter, or a mate . . . but rather the attempt to rule our passions—our internal desires and cravings. If they are not contained by meditative practice, or restrained by practical reason, or expressed by wholesome habits, or transcended by conscious awakening, the incessant grasping gives rise to attachments, which are thought to be the source of all our suffering. (Marinoff, 2003, p. 58)

According to Lou Marinoff, the Jewish cabalists, the Christian Gnostics, the Islamic Sufis, the Hindu Brahmanas and the Buddhist awakened ones all teach theories, techniques, and methods for reasonably guiding the self's passions (Marinoff, 2003). Sooner or later they all lead to the center of oneself, the concept described above as awakening.

Appendix F
Passion Model TL Responses

Passion is an emergent phenomenon. External and internal inducers make up a set of stimuli that result in passion. This passion is both externally observed and internally felt in a variety of ways, and is also correlated to the larger aspects of self. The definition of passion, the internal inducers, lists of elements externally observed and internally felt, and a list of correlates to the larger self are all developed from the characteristics of passion. These characteristics emerge from the literature. See Appendix E and Chapter 18 for the passion model.

Specific external events and stimuli that trigger thought leader passions include the field itself (breakthroughs, the nature of knowledge), the breadth of the field (richness of multidimensionality of experience), the changing nature of the field, the value (growing collaborative advantage of knowledge in the world), the transfer and reuse of knowledge (improving organizational memory, not repeating mistakes), new thinking (intellectually exciting, new way of looking at things) and challenges and opportunities (incredible challenge, confronting moral and political dilemmas very openly).

The thought leader responses to **"What about their field of work excites their passion?"** that fall into the Externally Observed, Correlation to Larger Picture, Internally Felt, and Internal Inducers are included in the tables below.

As can be seen, all areas of the passion model are represented in this thought leader response, demonstrating that the passion model well represents the passion with which thought leaders lead.

Table E-1: *TL Responses: Externally Observed*

EXTERNALLY OBSERVED	
Passionate commitment, action and a sense of urgency Leadership in terms of unleashing energy, building, freeing and growing A passion to serve Speaking from the heart and drawing out other people and engaging them Joy	Need to integrate, synthesize, bring it all together Impacting performance in the moment Changes KM brings to leadership and management To get people to build knowledge and get into situations where you create an environment for creativity and innovation Networking and knowledge sharing (the whole is greater than the sum of the parts) Changing the way people collaborate Living networks Watching the energy transfer Enabling conversations Wireless technology connecting people Network ideas Simple things create unexpected outcomes thinking together Working with people Power of theory to help people become intentional about what they know Building tools that engage more of the whole person People's ability to create extraordinary results with the right environment created by the proper knowledge-based strategy If you look at people from the knowledge perspective you start seeing their capabilities and aspirations Passion is catching Fun Enables people to be happier human beings Joy dimension Makes work easier and more enjoyable It makes work fun, frankly.

Table E-2: *TL Responses: Correlation to Larger Picture*

CORRELATION TO LARGER PICTURE	
Part of larger picture What it means to be alive Flow experience Spiritual awakening Making one's life meaningful	If these ideas take hold and work takes us to a more hopeful future for the planet Nourishment and cultivation of the future Something in it that's more Human nature of these systems There was a sense of suddenly being a participant in some incredibly rapidly evolving, passionate ecologies, knowledge ecologies Transformative nature Energizer for what I do One of those questions that can take you to another world I love it Suddenly see the world differently New way to look at the world, actually gives you new lenses and ways to look at the world Changes our perspectives and perceptions, our point of view Shift is underway The paradigm shift It provides meaning to our own life People fulfilling something worthwhile in their lives Creates meaning

Table E-3: *TL Responses: Internally Felt*

INTERNALLY FELT	
Promoting the greater good Doing the right things right Duty toward others Intersects with goals and needs It is "precious," of higher interest and great Optimism and confidence in the future Demands attention	Helping people make good decisions … getting people to sense beyond short-term decisions Instilling appreciation for learning, knowledge sharing and application of knowledge through teams and individuals for organizational and personal growth It does a whole lot of good Building organizations that perform well on a sustainable basis and where people actually have a sense of fulfillment that they're doing the right thing of interpretation, it's so right to help people view organizations in a different way I love the connectedness with myself, with my own thought, my own interest in life Advancing my own thinking Changes aspects of who we are Intellectually stimulating and challenging Value of knowledge and what it can do for society, for individuals, for interactions between individuals From the knowledge perspective you have a very optimistic view of the future Attention as a constraint on KM and how it needs to be managed

Table E-4: *TL Responses: Internal Inducers*

INTERNAL INDUCERS	People's beliefs are the group's knowledge
Morals	Overall human value
Values	Work really worthy
Purpose beyond ourselves	Value creation
Goals and needs	Learning things you feel are important and can contribute
Deep longing to make a difference	to the world
	Seeing ideas light people's eyes up
	Creating the context for ordinary people to discover the extraordinary ways that they can
	co- create innovation and actionable knowledge around the things they care most about
	I'm not wasting my time. I'm making a contribution.
	Seeing the fruits of your labors
	I'm doing some real good here

Endnotes

Chapter 4
[1] Content in this chapter appeared in Bennet & Bennet (2004) as an appendix.

Chapter 7
[1] Content in this chapter appeared in the first chapter of Bennet & Bennet (2004).
[2] The CUCA organization was first introduced by Bennet and Bennet in *Organizational Survival in the New World: The Intelligent Complex Adaptive System* (Bennet and Bennet, 2004).

Chapter 8
[1] Connected of choices means that decisions made at all levels of the organization, while different, are clearly based not only on a clear direction for the future, but made in a cohesive fashion based on an understanding of both why that direction is desirable and the role that individual decisions play with respect to immediate objectives and their support of the shared vision. This term was coined in the U.S. Department of the Navy in the late 1990's (Bennet & Bennet, 2004).
[2] The environmental opportunity space, introduced in Chapter 7, is a window of opportunity in terms of space and time. While the company may not be able to define this space, nor can it go there before it exists, the organization's direction and agility is such that it can scan the environmental opportunity space and take advantage of opportunities as they emerge.

Chapter 9
[1] fMRI is used for neuroimaging to produce precise measurements of brain structures (Hyman, 2007). EEG is another noninvasive technique that measures the average electrical activity of large populations of neurons (Nicolelis & Chapin, 2007). TMS uses head-mounted wire coils that send very short but strong magnetic pulses directly into specific brain regions that induce low-level electric currents into the brain's neural circuits. This technology is very young but appears to be able to "turn on and off particular parts of the human brain" (George, 2007, p. 21).

Chapter 10
[1] A deeper treatment on types of knowledge is included in *The Course of Knowledge: A 21st Century Theory* (Bennet & Bennet, 2015a).

Chapter 11
[1] This treatment first published in Bennet and Bennet (2009).
[2] The ADIIEA model was first published in the first edition of *The Explanation Age* (2010), where it is also referred to as the innate lesson cycle. ADIIEA is also commercially referred to as the CoHero Change Cycle at the CoHero Institute for Collaborative Leadership.

Chapter 12

[1] Hemispheric Synchronization is bringing both hemispheres of the brain into coherence. This can be accomplished through the use of sound coupled with a binaural beat. The result is a physiologically reduced state of arousal, quieting the body *while maintaining conscious awareness* (Bennet & Bennet, 2008e; Mavromatis, 1991; Atwater, 2004; Jevning et al., 1992).
[2] Henri-Louis Bergson, a French philosopher whose third major work, *Creative Evolution*, published in 1907, contributed profound thoughts to the understanding of evolution.
[3] Ray Kurzweil (2005) proposes that the computational power of supercomputers will equal that of the human brain around 2020, what he calls the point of singularity:

> Biological evolution for animals as complex as humans takes tens of thousands of years to make noticeable, albeit small, differences. The entire history of human culture and technological evolution has taken place on that timescale. Yet we are now poised to ascend beyond the fragile and slow creations of biological evolution in a mere several decades. Current progress is on a scale that is a thousand to a million times faster than biological evolution. (p. 94)

Kurzweil (2005) also argued that the computational power (1016 computations per second) "required for human brain functional simulation" would be achieved in 2013 (p. 71). While clearly the exact date was not right, the timeframe is reasonable and indicates just how fast the future is accelerating toward us. It also emphasizes the need for maximizing the knowledge worker's learning capacity to deal with CUCA. Impey considers singularity to be a "hypothetical time in a few decades when exponential progress in nanotechnology, genetic engineering, and computing leads to a post-biological race of humans." (Impey, 2010, p. 298)

While for the most part technologies are not yet part of the physical body, they are close at hand. What today's (and tomorrow's) knowledge workers need to know is very different from the workers in a separated (often stove-piped), control-oriented organization within a stable, predictable environment. When uncertainty increases, problem solutions take on a different character requiring flexibility, adaptability, and a larger systems perspective. Employees must now think for themselves, collaborate as needed, and carefully study their environment while they co-evolve with that environment in order to develop an intuitive ability to make effective decisions and take the right actions. In other words, as situations become more complex, the nature of learning, knowledge, and action shift. Building capacity lays the groundwork for those shifts.
[4] Attributed to Henry Ford.

Section V: Thought Leadership
[1] This refers to the threshold within which knowledge and events make sense to us. If a proposed new idea or strategy or initiative is above our threshold, it is not comprehended and has no perceived value. If a proposed new idea or strategy or initiative is below our threshold, it is so well-understood that it is dismissed as unimportant. This concept was introduced in Chapter 3.

Chapter 15
[1] The KMTL Study involved 34 KM thought leaders spanning four continents. Initial contacts were to those who appeared most often in KM literature and appeared at conferences to share their work. For purposes of this study, a thought leader was considered those individuals (a) whose focus has been in the area of KM for several years and continues in this or a related

field, (b) who have published or edited books or multiple articles in the field, (c) who have developed and taught academic or certification courses in the area of KM, and (d) who have spoken about KM at multiple symposia and conferences. By definition, this means that thoughts leaders are both learners and educators.

Chapter 18

[1] The bank account of self is detailed in Chapter 11. Self is also discussed in Chapter 10 in terms of the importance of Self knowledge.

[2] The term "incluessence" was coined by Jo Dunning (August 12, 2015, email to Alex). Jo talks about "True Incluessence" as the state of our Being that is far beyond the small drop of possibility was have come to accept as true. In our usage we infer a future state that is far beyond that which we know to dream.

Appendix A

[1] This story first appeared in Bennet and Bennet (2004). Used with permission.

References

Adler, M. J. (1992). *The Great Ideas: A Lexicon of Western Thought*. New York: Scribner Classics

Adolphs, R. (2004). "Processing of Emotional and Social Information by the Human Amygdala" in M. S. Gazzaniga (Ed.), *The Cognitive Neurosciences III* (pp. 1017-1030). Cambridge, MA: The Bradford Press.

Almaas, A. H. (2004). *The Inner Journey Home: Soul's Realization of the Unity of Reality*. Boston: Shambhala.

Amabile, T. M. (1997). "Motivating Creativity in Organizations: On Doing What You Love and Loving What You Do" in *California Management Review*, 40(1), 39-58.

Amen, D.G. (2005). *Making a Good Brain Great*, New York: Harmony Books.

Aquinas, Thomas (2015). Summa Theologiae of the Catholic Church. Downloaded July 28, 2015, from http://www.newadvent.org/summa/2026.htm#article4

American Heritage Dictionary 4th Ed. (2006). Boston: Houghton Mifflin Company

American Heritage Dictionary 4th Ed. (2000). Boston: Houghton Mifflin Company.

AMSA/AMWA Checklist (2004). *The Changing Workforce...Crisis & Opportunity*. Association of Metropolitan Sewerage Agencies (AMSA) and the Association of Metropolitan Water Agencies (AMWA).

Andreason, N. (2005). *The Creating Brain: The Neuroscience of Genius*. New York: The Dana Foundation.

Ardagh, A. (2005). *The Translucent Revolution: How People Just Like You Are Waking Up and Changing the World*. Novato, CA: New World Library.

Argyris, C. and Schon, D. A. (1978) *Organizational Learning: A Theory of Action Perspective*. Philippines: Addison-Wesley Publishing Co.

Argyris, C. (1993). *Knowledge for Action*. San Francisco: Jossey Bass.

Ashby, W. R. (1964). *An Introduction to Cybernetics*. London: Methuen.

Atwater, F.H. (2004). *The Hemi-Sync Process*. Faber, VA: The Monroe Institute.

Avedisian, J. and Bennet, A. (2010). "Values as Knowledge: A New Frame of Reference for a New Generation of Knowledge Workers" in *On the Horizon*, Vol. 18, No. 3, pp. 255-265.

Axelrod, R. and Cohen, M. (1999). *Harnessing Complexity: Organizational Implications of a Scientific Frontier*. New York: The Free Press.

Barnhart, R. K. & Steinmetz, S. (1988). *Chambers Dictionary of Etymology*. New York: Chambers.

Bass, B. M. (Ed.) (1981). *Stogdill's Handbook of Leadership: A Survey of Theory and Research*. New York: The Free Press.

Batten, J. (1998). "Servant-Leadership: A Passion to Serve" in Spears, L.C. (Ed.). *Insights on Leadership: Service, Stewardship, Spirit, and Servant-leadership*. New York: John Wiley & Sons.

Battram, A. (1996). *Navigating Complexity: The Essential Guide to Complexity Theory in Business and Management*. Sterling, VA: The Industrial Society.

Begley, S. (2007). *Train Your Mind Change Your Brain: How a New Science Reveals Our Extraordinary Potential to Transform Ourselves*. New York: Ballantine Books.

Belasco, J.A. (1997). "Leading the New Organization" in Shelton, K. (Ed.). *A New Paradigm of Leadership: Visions of Excellence for 21st Century Organizations*. Provo, UT: Executive Excellent Publishing.

Belitz, C. & Lundstrom, M. (1997). *The Power of Flow*. New York: Harmony Books.

Bell, C. R. (1997). "Passionate Leadership" in Shelton, K. (Ed.). *A New Paradigm of Leadership: Visions of Excellence for 21st Century Organizations*. Provo, UT: Executive Excellence Publishing.

Bennet, A. (2006) "The Learning Organization: Setting the Stage for Exploration" in *VINE: The Journal of Information and Knowledge Management Systems*, Vol. 36. No. 1, 2006, pp. 7-11.

Bennet, A. and Bennet, D. (2015a). *The Course of Knowledge: A 21st Century Theory*. Frost, WV: MQIPress.

Bennet, A. and Bennet, D. (2013). *Decision-Making in The New Reality: Complexity, Knowledge and Knowing*. Frost, WV: MQIPress.

Bennet, A. and Bennet, D. (2010). 'MULTIDIMENSIONALITY: Building the Infrastructure for the Next Generation Knowledge Worker" in "The Future of Knowledge Workers," a special issue of *the International Journal On the Horizon*, Vol. 18, No. 3., pp. 240-254.

Bennet, A. and Bennet, D. (2009). "Managing Self in Troubled Times: Banking on Self-Efficacy" in *Effective Executive* Vol. XII, No. 04 (April). India: The Icfai University Press, pp 56-82.

Bennet, A. and Bennet, D. (2009b). "Associative Patterning: The Unconscious Life of an Organization" in Girard, John, *Building Organizational Memories*. Hershey, PA: IGI Global, pp. 201-224.

Bennet, A. and Bennet, D. (2008c). "A New Change Model: Factors for Initiating and Implementing Personal Action Learning" in *VINE: The Journal of Information and knowledge Management Systems*, Vol. 38, No. 4, pp. 378-387.

Bennet, A. and Bennet, D. (2008d). "eLearning as Energetic Learning" in *VINE: The Journal of Information and Knowledge Management Systems*, Vol. 38, No. 2.

Bennet, A. and Bennet , D. (2007a). *Knowledge Mobilization in the Social Sciences and Humanities: Moving from Research to Action,* Frost, WV: MQIPress.

Bennet, A. and Bennet, D. (2007b). "CONTEXT: The Shared Knowledge Enigma", in *VINE: The Journal of Information and Knowledge Management Systems*, Vol. 37, No. 1, pp. 27-40.

Bennet, A. & Bennet, D. (2007c). "The Knowledge and Knowing of Spiritual Learning" in *VINE: The Journal of Information and Knowledge Management Systems*, Vol. 37, No. 2, 2007, pp. 150-168.

Bennet A. and Bennet, D. (2006). "Learning as Associative Patterning" in *VINE: The Journal of Information and Knowledge Management Systems*, Vol. 36. No. 4, pp. 371-376.

Bennet, A. & Bennet, D. (2004). *Organizational Survival in the New World: The Intelligent Complex Adaptive System*. Burlington, MA: Elsevier.

Bennet, D. (2006) "Expanding the Knowledge Paradigm" in *VINE: The Journal of Information and Knowledge Management Systems*, Vol. 36. No. 2, pp. 175-181.

Bennet, D. (1997). *IPT learning Campus: Gaining Acquisition Results through IPTs*. Alexandria, VA: Bellwether Learning Center.

Bennet, D. & Bennet, A. (2015b). *Expanding the Self: The Intelligent Complex Adaptive Learning System*. MQIPress, Frost, WV.

Bennet, D. and Bennet, A. (2008a). "Engaging Tacit Knowledge in Support of Organizational Learning', in *VINE: The Journal of Information and Knowledge Systems*, Vol. 38, No. 1, pp. 72-94.

Bennet, D. and Bennet, A. (2008b). "The Depth of KNOWLEDGE: Surface, Shallow or Deep?" in *VINE: The Journal of Information and Knowledge Management Systems*, Vol. 38, No. 4 (December), pp. 405-420.

Bennett-Goleman, T. (2001). *Emotional alchemy: How the mind can heal the heart*. New York: Harmony Books.

Bennis, W. (1995). *Beyond Leadership: Balancing Economics, Ethics and Ecology*. Cambridge, MA: Blackwell Publishers.

Birkinshaw, J. and Gibson, C. (2004). "Build Ambidexterity into Your Organization" in *MIT Sloan Management Review, Summer* 2004, Vol. 45 No 4.

Blake, R.R. and Moulton, J.S. (1994). *The Managerial Grid*. Houston, TX: Gulf Publishing.

Bohm, D. (1992). *Thought as a System*. New York: Routledge.

Bortoft, H. (1996). *The Wholeness of Nature: Goethe's Way toward a Science of Conscious Participation in Nature*. Barrington, MA: Lindisfarne Books.

Bownds, M.D. (1999). *The Biology of Mind: Origins and Structures of Mind, Brain, and Consciousness*. Bethesda, MD: Fitzgerald Science Press.

Brandenburger, A.M. and Nalebuff, B.J. (1997). *Co-opetition*. New York: Currency Doubleday.

Brussat, F. and Brussat, M. A. (2000). *Spiritual RX: Prescriptions for Living a Meaningful Life*. New York: Hyperion.

Buonomano, D.V. and Merzenich, M.M.. (1998). "Cortical Plasticity: From Synapses to Maps" in *Annual Review of Neuroscience*, 21.

Burnes B. (2004). "Kurt Lewin and the Planned Approach to Change: A Re-appraisal" in *Journal of Management Studies* (41:6, September), Manchester.

Buzsaki, G. (2006). *Rhythms of the Brain*. New York: Oxford University Pressi.

Byrne, R. (2006). *The Secret*. New York: ATRIA Books.

Byrnes, J. P. (2001). *Minds, Brains, and Learning: Understanding the Psychological and Educational Relevance of Neuroscientific Research*. New York: The Guilford Press.

Capra, F., Juarrero, A., Sotolongo, P. and van Uden, J. (2007). Exploring Complexity: Volume One in *Reframing Complexity: Perspectives from the North and South*. Mansfield MA: ISCE Publishing.

Cardozo, B.N. (1921). *Nature of the Judicial Process*. New Haven, CN: Yale University Press, pp. 167-170.

Carey, K. (1996). *The Third Millennium: Living in the Posthistoric World*. New York: HarperCollins Publishers.

Carpenter, H. (2009). "Designing for innovation through competitive collaboration". Downloaded on 11/02/14 from http://www.cloudave.com/1036/designing-for-innovation-through-competitive-collaboration/

Champy, J. and Nohria, N. (2000). The Arc of Ambition: Defining the Leadership Journey (1st Ed). New York: Basic Books.

Chickering, A. W., Dalton, J. C. and Stamm, L. (2006). *Encouraging Authenticity & Spirituality in Higher Education*. San Francisco: Jossey-Bass.

Church, D. (2006). *The Genie in Your Genes: Epigenetic Medicine and the New Biology of Intention*. Santa Rosa, CA: Elite Books.

Cleveland, H. (2002). *Nobody in Charge: Essays on the Future of Leadership*. San Francisco: Jossey-Bass.

Cohn, K.H. (2008). "Collaborative co-mentoring" downloaded on 03/15/08 from http://www.biomedsearch.com/article/lifelong-iterative-process-physician-retention/204857941.html

Collins, J. (2001). *Good to Great*. New York: HarperCollins Publishers.

Colvin, G. (2015). "Humans are Underrated" in *Fortune*, 8.1, pp. 100-113.

Conner, D.R. (1998). *Leading at the Edge of Chaos: How to Create the Nimble Organization*. New York: John Wiley & Sons.

Corbin, C. (2000). *Great Leaders See the Future First: Taking Your Organization to the Top in Five Revolutionary Steps*. Chicago, IL: Dearborn Books.

Cousins, E. (1999). "Spirituality on the Eve of a New Millenium: An Overview" in *Chicago Studies*, 38 (1), pp. 5-14.

Covey, S.R. (2004). *The 8th Habit: From Effectiveness to Greatness*. New York: Free Press.

Covey, S.R.. (1997). "Leading by Compass" in Shelton, K. (Ed.). *A New Paradigm of Leadership: Visions of Excellence for 21st Century Organizations*. Provo, UT: Executive Excellent Publishing.

Cowan, W. M., & Kandel, E. R. (2001). "A Brief History of Synapses and Synaptic Transmission" in Cowan, W.C., Sudhof, T.C. and Stevens, C.F. (Eds.). *Synapses*. Baltimore: Johns Hopkins Press.

Cozolino, L. (2006). *The Neuroscience of Human Relationships: Attachment and the Developing Social Brain* New York: Norton & Company.

Cozolino, L.J. (2002). *The Neuroscience of Human Relationships: Building and Rebuilding the Human Brain*, New York: Norton.

Cozolino, L. and Sprokay, S. (2006). "Neuroscience and Adult Learning" in Johnson, S. and Taylor, K. (Eds.). *The Neuroscience of Adult Learning*. San Francisco: Jossey-Bass.

Crandall, B., Klein, G., & Hoffman, R. R. (2006). *Working Minds: A Practitioner's Guide to Cognitive Task Analysis*. Cambridge, MA: The MIT Press.

Crowley, V. (1999). *Jung: A Journey of Transformation*. Wheaton, IL: Quest Books.

Csikszentmihalyi, M. (2003). *Good Business: Leadership, Flow, and the Making of Meaning*. New York: The Penguin Group.

Csikszentmihalyi, M. (2003). *Good Business: Leadership, Flow and the Making of Meaning*. New York: Viking.

Csikszentmihalyi, M. (1996). *Creativity: Flow and the Psychology of Discovery and Invention*. New York: HarperCollins Publishers, Inc.

Csikszentmihalyi, M. (1990). *Flow: The Psychology of Optimal Experience*. New York: Harper Perennial.

Cummings, T.G. and Huse, E.F. (1989). *Organization Development and Change* (4th ed.). New York: West Publishing Company.

Damasio, A. (1999). *The Feeling of What Happens: Body and Emotion in the Making of Consciousness*. New York: Harcourt Brace & Co.

Darwin, C. (1998). *The Descent of Man*. Amherst, NY: Prometheus Books.

Dass, R. (1980). "Relative Realities" in Walsh, R. N. and Vaughan, F. *Beyond Ego: Transpersonal Dimensions in Psychology*. Los Angeles: Jeremy P. Tarcher, Inc.

Dauphinais, G. W., Means, G., and Price, C. (2000). *Wisdom of the CEO*. New York: John Wiley & Sons, Inc.

Davenport, T. H. (2001). "Knowledge Work and the Future of Management" in Bennis, W., Spreitzer, G.M., and Cummings, T.G. (Eds). *The Future of Leadership: Today's Top Leadership Thinkers Speak to Tomorrow's Leaders*. San Francisco, CA: Jossey-Bass.

de Chardin, T. (1966). *The Vision of the Past*. Collected Works of Teilhard de Chardin in English translation (Collins). UK: Harper and Row.

De Furia, G. (1997). *Interpersonal Trust Surveys*. San Francisco: Jossey-Bass.

De Geus, A. (1997). *The Living Company: Habits for Survival in a Turbulent Business Environment*. Boston: The Harvard Business School Press.

De Mello, A. (1990). *Awareness: The Perils and Opportunities of Reality*. New York: Doubleday.

Demming, W. E. (1997). "Quality Leaders" in Shelton, K. (Ed.) *A New Paradigm of Leadership: Visions of Excellence for 21st Century Organizations*. Provo, UT: Executive Excellent Publishing.

Dewey, J. (1938/1997). *Experience and Education*. New York: Simon & Schuster.

Dobbs, D. (2007). "Turning Off Depression" in Bloom, F.E. (Ed.) *Best of the Brain from Scientific American: Mind, Matter and Tomorrow's Brain*. New York: Dana Press.

Dotlich, D. and Cairo, P. (2002). *Unnatural Leadership: Going Against Intuition and Expeience to Develop Ten New Leadership Instincts*. San Francisco: Jossey-Bass.

Drath, W. (2001). *The Deep Blue Sea: Rethinking the Source of Leadership*. San Francisco: Jossey-Bass.

Drath, W.H. and Palus, C.J. (1994). *Making Common Sense: Leadership as Meaning-Making in a Community of Practice*. Greensboro, NC: Center for Creative Leadership.

Drucker, P. (1998). "Management's New Paradigms" in *Forbes* Magazine, October 5, 1998.

Dummett, M. (1991). *The Logical Basis of Metaphysics*. Cambridge: Harvard University Press.

Dunlap, A. J. (1996). *Mean Business: How I Save Bad Companies and Make Good Companies Great*. New York: Fireside.

Dyer, W. W. (2001). *There's a Spiritual Solution to Every Problem*. New York: Harper Collins.

Ebrey, P. B. (Ed.) (1993). *Chinese Civilization: A Sourcebook*. New York: The Free Press.

Eccles, R. G. and Nohria, N. (1992). *Beyond the Hype: Rediscovering the Essence of Management*. Boston: Harvard Business School Press.

Edelman, G. and Tononi, G. (2000). *A Universe of Consciousness: How Matter Becomes Imagination*. New York: Basic Books.

Elbert, J. W. (2000). *Are Souls Real?* New York: Prometheus Books.

Ellinor, L. and Gerard, G. (1998). *Dialogue: Rediscover the Transforming Power of Conversation*. New York: John Wiley & Sons.

Elmore, T. (2010). *More Predictions for Generation iY in the Workplace*. Retrieved 09/13 from: www.savetheirfuturenow.com/predictions

Emanuel, E.J. (2013). "Online Education: MOOCs Taken by Educated Few" in *Nature,* Vol. 503, November 21, p. 342.

English, L. M. and Gillen, M. A. (Eds.) (2000). *Addressing the Spiritual Dimensions of Adult Learning: What Educators Can Do.* San Francisco: Jossey-Bass Publishers.

Fairholm, ,G.W. (1997). *Capturing the Heart of Leadership: Spirituality and Community in the New American Workplace.* Westport, CT: Praeger Publishers.

Fiedler, F. (1967). *A Theory of Leadership Effectiveness.* New York: McGraw-Hill.

Frager, R. and Fadiman, J. (1998). *Personality and Personal Growth* (4th Ed.). New York: Longman.

Frick, D. M. and Spears, L.C. (1996). *The Private Writings of Robert K. Greenlead: On Becoming a Servant Leader.* San Francisco: Jossey-Bass.

Friedman, T.L. (2005). *The World Is Flat: A Brief History of the Twenty-First Century.* New York: Farrar, Straus and Giroux.

Frijda, N. H. (2000). "The Psychologists' Point of View" in M. Lewis, M. and. M. Haviland-Jones, M. *Handbook of Emotions* (2nd Ed). New York: The Guilford Press, pp. 59-74.

Frydman, B., Wilson, I., and Wyer, J. (2000). *The Power of Collaborative Leadership: Lessons for the Learning Organization.* Boston: Butterworth Heinemann.

Gardner, H. (1995). *Leading Minds: An Anatomy of Leadership.* Nashville: Reed Business Information, Inc.

Gardner, J. W. (1990). *On Leadership.* New York: The Free Press.

Gazzaniga, M.S. (Ed.) (2004). *The Cognitive Neurosciences III.* Cambridge, MA: The MIT Press.

George, M. S. (2007). "Stimulating the Brain" in F. E. Bloom (Ed.). *Best of the Brain from Scientific American: Mind, Matter, and Tomorrow's Brain* (pp. 20-34). New York: The Dana Foundation.

Gert, B. (1998). *Morality: Its Nature and Justification.* New York: Oxford University Press.

Gerth, H.H. and Mills, C.W. (Eds. and Trans.). From *Max Weber: Essays in Sociology.* New York: Oxford University Press.

Gold, M. and Douvan, E. (1997). *A New Outline of Social Psychology.* Washington, DC: American Psychological Association.

Goldsmith, M. and Walt, C. (1999). "New Competencies for Tomorrow's Global Leaders" in Hesselbein, F., Goldsmith, M., and Somerville, I. (Eds) *Leading Beyond the Walls.* San Francisco: Jossey-Bass, pp. 164-5.

Goleman, D. (2000). "Leadership That Gets Results" in *Harvard Business Review*, March-April, pp. 78-90.

Goleman, D. (1998). What Makes a Leader? in *Harvard Business Review*, pp. 93-102.

Goleman, D., Kaufman, P., and Ray, M. (1992). *The Creative Spirit: Companion to the PBS Television Series.* New York: Penguin Books.

Greenleaf, R.K. (1977; 2002). *Servant Leadership*: A Journey into the Nature of Legitimate Power & Greatness (25th Anniversary Ed.). New York: Paulist Press.

Gyatso, T. and the Fourteenth Dalai Lama (1992). *The Meaning of Life: Buddhist Perspectives on Cause and Effect.* Boston: Wisdom Publications.

Haas, H. G. and Tamarkin, B. (1992). *The Leader Within.* New York: Harper-Collins.

Haberlandt, K. (1998). *Human Memory: Exploration and Application.* Boston: Allyn & Bacon.

Hadar, G. (2009). "Reaching across Generational Lines" in *ei: Managing the Enterprise Information Network.*

Hamel, G. (2000). *Leading the Revolution.* Boston: Harvard Business School Press.

Hammond, S.A. and Hall, J. (1996). "What is AI?" Downloaded 09/06 from www.thnbook.com

Handy, C. (1999). "The Search for Meaning" in Hesselbein, F and Cohen, P.M. *Leader to Leader: Enduring Insights on Leadership* from the Drucker Foundation's award-winning journal. New York: Drucker Foundation Leaderbooks, pp. 121-132.

Harris, T. G. (1999). "The Post-Capitalist Executive: An Interview with Peter F. Drucker" in Magretta, J. (Ed.) *Managing in the New Economy.* Boston: Harvard Business Review Press.

Hawkins, J. (2004). *On Intelligence: How a New Understanding of the Brain will Lead to the Creation of Truly Intelligent Machines*. New York: Henry Holt & Company.

Hawkins, J. and Blakeslee, S. (2004). *On Intelligence: How a New Understanding of the Brain will Lead to the Creation of Truly Intelligent Machines*. New York: Times Books.

Hector, P.G.C. (2015). "Helping Cities in the Developing World Find Success: Designing a Knowledge Maturity Model", a draft Ph.D. dissertation presented to the Institute for Knowledge and Innovation Southeast Asia (IKI-SEA) Business School of Bangkok University, Thailand.

Helgesen, S. (1996). "Leading from the Grass Roots" in Hesselbein, F., Goldsmith, M. and Beckhard, R. (Eds) *The Leader of the Future*. San Francisco: Jossey-Bass.

Helgesen, S. (1999). "Dissolving Boundaries in the Era of Knowledge and Custom Work" in Hesselbein, F., Goldsmith, M., Somerville, I. (Eds). *Leading Beyond the Walls*. San Francisco: Jossey-Bass.

Henderson, M. and Thompson, D. (2003). *Values at Work*. New Zealand: HarperCollinsPublishers.

Hendricks, G. (2000). *Conscious Living: Finding Joy in the Real World*. San Francisco: Harper.

Hershey, P. (1985). *The Situational Leader*. New York: Warner Books.

Hershey, P. and Blanchard, K.H. (2012). *Management of Organizational Behavior* (10th Ed). Upper Saddle River: Prentice Hall.

Hesselbein, F. and P. Cohen (Eds.) (1999*). Leader to Leader: Enduring Insights on Leadership* from the Drucker Foundation's Award-Winning Journal. San Francisco: Jossey-Bass Publishers.

Hesselbein, F., Goldsmit, M. and Beckhard, R. (Eds) (1996). *The Leader of the Future: New Visions, Strategies, and Practices for the Next Era*. San Francisco: Jossey-Bass Publishers, 1996.

Hesselbein, Fr., Goldsmith, M., and Somerville, I. (2002). *Leading for Innovation and Organizing for Results*. San Francisco: Jossey-Bass.

Hine, D. and Kapeleris, J. (2008). *Innovation and Entrepreneurship in Biotechnology, An International Perspective.* Northampton, MA: Edward Elgar Publishing, Inc.

Holmes, J. and Pollock, F. (1961). *Holmes-Pollock Letters: The Correspondence of Mr. Justice Holmes and Sir Frederick Pollock*, 1874-1932 (2nd Ed.) Boston: Belknap Press (Harvard University).

Honderich, T. (1999). *The Philosophers: Introducing Great Western Thinkers*. Oxford: Oxford University Press.

Humphrey, J. W. (1997). "A time of 10,000 Leaders" in Shelton, K. (Ed.). *A New Paradigm of Leadership: Visions of Excellence for 21st Century Organizations.* Provo, UT: Executive Excellent Publishing.

Hyman, S. E. (2007). "Diagnosing Disorders" in Bloom, F.E. (Ed.). *Best of the Brain from Scientific American: Mind, Matter, and Tomorrow's Brain*. New York: Dana Press, pp.132-141.

Impey, C. (2010). *How It Ends: From You to the Universe*. New York: W.W. Norton & Company.

Inglehart, R., Basanez, M. and Moreno, A. (1998). *Human Values and Beliefs: A Cross-cultural Sourcebook*. Ann Arbor: The University of Michigan Press.

Ingram, C. (2003). *Passionate Presence: Experiencing the Seven Qualities of Awakened Awareness*. New York: Gotham Books.

Issacs, W. (1999). *Dialogue and the Art of Thinking Together*. New York: Doubleday.

Jacobs, T.O. and Jaques, E. (1991). "Executive Leadership" in Gal, R. and Manglesdorff, A.D. (Eds.) *Handbook of Military Psychology*. Chichester, England: Wiley.

James, W. (1890). "Grundzuge der physiologiscen Psychologie" in *North American Review*, 1875, 121, 195-201.

Jensen, E. (2006). *Enriching the Brain: How to Maximize Every Learner's Potential*. San Francisco: Jossey-Bass.

Jensen, E. (1998). *Teaching with the Brain in Mind*. Alexandria, VA: Association for Supervision and Curriculum Development.

Jevning, R., Wallace, R.K. and Beidenbach, M. (1992). "The Physiology of Meditation: A Review".

Johnson, S. (2006). "The Neuroscience of the Mentor-Learner Relationship" in Johnson, S. and Taylor, K. (Eds.) *The Neuroscience of Adult Learning*. San Francisco: Jossey-Bass.

Johns, K. (2003). *Managing Generational Diversity in the Workforce*. Trends and Tidbits. Retrieved September 2013 from www.workindex.com

Joyce, S.J. (2007). *Teaching an Anthill to Fetch: Developing Collaborative Intelligence @ Work*. Canada: Creative Commons.

Kahneman, D. (2011). *Thinking, Fast and Slow*. New York: Farrar, Straus and Giroux.

Kandel, E. R. (2007). "The New Science of Mind" in F. E. Bloom, F.E. (Ed.). *Best of The Brain from Scientific American: Mind, Matter, and Tomorrow's Brain*. New York: Dana Press.

Kandel, E. R. (2006). *In Search of Memory: The Emergence of a New Science of Mind*. New York: W.W. Norton & Company.

Kanter, R. (1997). "Restoring People to the Heart of the Organization" in Hesselbein, F., Goldsmith, M., and Beckhard, R. (Eds.), *The Organization of the Future*. San Francisco: Jossey-Bass.

Katzenbach, J.R. and Smith, D.K. (1993). *The Wisdom of Teams: Creating the High-Performance Organization*. Boston: Harvard Business School Press.

Kayser, T. A. (1994). *Building Team Power: How to Unleash the Collaborative Genius of Work Teams*. Burr Ridge, IL: Irwin Professional Publishing.

Kelley, R. E. (1985). *The Gold-Collar Worker*. New York: Addison-Wesley.

Kluwe, R.H., Luer, G. and Rosler, F. (Eds.) (2003). *Principles of Learning and Memory.*, Basel, Switzerland: Birkhauser Verlag.

Kolb, D. A. (1984). *Experiential Learning: Experience as the Source of Learning and Development*. New Jersey: Prentice-Hall.

Komives, S.R., Lucas, N. and McMahon, T.R. (1998). *Exploring Leadership*. San Francisco: Jossy-Bass.

Kouzes, J.M. and Posner, B.Z. (1995) *The Leadership Challenge: How to Keep Getting Extraordinary Things Done in Organizations*. San Francisco: Jossey-Bass.

Kouzes, J. M. and Posner, B. Z. (1993). *Credibility: How Leaders Gain and Lose It, Why People Demand It*. San Francisco: Jossey-Bass.

Kouzes, J. M. (1998). "Finding Your Voice" in Spears, L.C. (Ed.) *Insights on Leadership: Service, Stewardship, Spirit, and Servant-Leadership*. New York: John Wiley & Sons.

Kropotkin, P. (1902). *Mutual Aid: A Factor of Evolution*, downloaded on 01/26/15 from http://libcom.org/files/Peter%20Kropotkin-%20Mutual%20Aid;%20A%20Factor%20of%20Evolution.pdf

Kuntz, P.G. (1968). *The Concept of Order*. Seattle, WA: University of Washington Press.

Kurzweil, R. (2005). *The Singularity Is Near: When Humans Transcend Biology*, New York: Viking.

Lad, L. J. and Luechauer, D. (1998). "On the Path to Servant-Leadership" in L. C. Spears (Ed.). *Insights on Leadership: Service, Stewardship, Spirit, and Servant-Leadership*. New York: John Wiley & Sons.

Lakoff, G. (2006). *Thinking Points: Communicating Our American Values and Vision*. New York: Farrar, Straus and Giroux.

Lawler, E. (2001). "The Era of Human Capital Has Finally Arrived" in Bennis, W., Spreitzer, G. and Cummings, T. (Eds.). *The Future of Leadership*. San Francisco: Jossey-Bass.

LeDoux, J. (1996). *The Emotional Brain: The Mysterious Underpinnings of Emotional Life*. New York: Touchstone.

Lee, B. N. (1997). "Leading with Power" in Shelton, K. (Ed.). *A New Paradigm of Leadership: Visions of Excellence for 21st Century Organizations*. Provo, UT: Executive Excellent Publishing.

Leonard, D. and Swap, W. (2004). *Deep Smarts: How to Cultivate and Transfer Enduring Business Wisdom*. Boston: Harvard Business School Press.

Lerner, M. (2000). *Spirit Matters*. Charlottesville, VA: Hampton Roads.

Lesser, E. (1999). *The New American Spirituality: A Seeker's Guide*. New York: Random House.

Lewis, J. (July 2014) "ADIIEA: An Organizational Learning Model for Business Management and Innovation" in *The Electronic Journal of Knowledge Management* - Volume 12 Issue 2 Available online: http://www.ejkm.com/volume12/issue2

Lewis, J. (2013). *The Explanation Age* (3rd Ed). Charleston: Amazon Create Space. Available online: http://www.amazon.com/dp/1452811067/

Lipton, B. (2005). *The Biology of Belief: Unleashing the Power of Consciousness, Matter & Miracles*. Santa Rosa, CA: Mountain of Love/Elite Books.

Llinas, R.R. (2001). *I of the Vortex: From Neurons to Self*. Cambridge, MA: The MIT Press.

Maccoby, M. (1981). *The Leader: A New Face for American Management*. New York: Simon and Schuster.

Machlup, F. (1962). *The Production and Distribution of Knowledge in the United States*. Princeton: Princeton University Press.

Makridakis, S. G. (1990). *Forecasting, Planning, and Strategy for the 21st Century*. New York: The Free Press.

Malafsky, G.P. and Newman, B.D. (2008). "Organizing Knowledge with Taxonomies and Ontologies" (unpublished manuscript).

Mannheim, K. (1980). *Structure of Thinking*. London: Routledge and Kegan Paul.

Manz, C. C. and Sims, H.P. (2000). *The New SuperLeadership: Leading Others to Lead Themselves,* San Francisco: Berrett-Koehler Publishers, Inc.

Marinoff, L. (2003). *The Big Questions: How Philosophy Can Change Your Life*. New York: Bloomsbury.

Marion, R. (1999). *The Edge of Organization: Chaos and Complexity Theories of Formal Social Systems*. Thousand Oaks, CA: SAGE Publications, Ltd.

Maturana, H. R. and F. J. Varela. (1887). *The Tree of Knowledge: The Biological Roots of Human Understanding.* Boston: Shambhala.

Mavromatis, A. (1991). *Hypnagogia*. New York: Routledge.

Maxwell, J. C. (1999). *The 21 indispensable qualities of leaders: Becoming the person others will want to follow*. Nashville: Thomas Nelson Publishers.

May, R. (1953). *Man's search for himself.* New York: Dell Publishing.

Mayer, R.E. (2009). Multi-Media Learning (2nd Ed.). New York: Cambridge University Press.

Mayer-Schönberger, V. & Cukier, K. (2013). *Big data: A revolution that will transform how we live, work, and think*. New York: Houghton Mifflin Harcourt.

McFadden, JJ and Al-Khalili, J. (2014). *The Coming of Age of Quantum Biology: Life on the Edge*. New York: Crown Publishers.

Medina, J. (2008). *Brain rules: 12 Principles for Surviving and Thriving at Work, Home and School*. Seattle: Pear Press.

Melendez, S. E. (1996). An 'Outsider's' View of Leadership" in Hesselbein, F., Goldsmith, M. & Beckhard, R. *The Drucker Foundation: The Leader of the Future* (pp. 293 – 302). San Francisco: Jossey-Bass.

Menkes, J. (2005). *Executive Intelligence: What All Great Leaders Have*. New York: Harper Collins Publishers.

Merry, U. (1995). *Coping With Uncertainty: Insights from the New Sciences of Chaos, Self-Organization, and Complexity*. London: Praeger.

Moon, J.A. (2004). *A Handbook of Reflective and Experiential Learning: Theory and Practice*. New York: Routledge-Falmer.

Mulvihill, M.K. (2003). "The Catholic Church in Crisis: Will Transformative Learning Lead to Social Change Through the Uncovering of Emotion?" in Weissner, C.A., Meyers, S.R., Pfhal, N.L. and Neaman, P.J. (Eds.) *Proceedings of the 5th International Conference on Transformative Learning.* New York: Teachers College, Columbia University, pp 320-325.

Neff, T. J., & Citrin, J. M. (1999). *Lessons from the Top: The Search for America's Best Business Leaders.* New York: Currency Doubleday.

The New York Times, June 24, 1993, New York. pp. 1, 9.

Nicolelis, M.A.L. and Chapin, J.K. (2007). "Controlling Robots with the Mind" in Bloom, F.E. (Ed.). *Best of the Brain from Scientific American: Mind, Matter, and Tomorrow's Brain.* New York: Dana Press, pp. 197-212.

Noer. D. M. (1997). "Images of Cowboys and Leaders" in Shelton, K. (Ed.) *A New Paradigm of Leadership: Visions of Excellence for 21st Century Organizations*. Provo, UT: Executive Excellent Publishing,.

Nonaka, I. and Scharmer, C.O. (1996). *Knowledge Has to Do with Truth, Goodness, and Beauty: Conversation with Professor Ikujiro Nonaka*. http://www.dialogonleadership.org/Nonaka-1996.html.

Nouwen, H. J. M. (1975). *Reaching Out: The Three Movements of the Spiritual Life*. New York: Doubleday

Northwrite 2013 (Competition website), downloaded on 01/26/15 from http://northwrite.co.nz/northwrite2013-collaborative-competition/

Orr, J. A. (2000). "Learning from Native Adult Education" in English, L. M. and Gillen, M. A. (Eds.) *Addressing the Spiritual Dimensions of Adult Learning: What Educators Can Do*. San Francisco: Jossey-Bass Publishers, pp. 59-66.

Outhwaite, W. and Bottomore, T. (Eds.), *The Blackwell Dictionary of Twentieth-Century Social Thought*. Malden, MA: Blackwell.

Oxford English Dictionary (1933). London: Oxford University Press, London, 1933.

Oxford English Dictionary (5th Ed) (2002). Volumes 1 and 2. Oxford: Oxford University Press.

Pert, C. (1997). *Molecules of Emotion: The Science Behind Mind-Body Medicine*. New York: Simon & Schuster.

Peters, T., and Austin, N. (1985). *A Passion for Excellence: The Leadership Difference*.
New York: Random House.

Piaget, J. (1968). *Structuralism*. New York: Harper Torchbooks.

Pinker, S. (1997). *How the Mind Works*. New York: W. W. Norton and Company.

Polanyi, M. (1967). *The Tacit Dimension*. New York: Anchor Books.

Polanyi, M. (1958). *Personal Knowledge: Towards a Post-Critical Philosophy*, Chicago: The University of Chicago Press.

Porter, D., Bennet, A., Turner, R., Wennergren, D. (2002). *The Power of Team: The Making of a CIO*. U.S. Department of the Navy, Washington, D.C.

Posner, M. (1999). "Spirituality Inc." in *Enroute*, April 1999, pp. 70-77.

Prahalad, C.K. (1999). "Preparing for Leadership" in Hesselbein, F., Goldsmith, M., Somerville, I. (Eds.) *Leading Beyond the Walls*. San Francisco: Jossey-Bass.

Quigley, M. E. (1997). "Leader as Learner" in Shelton, K. (Ed.), *A New Paradigm of Leadership: Visions of Excellence for 21st Century Organizations*. Provo, UT: Executive Excellent Publishing.

Quinn, R. E. and G. M. Spreitzer. (1997). "The Road to Empowerment: Seven Questions Every Leader Should Consider" in *Organizational Dynamics*, Autumn.

Rasha (2003). *Oneness: The Teachings*. San Diego, CA: Jodere Group.

Ratey, J.J. (2001). *A User's Guide to the Brain: Perceptions, Attention, and the Four Theaters of the Brain*. New York: Pantheon Books.

Reik, W. and Walter, J. (2001). Genomic Imprinting: Parental Influence on the Genome, in *Nature Reviews Genetics* 2: 21;

Roaf, M. (1999). *Cultural Atlas of Mesopotamia and the Ancient Near East*. Oxford: Andromeda.

Roberts, J.A.G. (1999). *A Concise History of China*. Cambridge: Harvard University Press.

Rockwell, I. (2002). *The Five Wisdom Energies: A Buddhist Way of Understanding Personalities, Emotions, and Relationships*. Boston: Shambhala.

Rohmann, C. (1999). *A World of Ideas: A Dictionary of Important Theories, Concepts, Beliefs, and Thinkers*. New York: Ballantine Books.

Rose, S. (2005). *The Future of the Brain: The Promise and Perils of Tomorrow's Neuroscience*. New York: Oxford University Press.

Rosen,, R., Digh, P., Singer, M. and Phillips, C. (2000). *Global Literacies: Lessons on Business Leadership and National Cultures*. New York: Simon & Schuster.

Rosenberg, J. (20th Century History Expert) *Franklin D. Roosevelt Quotes*, downloaded on 01/26/15 from http://history1900s.about.com/od/people/a/Roosevelt-Quotes.htm

Rosenthal, N. E., M.D. (2002). *The Emotional Revolution: How the New Science of Feelings Can Transform Your Life*. New York: Citadel Press Books.

Ross, C.A. (2006). "Brain Self-Repair in Psychotherapy: Implications for Education" in Johnson, S. and Taylor, K. (Eds.) *The Neuroscience of Adult Learning: New Directions for Adult and Continuing Education*. San Francisco, CA: Jossey-Bass.

Russell, P. (1995). *The Global Brain Awakens*. Saline, MI: McNaughton & Gunn.

Ryle, G. (1949), *The Concept of Mind*, Hutchinson, London.

Saint-Onge, H. (2000). "Shaping Human Resource Management Within the Knowledge-Driven Enterprize" in Phillips, J. and Bonner, D. (Eds). *Leading Knowledge Management and Learning*. Alexandria, VA: ASTD.

Schore, A. (1994). *Affect Regulation and the Origin of the Self: The Neurobiology of Emotional Development*. Mahway, NJ: Erlbaum.

Schrodinger, E. (1944/2015). *What is Life?* Downloaded 09/13/2015 from http://whatislife.stanford.edu/LoCo_files/What-is-Life.pdf

Schwartz, P. (2003). *Inevitable Surprises: Thinking Ahead in a Time of Turbulence*. New York: Penguin Group, Inc.

Senge, P., Scharmer, C.O., Jaworski, J. and Flowers, B.S. (2004). *Presence: Human Purpose and the Field of the Future*. Cambridge, MA: The Society for Organizational Learning.

Senge, P. M. (1999). "The Practice of Innovation" in Hesselbein, F. & Cohen, P.M. *Leader to Leader: Enduring Insights on Leadership from the Drucker Foundation's Award-Winning Journal*. New York: Drucker Foundation Leaderbooks, pp. 121-132.

Senge, P. (1990). *The Fifth Discipline: The Art andPpractice of the Learning Organization*. NewYork: Doubleday.

Shafer, I. H. (1999). "World Commission on Global Consciousness and Spirituality." [http//globalspirit.org/home.htm.] June 29, 1999.

Shechtman, M. R., *Fifth Wave Leadership: the Internal Frontier,* Facts On Demand Press, Tempe, AZ, 2002, p. xiv.

Shelley, A.W. (2016). KNOWledge SUCCESSion. Business Expert Press Project Management Series. New York: Business Expert Press.

Shelley, A.W. (2006). The Organizational Zoo: A Survival Guide to Work Place Behavior. Australia: Aslan Pub

Shelton, K. (ed.) (1997). *A New Paradigm of Leadership: Visions of Excellence for 21st Century Organizations*. Provo, UT: Executive Excellence Publishing.

Silberman, M. (2007). *The Handbook of Experiential Learning*. San Francisco: Pfeiffer.

Silverman, D. P. (Ed.) (1997). *Ancient Egypt*. New York: Oxford University Press.

Sousa, D. A. (2006). *How the Brain Learns*. Thousand Oaks, CA: Corwin Press.

Sousa, M. & van Dierendonck, D. (2015). "Servant Leadership and the Effect of the Interaction Between Humility, Action and Hierarchical Power on Follower Engagement" in *Journal of Business Ethics*, pp. 1-13.

Souter, D. (2010). *Towards Inclusive Knowledge Societies: A Review of UNESCO's Action in Implementing the WSIS Outcomes*. Paris, France: UNESCO.

Spears, L. C. (ed.) (1998). *Insights on Leadership: Service, Stewardship, Spirit, and Servant-Leadership*. New York: John Wiley & Sons, 1998.

Srivastva, S. and Cooperrider, D.L. (Eds.) (1990). *Appreciative Management and Leadership*. San Francisco: Jossey-Bass.

Stacey, R.D. (1996). *Complexity and Creativity in Organizations*. San Francisco: Berrett-Koehler.

Sternberg, R. J. (2003). *Wisdom, Intelligence, and Creativity Synthesized*. Cambridge: Cambridge University Press.

Stewart. T. A. (2001*). The Wealth of Knowledge: Intellectual Capital and the Twenty-First Century Organization*. New York: Currency.

Stogdill, R. M. (1948). "Personal Factors Associated with Leadership: A Survey of the Literature" in *Journal of Psychology*, 1948, 25, p. 71.

Stonier, T. (1997). *Information and Meaning: An Evolutionary Perspective*. New York: Springer.

Stonier, T. (1992). *Beyond Information: The Natural History of Intelligence*. London: Springer-Verlag.

Stonier, T. (1990). *Information and the Internal Structure of the Universe: An Introduction into Information Physics*. New York: Springer-Verlag.

Surani, M.A. (2006). "Reprogramming of Genome Function through Epigenetic Inheritance" in *Nature* 414, 2001, 122.

Swomley, J. (2000). "Violence: Competition or cooperation" in *Christian Ethics Today* 26, Vol. 6, No. 1.

Tapscott, D. (2010). *Grown Up Digital*. New York: McGraw Hill.

Taylor, K. (2006). "Brain Function and Adult Learning: Implications for Practice", in Johnson, S. and Taylor, K. (Eds.) *The Neuroscience of Adult Learning*. San Francisco, CA: Jossey-Bass.

Teasdale, W. and the Dali Lama (1999). *The Mystic Heart: Discovering a Universal Spirituality in the World's Religions*. Novato,CA: New World Library.

Teck, T.P. (SIA senior vice president for product services), downloaded on 01/26/15 from http://www.dnaindia.com/money/report-venture-with-tata-group-competitive-collaboration-sia-1994195

Tichy, N. M. with Cardwell, N. (2002). *The Cycle of Leadership: How Great Leaders Teach Their Companies to Win*. New York: Harper Business.

Topping, P. A. (2002). *Managerial Leadership*. New York: McGraw-Hill.

UNESCO (2005). *Towards Inclusive Knowledge Societies: UNESCO World Report*. Paris, France: UNESCO.

Ury, W. (2002). "The Negotiation Revolution" in Marshall, G., Govindarajan, V., Kaye, B. and Vicere, A.A. (Eds.) *Many Facets of Leadership*. Upper Saddle River, NJ: Pearson Education, Inc.

Van Ness, P.H. (Ed.) (1996). *Spirituality and the Secular Quest*. Vol. 22: *World Spirituality: An Encyclopedic History of the Religious Quest*. New York: Crossroad.

Vicere, A.A. and Fulmer, R.M. (1997). *Leadership by Design*. Boston: Harvard Business School Press.

Vogel, L. J. (2000). "Reckoning with the Spiritual Lives of Adult Educators" in English, L. M. and Gillen, M. A. (Eds.) *Addressing the Spiritual Dimensions of Adult learning: What Educators Can Do*. San Francisco: Jossey-Bass Publishers, pp. 17-28.

von Krogh, G. and Roos, J. (1995). *Organizational Epistemology*. New York: St. Martin's Press, Inc.

Wagner, R. and R. Sternberg, R. (1990). "Street Smarts" in Clark, K. and Clark, M. (Eds) *Measures of Leadership*. West Orange, NJ: Leadership Library of America.

Walsh, R. and Shapiro, D. H. (1983). *Beyond Health and Normality: Explorations of Exceptional Psychological Well – Being*. New York: Van Nostrand Reinhold Company.

Watts, A. (2002). *ZEN: The Supreme Experience: The Newly Discovered Scripts*. London: Vega.

Ward, J. (2006). *The Student's Guide to Cognitive Neuroscience*. New York: Psychology Press.

Wenger, E. (2009). "Communities of Practice and Social Learning Systems: The Career of a Concept" in Blackmore, C. (Ed.) *Social Learning Systems and Communities of Practice*. London: Springer Verlag and the Open University.

Wenger, E. (1999). *Communities of Practice: Learning, Meaning, and Identity*. New York: Cambridge University Press.

Wenger, E., McDermott, R. and Snyder, W. M. (2002). *A Guide to Managing Knowledge: Cultivating Communities of Practice*. Boston: Harvard Business School Press.

White, R.P., Hodgson, P. and Crainer, S. (1996). *The Future of Leadership: Riding the Corporate Rapids into the 21st Century*. Washington, D.C.: Pitman Publishing.

White, R. W. (1959). "Motivation Reconsidered: the Concept of Competence" in *Psychological Review*, 1959, 66, p. 297-333.

Whyte, W.H. (1956). *The Organization Man*. New York: Simon and Schuster, Inc..

Wickett, R.E.Y. (2000). "The Learning Covenant" in English, L. M. and Gillen, M. A. (Eds.) *Addressing the Spiritual Dimensions of Adult learning: What Educators Can Do*. San Francisco: Jossey-Bass Publishers, pp. 39-48.

Wigglesworth, C. (2014). *SQ21: The Twenty-One Skills of Spiritual Intelligence*. New York: SelectBooks.

Wiig, K.M. (2004). *People-Focused Knowledge Management: How Effective Decision Making Leads to Corporate Success*. New York, NY: Elsevier.

Wiig, K. M. (1993). *Knowledge Management Foundations: Thinking about Thinking—How People and Organizations Create, Represent, and Use Knowledge*. Arlington, TX: Schema Press, 1993.

Williamson, M. (2002). *Everyday Grace: Having Hope, Finding Forgiveness, and Making Miracles*. New York: Riverhead Books.

Wilson, E.O. (1998). *Consilience: The Unity of Knowledge*, Alfred A. Knopf, New York.

Wlodkowski, R. J. (1998). *Enhancing Adult Motivation to Learn: A Comprehensive Guide for Teaching All Adults*. San Francisco: Jossey-Bass Publishers.

Yates, J.F. and Tschirhart, M.D. (2006). "Decision-Making Expertise" in Ericsson, K, Charness, N., Feltovich, P. & Hoffman, R., *The Cambridge Handbook of Expertise and Expert Performance*. New York: Cambridge University Press.

Zand, D. E. (1997). *The Leadership Triad: Knowledge, Trust, and Power*. New York: Oxford University Press.

Zhu, X. O. and Waite, P. M. E. (1998). "Cholinergic Depletion Reduces Plasticity of Barrel Field Cortex" in *Cerebral Cortex, 8*, 63-72.

Zimmer, C. (2005). "The Neurobiology of the Self" in *Scientific American*, November.

Zohar, D. & Marshall, I. (2012). *Spiritual Intelligence: The Ultimate Intelligence*. London: Bloomsbury Paperbacks

Zohar, D. and Marshall, I. (2000). *Connecting with our Spiritual Intelligence*. New York: Bloomsbury.

Zohar, D. and Marshall, I. (2003). *Spiritual Capital: Wealth We Can Live By*. San Francisco: Berrett-Koehler Publishers, Inc

Zubko, A. (1996). *Treasury of Spiritual Wisdom*. San Diego, CA: Blue Dove Press.

Zull, J. E. (2002). *The Art of Changing the Brain: Enriching the Practice of Teaching by Exploring the Biology of Learning*. Sterling, VA: Stylus.

Subject Index

About the Mountain Quest Institute

MQI is a research, retreat and learning center dedicated to helping individuals achieve personal and professional growth and organizations create and sustain high performance in a rapidly changing, uncertain, and increasingly complex world.

Current research is focused on Human and Organizational Development, Knowledge, Knowledge Capacities, Adult Learning, Values, Complexity, Consciousness and Spirituality. MQI has three questions: The Quest for Knowledge, The Quest for Consciousness, and The Quest for Meaning. **MQI is scientific, humanistic and spiritual and finds no contradiction in this combination**. See www.mountainquestinstitute.com

MQI is the birthplace of Organizational Survival in the New World: The Intelligent Complex Adaptive System (Elsevier, 2004), a new theory of the firm that turns the living system metaphor into a reality for organizations. Based on research in complexity and neuroscience—and incorporating networking theory and knowledge management—this book is filled with new ideas married to practical advice, all embedded within a thorough description of the new organization in terms of structure, culture, strategy, leadership, knowledge workers and integrative competencies.

Mountain Quest Institute, situated four hours from Washington, D.C. in the Monongahela Forest of the Allegheny Mountains, is part of the Mountain Quest complex which includes a Retreat Center, Inn, and the old Farm House, Outbuildings and mountain trails and farmland. See www.mountainquestinn.com The Retreat Center is designed to provide full learning experiences, including hosting training, workshops, retreats and business meetings for professional and executive groups of 25 people or less. The Center includes a 26,000 volume research library, a conference room, community center, computer room, 12 themed bedrooms, a workout and hot tub area, and a four-story tower with a glass ceiling for enjoying the magnificent view of the valley during the day and the stars at night. Situated on a 430 acres farm, there is a labyrinth, creeks, four miles of mountain trails, and horses, Longhorn cattle,

Llamas and a myriad of wild neighbors. Other neighbors include the Snowshoe Ski Resort, the National Radio Astronomy Observatory and the CASS Railroad.

About The CoHero Institute

The CoHero Institute was founded on the principle that there is a relationship between *leadership* and *learning*. Leadership does not occur in a vacuum; it takes place within organizations of all sizes. And these organizations are all *learning* organizations, with varying degrees of learning *disabilities*. To address the **transformational leadership needs of today's organizations**, The CoHero Institute was formed by Doug Moran and John Lewis – two leaders with expertise in both areas: leadership and organizational learning. Collaborative Leadership requires more than just "getting along." It requires each leader knowing their strengths, and being aware of the relationships they need to build to complete the strengths needed by the organization. The CoHero Leadership Framework Profile (CHLFP) assessment and certified change leader course provide the leadership skills essential in today's dynamic organizations. See www.cohero-institute.com

About the Authors

Drs. Alex and David Bennet are co-founders of the Mountain Quest Institute. They may be contacted at alex@mountainquestinstitute.com

Alex Bennet, a Professor at the Bangkok University Institute for Knowledge and Innovation Management, is internationally recognized as an expert in knowledge management and an agent for organizational change. Prior to founding the Mountain Quest Institute, she served as the Chief Knowledge Officer and Deputy Chief Information Officer for Enterprise Integration for the U.S. Department of the Navy, and was co-chair of the Federal Knowledge Management Working Group. Dr. Bennet is the recipient of the Distinguished and Superior Public Service Awards from the U.S. government for her work in the Federal Sector. Alex is a Delta Epsilon Sigma and Golden Key National Honor Society graduate with a Ph.D. in Human and Organizational Systems; degrees in Management for Organizational Effectiveness, Human Development, English and Marketing; and certificates in Total Quality Management, System Dynamics and Defense Acquisition Management.

David Bennet's experience spans many years of service in the Military, Civil Service and Private Industry, including fundamental research in underwater acoustics and nuclear physics, frequent design and facilitation of organizational interventions, and serving as technical director of two major DoD Acquisition programs. Prior to founding the Mountain Quest Institute, Dr. Bennet was CEO, then Chairman of the Board and Chief Knowledge Officer of a professional services firm located in Alexandria, Virginia. He is a Phi Beta Kappa, Sigma Pi Sigma, and Suma Cum Laude graduate of the University of Texas, and holds degrees in Mathematics, Physics, Nuclear Physics, Liberal Arts, Human and Organizational Development, and a Ph.D. in Human Development focused on Neuroscience and adult learning. He is currently researching the nexus of Science, the Humanities and Spirituality.

John Lewis is a speaker, business consultant, and part-time professor on the topics of organizational learning, thought leadership, and knowledge & innovation management. John is a proven leader with business results, and was acknowledged by Gartner with an industry "Best Practice" paper for an innovative knowledge management implementation. He is a co-founder at The CoHero Institute, creating collaborative leadership in learning organizations. John holds a Doctoral degree in Educational Psychology from the University of Southern California, with a dissertation focus on mental models and decision making, and is the author of *The Explanation Age*, which Kirkus Reviews described as "An iconoclast's blueprint for a new era of innovation." John may be contacted at john@cohero-institute.com

Other Books by These Authors

Possibilities that are YOU!

These little **Conscious Look Books** are focused on sharing 22 large concepts from *The Profundity and Bifurcation of Change.* Conversational in nature, each with seven ideas offered for the graduate of life experience. Available in soft cover from Amazon.

eBooks available in PDF format from MQIPress (US 304-799-7267 or alex@mountainquestinstitute.com) and Kindle format from Amazon. (Softback copies available mid-2019)

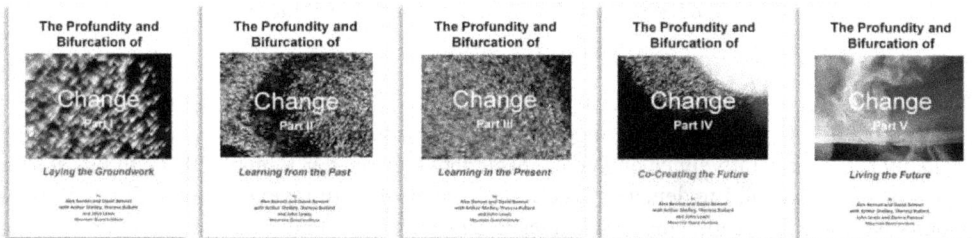

Five in-depth eBooks, ***The Profundity and Bifurcation of Change***, heavily referenced and resourced. These books lay the groundwork for the **Intelligent Social Change Journey** (ISCJ), a developmental journey of the body, mind and heart, moving from the heaviness of cause-and-effect linear extrapolations, to the fluidity of co-evolving with our environment, to the lightness of breathing our thought and feelings into reality. Grounded in development of our mental faculties, these are phase changes, each building on and expanding previous learning in our movement toward intelligent activity. Available as eBooks from Amazon. (Available 2019 in soft cover.)

Other eBooks available from in PDF format from MQIPress (US 304-799-7267 or alex@mountainquestinstitute.com) and softback cover or Kindle format from Amazon.

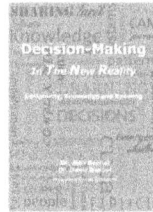

The Course of Knowledge: A 21st Century Theory

by Alex Bennet and David Bennet with Joyce Avedisian (2015)

Knowledge is at the core of what it is to be human, the substance which informs our thoughts and determines the course of our actions. Our growing focus on, and understanding of, knowledge and its consequent actions is changing our relationship with the world. Because **knowledge determines the quality of every single decision we make**, it is critical to learn about and understand what knowledge is. **From a 21st century viewpoint,** we explore a theory of knowledge that is both pragmatic and biological. Pragmatic in that it is based on taking effective action, and biological because it is created by humans via patterns of neuronal connections in the mind/brain.

In this book we explore *the course of knowledge*. Just as a winding stream in the bowls of the mountain's curves and dips through ravines and high valleys, so, too, with knowledge. In a continuous journey towards intelligent activity, context-sensitive and situation-dependent knowledge, imperfect and incomplete, experientially engages a changing landscape in a continuous cycle of learning and expanding. *We are in a continuous cycle of knowledge creation such that every moment offers the opportunity for the emergence of new and exciting ideas, all waiting to be put in service to an interconnected world.* Learn more about this **exciting human capacity**!

Expanding the Self: The Intelligent Complex Adaptive Learning System

by David Bennet and Alex Bennet (2015)

We live in unprecedented times; indeed, turbulent times that can arguably be defined as ushering humanity into a new Golden Age, offering the opportunity to embrace new ways of learning and living in a globally and collaboratively entangled connectedness (Bennet & Bennet, 2007). In this shifting and dynamic environment, life demands accelerated cycles of learning experiences. Fortunately, we as a humanity have begun to look within ourselves to better understand the way our mind/brain operates, the amazing qualities of the body that power our thoughts and feelings, and the reciprocal loops as those thoughts and feelings change our physical structure. This emerging knowledge begs us to relook and rethink what we know about learning, providing a new starting point to expand toward the future.

This book is a treasure for those interested in how recent findings in neuroscience impact learning. The result of this work is an expanding experiential learning model call the Intelligent Complex Adaptive Learning System, adding the fifth mode of social engagement to Kolb's concrete experience, reflective observation, abstract conceptualization and active experimentation, with the five modes undergirded by the power of Self. A significant conclusion is that should they desire, adults have much more control over their learning than they may realize.

Decision-Making in The New Reality: Complexity, Knowledge and Knowing

by Alex Bennet and David Bennet (2013)

We live in a world that offers many possible futures. The ever-expanding complexity of information and knowledge provide many choices for decision-makers, and we are all making decisions every single day! As the problems and messes of the world become more complex, our decision consequences are more and more difficult to anticipate, and our decision-making processes must change to keep up with this world complexification. This book takes a consilience approach to explore decision-making in The New Reality, fully engaging systems and complexity theory, knowledge research, and recent neuroscience findings. It also presents methodologies for decision-makers to tap into their unconscious, accessing tacit knowledge resources and increasingly relying on the sense of knowing that is available to each of us.

Almost every day new energies are erupting around the world: new thoughts, new feelings, new knowing, all contributing to new situations that require new decisions and actions from each and every one of us. Indeed, with the rise of the Net Generation and social media, a global consciousness may well be emerging. As individuals and organizations we are realizing that there are larger resources available to us, and that, as complex adaptive systems linked to a flowing fount of knowing, we can bring these resources to bear to achieve our ever-expanding vision of the future. Are we up to the challenge?

Other books available from the authors and on Amazon...

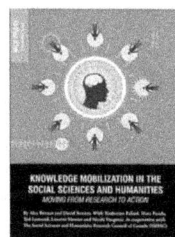

The Explanation Age

by John Lewis (2013) (3rd Ed.), available in hard and soft formats from Amazon.

The technological quest of the last several decades has been to create the information age, with ubiquitous and immediate access to information. With this goal arguably accomplished, even from our mobile phones, this thought-provoking book describes the next quest and provides a blueprint for how to get there. When all organizational knowledge is framed as answers to our fundamental questions, we find ubiquitous and visual access to knowledge related to who, where, how, etc., yet the explanations are still buried within the prose. The question of "why" is arguably the most important question, yet it is currently the least supported. This is why business process methodologies feel like "box-checking" instead of "sense-making." This is why lessons learned are not actually learned. And this is why the consequential options and choices are captured better within a chess game than within the important decisions faced by organizations and society. With implications for business, education, policy making, and artificial intelligence, Dr. Lewis provides a visualization of explanations which promotes organizational sense-making and collaboration. AVAILABLE online FROM AMAZON http://www.amazon.com/dp/1452811067

Organizational Survival in the New World: the Intelligent Complex Adaptive System

by Alex and David Bennet (Elsevier, 2004), available in hard and soft formats from Amazon.

In this book David and Alex Bennet propose a new model for organizations that enables them to react more quickly and fluidly to today's fast-changing, dynamic business environment: the Intelligent Complex Adaptive System (ICAS). ICAS is a new organic model of the firm based on recent research in complexity and neuroscience, and incorporating networking theory and knowledge management, and turns the living system metaphor into a reality for organizations. This book synthesizes new thinking about organizational structure from the fields listed above into ICAS, a new systems model for the successful organization of the future designed to help leaders and managers of knowledge organizations succeed in a non-linear, complex, fast-changing and turbulent environment. Technology enables connectivity, and the ICAS model takes advantage of that connectivity by fostering the development of dynamic, effective and trusting relationships in a new organizational structure. AVAILABLE as a hardback and as an eBook FROM AMAZON.

Knowledge Mobilization in the Social Sciences and Humanities: Moving from Research to Action

by Alex Bennet and David Bennet (2007), available in hard and soft formats from Amazon.

This book takes the reader from the University lab to the playgrounds of communities. It shows how to integrate, move and use knowledge, an action journey within an identified action space that is called knowledge mobilization. Whether knowledge is mobilized through an individual, organization, community or nation, it becomes a powerful asset creating a synergy and focus that brings forth the best of action and values. Individuals and teams who can envision, feel, create and apply this power are the true leaders of tomorrow. When we can mobilize knowledge for the greater good humanity will have left the information age and entered the age of knowledge, ultimately leading to compassion and—hopefully—wisdom. AVAILABLE as an eBook (Kindle and PDF) FROM AMAZON

Also available in PDF format from MQIPress (US 304-799-7267 or alex@mountainquestinstitute.com) and Kindle format from Amazon.

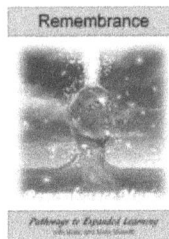

REMEMBRANCE: *Pathways to Expanded Learning with Music and Metamusic®*

by Barbara Bullard and Alex Bennet (2013)

Take a journey of discovery into the last great frontier—the human mind/brain, an instrument of amazing flexibility and plasticity. This eBook is written for brain users who are intent on mining more of the golden possibilities that lie inherent in each of our unique brains. Begin by discovering the role positive attitudes play in learning, and the power of self affirmations and visualizations. Then explore the use of brain wave entrainment mixed with designer music called Metamusic® to achieve enhanced learning states. Join students of all ages who are creating magical learning outcomes using music and Metamusic.® AVAILABLE as an eBook (Kindle and PDF) FROM AMAZON

The Journey into the Myst (Vol 1 of The Myst Series)

by Alex Bennet and David Bennet (2012)

What we are about to tell you would have been quite unbelievable to me before this journey began. It is not a story of the reality either of us has known for well over our 60 and 70 years of age, but rather, the reality of dreams and fairytales." This is the true story of a sequence of events that happened at Mountain Quest Institute, situated in a high valley of the Allegheny Mountains of West Virginia. The story begins with a miracle, expanding into the capture and cataloging of thousands of pictures of electromagnetic spheres widely known as "orbs." This joyous experience became an exploration into the unknown with the emergence of what the author's fondly call the Myst, the forming and shaping of non-random patterns such as human faces, angels and animals. As this phenomenon unfolds, you will discover how the Drs. Alex and David Bennet began to observe and interact with the Myst. This book shares the beginning of an extraordinary *Journey into the Myst*. AVAILABLE as an eBook (Kindle and PDF) FROM AMAZON

Patterns in the Myst (Vol 2 of The Myst Series)

by Alex Bennet and David Bennet (2013)

The Journey into the Myst was just the beginning for Drs. Alex and David Bennet. Volume II of the Myst Series brings Science into the Spiritual experience, bringing to bear what the Bennets have learned through their research and educational experiences in physics, neuroscience, human systems, knowledge management and human development. Embracing the paralogical, patterns in the Myst are observed, felt, interpreted, analyzed and compared in terms of their physical make-up, non-randomness, intelligent sources and potential implications. Along the way, the Bennets were provided amazing pictures reflecting the forming of the Myst. The Bennets shift to introspection in the third volume of the series to explore the continuing impact of the Myst experience on the human psyche. AVAILABLE as an eBook (Kindle and PDF) FROM AMAZON

MQIPress is a wholly-owned subsidiary of Mountain Quest Institute, LLC, located at 303 Mountain Quest Lane, Marlinton, West Virginia 24954, USA.

The authors may be contacted at

Mountain Quest Institute
303 Mountain Quest Lane
Marlinton, WV 24954

304-799-7267

alex@mountainquestinstitute.com

www.ingramcontent.com/pod-product-compliance
Lightning Source LLC
Chambersburg PA
CBHW061801210326
41599CB00034B/6842